Economic
and
Business Forecasting

Wiley & SAS Business Series

The Wiley & SAS Business Series presents books that help senior-level managers with their critical management decisions.

Titles in the Wiley & SAS Business Series include:

Activity-Based Management for Financial Institutions: Driving Bottom-Line Results by Brent Bahnub

Big Data Analytics: Turning Big Data into Big Money by Frank Ohlhorst

Branded! How Retailers Engage Consumers with Social Media and Mobility by Bernie Brennan and Lori Schafer

Business Analytics for Customer Intelligence by Gert Laursen

Business Analytics for Managers: Taking Business Intelligence beyond Reporting by Gert Laursen and Jesper Thorlund

The Business Forecasting Deal: Exposing Bad Practices and Providing Practical Solutions by Michael Gilliland

Business Intelligence Success Factors: Tools for Aligning Your Business in the Global Economy by Olivia Parr Rud

CIO Best Practices: Enabling Strategic Value with Information Technology, second edition by Joe Stenzel

Connecting Organizational Silos: Taking Knowledge Flow Management to the Next Level with Social Media by Frank Leistner

Credit Risk Assessment: The New Lending System for Borrowers, Lenders, and Investors by Clark Abrahams and Mingyuan Zhang

Credit Risk Scorecards: Developing and Implementing Intelligent Credit Scoring by Naeem Siddiqi

The Data Asset: How Smart Companies Govern Their Data for Business Success by Tony Fisher

Delivering Business Analytics: Practical Guidelines for Best Practice by Evan Stubbs

Demand-Driven Forecasting: A Structured Approach to Forecasting, Second Edition by Charles Chase

Demand-Driven Inventory Optimization and Replenishment: Creating a More Efficient Supply Chain by Robert A. Davis

Economic and Business Forecasting: Analyzing and Interpreting Econometric Results by John Silvia, Azhar Iqbal, Kaylyn Swankoski, Sarah Watt, and Sam Bullard

The Executive's Guide to Enterprise Social Media Strategy: How Social Networks Are Radically Transforming Your Business by David Thomas and Mike Barlow

For more information on any of the above titles, please visit www.wiley.com.

Economic and Business Forecasting

Analyzing and Interpreting Econometric Results

John Silvia
Azhar Iqbal
Kaylyn Swankoski
Sarah Watt
Sam Bullard

WILEY

Published by John Wiley & Sons, Inc., Hoboken, New Jersey.

Published simultaneously in Canada.

Library of Congress Cataloging-in-Publication Data:

Silvia, John.
    Economic and business forecasting : analyzing and interpreting econometric results /
  John Silvia, Azhar Iqbal, Kaylyn Swankoski, Sarah Watt, Sam Bullard.
        pages cm.   (Wiley & SAS business series)
      ISBN 978-1-118-49709-8 (cloth); ISBN 978-1-118-56980-1 (ebk);
      ISBN 978-1-118-56954-2 (ebk)
        1. Economic forecasting. 2. Business forecasting. 3. Decision-making.
    4. Econometrics. I. Title.
    HB3730.S484 2014
    330.01'5195—dc23
                                                                    2013039764

Printed in the United States of America
10 9 8 7 6 5 4 3 2 1

To Tiffani Kaliko, Penny and Sherman
Shahkora and Mohammad Iqbal, Nargis, Saeeda, Shahid and Noreen
And to the family and friends who remain our wellsprings of inspiration

If a man will begin with certainties,
he shall end in doubts,
but if he will content to begin with doubts,
he shall end in certainties.

—Francis Bacon, *The Advancement of Learning*, 1605

Contents

Preface

Due to the Great Recession (2007–2009) and the accompanying financial crisis, the premium on effective economic analysis, especially the identification of time series and then accurate forecasting of economic and financial variables, has significantly increased. Our approach provides a comprehensive yet practical process to quantify and accurately forecast key economic and financial variables. Therefore, the timing of this book is appropriate in a post-2008 world, where the behavior of traditional economic relationships must be reexamined since many appear out of character with the past. The value proposition is clear: The framework and techniques advanced here are the techniques we use as practitioners. These techniques will help decision makers identify and characterize the patterns of behavior in key economic series to better forecast these essential economic series and their relationships to other economic series.

This book is for the broad audience of practitioners as well as undergraduate and graduate students with an applied economics focus. This book introduces statistical techniques that can help practitioners characterize the behavior of economic relationships. Chapters 1 to 3 provide a review of basic economic and financial fundamentals that decision makers in both the private and public sectors need to know. Our belief is that before an analyst attempts any statistical analysis, there should be a clear understanding of the data under study. Chapter 4 provides the tools that an analyst will employ to effectively characterize an economic series. One relationship of interest is the ability of leading indicators to predict the pattern of the business cycle, particularly the onset of a recession. Another way to characterize economic relationships is to reflect on the current trend of any economic series of interest relative to the average behavior over prior cycles. In a third approach, we may be interested in identifying the possibility of a structural change in an economic time series to test if the past history of a variable would be different over time.

Different economic and financial variables exhibit differential behavior over the business cycle and over time. In this book we focus on a select set of major economic and financial variables, such as economic growth, final sales, employment, inflation, interest rates, corporate profits, financial ratios, and the exchange value of the dollar.

Our analysis then extends the text into the relationships between different time series. This analysis begins with Chapter 5, and then in Chapters 6 and 7 we take a look at the SAS® software employed in our analysis. We also examine these variables' patterns over the business cycle, with an emphasis on their recent history, using econometric techniques and the statistical software SAS as a template for the reader to apply to variables of interest. These variables form the core of an effective decision-making process in both the private and public sectors. Chapter 8 provides techniques that an analyst can employ and contains numerous examples of our techniques in action.

Our approach has several advantages. First, effective decision making involves an analysis of the behavior of select economic and financial variables. By choosing a small set of economic factors, we provide a template for decision making that can be easily applicable to a broader set of variables for future study in many economic fields. Our focus is on the importance of a limited, but central, set of select economic and financial variables that provide special insights into economic performance, along with the empirical evidence of their vital role to the economy and financial markets.

Second, using a small set of simple data descriptors and econometric techniques to characterize and describe the behavior of economic variables provides value in a number of contexts. We can examine the behavior of any particular economic series in numerous ways so that the analysis is less subject to personal beliefs and biases. This helps overcome the confirmation bias of many decision makers who *search* for the results they want to see from any analysis. Many analysts may search for the comfortable, familiar historical statistical relationships in a post-2008 era when, in fact, many of those relationships have vanished.

Third, our detailed discussion about SAS and its applications creates a valuable starting point for researchers. We provide a practical forecasting framework for important everyday applications. Finally, our work discusses SAS results and identifies econometric issues and solutions that are of interest to addressing a number of economic and business issues. One outgrowth of our experience with many of these issues is reviewed in Chapter 9, where we focus on our 10 commandments of applied time series forecasting. Chapters 10 and 11 build on these commandments with a focus on single equations in Chapter 10 and multiple equations in Chapter 11.

The net result is the application of econometrics in a way that contributes to effective decision making in both the private and public sectors. In Chapter 12 we focus on model-based forecasting applied to make long-term forecasts for the next five to 10 years, which reflects the reality of determining the real sustainability of projects and their profitability overtime. Chapter 13 then highlights the risks and challenges of such forecasting. Finally in Chapter 14 we illustrate some of the lessons we have learned in recent years as we identify and understand the changes that are ongoing in the twenty-first-century economy. As an additional resource, there is a test bank to accompany this text.

This book is dedicated first to young professional economists and aspiring students who wish to provide a thoughtful statistical basis for better decision making in their careers, whether it is in the public or the private sector. This book is also aimed to serve professional analysts who wish to provide statistical support for effective decision making. This work reflects the years of experience of the authors whose work contains a focus on simple yet practical techniques needed for efficient decision making without extensive theoretical and mathematical refinements that are ancillary to effective decision making. That we leave for authors with the luxury of time and tenure. The techniques in the text are being used in our work every day. They have brought us numerous forecasting awards and published papers that reflect the practical undertakings required of young professionals who wish to add value to the decision-making process in their organizations.

Acknowledgments

We would like to thank all the people who have supported us through the writing and publication of this book. Special thanks to Larry Rothstein and Zachary Griffiths, for without their help this book would not have been possible. We also wish to express our gratitude for the many people at Wells Fargo who have supported this project, including Diane Schumaker-Krieg and John Shrewsberry, as well as the technical support staff at Wells Fargo. Thank you Robert Crow, editor of *Business Economics*, and the referees of that journal as well as the referees of articles that have appeared in other journals; you have improved the quality of our research over the years. We are grateful for the instructors and students who have come into our lives and taught and inspired us (Nuzhat Ahmad, M. S. Butt, Kajal Lahiri, Asad Zaman, Adil Siddique, Ambreen Fatima, Hasan N. Saleem, Jon Schuller, and Anika Khan).

CHAPTER 1

Creating Harmony Out of Noisy Data

By the spring of 2012, the economic performance of the United States was operating at a much different pace from what many analysts had expected. Decision makers in both private and public sectors faced a set of mixed and unclear economic and financial indicators that offered a confused picture of the state of the economic recovery, the pace of that recovery, and the character of the structural challenges facing the economy.

Three major trends characterized the confusion. First, top-line economic growth had been unusually low and uneven relative to past economic recoveries since World War II. During the recovery, the economy accelerated after an initial stimulus but then lost momentum as the stimulus generated no follow-on growth. Decision makers had the difficult challenge of identifying what the true trend in the economy was and what the cycle around that trend was. Had trend economic growth downshifted in the United States?

Second, job growth had become the number one political issue. But the lack of job growth appeared out of line with traditional economic models on a cyclical basis. Further, weak job growth intimated a sharp structural break in both private and public sector decision makers' preconceived understanding of the relationship between employment and population growth. Had there been a structural break between employment and population growth, and/or between employment and output growth? Why have exceptionally low mortgage interest rates not spurred a pickup in housing, as in prior recoveries? Had this relationship experienced a structural break as well?

Third, corporate profits, business equipment spending, and industrial production had improved in this cycle in a way reminiscent of prior recoveries despite the overall perception that the economic recovery had been subpar. How can we identify economic series that appear to be behaving in typical cyclical fashion compared to those that are not?

In this book, we test whether certain series, such as output, employment, profits, and interest rates, exhibit a steady pace of growth over time, or if that pace has drifted. In statistical terms, is the series stationary or not? If not, then oft-used statistical tools cannot be employed to evaluate the behavior of an economic series without introducing statistical bias.

To address these issues effectively, we examine many economic and business series and pursue alternative statistical approaches to make effective decisions based on the application of simple economic and statistical methods. Our work here is in contrast to two common approaches: econometric-only approaches or economic theory-only approaches. Our work returns to an earlier tradition of applied research rather than mathematical elegance, which is an alternative to econometrics that uses all technique with little to no real-world application or all-theory approaches with no technique and only hypotheses about the real world.

EFFECTIVE DECISION MAKING: CHARACTERIZE THE DATA

The first task for many analysts is to characterize the behavior of a particular time series. For example, is there a cyclical component to the data? Many economic data series show some cyclicality, but, alternatively, some are driven more by secular changes in our economy—for example, the labor force participation rate trended steadily higher between the early 1960s and late 1990s as women joined the workforce. Yet often a time series, such as employment, is influenced by both cyclical and secular factors, where the cyclical element may change the pace but not derail longer-term secular shifts in the economy.

If a time series does display a cyclical component, how does it behave as we move through the business cycle? Does the data in the time series decline when the economy is in a recession, or is it countercyclical and increase during a recession, such as the saving rate for households? How distinguishable are turning points in the series? If the series is volatile on a period-to-period basis, a large move in one direction or another may not be enough to signify a turning point, but instead care must be taken with a few recent data points in order to smooth out any volatility and distinguish the true trend. Moreover, do turning points in the time series lead or lag those of other series? Is the time series linear or nonlinear over the period of study?

Part IA: Identifying Trend in a Time Series: GDP and Public Deficits

Throughout the recovery from the Great Recession of 2007 to 2009, the pace of economic growth has been below par, and public sector deficits have persisted. This has led to a greater problem of public debt than many policy makers anticipated when the recovery began. Today, perceptions of the effectiveness of fiscal policy actions and the competitiveness of the U.S. economy have been brought into question. Both are critically dependent on the estimates of the underlying trend in essential economic variables like growth, inflation, interest rates, corporate profits, and the dollar exchange rate as well as other financial variables. For example, one key issue since the recession of 2007 to 2009 has been to identify the trend pace of economic growth, which, in turn, reflects the influence of underlying economic forces, such as productivity growth and labor force participation. Identifying the trend of these series helps to characterize the pattern of sustainable federal, state, and local revenues that will make for better budgeting in government and help guide policy makers over time.

The question is: What is the trend pace of economic growth, and has that pace downshifted in the United States over recent years? This issue is critical at both federal and state levels of government as well as for the strategic vision of private sector firms when they estimate their top-line revenue growth. Trend growth in the United States is a primary driver of tax revenues and thereby influences the outlook for budget deficits—a key focus of policy today. The ability of federal and state policy makers to balance their budgets depends critically on the pace of economic growth. Trend growth reflects the underlying influence of productivity and labor force participation rates at the national level.

But unfortunately, many decision makers suffer from an anchoring bias.[1] They base decisions on estimates anchored on historical growth rates without consideration that the model of economic growth they are using may have been altered. Nor do they consider that the potential growth of the economy, and therefore federal revenues, has downshifted compared to past estimates.

It is also important to distinguish whether the pace of economic growth, for example, can be described as a linear trend or as a nonlinear trend. If it is a linear trend, then the average pace of growth would provide a useful benchmark for anticipating revenues over time and thereby improve budget forecasts. If the trend is nonlinear, however, then estimating the growth of public revenues becomes more difficult, as will forecasting top-line revenue for private sector businesses. It is also important to know whether the average rate of economic growth has changed over time and whether its volatility has altered as well. Interpreting econometric issues of trend and volatility in a useful context is vital to practical decision making. For example, if the average rate of economic growth has downshifted, private firms are likely to become more cautious in hiring and equipment spending while also increasing oversight on inventories. Similarly, rising volatility for any series suggests a heightened sense of risk in using that series, which will also alter the behavior of decision makers toward an emphasis on avoiding risk.

---

[1]For a review of the role of bias in decision making, see John E. Silvia (2011), *Dynamic Economic Decision Making* (Hoboken, NJ: John Wiley & Sons).

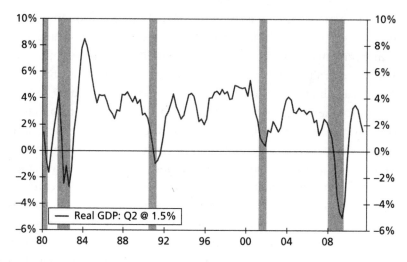

FIGURE 1.1   Real GDP (Year-over-Year Percentage Change)
Source: U.S. Bureau of Economic Analysis

Therefore, the first step in an econometric analysis is to identify the character of a trend in a time series—that is, whether a time series follows a linear or a nonlinear trend. A linear trend indicates a constant growth rate in a series and a nonlinear trend represents a variable growth rate. For trend selection, we will employ different types of methods, including t-value, R-squared, Akaike Information Criteria (AIC), and Schwarz Information Criteria (SIC).[2] A complete estimation process to identify the time in a time series is discussed in Chapter 6, and the U.S. unemployment rate is used as a case study.

Here we focus on the real gross domestic product (GDP) growth rate and determine the type of trend. The results indicate that the real GDP growth rate follows a nonlinear—more likely inverted U-shaped—time trend since 1980. The nonlinear trend implies that the average growth rate of real GDP is not constant over time, and it increases at a faster rate for some periods than others (see Figure 1.1). Since the average growth rate is not constant over time, it is therefore not an easy task to forecast the future real GDP trend.

Another way to characterize the rate of GDP growth is to calculate the mean, standard deviation, and stability ratio for different business cycles. Using a trough-to-trough definition of a business cycle, there were three business cycles between 1982 and 2009. As shown in Table 1.1, the average growth rate for the entire sample is 2.98 percent and the standard deviation is 2.1 percent, which is smaller than the mean. The stability ratio—the standard deviation relative to the mean—is 70.47 percent. However, when we break the series down into periods of individual business cycles, the stability ratio changes. For

---

[2]The AIC and SIC are information criteria, which help users to choose a better model among their competitors. See Chapter 5 of this book for more details about AIC and SIC.

TABLE 1.1   Real Gross Domestic Product (Year-over-Year Percentage Change)

Period	Mean	Std. Dev.	Stability Ratio	Trend
1982:Q4–1991:Q1	3.71	2.14	57.68	
1991:Q1–2001:Q4	3.20	1.61	50.31	Nonlinear, more similar to to an inverted U-shape
2001:Q4–2009:Q2	1.66	2.24	134.94	
1982:Q4–2009:Q2	2.98	2.10	70.47	

instance, the highest average growth rate during 1982 to 2009 is attached to the 1982 to 1991 business cycle; after that, the average growth rate declined in each subsequent business cycle. The most volatile business cycle is the 2001 to 2009 cycle, as this period experienced the smallest average growth rate along with the highest standard deviation.

Both trend and business cycle analysis reveal that the average real GDP growth varies over time, with some periods having a higher average growth rate than others, as shown in Table 1.1. Moreover, the average growth rate has a decreasing trend over time, while swings in GDP growth—evidenced by the stability ratio—have gotten larger. Note the growth rate for the 2001 to 2009 period is far below the pace of 1982 to 1991 and 1991 to 2001 periods. Meanwhile, the stability ratio for the 2001 to 2009 period exceeds that of the two earlier periods.

Part IB: Identifying the Cycle for a Time Series

In recent years, decision makers have been challenged to identify the changes in the stage of the business cycle—recession, recovery, expansion, slowdown—in the U.S. economy along the lines of the stylized economic cycle pictured in Figure 1.2 using industrial production. This identification is essential for business management in terms of planning production schedules, adjusting inventories and ordering inputs for the production process. In government, identifying the stage of the economic cycle will allow for better preparation for the cyclical rhythms of revenues and spending flows. Here again we see the importance of simple data description to improve decision making.

To identify a cycle in an economic or financial time series, we recognize first that many, but not all, macroeconomic time series follow a predictable pattern over the business cycle and, as such, can be characterized by certain statistical properties. In this sense, econometrics can provide a solution to identifying changes in a series over the economic cycle and can allow decision makers to anticipate those changes and alter their business plans accordingly. We employ a number of techniques to identify and characterize a cycle, such

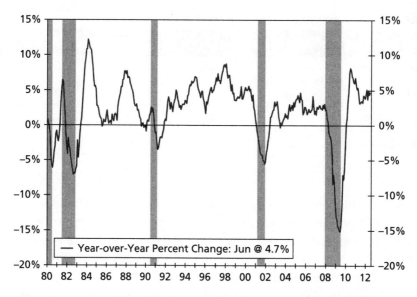

FIGURE 1.2 Total Industrial Production Growth (Output Growth by Volume, Not Revenue)
Source: Federal Reserve Board

as the mean, variance, autocorrelation, and partial autocorrelation. A complete econometric analysis to identify the cyclical elements in a time series is presented in Chapter 6. Other important macroeconomic variables with cyclical properties are GDP growth, the consumer price index (see Figure 1.3), corporate profits (see Figure 1.4), productivity (see Figure 1.5), employment (see Figure 1.6), federal budget deficit/surplus (see Figure 1.7), the yield curve (10 year/2 year, see Figure 1.8), and the credit spread (AA/5 year, see Figure 1.9).

In the following section we characterize nonfarm payrolls growth using autocorrelations and partial autocorrelations functions.[3] A simple plot of the payrolls growth (see Figure 1.10) suggests that it may not contain an explicit (linear) time trend, but it does contain a strong cyclical element. During an economic expansion, the rate of employment growth is greater than zero, and during a recession, the rate of employment growth turns negative. To confirm the cyclical behavior of payrolls growth, we plot autocorrelations and partial autocorrelations along with two-standard deviation error bands (standard errors). A good rule of thumb to determine whether a series contains a cyclical element is to check whether: (1) autocorrelations are large relative to their standard errors, (2) autocorrelations have a slow decay, and (3) partial autocorrelations spike at first few lags and are large compared to their standard errors.

---

[3]We provide a detailed discussion about autocorrelation and partial autocorrelation functions in Chapter 4 and application of the process in Chapter 6.

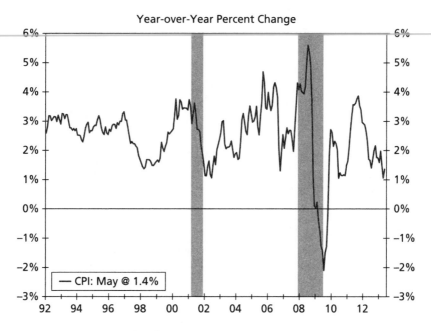

FIGURE 1.3 U.S. Consumer Price Change
Source: U.S. Bureau of Labor Statistics and U.S. Bureau of Economic Analysis

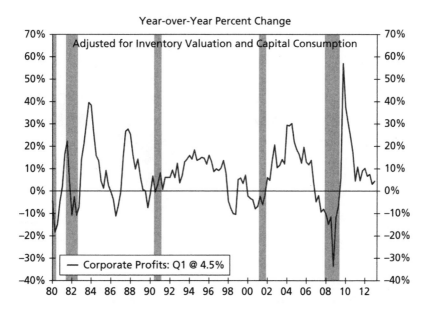

FIGURE 1.4 Corporate Profits Growth
Source: U.S. Bureau of Labor Statistics and U.S. Bureau of Economic Analysis

As shown in Table 1.2, the autocorrelations (column 3) for nonfarm payroll growth are large compared to their standard errors. The autocorrelations display slow, one-sided decay, which is represented by asterisks in column 4. The partial autocorrelations (Table 1.3) show a spike at lag-one, and this spike is large for first four lags relative to their standard errors. Taken together, both

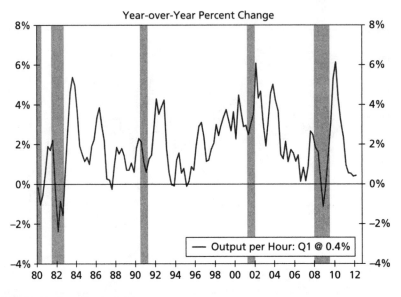

FIGURE 1.5 Nonfarm Productivity
Source: U.S. Bureau of Labor Statistics

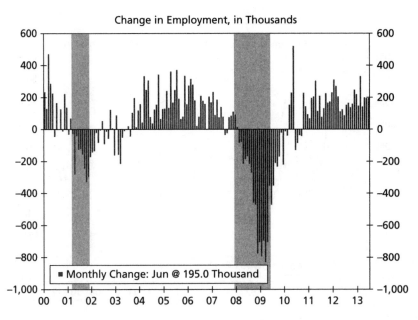

FIGURE 1.6 Nonfarm Productivity Change
Source: U.S. Bureau of Labor Statistics

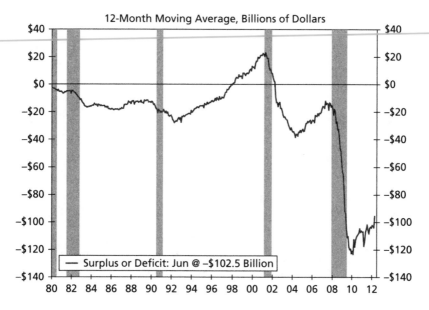

FIGURE 1.7 Federal Budget Surplus or Deficit
Source: U.S. Department of the Treasury and Federal Reserve Board

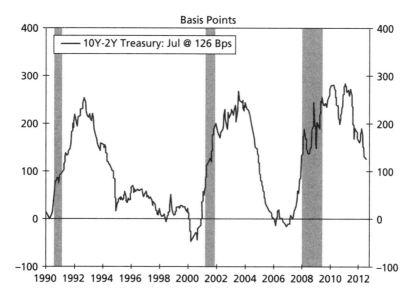

FIGURE 1.8 Yield Curve Spread
Source: U.S. Department of the Treasury and Federal Reserve Board

autocorrelations and partial autocorrelations suggest that nonfarm payroll growth has a strong cyclical behavior.

However, while the cyclical character of the economy is evident, we also recognize that often decision makers fall for recency bias in their thinking. That is, many decision makers in the midst of an economic expansion see that expansion as the most recent experience of the business cycle and thereby project that experience into the future. In contrast, when facing a recession,

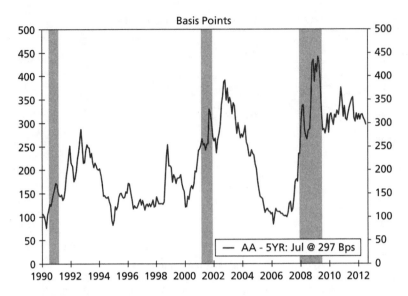

FIGURE 1.9 AA Five-Year Spread
Source: Federal Reserve Board and IHS Global Insight

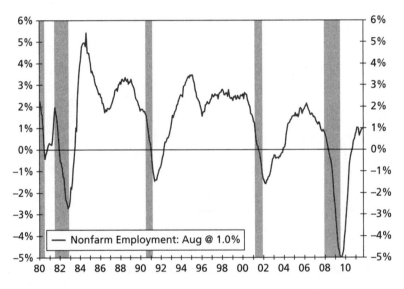

FIGURE 1.10 Nonfarm Employment Growth (Year-over-Year Percentage Change)
Source: U.S. Bureau of Labor Statistics

decision makers project that the recession will continue for the foreseeable future. The recency bias then leads decision makers to project the most recent experience into the future and thereby fail to recognize that the cyclical pattern within the economy actually changes over time, as we have seen with the employment series in Figure 1.10.

TABLE 1.2 Autocorrelation Functions for Nonfarm Payrolls

Lag	Covariance	Correlation		Standard Error
1	3.478113	0.99064	********************	0.050965
2	3.412676	0.97200	******************	0.087723
3	3.312945	0.94359	******************	0.112265
4	3.183517	0.90673	*****************	0.131258
5	3.033285	0.86394	****************	0.146627
6	2.864489	0.81586	***************	0.159301
7	2.680619	0.76349	**************	0.169808
8	2.485137	0.70782	*************	0.178502
9	2.277920	0.64880	************	0.185649
10	2.064523	0.58802	************	0.191448

TABLE 1.3 Partial Autocorrelation Functions for Nonfarm Payrolls

Lag	Correlation	
1	0.99064	********************
2	−0.50231	*********
3	−0.38539	********
4	−0.19967	****
5	0.02576	*
6	−0.01864	.
7	−0.05064	*
8	−0.04183	*
9	−0.0928	**
10	0.01544	.

The asterisks "*" signal a visual representation of the autocorrelation.

Part IC: Identifying the Subcycles of Economic Behavior: Use of the HP Filter

During the 2010–2011 period, the pace of job and economic growth appeared to move up and down without entering into the extremes of recession or economic boom as growth remained below the pace of prior economic expansions.

Yet this subcycle pattern occurred within the expansion phase itself and introduced considerable uncertainty for decision makers. Decision makers need to identify how the current cyclical behavior in any economic series stands relative to its underlying trend behavior. For example, is the series above or below trend during the current economic expansion? One simple technique to analyze any time series is through filtering and decomposing the series by applying the Hodrick-Prescott (HP) filter,[4] as one among several filters. A key advantage of the HP filter is that we can observe at any point in time whether a series is moving below trend or above trend relative to the historical values of that series.

This feature of the HP filter contains a useful policy implication that will help decision makers identify the stage of the cycle—slowdown or acceleration around a trend—in any economic time series. For example, in the spring of 2012 and often in the prior two years of the economic recovery, decision makers had been challenged to read the tea leaves and to ferret out the trend of the economy and labor market. Was the economy slowing down? Speeding up? What was the trend pace of growth over time? Had the trend pace changed over time? These questions were asked many times in relationship to the pace of GDP growth, job growth, and inflation between 2009 and 2012. These subcycles in the economy are not characterized by all-or-nothing boom-or-bust metrics. Instead, there is a constant acceleration and deceleration of economic activity. An effective decision maker needs to be able to identify these subcycles, which is another case of the use of econometric techniques in a practical setting. In addition, many decision makers succumb to the confirmation bias, expecting a stronger recovery, and so will jump at the opportunity to point out that when growth peaks above trend, this is a signal of permanent prosperity—the perma-bull in the financial markets. In contrast, any slowdown in the cycle below trend leads the perma-bear to declare the emergence of the next great depression. The careful implementation of econometrics can make for better decision making even in the financial markets when faced with claims by the perma-bull or perma-bear.

We begin the HP analysis by recognizing that an economic series, such as real GDP, termed y_t (log form), with g_t its long-run growth path, can continuously grow, but that growth may be less than its long-run growth path-term rate, g_t, for a period of time—this has in fact been the U.S. experience for several years now. So while there is no recession, usually approximated by a negative growth rate of GDP (more specifically, roughly gauged as two consecutive quarters of negative growth rate, although that was not precisely true for the 2001 U.S. recession), there are periods of time during any economic expansion that the acceleration of the economy would lead some to project a speculative

[4]R. J. Hodrick and E. C. Prescott (1997), "Postwar U.S. Business Cycle: An Empirical Investigation," *Journal of Money Credit and Banking* 29, no. 1: 1–16.

boom, while a decelerating economy will lead some to project the onset of recession. Yet decision makers who recognize that periods of below- or above-trend growth are typical of every cycle will first analyze the pattern of the data and then make the correct assessments necessary for effective employment and production decisions. The economy has at times suffered a major slowdown in the rate of growth while the actual pace of growth remains positive, such as during the mid-1990s. These midcycle slowdowns are ripe for the confirmation bias. It is certainly possible to conceive a severe and long slowdown causing more hardship than a mild and short recession, the 2009 to 2011 period being a precise example. In fact, long slowdowns in employment and demand growth have occurred repeatedly in recent times, even while output and supply growth held up well, supported by the process of technology and productivity. Note that the patterns of cycle and trend can differ between economic series, evident in the current cyclical behavior of output gains in manufacturing despite manufacturing employment declining in the early phase of the recovery. With the help of the HP filter, we can see where any series stands relative to trend and therefore make better decisions for investment spending, inventories, and hiring.

Rather than waiting for a public announcement of a recession, any economic slowdown merits serious consideration by decision makers. For example, a slowdown in employment and demand growth can lead to an overall slowdown in economic output or, perhaps, to recession ahead. A decision maker may thus want to alter production and inventory levels today.

Over longer periods of time than just a single business cycle, both private and public decision makers must distinguish between the long-term trends of any business series from that of the short-term cycle for that series. For instance, 10-year Treasury rates are constantly moving during the business cycle. But are the ups and downs in Treasury rates simply the representations of a cycle around a longer-term trend? In a similar way, are the movements of labor force growth and labor force participation partly due to the current phase of the business cycle, but also are they moving within a band that indicates a longer-term trend?

Therefore, an effective analysis must separate cyclical movements from long-term trend growth in a time series. As an example, we apply the HP filter on the 10-year Treasury yield, shown in Figure 1.11, to separate cyclical movements from a long-term trend component. The log of the 10-year Treasury along with a long-run trend, based on the HP, is plotted. Since 1980, the 10-year Treasury yield has trended downward. Yet, since 2008, the plot shows a volatile pattern, which may represent uncertainty in the financial market as well as in the economic outlook. The HP filter also helps to identify periods of expansion, as evidenced by the log of the 10-year Treasury yield typically running above the long-run trend (1995), and periods of weakness in the series when rates are below their long-run trend (1986, 1994, and 2012).

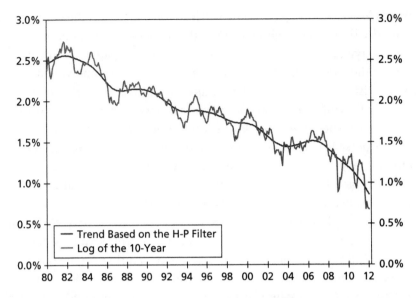

FIGURE 1.11 Decomposing the 10-Year Treasury (Using the HP Filter)
Source: Federal Reserve Board

Part ID: Spotting Structural Breaks in a Time Series

Over the past 40 years, a number of instances have appeared where the basic character of an economic series, or the relationship between two series, has changed. Yet decision makers appear to have anchored their expectations of the behavior of a series in the distant past, generating an anchoring bias. For example, the growth rate of productivity appeared to change during the 1970s in response to the rapid rise in the price of oil. Employment gains in each economic recovery since 1990 appear to be much slower than employment gains prior to that time. In recent years, considerable discussion has centered on whether the entry of China into the global trading environment has altered the behavior of inflation. In contrast, the recency bias leads a researcher to emphasize that this time is different. Perhaps it is, but the assumption must be tested to determine if this time really is different.

Essentially, the questions in 2012 became: Are interest rates permanently lower today than in the past? Is there a structural break in the behavior of interest rates? If a time series experiences a sudden shift (upward or downward) in its mean and/or variance, then we characterize that shift as a structural break. Yet if decision makers are hindered by an anchoring bias, then the implementation of statistical tests will help provide evidence to overcome that bias. Similarly, statistical tests will help to overcome the recency bias, showing whether there is a structural break in the series from long-term trends. The three primary tests of a structural break in a time series—the dummy variable approach, the Chow approach, and the state-space approach—are discussed in

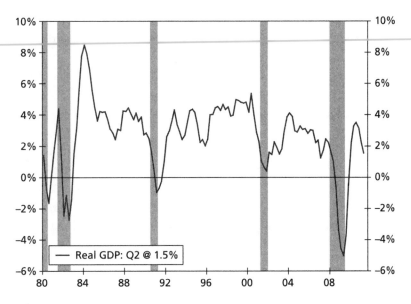

FIGURE 1.12   Real GDP (Year-over-Year Percentage Change)
Source: U.S Bureau of Economic Analyses

more detail in Chapter 4. These tests have a null hypothesis that the underlying series contains a break and the alternative hypothesis is that the series does not contain a structural break. Chapter 6 provides applications and SAS codes for these tests.

We apply the Chow test to determine whether there has been a structural break in GDP growth (see Figure 1.12). The results indicate that, indeed, GDP has experienced a structural break, which occurred in the fourth quarter of 2007, as suggested by the sharp decline shown in Figure 1.12. Evidence of a structural break has important implications for those who are interested in forecasting GDP and testing a relationship between GDP and another series, such as personal consumption expenditure. For a forecaster, evidence of a break implies that extra care is needed when making a call because the forecast bands (upper and lower forecast limits) will not be accurate from traditional estimation techniques. A structural break also signals caution on the part of the researcher and the user of that research in a statistical analysis between GDP and another variable that may not have suffered a structural break. Traditional estimation methods assume that there is not a structural break in the variables, leading to unreliable results if in fact there is a structural break, as in the case the GDP.

Part IE: Unit Root Tests

For many economic series, individual values drift over time since the series, when expressed in level form, will have a tendency to rise or fall over time. This is typical of aggregate measures of economic activity, such as GDP, industrial production, and personal income. To avoid making a bad decision based on data that exhibits an underlying drift, we want to identify if a series possesses a unit root. That is, we wish to identify whether the values of a series tend to move higher or lower over time, making them nonstationary and therefore prone to bias in the statistical analysis of the series over time. Since a series with a unit root drifts over time, its use in a regression model would produce spurious results. However, the unit root introduces a bias in decision making that we can call an illusory correlation—two economic series appear to be related but such a relationship is simply a product of the existence of the series moving in the same direction over time. The existence of the unit root suggests that the time series needs to be restated as a first difference, or rate of growth.

A series, such as nonfarm employment, may also have stationary elements. This means that a series falls below its trend value but later returns to the level implied by the original trend, such that there is no permanent decline in employment. This is particularly an issue today when we wish to know if the job losses of the Great Recession will ever be reclaimed or if the pace of monthly job gains permanently slowed. During the Great Recession, interest rates also fell sharply to levels that we have not witnessed since the early 1950s. Have these interest rates also entered new territory? Has inflation permanently downshifted as well?

Unit root testing is essential in time series analysis, as many macroeconomic data series are nonstationary in level form. Moreover, in the presence of a unit root, the ordinary least squares (OLS) results would not be reliable and would present an illusory correlation. Fortunately, there are a number of econometric tests that can be applied to identify a unit root. Among these are the augmented Dickey-Fuller (ADF); Phillips-Perron (PP); and Kwiatkowski, Phillips, Schmidt, and Shin (KPSS) tests.[5] Chapter 6 provides the SAS codes needed to apply these tests and guidance on how to interpret the SAS output.

Here, for example, we apply the ADF and PP tests of unit root on the consumer price index (CPI) (see Table 1.4 and Figure 1.13). Both tests have a null hypothesis of a unit root, which would indicate a series is nonstationary, and the detailed results do indeed suggest that the CPI is nonstationary. As a result, a researcher should not use OLS to analyze or forecast the level of the CPI because OLS assumes that the series are stationary and if they are not, then the results would be spurious. In simple words, if one or more series are nonstationary, then a researcher should employ cointegration and an error correction

---

[5]For information on these tests, see: D. Dickey and W. Fuller (1981), "Likelihood Ratio Tests for Autoregressive Time Series with a Unit Root," *Econometrica* 49: 1057–1072; P.C.B. Phillips and P. Perron (1988), "Testing for a Unit Root in Time Series Regression," *Biometrika*, 75: 335–346; and D. Phillips Kwiatkowski, P. Schmidt, and Y. Shin (1992), Testing the Null Hypothesis of Stationarity against the Alternative of a Unit Root," *Journal of Econometrics* 54: 159–178.

TABLE 1.4 CPI, Unit Root Test Results

Test Name	Constant	Constant and Trend	None
ADF	Yes	Yes	Yes
PP	Yes	Yes	Yes

Yes: Unit Root, Nonstationary
No: No Unit Root, Stationary

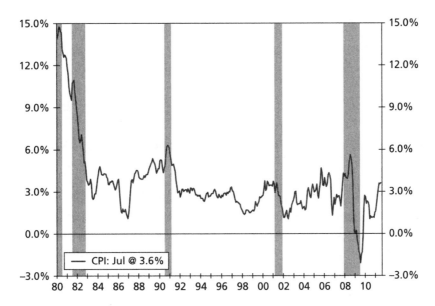

FIGURE 1.13 U.S. Consumer Price Index (Year-over-Year Percentage Change)
Source: U.S. Bureau of Labor Statistics

model (ECM), both reviewed in Chapter 5, for analysis as well as for forecasting of CPI instead of OLS.[6]

Part IF: Modeling the Cycle

For equity investors, earnings growth, as measured by growth in corporate profits, varies over the economic cycle, and as such, it must be modeled over that cycle. Therefore, to make successful investment decisions in both private and public sectors, we must identify cycles in a time series and then model these cycles to understand their typical amplitude and longevity. The purpose for modeling the cycle is to develop a framework for identifying the current phase of the business cycle for planning purposes, such as future financial investment decisions. For this, we can use autoregressive moving average

---

[6]In Chapter 4, we provide more details about unit root testing.

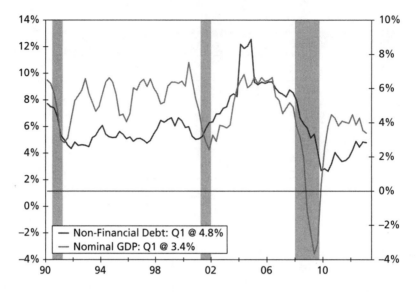

FIGURE 1.14 GDP versus. Total Domestic Nonfinancial Debt (Year-over-Year Percentage Change)
Source: U.S. Bureau of Economic Analysis and Federal Reserve Board

(ARMA) / autoregressive intergrated moving average (ARIMA), autoregressive (AR), integrated (I), and moving average (MA) techniques to model cyclical behavior of a variable of interest.[7] Autoregressive refers to the pattern of the data where the current value of an economic series is linearly related to its past values, that is, consumer spending today is related statistically to its prior value(s). The moving average simply represents that the current value of any economic time series can be expressed as a function of current and lagged unobservable shocks. The integration (I) simply allows for both behaviors to be a characteristic of a time series. SAS codes for modeling the cycle of a time series are provided in Chapter 6.

Part IG: Cointegration and Error Correction Model

Over the last 20 years, the growth of nonfinancial corporate debt and growth in the economy, as measured by GDP, were considered to be linked, as illustrated in Figure 1.14. Yet, could growth in both variables reflect other forces such that there is no actual link between debt and GDP themselves? Moreover, for certain periods, growth of GDP picked up while that of debt fell, such as during the 2000–2001 period. Then again from 2009 to 2012, economic growth appeared to recover while debt weakened.

---

[7]See Chapters 4 and 6 for more details about the AR and MA process. A comprehensive discussion about ARMA/ARIMA can also be found in Francisco Diebold (2007), *Elements of Forecasting,* 4th ed. (Boston, MA: South-Western).

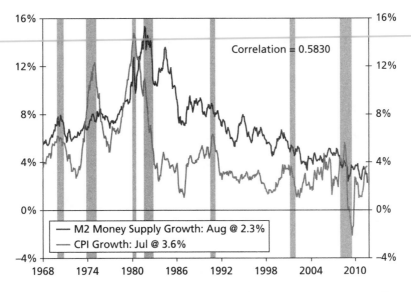

FIGURE 1.15 M2 Money Supply Growth versus CPI Growth (Year-over-Year Percentage Change)
Source: Federal Reserve Board and U.S. Bureau of Labor Statistics

Often economic series, especially when expressed in level terms, appear to be related when, in fact, the two series are simply influenced by a similar but distinct long-run trend. The apparent link is simply a coincidence of the movement of two variables and does not reflect a real underlying relationship. In contrast, over the short run, there may be little or no apparent relationship between two series so that decision makers will ignore any link between two series, yet over time the relationship will reassert itself. The actual link between two variables is simply not reflected in the current period.

Moreover, if two series have a trend or unit-root component, then it may appear that there is a statistically significant relationship between the variables when, in fact, there is no relationship.

In recent years, there has been a question of whether the economy and measures of the financial sector, such as nonfinancial debt, have a meaningful relationship to overall economic growth. Other economic relationships have taken on the aura of sacred truth, such as the link between the money supply and inflation (see Figure 1.15) as well as federal spending and economic growth (see Figure 1.16). Money M2 consists of currency, checking accounts, savings deposits, small-denomination time deposits and retail money-market funds.

ECMs take account of the deviation of the current value of a series from its long-run relationship and use that deviation, or error, to correct the estimates coming from the model going forward.

As noted earlier, if a series contains a unit root, then OLS cannot be used in the analysis. However, cointegration and ECM can be used as solutions to this

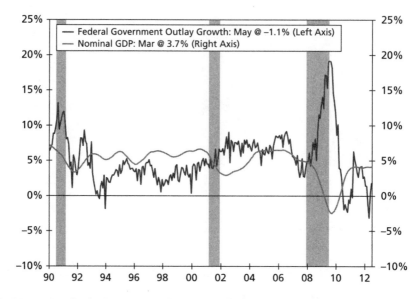

FIGURE 1.16 Federal Government Outlays and Nominal GDP (Year-over-Year Percentage Change, 12-Month Moving Average)
Source: U.S. Department of Treasury and U.S. Bureau of Economic Analysis

problem.[8] In this book, the Engle-Granger and Johansen tests for cointegration will be applied.[9] SAS codes of these tests are presented in Chapter 7.

Part IH: Causality—What Drives What?

While many economic series appear to follow similar paths over the economic cycle, it is important to determine if one economic variable really drives another. For example, during the 1970s and 1980s, movements in money growth were interpreted as causing a change in inflation; this decade, fiscal stimulus is implemented on the expectation that increased federal spending will lead to faster economic growth; higher inflation will lead to a weak dollar; finally, faster economic growth is thought to cause an increased pace of inflation. One way of looking at this is whether lagged values of an economic series provide statistically significant information about the future values of another series.

In many statistical applications, regressions are run between variables as if there is some underlying link between the variables, and yet the results of such regressions may reflect a mere correlation between the two time series, not that one series can be said to cause the other series. Here again, in many

---

[8] See Chapter 5 for more details about cointegration and ECM.
[9] See Robert E. Engle and C.W.J. Granger (1987), "Co-Integration and Error Correction: Representation, Estimation and Testing," *Econometrica* 55, no. 2: 251–276; Søren Johansen (1991), "Estimation and Hypothesis Testing of Cointegration Vectors in Gaussian Vector Autoregressive Models," *Econometrica* 59, no. 6: 1551–1580.

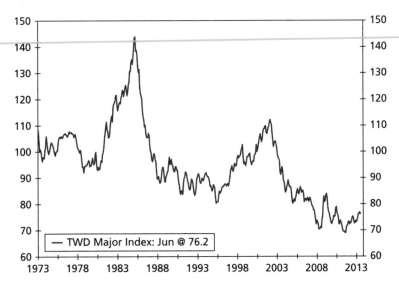

FIGURE 1.17 Trade Weighted Dollar (March 1973 = 100)
Source: Federal Reserve Board

economic relationships, the behavior of a series is commonly assumed to lead to a change, or cause, a change in another variable.

We use the Granger causality test to determine causality between money supply and inflation to find whether there is a causal relationship between above mentioned variables. We also discuss whether the causality is unidirectional (one way) or bidirectional (two ways). See Chapters 5 and 7 for more details about the causality test.

Part II: Measuring Volatility: ARCH/GARCH

Many economic series are characterized as volatile in some sense since values appear to swing up and down widely—this is particularly true of equity values and exchange rates (see Figure 1.17). Moreover, the volatility of these series can also be . . . volatile. In other words, the variability of the series is not steady but instead varies over time and therefore gives rise to the problem of trying to test for statistical significance. Economic series that exhibit periods of volatility followed by periods of small change are subject to this problem of volatility varying over time. Certainly many financial series, such as stock prices, exhibit such behavior and therefore are ideal candidates for this ARCH/GARCH approach that allows for variance (volatility) of a series over time. ARCH (autoregressive conditional heteroskedasticity) refers to modeling the volatility of an economic series. GARCH (generalized ARCH) refers to the possibility of both the autoregressive and moving average properties of the series.

Estimating volatility is crucial to the financial world. Engle provided a way to estimate volatility and it is called the autoregressive conditional

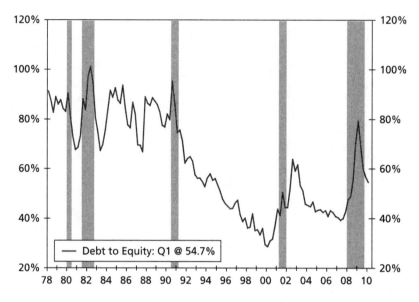

FIGURE 1.18   Ratio: Debt to Equity (Nonfarm Nonfinancial Corporation)

heteroskedasticity (ARCH) approach.[10] A useful generalization of the ARCH model is provided by Bollerslev and is known as generalized autoregressive conditional heteroskedasticity (GARCH).[11] ARCH/GARCH methods will be applied to the Standard & Poor's 500 Index and on financial ratios such as debt to equity (see Figure 1.18) in Chapter 7.

Part IIA: Forecasting with a Regression Model

Forecasting interest rates appears to be a thankless job. As someone once quipped, "We forecast interest rates, not because we can but because we are asked to." Our focus here is on the promises and pitfalls of forecasting interest rates using a regression model.

One standard practice in the industry and in the academic world is forecasting with regression models. With the help of regression analysis, a researcher can generate different types of forecasts, such as a point forecast, an interval forecast, and an unconditional and a conditional forecast. We review each in Chapter 9 of this book. We look at each type of forecast on quality spreads (see Figure 1.19), the 10-year Treasury yield, and the yield curve (see Figure 1.20).

---

[10]R. F. Engle (1982), "Autoregressive Conditional Heteroskedasticity with Estimates of the Variance of U.K. Inflation," *Econometrica* 50: 987–1008.

[11]A detailed discussion about the ARCH/GARCH is presented in Chapter 5. For technical details about ARCH/GARCH, see T. Bollerslev (1986), "Generalized Autoregressive Conditional Heteroskedasticity," *Journal of Econometrics* 31: 307–327.

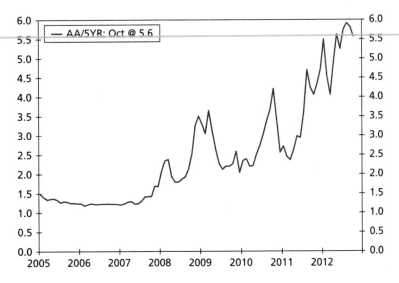

FIGURE 1.19 Ratio of the AA Corporate Yield to the 5-Year Treasury Yield

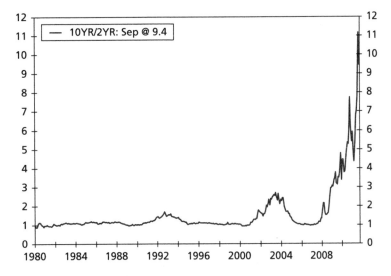

FIGURE 1.20 Ratio of the 10-Year Treasury Yield to the 2-Year Treasury Yield

The discussion in the text focuses on forecasting in a single-equation frame-work, with one dependent variable and one or more predictors (sometimes just one variable and no predictor). The unconditional forecasting approach follows ARMA and ARIMA methods. It is unconditional forecasting because ARMA/ARIMA frameworks usually do not involve any predictors.[12] That is, an ARMA

---

[12]The ARMA/ARIMA (autoregressive integrated moving average) is a pure statistical approach, which characterizes a time series into orders of AR and MA and then generates forecasts based on these orders. Chapter 9 of this book sheds light on ARMA/ARIMA and conditional/unconditional forecasting approaches.

approach uses lag(s) of a dependent variable along with lag(s) of the error term as regressors to generate a forecast for a dependent variable. In a conditional forecasting approach, forecasts for a dependent variable are generated by assuming (or sometimes using actual) values of predictors. Conditional and/or scenario-based forecasts are getting more popular nowadays because they create several more likely scenarios of the future path of a dependent variable. Typically, a researcher generates three scenarios: a base case (usually trend growth), a mild case (recession or expansion), and a severe case (severe recession or an economic boom). One example of conditional forecasting would be, at a given/assumed value of real GDP and the unemployment rate (as predictors), what would the 10-year Treasury yield (dependent variable) at that time?

Part IIB: Forecasting Recession/Regime Switch as Either/or Outcomes

One of the major objectives for decision makers is to forecast key economic and financial variables accurately. In this regard, we are interested in why a forecast breaks down and how this may relate to a change in the framework (regime) of our model of economic and financial behavior where the outcomes are one of two types—binomial. In Part IIB of this book, we examine key steps to an accurate economic and business forecasting approach when faced with a binomial (either/or)—possible outcomes are:

1. Forecasting techniques
2. How to identify the best predictors (independent variables) for a binomial model
3. Issues related with the data (e.g., cyclicity, structural changes, outliers)
4. Forecast evaluation

Overall, this book provides comprehensive and practical analysis as well as accurate forecasting procedures for business analysts, researchers, practitioners, and graduate students using SAS software.

How do we deal with events where the outcomes are binomial (i.e., events where there are only two mutually exclusive outcomes)? In economics, this problem appears when we go to estimate the probability of having a recession or not at some time in the future.[13]

Seeing a recession coming is one of the most important elements in forecasting for decision makers, investors and the academic world. In this book, a Probit

---

[13]J. Silvia, S. Bullard, and H. Lai (2008), "Forecasting U.S. Recessions with Probit Stepwise Regression Models," *Business Economics* 43, no. 1, pages 7-18. M. Vitner, J. Bryson, A. Khan, A. Iqbal, and S. Watt (2012), "The State of States: A Probit Model," presented at the 2012 Annual Meeting of the American Economic Association, January 6–8, Chicago, Illinois.

model will be employed to generate recession probabilities for the United States as an illustration of the binomial outcomes that occur in decision making.

Part IIC: Forecasting with Vector Autoregression

Often the relationship between economic variables is not theoretically clear. Moreover, we are frequently interested in several variables at the same time, and we are not sure how to build a model for the relationships for all these variables. For this we turn to the vector autoregression (VAR) approach.[14] A VAR treats all economic variables symmetrically by including an equation explaining each variable's evolution based on its own lags and the lags of all the other VAR models as a theory-free method to estimate economic relationships. The approach is theory-free in the sense that, in a VAR model, every variable is interrelated with each other, and therefore there are no specific dependent and independent variables. However, economic theory usually suggests a typical pattern among different variables, such as short-term interest rates being dependent on output growth and the expected rate of inflation.

The VAR approach is one of the most important and common approaches being used for forecasting and econometric analysis in the market and in the academic world. We employ VAR to generate a forecast for nonfarm payrolls. Furthermore, we provide a systematic approach to forecasting with VAR including, data and model specification selection in Chapter 10 of this book.

Part IID: Forecast Evaluation

Finally, how do we know how well a model performs, and how can we compare the performance of different models? A comprehensive methodology for in-sample and out-of-sample forecast evaluations is presented for the employment model developed in Chapter 11. Methods include root mean squared error (RMSE), mean absolute error (MAE), and directional accuracy.

---

[14]Chapter 10 explains the VAR approach in more detail. A good source of the VAR approach is Christopher A. Sims (1980), "Macroeconomics and Reality," *Econometrica* 48, no. 1: 1–48.

CHAPTER 2

First, Understand
the Data

Large amounts of data can be cumbersome and daunting, frustrating users and turning them away from rich information that can provide insight into the world. During, as well as long after the Great Recession of 2007 to 2009, anecdotes abounded about the weakness of the labor market: laid-off workers finding a new job only to be laid off again weeks later; job seekers unable to obtain employment for years; and workers taking pay cuts to help companies as they struggled to survive. How representative were these stories? Were they a few people's experience, or did they indicate broader labor market troubles? Moreover, who were these laid-off workers unable to find jobs for more than a year? Were they the least educated in our society, the oldest, or a member of a minority? How long was the average person out of work? How many people continued to look for work and how many just gave up? Were the employed immune from the downturn, or were they seeing their wages crumble in the weak economy? Were the employed working harder for fear of losing their job? All these questions can be answered, if an analyst dives into the wealth of economic information available on the economy and knows the techniques to filter though the noise of any data series. This chapter presents a review of the major economic indicators used in both public and private sectors. For the serious analyst, understanding the data is essential before attempting to apply any sophisticated statistical software. That is the focus of this chapter.

In October 2009, the unemployment rate in the United States reached 10 percent, a 26-year high (see Figure 2.1). Three months later, in January 2010, the unemployment rate had come off its cycle high and fallen to 9.7 percent, suggesting that the labor market was beginning to recover. But had it? Taking the unemployment rate at face value suggested it had, but other measures

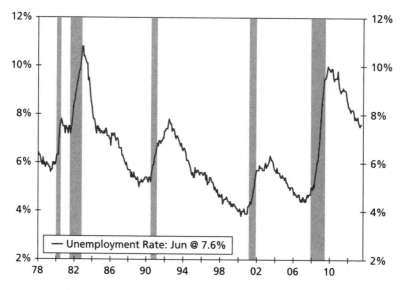

FIGURE 2.1 Unemployment Rate (Seasonally Adjusted)
Source: U.S. Bureau of Labor Statistics

painted a different picture. Analysts needed to look deeper at the data to determine if the usual benchmarks were accurately portraying the economic environment, or if something had shifted, making traditional measures ineffective. Was this cyclical turn a real change in the trend? Or was there a new model for the labor market that was bringing the unemployment rate down? How can an analyst decide?

Although the unemployment rate was falling in late 2009, firms still were reducing jobs and the number of workers being laid off or discharged was still running above the number of workers quitting jobs. What was helping to drive the unemployment rate down was that fewer people were looking for work—a sign that labor market conditions were not improving but instead so dire that many had given up hope of finding a new job (see Figure 2.2). The unemployment rate, in this case, was not comparable to the previous two decades when the labor force was consistently growing and participation in the economy—particularly among women—was rising. Was there a new structure in the labor market?

The discrepancy between the unemployment rate and other measures of the labor market back in late 2009 and early 2010 was observable to analysts familiar with other key indicators of the economy. However, graduates of college economics courses are exposed to very few of the data series they will later encounter in the business world, let alone the statistical means to test the observed data. Instead, college curriculum often emphasizes theory and elegant statistics—the foundation for the field of economics—but glosses over key data that many students actually will analyze in their professional careers.

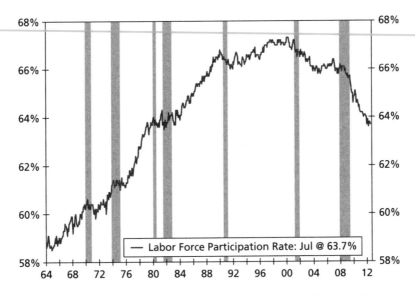

FIGURE 2.2 Labor Force Participation Rate (16 Years and Over, Seasonally Adjusted)
Source: U.S. Bureau of Labor Statistics

At the same time, economists in the workplace often interpret data without carefully examining the underlying structural models that generate the data. For new professionals to use this data effectively, they must have a basic working knowledge of its composition and an understanding of its historical relationship to the performance of the economy and their own organization. Therefore, in this chapter we introduce variables that serve as benchmarks for decision making at all levels to many professional analysts and offer an essential review of the character of these variables. For example, these benchmarks include economic series that are used at the federal level for budget projections by the Congressional Budget Office and by the Federal Reserve in providing guidance to the markets on policy.

In today's sophisticated economy, decision makers have available hundreds of economic indicators. Data encompasses all sectors of the economy, from financial, real estate, and labor markets to output and business conditions. Analysts and practitioners can drill down to detailed levels of information to gain insight into their fields of interest; but understanding a few key economic variables can help decision makers save time in analyzing market conditions. Both private and public organizations collect data series. Data collected by public institutions usually is available at no cost to users. Private industry and nonprofits fill gaps in government coverage as the need and opportunity for additional data has risen.

In this chapter, we discuss some of the key economic variables for decision makers across all areas of the economy. These variables provide insight into the five primary economic indicators that are the basis for good decision making: growth, inflation, interest rates, profits, and exchange rates.

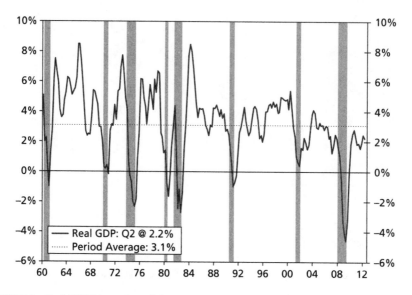

FIGURE 2.3   Real GDP, Volume Growth (Year-over-Year Percentage Change)
Source: U.S. Bureau of Economic Analysis

GROWTH: HOW IS THE ECONOMY DOING OVERALL?

Gross domestic product (GDP) is the broadest measure of the economy's performance. The GDP report provides a snapshot of the total output in the economy, combining the performance measures of all major sectors in the economy into a single measure. GDP is the sum of the final value (price) of total goods and services produced *within* a given geography. It is similar to, but not to be confused with, gross national product (GNP), which is the sum of output produced *by* a nation's population and related capital, whether it was produced within the nation's borders or not. In order to avoid double counting, GDP does not include intermediate stages of production, but only the final value of finished goods and services within the economy.

Given the scope of GDP, it is a highly influential report for businesses, policy makers, and investors. It shows whether the economy is contracting or expanding, which can influence actions of business leaders and policy makers throughout the business cycle (see Figure 2.3). Moreover, the long-term trend in GDP can affect how much businesses can expect to grow, the ability of the federal government to spend, and a country's standard of living. Therefore, analysts should be familiar with the major components of GDP. For this we turn back to the equation first seen in introductory macroeconomics, where we learned that GDP = C + I + G + NX (see Figure 2.4),

where

C = personal consumption

I = business investment

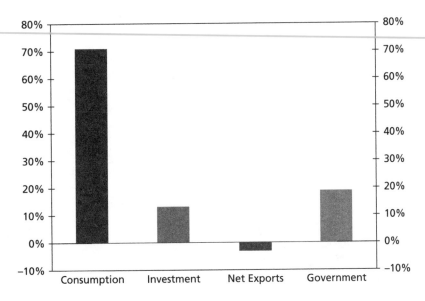

FIGURE 2.4 GDP Share by Major Components
Source: U.S. Bureau of Economic Analysis

$$G = \text{Government}$$
$$NX = \text{Net Exports}$$

PERSONAL CONSUMPTION

The first, and largest, component of GDP is personal consumption or C in the basic GDP equation. Goods and services for personal consumption account for just over 70 percent of total output in the economy. Included are final sales of goods and services purchased by households as well as the operating expenses of nonprofit institutions and imputed value of in-kind services received by individuals.

Personal consumption spending is divided into three groupings that each act differently throughout the business cycle: durable goods, nondurable goods, and services. Analysts must be aware of where the economy is in a business cycle in order to separate the trend in these components from what is a typical cyclical change and what may point to a long-term shift in the trend of the economy. As shown in Figure 2.5, for example, durable goods are the most volatile component of personal consumption as households will delay big-ticket purchases (e.g., cars, furniture, and major appliances) when the economy is weak and consumer confidence in the future is quite low. In periods of recession, consumers increase saving to guard against a potential loss of income as personal income growth slows and layoffs mount. Nondurable goods, such as food and gasoline, are more difficult to do without and are a steadier base of spending

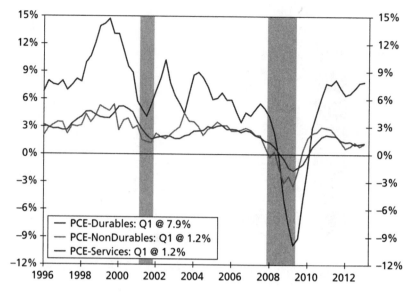

FIGURE 2.5 Real Personal Consumption Expenditures (Year-over-Year Percentage Change, Durables 4Q Moving Average)
Source: U.S. Department of Commerce

throughout the business cycle. Spending in this category will still fluctuate as consumers substitute goods or pull back on some nondurable purchases, such as clothing, when times get tough. Services account for about two-thirds of consumer spending and about 45 percent of all spending in the economy. Many of these items, such as medical care, housing, and transportation, cannot be postponed during a downturn. They are less sensitive to phases of the business cycle and provide a certain base of support for spending during a recession.

The pace of personal consumption growth is based on households' ability and willingness to consume. That, in turn, is a function of income growth, the saving rate, and the availability of credit. While GDP is only released quarterly, numerous monthly measures on the state of the consumer can help businesses and policy makers track consumer spending. One such source is the monthly personal income and spending report, which details income growth from all sources—everything to wages and salaries from work to rental and dividend incomes—what consumers spent, and how much they saved. Monthly reports are also available for retail sales, which give an earlier look at how much goods consumers are buying, and consumer credit, which provides an additional source for consumer purchases outside income. In addition, numerous surveys of consumer confidence are available, which can illustrate households' propensity to spend in the months ahead based on their outlook on the economy. All of these reports can provide analysts with an early look at the largest component of GDP and help them anticipate turns in the market that will affect their business.

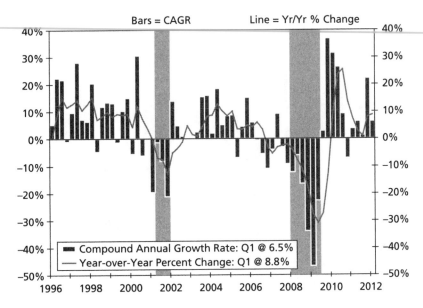

Bars = CAGR   Line = Yr/Yr % Change

Compound Annual Growth Rate: Q1 @ 6.5%
Year-over-Year Percent Change: Q1 @ 8.8%

FIGURE 2.6   Real Private Domestic Investment
Source: U.S. Department of Commerce

GROSS PRIVATE DOMESTIC INVESTMENT

Investment by private businesses is a second major source of spending in the economy. Although much smaller than personal consumption expenditures—about 13 percent of GDP—business investment spending provides insight into how businesses assess the economic outlook as well as their own general health. Private investment is based on the cost and the expected return of capital. For an investment to be profitable, the return on capital must exceed the cost. Interest rates—a simple, first-step proxy for the cost of capital—fall when the economy weakens as the central bank tries to ease financial conditions. But this might not be enough to offset weakening demand in final sales which impacts the return on capital. Since businesses often hold off on investment when the economic outlook darkens, this series can be fairly volatile (see Figure 2.6).

Investment spending can be broken down between fixed investments and changes to private inventories. Fixed investment includes spending on equipment and software by businesses. Spending in this category can greatly improve productivity in the economy but is also extremely sensitive to interest rates, credit availability, and expected profits. Investment in structures is also included under fixed investment and can be divided between nonresidential and residential structures. Nonresidential structures include spending by businesses for new commercial space, such as offices, warehouses, and utility plants. Residential investment includes private purchases for residences, whether they are owned by the occupant or rented out. Residential structures historically have accounted

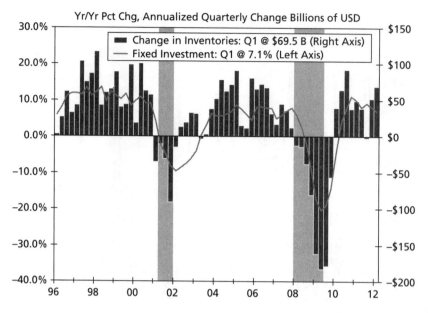

FIGURE 2.7   Real Inventory Change versus Business Investment (Year-over-Year Percentage Change)
Source: U.S. Bureau of Economic Analysis

for 30 percent of private investment, although this share increased to 35 percent between 2002 and 2006 as the housing sector became out of balance. Since the official end of the 2007 to 2009 recession, residential investment has averaged only 20 percent of private investment as the imbalance between current supply and demand in the housing market is reconciled.

The change to private inventories makes up the other major component of investment in the economy. As GDP measures everything produced in the economy over a given time period, not just what is sold, changes to inventory levels also must be accounted for to reflect total output in the economy. As the outlook for the economy changes, inventory levels also change. Here it is not the inventory level that matters in relation to GDP growth but rather the change throughout the quarter (see Figure 2.7).

The degree of these changes may be planned or forced, depending on how quickly the economic outlook and environment change. For example, inventories may decline if growth accelerated more quickly than businesses antici-pated or if businesses lowered production under the expectation that future sales would slow. The inventory-to-sales ratio can be a helpful gauge of appro-priate inventory levels. As the economy heats up, a lower inventory-to-sales ratio will signal the need for additional production in the near term to keep pace with demand; otherwise businesses may miss out on customer purchases. In contrast, the inventory-to-sales ratio will rise if sales slow more quickly than inventory building. Although there is a cyclical component to inventory

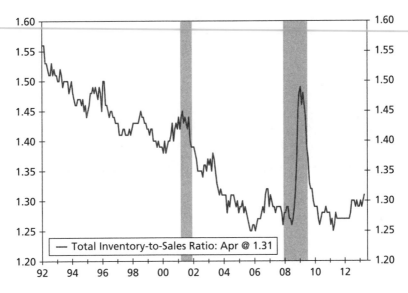

FIGURE 2.8 Business Inventories: Inventory-to-Sales Ratio
Source: U.S. Census Bureau

building, this ratio has shifted down over time as technology and management methods have changed the amount of inventories needed and desired by firms, which analysts must consider when evaluating changes over the course of the business cycle (see Figure 2.8).

GOVERNMENT PURCHASES

Government consumption comprises the final large component of GDP at around 18 percent. This category reflects spending by the government at the federal, state, and local levels. Federal government spending consists of defense and nondefense spending, with defense spending including military equipment and salaries for military personnel and nondefense spending incorporating spending by other agencies. Not included, however, are transfer payments from the government, such as Social Security income, since transfer payments are a reallocation of income, not a final purchase in the economy and not income for current production.

State and local government spending historically accounts for about two-thirds of government spending. That said, the state and local component can fluctuate more due to the requirement for states and localities to run balanced budgets. As such, during economic expansions, state and local spending often will rise in response to increased tax revenues, generating a larger contribution to GDP. In contrast, during recessions and in times of weak growth, state and local spending will contract. This was the case in the wake of the 2007 to 2009 recession, where rainy day funds and federal government aid was not enough

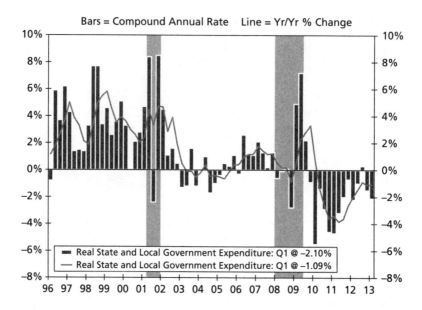

FIGURE 2.9 Real Estate and Local Government Expenditure
Source: U.S. Bureau of Economic Analysis

to shore up spending at the state and local level. State and local spending con-tracted in 14 out of 17 quarters between 2008 and the first quarter of 2012 (see Figure 2.9).

NET EXPORTS OF GOODS AND SERVICES

As globalization shows no signs of abating, trade is becoming increasingly impor-tant to the economy (see Figure 2.10). Exports are derived from foreign demand for products and services produced domestically. Demand can be affected by the strength of the receiving country's economy and currency. When a foreign country's economy slows, demand for products softens, reducing exports to that nation. The strength of a country's currency also will affect how much it imports or exports since that can change the relative cost of goods and services.

Exports must be included in GDP since production of those goods and ser-vices uses domestic resources, even if the products are not consumed within U.S. borders. Meanwhile, the United States imports more than it exports, and the sale of imported goods in the United States must be accounted for in other countries' GDP as imported goods were not produced domestically, and there-fore cannot contribute to domestic production.

When factoring in the adjustments to GDP based on what is produced but not consumed domestically (exports) and what is consumed but not produced domestically (imports), we end up with net exports. Net exports are simply exports minus imports of goods and services. Since the United States is a net

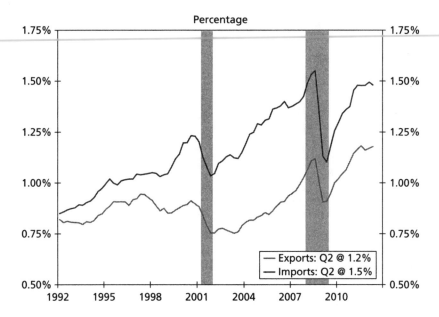

FIGURE 2.10 Imports and Exports as Percentage of GDP
Source: U.S. Census Bureau

importer of goods and services—that is, domestic demand for foreign goods exceeds foreign demand for domestically produced goods—net exports tend to be a drag on GDP growth, although that is not always true on a quarterly basis.

REAL FINAL SALES AND GROSS DOMESTIC PURCHASES

A final number to watch within the GDP report is "real final sales." As discussed earlier, inventories can jump around on a quarterly basis, and not always for the same reason. Therefore, real final sales can provide a more accurate picture of underlying final demand in the economy. Real final sales is GDP minus inventories. It includes exports, which reflect demand outside the United States. To get the best sense of final U.S. demand, we look at gross domestic purchases, which is GDP minus inventories and exports (see Figure 2.11). This measure helps businesses view the underlying trend in demand without adding the volatility of inventory building and it keeps separate outside markets which affect U.S. exports. This measure has trended lower over time, suggesting businesses cannot rely on the same pace of top-line sales growth as in prior economic cycles.

THE LABOR MARKET: ALWAYS A CORE ISSUE

Markets and policy makers closely watch the employment report. Indeed, in 2012, for many politicians, this report had become the measure of economic success or failure. This attention to the labor market is due to the effects it has

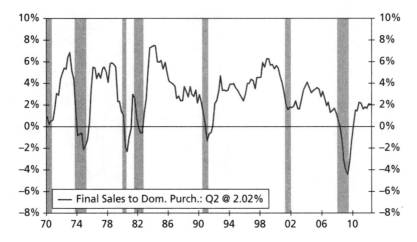

FIGURE 2.11 Real Final Sales to Domestic Purchasers (Year-over-Year Percentage Change)
Source: U.S. Bureau of Economic Analysis

on other areas of the economy. For example, employment is a means of income, and about half of income earned in the economy is derived from wages and salaries, with most households relying primarily on this source of income. As household spending accounts for more than two-thirds of total spending in the economy, the health of the labor market has great implications in regard to growth and the perceived success of the rest of the economy. Moreover, when households feel secure in their current source of income, they are more likely to purchase big-ticket items, such as autos and appliances. They are also apt to step up discretionary spending, such as going out to dinner and on vacation. Finally, households secure in their income prospects are more willing to buy a home, which generates business directly for those involved in the sale (real estate agents, appraisers, lenders, etc.) but also indirectly through retail purchases and contract work. Indeed, the labor market has been one of the major obstacles to the housing market's recovery following the 2007 to 2009 recession.

In addition to a source of income, the labor market represents one of the major inputs to growth in an economy. At a given level of capital investment and technology, additional labor can generate growth. To get an estimate of how much labor is being used, the Bureau of Labor Statistics (BLS) produces a measure of the aggregate hours worked in the economy, which takes into account the total number of people working and the average number of hours each person works. Yet what happens when the needs of an economy shift, and labor is a less desirable input compared to earlier years? It appears that this is the case today. More goods and services are being produced than before the Great Recession, but it is being done with less labor. With so much labor available in the economy not employed, the gap between potential GDP and actual GDP—the output gap—increases, leaving standards of living lower than they would be if all productive resources in the economy were engaged.

ESTABLISHMENT SURVEY

Of the indicators on the labor market, the most widely watched is the "Employment Situation" report published by the BLS at the beginning of each month. Based on surveys, this report offers a high level of detail on the labor market and provides a timely look at hiring, as it is usually released just a few weeks after the surveys are taken.

Decision makers sometimes overlook the fact that data comes from two separate surveys: the establishment survey and the household survey. The establishment survey, also known as the payroll survey, is based on data collected directly from companies. The most important number to come out of this report is the monthly change in the number of jobs at all firms (i.e., how many jobs on net did the economy create or destroy over the past month). This number is widely watched as it sheds light on where we are in the business cycle and is one of the four main measures the National Bureau of Economic Research (NBER) uses in dating U.S. recessions.[1] Typically when the number of jobs in the economy begins to fall on a sustained basis, the United States is entering a recession. However, firms tend to exhibit more caution in hiring when the economy comes out of a recession, as the scars of the past downturn are still fresh in the minds of management. Therefore, firms may be slower to add jobs than they were to cut jobs during a recession when companies go into survival mode. As a result, nonfarm payroll employment can be a coincident indicator when the economy falters and a lagging indicator of the economy healing (see Figure 2.12).

The details in this report are extremely rich. In addition to the headline figure of the number of jobs the economy has added, the payroll report provides a detailed breakdown by industry. This dissection can help analysts determine various points in the business cycle. Hiring in highly cyclical industries, such as manufacturing and temporary help services, can help determine turning points in the economy (see Figures 2.13 and 2.14). Details in hiring by industry can also show signs of structural shifts in the economy. In the 2007 to 2009 downturn, for example, losses in construction employment were outsized and protracted relative to other industries following the housing bust, suggesting a strong cyclical pattern (see Figure 2.15). Meanwhile, government employment declined for the longest stretch since the end of World War II as the Great Recession ushered in a new scale of fiscal challenges to state and local government, suggesting a structural break in the government employment trend (see Figure 2.16).

---

[1] On December 1, 2008, the NBER's Business Cycle Dating Committee (BCDC) announced December 2007 as a peak (beginning of a recession) in the U.S. economy. The announcement mentioned that one of the determining factors, with several others, to identify a peak month was payroll employment. See the NBER Web site for more detail: www.nber.org/cycles/dec2008.html.

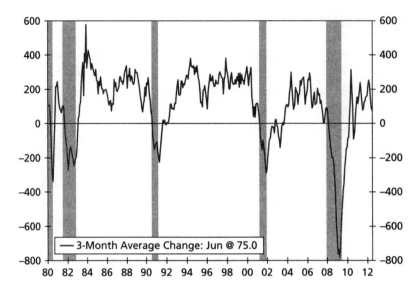

FIGURE 2.12 Nonfarm Employment Change (in Thousands)
Source: U.S. Bureau of Labor Statistics

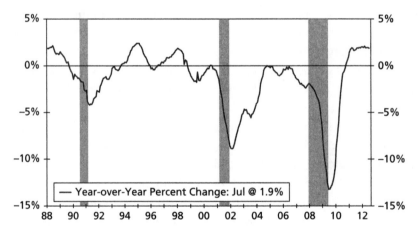

FIGURE 2.13 Manufacturing Employment Growth
Source: U.S. Bureau of Labor Statistics

The establishment survey also provides data on the number of hours worked in all jobs and earnings of workers over the course of the month. Data on hours is provided both for the aggregate number of hours worked (by an index) and the average number of hours worked per employee. Average hours worked can provide useful insight on the headline number of labor market conditions beyond the net change in jobs added to the economy. Firms may be reluctant to shed jobs immediately upon a slowdown in business and instead may cut hours worked, thereby reducing company costs and employee income. On the flip side, given the time and financial costs of hiring new workers, employers

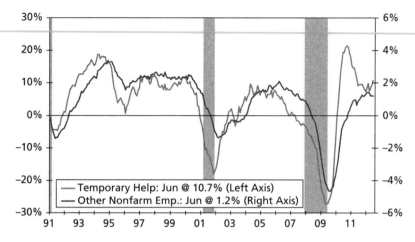

FIGURE 2.14 Temporary Help Employment (Year-over-Year Percentage Change)
Source: U.S. Bureau of Labor Statistics

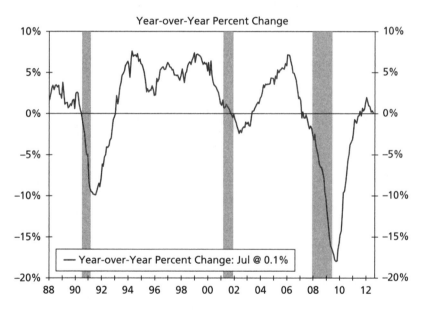

FIGURE 2.15 Construction Employment (Year-over-Year Percentage Change)
Source: U.S. Bureau of Labor Statistics

may add hours to current workers' schedules before taking on new hires. This still would boost households' income from earnings but would not be reflected in the headline employment number. In addition, the data provided from the establishment survey on average earnings can be a useful indication of future price pressures and, when combined with the total level of employment, can supply a proxy for personal income growth (see Figure 2.17).

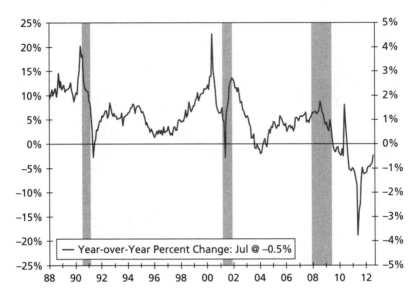

FIGURE 2.16 Government Job Growth (Year-over-Year Percentage Change)
Source: U.S. Bureau of Labor Statistics

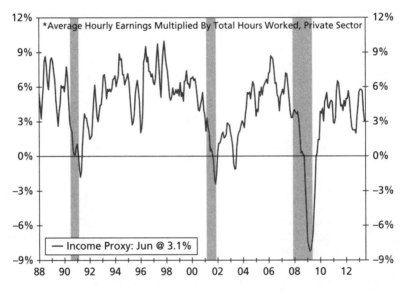

FIGURE 2.17 Income Proxy (Three-Month Annualized Rate of Three-Month Moving Average)
Source: U.S. Bureau of Labor Statistics

DATA REVISION: A SPECIAL CONSIDERATION

One noteworthy aspect of the payroll survey that creates a challenge for users of this data is that the headline number is often subject to substantial revisions in the months following the release of the survey. For example, revisions for a given month have averaged an absolute swing of 30,000 jobs in either direction in the second release of the data and 57,000 jobs between the first and third release since 1979, which is the first year available for data on revisions. This shift is due primarily to the survey collection period, where initially only 60 to 70 percent of firms surveyed submit their responses in time for the initial release of the data. As responses trickle in after the initial release, more accurate changes in the employment level of the economy can be obtained, which may paint a significantly different picture of the labor market. For example, in late summer of 2011, worries over whether the United States was headed back into a recession dominated markets. The first read of the August payroll survey showed that zero jobs were created over the month, a signal to markets that the economy was losing momentum. However, two months of revisions showed that employment had increased by 104,000 jobs, and subsequent annual revisions showed that employment increased by 200,000 jobs that month. Clearly, when conditions are even more uncertain than usual, users of the payroll survey data must be careful with how much weight to give a single month's payroll number upon its release.

THE HOUSEHOLD SURVEY

The second survey in the Employment Situation Summary is the household survey. As the name implies, the data derived from this survey is based on households' responses about their relationship to the labor market. Rather than measuring the number of *jobs* in the economy, this survey looks at the number of *people* working. Although the payroll survey's level of employment may capture the same person twice if he or she works two different jobs, the household survey does not double count these individuals. Moreover, in contrast to the payroll survey, the household survey also captures workers who are self-employed, work as domestic help, or work on farms. However, an individual's assessment of whether he or she is employed or not may be more subjective than a firm's assessment and therefore can lead to more volatility in the level of household employment—the number of people who report themselves as employed, as illustrated in Figure 2.18.

The most useful number to come out of the household survey report is the unemployment rate (see Figure 2.19). This measures the number of people who report themselves as unemployed as a percentage of the labor force. To be included in the labor force, an individual has to be either employed or actively seeking employment (i.e., applying for jobs). The unemployment rate is a useful measure in evaluating the overall health of the labor market. It provides a look at the slack in the labor market and is comparable across time periods since it is a rate, rather than a level, which accounts for level changes in the workforce. For example, an average monthly gain of 100,000 jobs in the 1950s would be more impactful on the labor market when the labor force was only

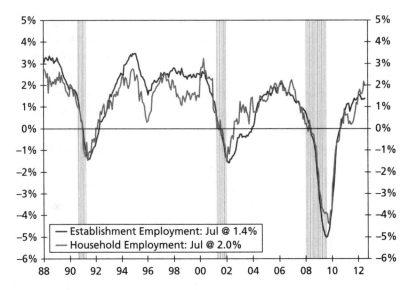

FIGURE 2.18 Household and Establishment Employment (Year-over-Year Percentage Change)
Source: U.S. Bureau of Labor Statistics

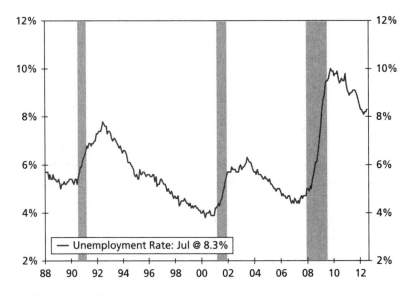

FIGURE 2.19 Unemployment Rate (Seasonally Adjusted)
Source: U.S. Bureau of Labor Statistics

about 65 million workers, compared to today when the labor force is approximately 154 million workers.

The unemployment rate, however, can be greatly affected by changes within the labor force. During recessions or other periods of weakness within the labor market, unemployed persons may drop out of the labor force as they believe no jobs are currently available, go back to school, or decide their time is better spent working in the home. This would push down the most commonly reported

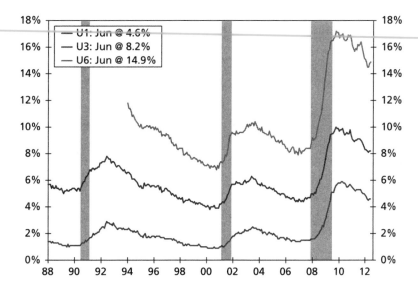

FIGURE 2.20 Unemployment Measures (Seasonally Adjusted)
Source: U.S. Bureau of Labor Statistics

measure of the unemployment rate—the U3 definition—as these workers are no longer counted in the labor force. Measures for such varying attachment to the labor force exist. The BLS calculates six measures of unemployment, ranging from vary narrow definitions of unemployment, such as the U1 calculation, which includes only persons unemployed 15 weeks or longer as a percentage of the labor force, to the U6 definition, which includes all persons unemployed, persons out of the labor force who are not looking for work but would take a job if it were available, and persons who are working part time because no full-time jobs are available (see Figure 2.20). Yet for each measure of unemployment, however narrow or wide, the rate remains well above the cyclical variations in prior business cycles. Is this merely the cyclical aftermath of the depth of the 2007 to 2009 recession, or does it represent a shift in the average unemployment rate?[2] This is the type of question we address in this book.

In the most basic terms, production in the economy is based on capital and labor inputs. Therefore, the household survey is a rich data source on the supply of labor within the economy. The rate of labor force growth can greatly impact the total growth rate in the economy. In the post–World War II period, the secular shift to more women working outside the home boosted the pace of growth in the labor force, but in recent years this trend has slowed, as has the rate of labor force growth (see Figures 2.21 and 2.22)

[2]For more on cyclical and structural unemployment, see John Silvia and Sarah Watt, "Long-Term Unemployment: Costs & Consequences," September 8, 2011, or John Silvia, Azhar Iqbal, and Sarah Watt, "Three Measures of a Healthy Labor Market," March 6, 2012, both of which are available from Wells Fargo Economics.

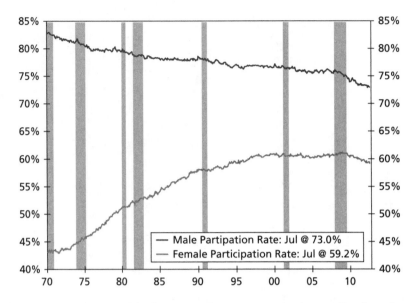

FIGURE 2.21 Labor Force Participation Rate: Males versus Females, (Seasonally Adjusted)
Source: U.S. Bureau of Labor Statistics

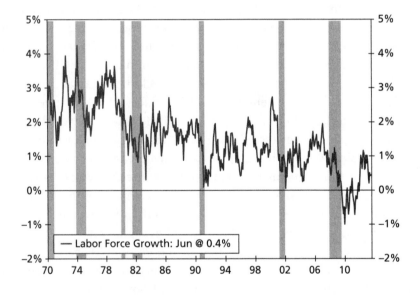

FIGURE 2.22 Labor Force Growth (Year-over-Year Percentage Change)
Source: U.S. Bureau of Labor Statistics

Another useful measure derived from the household survey is the labor force participation rate (see Figure 2.23). The participation rate looks at the percentage of the civilian population age 16 and over that is in the labor force. Given the sharp decline illustrated below in Figure 2.23 from 2009 to the present, the question arises: Is there a structural change in the share of the population that is even interested in working? This is another question we address with our statistical analysis.

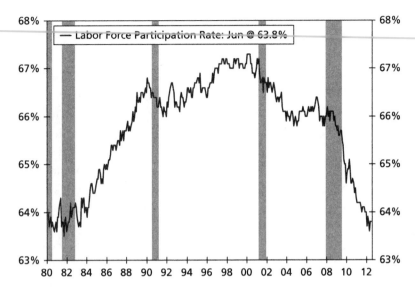

FIGURE 2.23 Labor Force Participation Rate: 16 Years or Over (Seasonally Adjusted)
Source: U.S. Bureau of Labor Statistics

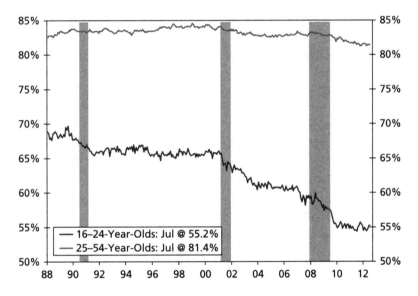

FIGURE 2.24 Labor Force Participation Rate (Seasonally Adjusted)
Source: U.S. Bureau of Labor Statistics

Since most Americans earn the bulk of their income from wages and salaries, the percentage of the population engaged in the labor market can impact the current level of earnings and spending in the economy. The participation rate can also affect the future level of earnings and spending in the economy, depending on why people may not be participating. For example, since the early 1990s, the labor force participation rate for 16- to 24-year-olds has steadily declined as higher education has become more common for younger members of the population (see Figure 2.24). Although this lowers the current supply of labor, the investment in education for this group should lead to better-quality labor production in the future and potentially higher incomes. On the other side, a decline in the participation of 25- to 55-year-olds may signal something more ominous, such as people dropping out of the labor force due to few job prospects. This could lower future productivity and income growth as the skills of those out of the workforce deteriorate. It could lead to lower overall spending in the economy as more people are dependent on income from elsewhere, whether it is a spouse, family, the government, or charity. The questions become: Is a decline in the labor force participation rate due to something less impactful, like an aging population where a higher percentage of the population over 16 is moving into retirement? How can we test structural breaks in cyclical trends?

In addition to the data series and measures just highlighted, the household survey provides rich details on these measures through demographic breakdowns, such as gender, age, race/ethnicity, and education. This data can help identify secular trends in the labor market, such as higher female participation rates, changes in educational attainment among the workforce, and labor market outcomes for certain target groups in business and marketing.

MARRYING THE LABOR MARKET INDICATORS TOGETHER

Confusing messages can arise between the data from the establishment and household surveys as they are based on measures from different surveys of the labor market, even if taken from the same month. Analysts need to decipher the noise stemming from these surveys by asking: Is the conflict between a decline in payrolls and a decline in the unemployment rate due to inconsistency between the household and establishment employment changes or due to a decline in the number of people looking for work, which also signals weakness in the economy? These are issues decision makers must be aware of when examining the employment situation.

JOBLESS CLAIMS

An issue with many economic indicators, including measures of the labor market, concerns the timely nature of their reporting. Although the monthly employment report offers a relatively timely look at the current state of the labor market, the weekly report on jobless claims can provide an even more up-to-date picture of labor market conditions and the broad economy. As seen in Figure 2.25, jobless claims are highly cyclical, and as such they can offer an early insight into whether an economy is shifting from one phase of the business cycle to another. But given the volatility of jobless claims, decision makers must ask: How can we tell when a rise in initial jobless claims is significant?

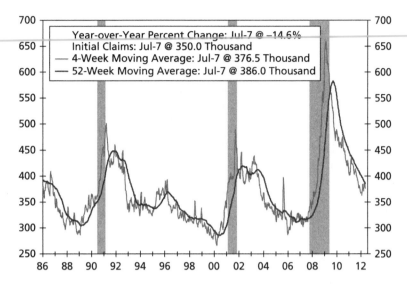

FIGURE 2.25 Initial Claims for Unemployment (Seasonally Adjusted, in Thousands)
Source: U.S. Bureau of Labor Statistics

Moreover, like any series, how much of the change is cyclical, and how much of the change might be due to a long-term shift in the data?

In a dynamic economy such as the United States, thousands of people lose their job at the same time new jobs are created every week. During the last two economic expansions, initial jobless claims averaged 340,000 per week. However, when this series is consistently above a certain level, it is often an early warning sign of the distress in the labor market. Initial claims, therefore, also signal potential weakness ahead for personal income, spending, confidence, and business investment. Due to the frequency of the release of this information, this series can be volatile on a week-to-week basis. A moving average for this series is helpful in determining trends and turning points. With this series, analysts must ask: How else can we better distinguish the signals of movements in jobless claims over time?

INFLATION

Price changes can have far-reaching consequences across the economy. For consumers, a rise in prices, if unaccompanied by a commensurate rise in income, can mean diminished real purchasing power and therefore a lower standard of living. For businesses, a rise in input prices could challenge profitability if the business cannot pass on the increase in its output prices to its consumers. Although substitutions and adjustments can be made in the shopping cart and production process, balancing changes to costs with changes to income/revenue is a constant challenge for all actors in the economy.

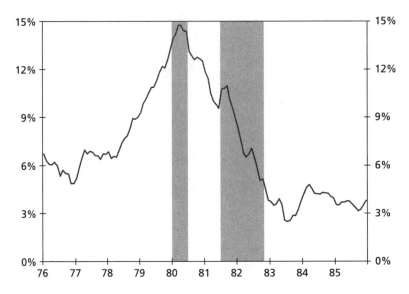

FIGURE 2.26 CPI Disinflation (Year-over-Year Percentage Change)
Source: U.S. Bureau of Labor Statistics

Importantly, changes in price do not always mean inflation. In a dynamic economy, prices are constantly changing to reflect the supply and demand of individual products. Inflation reflects a broad rise in prices across the whole economy. Moreover, a distinction should be made between *deflation* and *disinflation*. Deflation is a decline in the aggregate price level of the economy. This can have detrimental and widespread effects across an economy as consumers and businesses hold back on spending in anticipation of lower prices in the future. In this environment, output and demand falls, putting further downward pressure on prices and creating the potential for a harmful spiral, which will not be altered unless there is fiscal or monetary policy intervention or other shocks to the economy. Disinflation, in contrast, is a slowdown in the pace of inflation. Aggregate price levels continue to rise, but the pace of growth is slower than previously (see Figure 2.26).

Multiple measures of inflation exist and range from prices of imports, employment costs, and end products to consumers. The three most important measures of inflation are: the consumer price index, the producer price index, and the personal consumption expenditure index.

CONSUMER PRICE INDEX: A SOCIETY'S INFLATION BENCHMARK

The consumer price index (CPI) measures the price of final goods and services to consumers. The CPI is the most broadly watched measure of inflation. This series has a lengthy history dating back to 1913. It is reported on a monthly basis, making it a timely gauge of broad price changes. Moreover, the CPI is

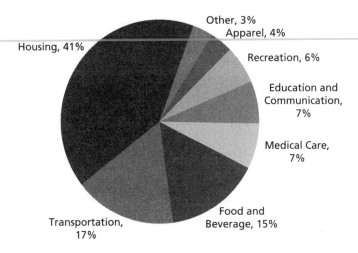

FIGURE 2.27 Consumer Price Index Weights, 2009–2010
Source: U.S. Bureau of Labor Statistics

widely used as a benchmark for inflation in many wage and benefit contracts, such as in collective bargaining and for indexing Social Security payments and tax brackets over time.

Each month, the CPI is calculated by sampling the prices of a fixed basket of goods and services. The basket includes goods such as groceries, clothing, gasoline, and cars. Services account for a little over half the products measured in the CPI and encompass housing, medical, and education services, among others. These products are then weighted within the basket based on the proportion of household budgets they comprise for a benchmark period, which is currently 2009–2010. Housing costs make up the largest portion of the CPI at over 40 percent weighting, followed by transportation and food and beverages (see Figure 2.27).

Although timely and broad in coverage, the CPI can misstate the rise in prices over time for several reasons. The "fixed basket" concept streamlines the calculation of the index but does not allow for the substitution of goods and services within the basket. As prices of individual goods change, consumers are apt to substitute one good for another based on their relative price, which would make their "basket" of goods and services less costly. A second issue with the CPI is that its adjustments for quality can be somewhat arbitrary. If the quality of an item is perceived to have increased over time, actual price changes may not be fully reflected within the CPI. The improved quality offsets the price increase because consumers are getting more out of that good or service.[3] Medical care illustrates the point. Nominal prices have increased rapidly, but so too has the quality of the service because of new scientific advancements and improved technology. Actual price increases may be adjusted downward by the CPI, but these quality enhancements are difficult to quantify precisely.

---

[3] See www.bls.gov/cpi/cpihqaitem.htm for more information on quality adjustment for the CPI.

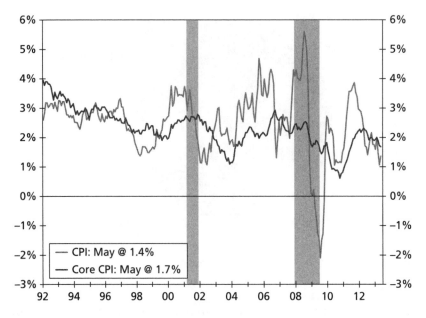

FIGURE 2.28 CPI versus Core CPI (Year-over-Year Percentage Change)
Source: U.S. Bureau of Labor Statistics

Changes in consumer prices are reported at the aggregate level (the headline) as well as for the index's subcomponents. Measures of inflation can be narrowed to categories such as food, transportation, shelter, apparel, recreation, and education and the subcomponents that feed into these broader categories—everything from white bread to women's dresses. In addition, the BLS computes a few special aggregates. Most important among these is the "core" CPI, which excludes food and energy items. The reasoning behind the core measure is that food and energy prices are historically much more volatile than other consumer prices, although this has changed over time. By leaving out these items, it is easier to determine the underlying trend in inflation (see Figure 2.28). Moreover, food and energy—particularly energy prices—feed into many of the other products in the CPI. Therefore, changes in these two components are at least partially reflected in the prices of other goods and services. Critics of the use of core inflation, particularly when used for determining monetary policy, argue that food and energy are consumer products. As such, the headline CPI should be used in decision making. This argument has some merit. Energy prices represent a growing share of consumer's disposable income, although food spending has declined as a share of total spending over the past two decades (see Figure 2.29).[4]

A casual examination of Figures 2.28 and 2.29 suggests a cyclical pattern for prices. It also demonstrates a shift in the long-term documented trend in core CPI and in the money spent on food at home. Meanwhile, overall CPI appears to be

---

[4]James Bullard, "Headline vs. Core Inflation: A Look at Some Issues," *Regional Economist* (April 2011), p. 3

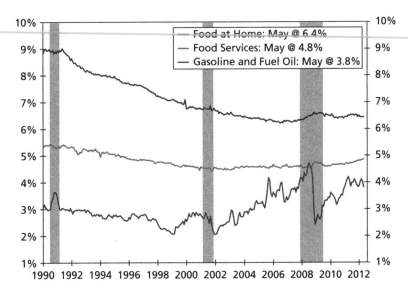

FIGURE 2.29 Food and Energy Spending (Share of Total Consumption)
Source: U.S. Bureau of Labor Statistics

more volatile than core CPI. These patterns are tested in later chapters for structural significance as these data patterns give better guidance for good decision making.

PRODUCER PRICE INDEX

The producer price index (PPI) is a measure of goods traded at the wholesale level or, in other words, goods prior to their purchase by end users. The PPI can provide early insight into cost pressures and whether these pressures are likely to reach the consumer. For businesses, the PPI is a measure of input costs as well as the prices of goods sold to the next level of production or on to the retail sector. The prices paid and received by producers and end use sellers will affect a company's revenue and profits, therefore making this a widely watched indicator by the business community.

The PPI report is broken into three sections representing different stages of production: crude goods, intermediate goods, and finished goods. The first stage, crude goods, measures the price of raw materials including food products, such as corn and livestock for slaughter, and nonfood products like cotton, timber, and crude petroleum. As shown in Figure 2.30, crude goods prices can swing dramatically. Supply of these goods can be influenced by weather, disease, and political factors (think petroleum) and therefore shift the market price. For decision makers, the difference in the volatility of prices at each stage of production is significant and offers a means of adding value that the analyst can bring to the discussion.

Changes at the crude stage of production will likely be felt at the intermediate stage, making price changes here still somewhat volatile. Intermediate

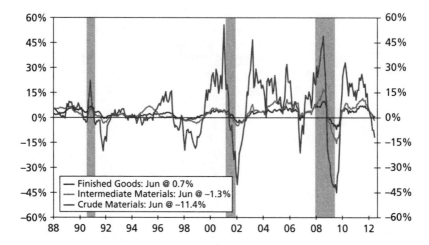

FIGURE 2.30 Producer Prices by Stage of Processing (Year-over-Year Percentage Change)
Source: U.S. Bureau of Labor Statistics

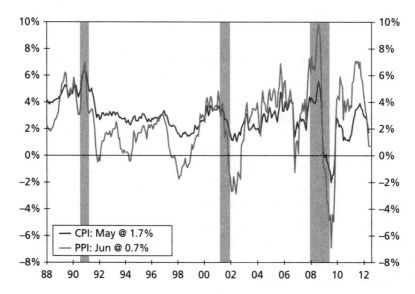

FIGURE 2.31 Consumer Price Index versus Producer Price Index (Year-over-Year Percentage Change)
Source: U.S. Bureau of Labor Statistics

goods are processed from raw materials one stage closer to their final component. An example here would be harvested wheat (a crude good) and grinding it so it can then be made into flour (an intermediate good).

The final stage of production is for finished goods before they are sold onto the retail sector to be sold to consumers. These are products that have completed the manufacturing process and have the most bearing on consumer prices. Although not a perfect relationship because, as mentioned previously, more than half of the CPI is based on services, the finished goods component can signal changes ahead for the price of goods sold to consumers (see Figure 2.31).

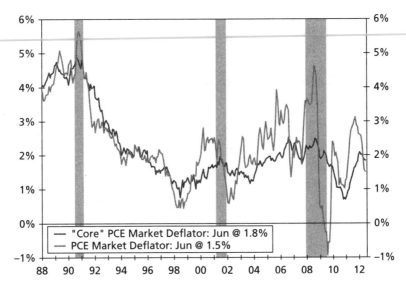

FIGURE 2.32 PCE Market Deflators (Year-over-Year Percentage Change)
Source: U.S. Bureau of Labor Statistics

One hypothesis we can test is whether changes at the consumer price level lag changes at the finished goods wholesale level and by how long.

Like the CPI, producer prices are broken into a few special aggregates. Among them is the "core" PPI, which like the core measure of CPI excludes food and energy prices. This measure helps identify the underlying trend in inflation, not just the movements of a few particular goods, as food and energy products are more likely to be affected by temporary changes in weather and political tensions. Other special groupings include crude materials less agricultural products and finished consumer goods less energy.

PERSONAL CONSUMPTION EXPENDITURE DEFLATOR: THE INFLATION BENCHMARK FOR MONETARY POLICY

The third measure of inflation worth noting is the personal consumption expenditure price deflator, or PCE deflator for short (see Figure 2.32). It is released monthly with the personal income and spending report and is used to adjust personal consumption for inflation, generating "real" personal spending. Although similar to the CPI in that it measures price changes for goods and services sold to consumers, the PCE deflator allows for ongoing substitution in consumer spending patterns, whereas the CPI relies on a fixed basket of goods that is adjusted only every few years. The PCE deflator provides a more accurate reading in the overall trend in inflation since it allows for the substitution effect, making it the preferred measure of inflation for the Federal Open Market Committee (FOMC) when developing monetary policy decisions. For this reason, the PCE can help gauge the path of interest rates and other monetary policy tools, such as asset purchases in recent years.[5]

INTEREST RATES: PRICE OF CREDIT

Interest rates and related risk measures are major factors in household and business finances. Although there are a vast number of fixed income instruments in the market, a few benchmark rates are telling of the interest rate environment across the yield curve.

Any discussion of interest rates begins with the federal funds target rate—the rate banks charge one another for overnight loans. This benchmark rate reflects the intentions of the FOMC and affects the movement of rates across the entire yield curve because it targets the shortest duration of loans. Since the Federal Reserve funds rate sets the benchmark for primary overnight bank credit, its impact extends outside the fixed income market and into loans for businesses, consumers, and nearly every other form of borrowing as the rate banks charge customers is dependent on their own borrowing costs. The 5- and 7-year Treasury rates are often used to benchmark corporate debt, while the 10-year Treasury acts as the benchmark for longer-term interest rates, such as residential mortgages in many cases.

Taken together, interest rates can indicate a great deal about the direction of the economy. Interest rates on securities of equal credit quality and different maturity dates are used in plotting yield curves (see Figure 2.33). The shape of the yield curve can indicate whether the economy is continuing to expand or likely to contract. A "normal" yield curve, the June 2009 and July 2012 curve, is upward sloping, as securities with a longer maturity date yield higher interest rates to compensate investors for the inflation risk they take and the love of liquidity. A relatively steep curve indicates that investors anticipate higher rates of inflation over their investment horizon. An inverted yield curve, when short-term interest rates are higher than long-term rates, signals that the economy is headed toward a recession and thereby the current economic/investment environment becomes relatively more risky in which to make a decision. When the yield curve begins to flatten and interest rates tend to become similar across maturity dates (the January 2008 series), the economy begins to head toward a recession/slower growth and inflation becomes less of a risk. However, depending on the current phase of the business cycle, a flat yield curve could indicate that the economy is headed toward more normal growth following a recession.[6]

---

[5] See the FOMC Summary of Economic Projections at www.federalreserve.gov/monetarypolicy.
[6] James C. Van Horne, *Function and Analysis of Capital Market Rates* (Englewood Cliffs, NJ: Prentice-Hall, 1970).

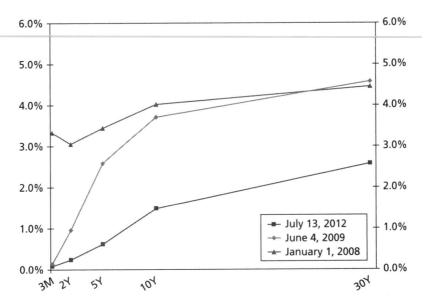

FIGURE 2.33 Yield Curve (U.S. Treasuries, Active Issues)
Source: Federal Reserve Board

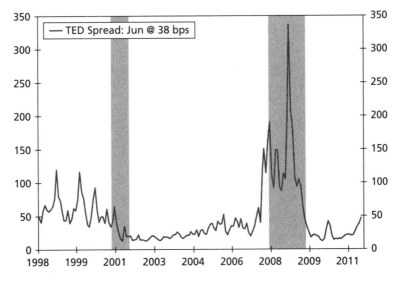

FIGURE 2.34 TED Spread (Three-Month LIBOR Minus Treasury Bill Yield in Basis Points)
Source: Federal Reserve Board and British Bankers Association

Interest rates can provide a quick assessment of perceived credit risk in the market. The TED (an acronym for T-Bill and ED, the ticker symbol for the eurodollar futures contract) spread is a prime example of this, as evidenced in the 2008 financial crisis (see Figure 2.34). It is measured as the difference in three-month Treasury bills, which are considered risk-free of default, and three-month eurodollar contracts (represented by three-month London

Interbank Offered Rate [LIBOR]), which reflect the credit risk of default in the market. During the 2008 financial crisis, the rate of interest financial institutions charged each other skyrocketed as demand for liquidity shot up and the credit risk of many financial institutions rose substantially due to the underlying value of assets on their balance sheet becoming highly unclear. Therefore, firms lending money demanded higher rates of interest in order to cover the heightened amount of risk they undertook when providing loans to other institutions. The Fed's provisions to insert additional liquidity in the market helped to bring down interest rates following the collapse of the investment bank Lehman Brothers, but risk in the market began to appear again in the spring of 2010, as the European sovereign debt crisis began to gain attention, and then again in late 2011, as interest rates rose to unsustainable levels on Greek debt payments and borrowing costs in Spain and Italy.

THE DOLLAR AND EXCHANGE RATES: THE UNITED STATES IN A GLOBAL ECONOMY

As the U.S. economy has become increasingly linked to international markets, the value of the dollar has taken on greater importance. A growing number of companies rely on inputs for their products that come from foreign countries, while many also look to foreign markets to sell their products. Many businesses are exposed to fluctuations in the value of the dollar—exchange rate risk—that can impact their bottom line.

Politicians and the media may discuss the value of the dollar, but in practice, there is no single value. Instead, the dollar is based on a series of bilateral relationships with other currencies, such as dollar/euro, dollar/pound, and dollar/peso. For many businesses, only a few of these exchange rates are pertinent to operations.

Most important, the value of the dollar is only a relative value as it represents the value of one currency, the dollar for example, expressed in units of another currency, for example the yen, subject to the laws of supply and demand based on the relative attractiveness of two currencies. That is, the dollar's value depends not only on factors originating in the United States but on factors occurring overseas. On the domestic front, an increasing appetite for imports in the United States will drive the dollar's value down as demand for foreign currencies to pay for the imports increases. U.S. importers buy foreign currency in order to buy foreign goods. As with any normal goods, the greater the demand for a product, the greater the price at a given supply. However, if the supply of a currency—the money supply—increases more rapidly than its demand, the expansion can drive down the price of the currency and therefore the currency's value. In contrast, increasing demand for products and services made in the United States will drive up the value of the dollar as overseas customers need to pay American companies in dollars, pushing up the demand for the currency.

However, since the dollar is perceived as a safe-haven relative to holding wealth in another currency, the value of the dollar is influenced by more than the demand for imported or exported goods and services. Financial turmoil abroad can influence the dollar's value, as investors move to it during times of uncertainty and drive up its value. On the flip side, more stable conditions internationally can drive down the value of the dollar as investors move into other currencies. This phenomenon can be seen in the wake of the 2008 financial crisis, when the depreciation of the dollar since the early 2000s was temporarily reversed as investors flocked to the greenback. When conditions calmed, the dollar continued its relative descent, but it crept upward again as the Eurozone crisis flared and investors again sought the safety of dollar assets (see Figure 2.35).

Although most businesses are interested in only a few specific relationships of the dollar, the Federal Reserve produces indexes of the dollar's value relative to other currencies. Among these indexes is the broad weighted index, shown in Figure 2.35, which includes the bilateral exchange rates for currencies of America's major trading partners, weighted by trading volume. This index can be helpful for companies that trade with many of the country's major trading partners. The Fed also produces two subindexes of the value of the dollar. The major currencies index reflects the value of the dollar relative to the value of currencies that are widely circulated outside their country of issuances, for example, the euro and yen. The other important trading partners (OITP) index reflects the value of the dollar relative to currencies in the broad index that do not circulate widely.

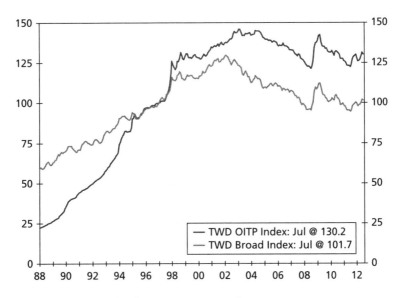

FIGURE 2.35 Trade-Weighted Dollar (January 1997 = 100)
Source: Federal Reserve Board

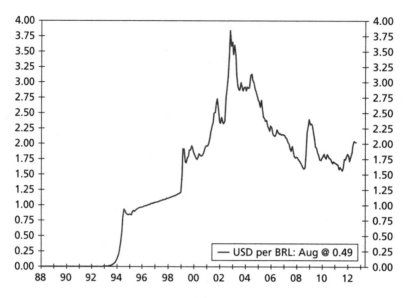

FIGURE 2.36 Brazilian Exchange Rate (USD per BRL)
Source: Federal Reserve Board

Policy in the United States lets the dollar float, but other countries may fix their exchange rates by restricting capital flows or relinquishing monetary policy independence and pegging their currency to the dollar, as in Hong Kong today. This may reduce exchange rate risk in the short term for businesses trading products in these currencies, but they run the risk of the peg being removed, as was the case in Argentina in 2001 and Brazil in 1999 (see Figure 2.36). In this graph we note the dollar and Brazil real by their market neumonics of USD and BRL respectively.

CORPORATE PROFITS

Of course, businesses exist to earn profits as a return to their investors. In addition to providing a return on previous investment, profits provide a source of funds for future investment. Moreover, they also represent income earned in the economy from production of goods and services. In today's economy, the major measures of profits include those reported for in the National Income and Product Accounts (NIPA) and profits reported to shareholders.

Profits reported in the NIPA accounts reflect the overall profitability of firms and are thus a barometer on how the economy is performing. Profit growth is highly cyclical, as downturns reduce revenues and force many companies to streamline costs, which increases profitability down the road, particularly when the economy heats back up and revenues rebound (see Figure 2.37). Profits as a share of GDP are also cyclical, with the greatest share typically occurring in

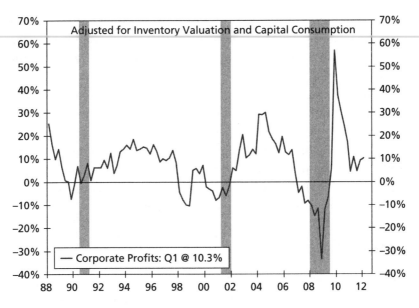

FIGURE 2.37 Corporate Profits Growth (Year-over-Year Percentage Change)
Source: U.S Bureau of Economic Analysis

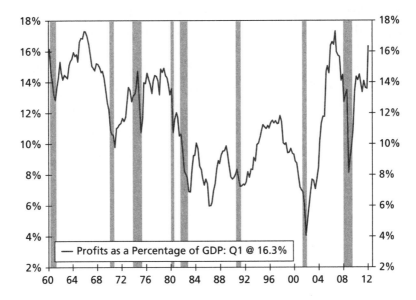

FIGURE 2.38 Profits as a Percentage of GDP (Pretax Profits Divided by Product of Nonfinancial Corporate Businesses)
Source: U.S Bureau of Economic Analysis

the middle of an expansion (see Figure 2.38). A decline in profits as a share of GDP often can signal that the economy is losing momentum.

NIPA data on profits stems from corporate income tax returns and are adjusted to account for national income accounting standards. The Bureau of Economic Analysis (BEA) adjusts profits to account for the current period's cost rather than the historical costs of accumulating inventory. This process is known as the inventory valuation adjustment (IVA). Depreciation expenses are also captured in the BEA's measure under capital consumption adjustments. Profits are then reported before taxes as to separate current tax policy's impact on overall operating performance. The BEA does, however, also report after-tax profits as well as net dividends earned.

Profits are also expressed in reports to shareholders. Here data is derived from financial accounting rather than from the tax-accounting measures used in the NIPA calculation of corporate profits. This allows for a more timely estimate of profits, as the BEA's measure can lag and includes a number of assumptions because tax returns are reported only annually.

SUMMARY

With hundreds of economic variables published on our economy from both public and private sources, the thoughtful analyst will find it daunting to sort through which indicators are most useful. There are, however, a number of key variables that provide a baseline to the time-constrained analyst. In this chapter, we looked at the crucial elements of the economy that relate to businesses: growth, labor, inflation, interest rates, the dollar, and corporate profits. Knowing both the basics and key issues surrounding these series produces better analysis and therefore better decisions by businesses and policy makers. In the next chapter we review the financial side indicators for the U.S. economy.

CHAPTER **3**

Financial Ratios

For business leaders and decision makers, financial ratios are indicators of financial performance as well as part of a broader financial and economic framework. Utilizing financial ratios within that framework provides business leaders with a context for making well-informed decisions about their firm and the economy in general.

Financial ratios serve several purposes. They can be targets that can trigger an action, such as an investment decision, or act as measures of financial performance for a firm, industry, or country.

It is important to note that a financial ratio describes what happened but not *why* it happened. When looking at companies, an analyst compares financial ratios of one company to its competitors to understand the underlying causes of divergence between firms and the industry. The same can be true when a decision maker evaluates a country's financial position.

When using a financial ratio, an analyst should decipher the numerator and the denominator to assess what the ratio is attempting to measure and how to interpret the results. Financial ratios enable a decision maker to determine past performance, assess current performance, and gain insights regarding future success.

Generally speaking, calculating ratios can be the easy part of the task. The real challenge is extracting the underlying meaning of the ratios. An analyst must establish a methodology to assess the direction, stability, and outlook for the trend in the data that makes up the ratio. Typically, analysts follow a process that identifies (1) the trend in the ratio (Is the value of the ratio increasing or decreasing over time?), (2) the drivers of the ratio's trend (What is causing the numerator and the denominator of the ratio to behave as they do?), and (3) an outlook for the ratio's trend (What is the most probable direction for the ratio based on the underlying drivers?).

In this chapter, we examine several important ratios designed to help ascertain financial performance. But two concerns regarding financial ratios and their interaction with the broader economy must be kept in mind: the interaction of cyclical and long-term secular patterns and how changes in the broader economy impact a financial ratio.[1]

Financial ratios have a cyclical component that is tied to the business cycle as well as a secular component that reflects longer-term trends. When analyzing financial ratios, cyclical and secular trends need to be distinguished. A decision maker assesseses the ratio over a period of time to determine whether changes in it imply cyclical movement around a series that has no trend or cyclical movement around a changing trend.

Trends in financial ratios may also reflect changes in the broader economy. Every financial ratio is not an independent indicator of the economic or financial performance of a firm, industry, or country. Strong correlations can exist between financial ratios and basic economic indicators, such as gross domestic product (GDP) growth, inflation, and interest rates.[2]

Business leaders utilize financial ratios, including leverage, liquidity, market value, and profitability/operating efficiency, to monitor the operating performance of their firms. A change in the magnitude or direction of a financial ratio can signal a significant change in the firm's operating landscape.

As decision makers determine which tools to use and before they make a final assessment, they should understand how the current behavior of an economic series or financial ratio stands relative to its underlying behavior. The technique we utilize to review important financial ratios is the Hodrick-Prescott (HP) filter. This filter removes the cyclical movements from the long-term trend of a financial ratio. Once the HP filter is applied to an economic series or financial ratio, a decision maker can observe if that series is moving below or above trend at any point in time compared to its historical values. The HP filter thus removes the so-called recency bias.

With more clarity about how to approach and utilize financial ratios, we now turn to several routinely utilized ratios.

PROFITABILITY RATIOS

Profitability ratios are important tools for business risk analysis. They indicate the effectiveness of a firm's operating management and describe its ability to consistently generate cash to meet its financial obligations. In this section, we review several essential profitability ratios.

Return on Equity

When investors and economists analyze a company, they often ask: How efficiently is this firm using its assets? A firm's return on equity (ROE) is a key ratio

---

[1] John Silvia, *Dynamic Economic Decision Making* (Hoboken, NJ: John Wiley & Sons, 2011).
[2] Ibid., p. 241.

to help determine this answer. ROE measures the return earned by a firm on its common and preferred equity capital. The company's return is measured as net income, or the difference between revenue and expenses. The ratio gauges how efficiently and profitably a business invests the shareholders' capital. The higher the ROE, the more efficient management is in utilizing shareholders' capital and the better the return to its investors.

As it is with many other types of ratios, it is important to evaluate any profitability ratio individually and as an industry group in order to gain a better understanding of what is driving a firm's success. In some cases, success can be found in its operating activities; in other cases, it can be discovered in its nonoperating activities. ROEs can vary significantly among different types of businesses. A firm's ROE should be evaluated and compared with companies in a similar line of business. For example, the semiconductor industry has exhibited a relatively high ROE; utilities, due in part to their capital-intensive nature, tend to have a relatively lower ROE.

In addition, a small equity capital base can mislead an analyst. A firm with a disproportionately large amount of debt in its capital structure could still produce a high ROE but with a modest equity base. ROE thus should not be viewed in isolation.

As seen in Figure 3.1, the ROE ratio has a cyclical pattern over time. During the dot-com boom of the 1990s and the housing-driven boom of the early to mid-2000s, the ROE of the Standard & Poor's 500 ran above its long-run trend growth rate. But as the ratio peaked just below the 3.00 level, the Great Recession of 2007 to 2009 unfolded, causing the ratio to drop dramatically as

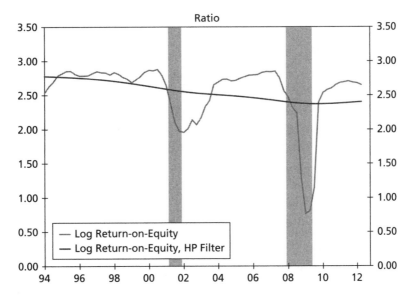

FIGURE 3.1 Return on Equity Ratio: HP Filter
Source: Factset

profitability fell. As of the second quarter of 2012, ROE has peaked at around 2.70 and has begun to moderate. This recent trend is in line with the softening in corporate profits over the past year as firms have found it more challenging to maintain high levels of profitability in a weak demand environment.

Return on Assets

A second measure of efficiency of corporate assets is the return on assets (ROA), which measures the return earned by a firm on its assets. The ROA ratio calculation is net income divided by a firm's average total assets, with net income measured as the return to stockholders, and assets can be financed by both debt and equity. The higher a firm's ROA, the more income that firm generates on a given level of assets.

Because interest expense, or the return to creditors, has already been deducted from net income, some analysts prefer to add it back into the calculation and use earnings before interest and taxes (EBIT). In this particular measure of ROA, returns are measured prior to deducting interest on debt capital and therefore reflect the return on all assets invested in the company, including both debt and equity. An analyst needs to be consistent with the specific form of ROA he or she is using when comparing companies, otherwise ratio results could be misleading.

As expected, the ROA ratio shows a similar result to the ROE ratio. Going back to 1994, ROA ran above its long-term trend during the boom times of the 1990s and 2000s (see Figure 3.2). The most recent peak in ROA occurs

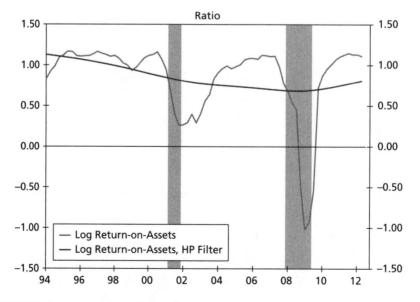

FIGURE 3.2 Return on Assets Ratio: HP Filter
Source: Factset

at around 1.15, before the Great Recession hit the U.S. economy. During the recession period of December 2007 through June 2009, the ROA ratio fell significantly below its long-run HP filtered trend.

Corporate Profits as a Percentage of GDP

Decision makers also need to analyze the profitability of the U.S. economy as a whole so they can assess how their company or industry is performing against this backdrop of the larger economy. One way to do this is to take the profits of all businesses and compare it to U.S. gross domestic product (GDP)—for example, calculate corporate profits as a percent of GDP. Figure 3.3 shows the cyclical trend of corporate profits throughout the various stages of the business cycle. During the recovery and early expansion phase of the business cycle, corporate profits as a percentage of GDP largely remained above trend. As the expansion phase of the business cycle lengthens, firms on average find it difficult to maintain their pace of profitability as productivity slows and cost structures rise.

Liquidity Ratios

Liquidity ratios, which focus on the firm's cash flow, measure a company's ability to meet its short-term financial obligations. A firm's liquidity measures how quickly its assets can be converted to cash. In day-to-day operations, liquidity management typically is achieved through efficient use of the firm's assets.

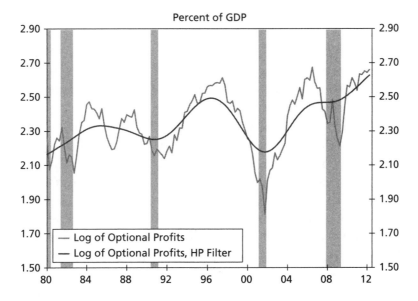

FIGURE 3.3 Corporate Profits: HP Filter
Source: U.S. Department of Commerce

Over a longer period of time, liquidity is addressed by managing the composite structure of liabilities.

A firm's level of liquidity can differ from one industry to the next as well as between firms within the same industry. Assessing whether a company has adequate liquidity requires analysis of its past funding requirements, current liquidity position, expected future funding needs, and all available options for attracting additional funds or reducing funding needs.

Typically, larger companies are in a better position to control the level and composition of their liabilities than smaller firms are. Larger firms thus usually have more available funding sources, including money markets and capital markets. This allows a firm to reduce the size of its liquidity buffer relative to businesses denied access to easily generated funds.

The data used to generate liquidity ratios is derived from a firm's balance sheet rather than from monthly or quarterly averages. There are three primary liquidity ratios: current, quick, and cash ratios. Each ratio reflects a firm's ability to pay current liabilities, and each progressively uses a stricter definition of what qualifies as a liquid asset. The higher the ratio, the larger the safety margin to repay short-term financial obligations. A company's liquidity also affects its capacity to take on additional debt.

The current ratio is a measure of a firm's current assets in relation to current liabilities. Current assets include cash, inventories, receivables, and short-term securities; current liabilities involve the ongoing interest expense of previous debt obligations as well as day-to-day operating expenses, such as electricity and water bills. Fundamental to the analysis, the current ratio implicitly assumes that a firm's account receivables and inventories are liquid. Depending on the stage of the business cycle, that assumption may not necessarily be true. A current ratio of 1.0 indicates that the book value of a business's current assets exactly matches the book value of its current liabilities. A higher ratio indicates a greater ability to meet short-term obligations; a lower ratio indicates less liquidity and therefore an increased reliance on a firm's operating cash flow and outside funding resources.

The quick ratio is a more conservative measure of liquidity than the current ratio. It includes a more strict definition of current assets, often referred to as quick assets. Like the current ratio, a higher quick ratio reflects greater liquidity within the firm. This stricter definition of assets reflects that, at certain points in time, inventory may not be converted as easily and quickly into cash as at other points in time. Moreover, it assumes a firm probably would not maximize the full carrying value of its inventory in periods of economic stress. When those periods occur, the quick ratio could be a better indicator of liquidity than the current ratio.

In extreme periods of economic stress, the cash ratio is the most reliable measure of a firm's liquidity. In this ratio, current assets include only highly marketable short-term investments, such as U.S. Treasuries and cash. Even in crisis times, however, the fair market value of marketable securities could decline significantly as a result of financial market forces and still not give decision makers a true picture of a firm's financial position.

As seen in Figure 3.4, over time, the current ratio has not strayed far above or below its HP filter trend unless the economy is in periods of great excess or great restraint. From 2001 through 2005, the current ratio grew in line with its long-run trend. The mid-2000s were a period of great excess because low interest rates helped fuel a boom led by residential housing, investment, and consumption. As the housing bubble burst in 2007–2008, the value of current assets fell at a faster rate than the value of current liabilities, leading to a significant pullback in the current ratio. When the economy bounced back in 2009 and firms rebuilt assets on their balance sheets, the current ratio rebounded sharply. After backsliding in 2011, the most recent data (as of mid-2012) suggests that firms have grown cautious primarily because of the so-called U.S. fiscal cliff. This situation involved President Barack Obama and Congress facing decisions regarding taxes, deficits, the national debt ceiling, and the sequester (impending across-the-board cuts to federal programs) without the ability to resolve these issues easily because of partisan gridlock. With uncertainty over how the fiscal cliff would be resolved, businesses, on balance, prepared for the worst. Not knowing whether they would be able to tap money or capital markets, firms topped off company coffers to sustain a period of financial market stress where financial options may be costly if not limited.

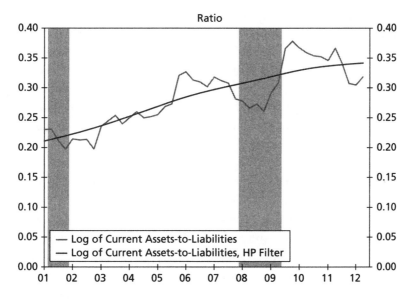

FIGURE 3.4 Current Assets to Liabilities: HP Filter
Source: Factset

Leverage Ratios

The third category of ratios useful to decision makers is leverage ratios, or solvency ratios. *Solvency* refers to a firm's ability to fulfill its debt obligations—its principal and interest payments—over the long term. Analysts want to understand a company's use of debt for several reasons. The amount of debt in a firm's capital structure is key to assessing the firm's risk and return characteristics, specifically its financial leverage. An analyst thus must perform an in-depth study on the components of the firm's capital structure. Leverage ratios provide an analyst with information regarding the relative amount of debt a firm has in its capital structure and the adequacy of its cash flow and earnings to cover interest and principal payments.

Leverage is the amplifying effect from the use of fixed costs. The first form of leverage is operating leverage, which is the use of fixed costs in conducting the firm's day-to-day business. The primary intent of operating leverage is to amplify the effect of changes in sales on operating income. When revenues increase, using operating leverage results in operating income increasing at a faster rate. Although variable costs will rise proportionately with revenue, fixed costs do not.

The second form of leverage is financial leverage. When a company finances itself using debt, that debt establishes financial leverage because the interest payments on the debt are basically fixed financing costs to the firm. Because a given percentage change in EBIT results in a larger percentage change in earnings before taxes, financial leverage tends to amplify the effect of changes in EBIT on stockholder returns. With the assumption that a firm can earn more on those funds than it can pay in interest, some level of debt in a firm's capital structure could lower its overall cost of capital and, in turn, increase the return to stockholders. On the flip side, a higher level of debt in the firm's capital structure increases the probability of default and results in higher borrowing costs for the company to compensate debt holders for assuming more credit risk.

In analyzing the data, the decision maker's goal is to better understand the levels and trends in a firm's use of financial leverage in relation to its past and its competitors, while recognizing the difference between operating and financial leverage. The greater a firm's operating leverage, the more a firm is at risk of having an insufficient income stream to cover debt payments. Therefore, operating leverage can limit a business's ability to use financial leverage.

There are two main types of leverage ratios: debt ratio and coverage ratio. Debt ratios focus on the balance sheet and measure the amount of debt capital relative to the amount of equity capital. Coverage ratios concentrate on the income statement, measuring a company's ability to cover its debt payments.

The debt-to-equity ratio measures the total amount of debt capital relative to the total amount of equity capital. Unlike profitability ratios, higher leverage ratios indicate weaker solvency and a greater propensity for firms to fall into financial trouble. Because corporate earnings fluctuate over the business cycle, higher levels of debt are associated with higher interest payments and therefore increased pressure on a given level of corporate earnings. As a decision maker analyzes the debt-to-equity ratio, he or she gains insight into the decisions made by company leadership on their capital structure.

As seen in Figure 3.5, a cyclical pattern in the debt-to-equity ratio has persisted over several business cycles. During the boom period of the 1990s, as stock valuations increased at a faster pace than the value of firms' debt, the debt-to-equity ratios fell precipitously. These low ratios gave business leaders the confidence to take on larger levels of debt. Business leaders often display a bias that recent success will continue without correction. Companies can get into trouble when changes in business fortunes occur, and earnings cannot accommodate higher interest payments.

As previously mentioned, analysts need to evaluate leverage ratios not only in comparison to a firm's history or to its competitors but also in a broad economic context. Generally speaking, companies with lower business risk and with operations that generate consistent cash flow streams can take on additional debt with a corresponding increase in credit risk. That appears to be what happened, on balance, as 2012 ended. Although firms have modestly increased debt burdens in recent quarters, they have taken advantage of the very low cost of borrowing. By retiring higher-interest-rate debt or bringing on additional capacity to finance acquisitions and future projects, companies have positioned their capital structures well in this uncertain economic environment.

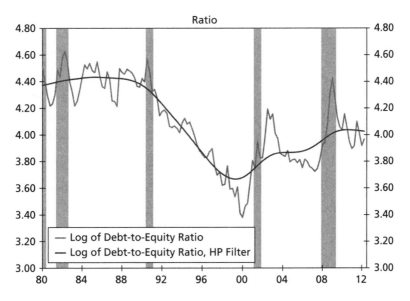

FIGURE 3.5 Debt-to-Equity Ratio: HP Filter
Source: Factset

Investment Valuation Ratio

Valuation ratios have long been used in the investment decision-making process. The most well-known and widely cited stock valuation indicator is the price-to-earnings (P/E) ratio. The P/E ratio is the ratio of the price per share of common stock to the earnings per share of common stock. Analysts frequently use this ratio as a quick proxy for investors' assessment of a particular company's ability to generate future cash flows. Explained differently, a P/E ratio tells how much in common stock an investor will pay for a dollar of future earnings. Firms that have a high P/E ratio tend to have strong earnings growth forecasts. On the flip side, businesses with a low P/E ratio are expected to have low future earnings growth potential.

The theory behind the P/E ratio is that the value of an asset is determined by the present value of the expected net earnings stream generated by the asset. The decision maker's expectations and the economic factors that shape those expectations are vital in making the assessment. When looking at the present value of the earnings stream, the outlook for inflation and interest rates are key and can have a substantial impact. In addition, the performance of the U.S. dollar exchange rate can play a pivotal role because so many companies, large and small, participate in international markets.

Market valuations are not set in an environment of certainty. The current P/E ratio indicates the prevailing sentiment of investors toward a firm's equity value. A decision maker must first decide if he or she agrees with the prevailing P/E ratio in comparision to the P/E ratio of the aggregate stock market, the

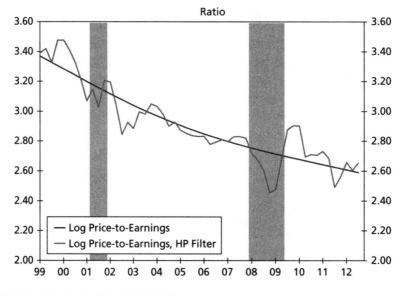

FIGURE 3.6 Price-to-Earnings Ratio: HP Filter
Source: Factset

firm's particular industry, and its specific competitors. Because each investor formulates his or her own expectations, a market is formed that allows buyers and sellers to trade, with each believing they have gotten a deal.

Figure 3.6 shows the P/E ratio over the past decade; it has steadily shrunk. Why? In our opinion, increased economic uncertainty increasingly plagues today's operating landscape. From political dysfunction to extraordinary monetary policy to general business outlook concerns, the sustainability of earnings has been cast into serious doubt. As economic and profit forecasts become less reliable, analysts and investors tend to focus on broader economic themes instead of firm-specific valuation considerations.

The bottom line (or rule): The more uncertainty there is in the market, the lower the P/E ratio.

SUMMARY

Ratio analysis can be a key tool in determining the financial performance of a firm, industry, or country. With thoughtful selection, evaluation, and interpretation of financial and economic data, a decision maker can use financial analysis tools, such as financial ratios, to assist in investment and financial evaluation. A decision maker must be aware that financial ratios should not be taken at face value and should be analyzed in the context of the broader economic framework as well as firm-specific situations. With that in mind, financial ratio analysis will give the decision maker a more informed answer on financial performance—past, present, and future.

CHAPTER 4

Characterizing a Time Series

In decision making, many rules of thumb are employed in economics and finance—for example, the relationship between gross domestic product (GDP) and the unemployment rate (Okun's law), the unemployment rate and the job vacancy rate (Beveridge curve), and the inflation rate and money supply (money neutrality).[1] In practice, however, these relationships need to be tested with the help of econometric techniques using real-world data. Why? Typically, economic theory suggests the *direction* of a relationship; for example, Okun's law suggests that a rise in GDP is associated with a decline in the unemployment rate. But how much? As a country's economy evolves, so do economic relationships. Furthermore, it is important to know the estimated magnitude of these economic relationships and how these relationships change over the business cycle and over time.

Knowledge of the magnitude of the relationship between GDP growth and the unemployment rate will help decision makers assess how jobs, income and thereby personal consumption follow the pace of GDP growth. For instance, during 2008 to 2010 of the Great Recession and early phase of the recovery, the Federal Reserve Board (monetary) and Presidents Bush and Obama (fiscal) introduced stimuli to boost the U.S. economy. U.S. GDP growth turned positive during 2009:Q3,[2] and real GDP surpassed its prerecession peak in 2011:Q4.

---

[1] For more detail about these relationships see, Gregory N. Mankiw, (2010), *Macroeconomics,* 7th ed. (New York, NY: Worth).

[2] The Federal Reserve Board reduced the Fed funds target rate to the 0 to 0.25 percent range on December 2008. In addition, the Fed implemented a large number of programs to support the financial markets (i.e., the Term Auction Facility and Term Securities Lending Facility, etc). In terms of fiscal stimulus, the 2008 tax stimulus and the American Recovery and Reinvestment Act of 2009, along with several others, were introduced to combat the Great Recession and to stimulate the recovery.

But as of August 2012, the unemployment rate remained well above its pre-recession level, with around 4.7 million fewer workers on payrolls compared to January 2008, the previous peak of employment. The divergence in the recovery period of output and the labor market suggest that these two parts of the economy do not move hand and hand and such a difference remains essential to estimating consumer spending.

Two different paths for the unemployment rate (labor market) and GDP (output) raise the question whether Okun's law is still valid for the United States. If it is still valid, what is the precise linkage in this relationship? That is, how much of an increase in GDP is needed to reduce unemployment rate? How long does it take an increase in GDP to affect the labor market and help bring down unemployment? Would a rise in GDP help reduce unemployment in the same quarter, the following quarter, or even later? And why has the unemployment rate behaved differently in terms of recovery time from GDP during the recovery from the Great Recession?

Econometric techniques using real-world data help to answer these questions and quantify any economic or financial relationship. This chapter centers on the characteristics of a time series: how do we identify and define trends, cyclicality, structural breaks, and other pertinent features of a data series? Before an analyst can fit an individual data series into a bigger picture, he or she must understand how certain characteristics of the data might influence the outcome and the reliability of a regression analysis. Chapter 5 explains how to analyze relationships between two or more time series and how to fit the series into a regression framework. Chapters 6 through 8 discuss how to employ these techniques in SAS as well as how to analyze the econometric results.

WHY CHARACTERIZE A TIME SERIES?

For any time series, the first step is to characterize the behavior of that series. Once the behavior of a series is understood, an analyst can determine the appropriate model to test for a statistical relationship between that variable and any other variables of interest. Why is the behavior of a time series important? Time series do not all act in the same way, and characterizing a time series helps an analyst to understand the behavior of a variable of interest. Some variables may have a dominant time trend, like the upward trend of U.S. GDP over time. Other variables have a dominant cyclical trend, like the upward trend of the U.S. unemployment rate during recessions followed by the downward trend during expansions.

For any time series, consider the next questions to determine its behavior. First, how does the variable of interest behave over time (e.g., does the variable show evidence of an explicit time trend and does the series have a cyclical pattern over the business cycle)? If the series has explicit trend over time, is the trend linear or nonlinear? What is the behavior of the series during a particular phase of a business cycle? Does the series act differently during varying phases of the business cycle? For example, does the unemployment rate increase (decrease) at the same rate during each of the last four recessions (recoveries)?

There are several ways to identify and test for such characteristics, the first being a simple plot of the data versus time. A plot allows an analyst to see if there are any explicit patterns that could cause problems later on, such as outliers, an explicit time trend, or a cyclical pattern. If an analyst observes such characteristics, statistical tests described in detail throughout the chapter can identify the precise mathematical pattern. Additionally, an analyst should observe the descriptive statistics of the data. The mean, the standard deviation, and the stability ratio—which is the standard deviation as percentage of the mean—are of particular interest, enabling an analyst to identify the data's basic behavior and how it changes over time.

Another question an analyst should examine is whether the data varies in a predictable pattern, such as over the course of a business cycle? This question can be answered by identifying the presence of autocorrelation, in which case the error terms are correlated and each observation is related to its prior observation in some way. Such correlation causes underestimation of the standard errors, thereby violating ordinary least squares (OLS) assumptions as well. We demonstrate how to test for cyclical behavior of a series using autocorrelation functions (ACFs) and partial autocorrelation functions (PACFs). In addition, we use the Hodrick Prescott (HP) filter to separate the long-run trend components from the cyclical components of a series.

Other time series characteristics an analyst should understand relate to the basic assumptions of simple regression analysis. For example, we demonstrate how to test for a unit root using the Dickey-Fuller test; the Phillips-Perron test; and the Kwiatkowski, Phillips, Schmidt, and Shin test. Testing for a unit root determines whether the data series is stationary and if the series has a constant mean and variance over time. A basic OLS analysis assumes that data are stationary.

Last, we identify whether the data series contains a structural break using the Chow test and state space approach. One of the most important assumptions of any time series model is that the underlying process is the same across all observations in the sample. Therefore, if a time series includes periods of violent change, the series has acted differently during varying periods of its long-term trend. Forecasting future data points becomes difficult when there is a structural break in the data.

HOW TO CHARACTERIZE A TIME SERIES

A simple, but important, way to begin the analysis of any economic or financial variable is to plot the data against time. For instance, Figure 4.1 compares the year-over-year changes in productivity growth against its long-run average.

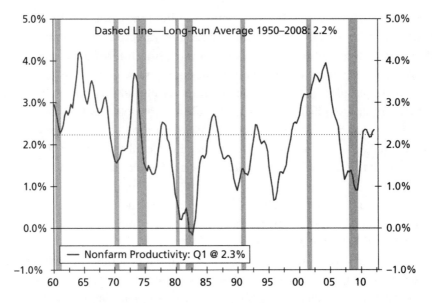

FIGURE 4.1 Productivity—Total Nonfarm (Year-over-Year Percentage Change, Three-Year Moving Average)

We define *productivity growth* as real nonfarm business output per hour of all persons, seasonally adjusted, and a year-over-year percentage change is used in the analysis. Shaded areas represent recessions declared by the National Bureau of Economic Research.

A plot of a time series provides a visual look at the data. This should be the first step of any applied time series analysis because this step allows the analyst to identify any unusual aspects of the data series.

First, a plot shows whether the series contains one or more extreme values in the time series, an outlier, which impacts calculations (e.g., mean, standard deviation) done on any series. An analyst should attempt to understand the reason for such an extreme value, such as an unusual event or simply a misprinted value that should be corrected in subsequent releases.

Second, a plot suggests whether the variable of interest contains an explicit time trend or an indication that the series may have a cyclical pattern. Finally, a plot may also provide visible signal of a structural break in the time series. A structural break suggests that the model defining the behavior of the variable of interest, such as the unemployment rate, is different before and after the break.[3]

Figure 4.1 indicates that the rate of U.S. productivity growth does not contain an outlier or an explicit time trend. However, a cyclical pattern is evident in the productivity growth rate, as it tends to fall during recessions and rise rapidly during the early phase of recoveries. By adding the long-run average growth rate—2.2 percent during the 1950 to 2008 period—as a dotted line, we can

---

[3] Detailed discussions about a time trend, cyclical pattern, and a structural break are provided in the next sections.

TABLE 4.1 Three Eras of U.S. Productivity

Period	Mean	S.D.	Stability Ratio
1948:Q1–2011:Q4	2.23	1.86	83%
1948:Q1–1973:Q4	2.81	1.93	69%
1974:Q1–1995:Q4	1.38	1.69	122%
1996:Q1–2011:Q4	2.46	1.53	62%

S.D. = Standard deviation

surmise that there is some evidence of a structural shift that should be tested. For instance, during the 1960s to early 1970s, productivity growth stays persistently above the average long-run growth rate, while during the mid-1970s to mid-1990s, average growth turns to less than 2.2 percent. Finally, the post–mid-1990s era appears to have a higher average growth rate than 2.2 percent.[4]

Putting Simple Statistical Measures to Work

Another way to characterize an economic or financial variable is to estimate its mean (represents central tendency of a data series), standard deviation (shows how much deviation exists from the mean), and stability ratio—the standard deviation as percentage of the mean. Moreover, a time series can be divided into different periods when it appears that the series has changed and then the mean, standard deviation, and stability ratio can be estimated for each subsample. We can also test if the mean is statistically significantly different between periods.[5] The data series can be divided between different business cycles, different decades, or even different eras, such as pre– and post–World War II.

So by what criteria, such as business cycles or decades, would an analyst divide a data series? The answer depends on the question he or she wants to answer. For instance, if an analyst wants to compare the real GDP growth rates between different business cycles, he or she separates the data into the dates corresponding with those business cycles, as in Chapter 1, Table 1.1. For productivity, the series has been split into three different eras (see Table 4.1 for results), following past work on productivity. The eras are: (1) the 1948 to 1973 era of strong productivity growth, (2) the 1974 to mid-1990s era of slow productivity growth, and (3) the post–mid-1990s era of "productivity

---

[4]Many studies confirm the idea of structural breaks in the U.S. productivity growth rate since the 1947. For more details, see John B. Taylor (2008), "A Review the Productivity Resurgence," paper presented at the American Economic Association Annual Meeting, January 8, New Orleans, Louisiana.
[5]See for more detail, D. Freedman, R. Pisani, and R. Purves (1997), *Statistics*, 3rd ed. (New York, NY: W. W. Norton).

resurgence."[6] These three eras are obvious in Figure 4.1.[7] One major benefit of dividing this data into different eras and then calculating the mean, standard deviation, and stability ratio for each era is that it reveals how differently the rate of productivity growth behaved during these three eras, thereby suggesting possible structural shifts in the series.

From Table 4.1, the mean for the complete sample period is 2.23 percent with a standard deviation of 1.86, while the stability ratio is 83 (standard deviation is 83 percent of the mean). The stability ratio represents the volatility of productivity growth in each era, where a higher value of the stability ratio is an indication of higher volatility. One benefit of the stability ratio compared to the standard deviation is that it identifies the magnitude of the difference in volatility of productivity growth by era. For instance, if we set the standard deviation instead of the stability ratio as the volatility criterion, then the 1948:Q1–1973:Q4 period has highest standard deviation and the 1996:Q1–2011:Q4 has lowest. If we link the analysis to the standard deviation criterion, then the 1948:Q1–1973:Q4 is most volatile and 1996:Q1–2011:Q4 is least volatile. But the problem with this standard deviation criterion is that the 1948:Q1–1973:Q4 period also has the highest mean. Therefore, the standard deviation alone is not the best measure of volatility, especially when comparing different eras or different subsamples, when the means of the series are also different. The stability ratio includes both the mean and standard deviation and gives us information about which subsample has a higher standard deviation relative to the mean for productivity growth. Therefore, the stability ratio better identifies which time series is more volatile.

Our results here indicate that productivity growth during the 1974:Q1–1995:Q4 period acts quite differently compared to the complete sample (1948:Q1–2011:Q4) and to other two sub-samples (1948:Q1–1973:Q4 and 1996:Q1–2011:Q4). The 1974:Q1–1995:Q4 period is associated with an average productivity growth rate of 1.38 percent, which is the lowest in our analysis. The standard deviation is higher than the mean for that period, and so the stability ratio is 122 percent. As a result, we would judge the 1974:Q1–1995:Q4 era to be the most volatile and the 1996:Q1–2011:Q4 to be the most stable era for productivity growth in our analysis.

In sum, these simple and easily applied techniques provide useful information and enable an analyst to observe the basic behavior of a time series over

---

[6]The post–mid-1990s era experienced a strong productivity growth compared to last couple of decades and thereby is known as the era of productivity resurgence; see Taylor (2008) for more detail.
[7]Basically, we use prior knowledge from other studies to divide the data series—productivity growth rate in this case—into three different eras.

FIGURE 4.2 10-Year Treasury Yield
Source: Federal Reserve Board

different periods or business cycles. An analyst can use SAS software to estimate a mean, standard deviation, and stability ratio.

Identifying a Time Trend in a Series

Another important feature of any economic series, such as GDP, the consumer price index (CPI), and industrial production, is its time trend.[8] In other words, if we plot a data series against time, does the series exhibit an explicit (upward or downward) trend over time? Using Figure 4.2, the U.S. 10-year Treasury note yield has a decreasing and, to some extent, linear trend since the mid-1980s. Many time series follow either a linear or a nonlinear trend. The existence of that trend influences the reliability of any forecast and statistical significance using that trended series. A linear trend implies that the series has a constant growth rate; a nonlinear trend exhibits a growth rate that is not constant over time. It is very important for an analyst to characterize a time trend in a time series, since the type of time trend reflects a different pattern of behavior over time and affects the statistical reliability of any measure of the behavior of that series. For instance, due to its constant growth rate, a linear time trend makes it easier to extrapolate future values compared to a series with a nonlinear time trend. However, the linear trend also creates nonstationarity (also known as trend stationary) in the data series, which makes OLS results unreliable, as we see later.

[8]Broadly speaking, a trend has two types: deterministic and stochastic. Here we discuss and characterize a deterministic trend into a linear and/or a nonlinear time trend. In the unit root section, we talk about a stochastic trend.

Testing for a Time Trend

We start by estimating a time trend in a data series by running a regression against time.

$$y_t = \beta_0 + \beta_1\, Time_t + \varepsilon_t$$
$$t = 1, 2, \dots T \tag{4.1}$$

where

y_t = variable of interest (e.g., GDP)

Time = time variable or time dummy

Time is generated artificially by setting *Time* equal to 1 for the first observation of the sample, to 2 for the second observation, and so on, up to T time periods. If the coefficient of *Time*, β_1, is statistically significant, we can hypothesize that the series has a linear trend. Moreover, at some level we can interpret the sign of the β_1 coefficient as to signal either an increasing (if positive) or decreasing (if negative) trend.

Some data series may not have a linear trend. Instead, a nonlinear trend may characterize the series better, or perhaps there is no trend at all. Using Figure 4.1, the U.S. productivity growth rate does not seem to follow a linear trend over time; thus a nonlinear trend may be a better fit for the data series. We employ a quadratic trend model to capture the nonlinearity and thereby will include a variable defined as $Time^2$, time squared.

If β_1 and β_2 in Equation 4.2 are both statistically significant, then the series appears to follow a nonlinear trend. Note, a t-value indicates the statistical significance of a variable. In addition, the signs of β_1 and β_2 will determine the shape of the curve, either U shaped (for employment) or inverted U shaped (for industrial production).[9] Figure 4.3 provides an idea of a U-shaped trend, and Figure 4.4 shows an inverted U-shaped trend.

$$y_t = \beta_0 + \beta_1 Time_t + \beta_2\, Time_t^2 + \varepsilon_t \tag{4.2}$$

Sometimes another type of nonlinear trend, other than the quadratic trend, may better fit a time series. A time series may be nonlinear in level form but linear in its growth rate. In another approach, we can take a logarithm of a time series, and the plot of that logged series may look like a linear trend. This case may be true for financial, business, and, sometimes, economic data series. This type of trend is known as exponential trend or log-linear trend.

$$Log(\, y_t) = \beta_0 + \beta_1\, Time_t + \varepsilon_t \tag{4.3}$$

---

[9]For more detail, see Francis X. Diebold (2007), *Elements of Forecasting*, 4th ed. (Mason, OH: Thomson), Chapter 5.

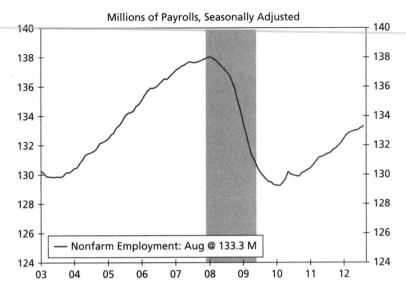

FIGURE 4.3 U-Shaped Trend Between 2008 and 2012: Nonfarm Employment (Millions)
Source: U.S. Bureau of Labor Statistics

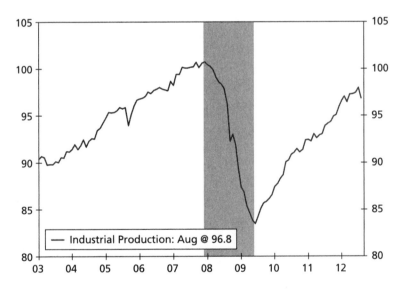

FIGURE 4.4 Inverted U-Shaped Trend Between 2003 and 2009: Industrial Production (2007 = 100, Seasonally Adjusted)
Source: Federal Reserve Board

A simple way to estimate an exponential or log-linear trend is to use the log form of a variable instead of the level form, shown in Figures 4.5 and 4.6. Since many variables are nonstationary at their level form, the growth rate of a series would provide not only a better fit of the trend but also provide more reliable statistical results. In the case of a nonstationary dataset, however, OLS results would be unreliable.

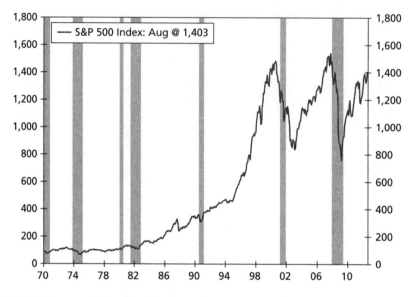

FIGURE 4.5 Exponential Trend, the S&P 500 Index
Source: Standard & Poor's

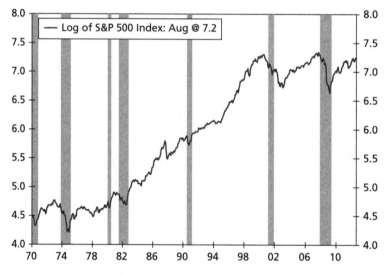

FIGURE 4.6 Log of the S&P 500 Index
Source: Standard & Poor's

Estimating a Time Trend

How can an analyst estimate a time trend? How can he or she determine whether the type of trend is linear or non-linear? Which trend type fits the data series best? The answer to these questions is that, with the help of SAS software, we can estimate an appropriate type of a time trend for any variable of interest. In the SAS framework, we generate a time trend variable and then test whether the time dummy is statistically significant. Furthermore, we utilize a number of statistical tests, including t-value, Akaike information criterion (AIC), and Schwarz information criterion (SIC), to determine what type of a trend is best fit for a particular variable.[10]

Identifying the Cycle in a Time Series

Another step for an analyst who wants to better understand a time series would be to determine whether an economic, financial, or business data series contains a cyclical pattern. For instance, a simple plot of the year-over-year percentage change in U.S. real GDP (see Figure 4.7) shows that GDP growth plunges during recessions, surges during the early years of recoveries, and then slows as the economic expansion ages. Therefore, the plot suggests that real GDP growth rate has a cyclical pattern.

Identifying cyclical behavior of a time series provides two major benefits for an analyst. Many economic, financial, and business variables evolve over time, and their growth rates usually fluctuate—or at least they do not follow a constant growth rate over time. Furthermore, the cyclical behavior of a series implies that changes in the growth rate of the series are temporary and that business cycle developments may be responsible for changes in values. Stated another way, the cyclical pattern of a series identifies the movements of that series around a long-run trend over time. The movements, the mean, and the standard deviation of any time series move away and then toward the trend growth, creating a cyclical (temporary) pattern as the series moves about its long-run trend growth rate. In contrast, if a change in a series is permanent and long lasting, then the series probably is characterized by a structural shift or a structural break in its growth rate.[11] In this case, the mean and/or standard deviation of the series would move away from the long-run trend either permanently or for at least an extended period.

Another major benefit to identifying the cyclical pattern of any time series is that it would help predict the values of that series during a specific phase of a business cycle. In this sense, the use of econometrics can identify changes in the values of a series over an economic cycle, allowing decision makers to anticipate those changes and alter their business plans if necessary. Looking at Figure 4.7, the real GDP growth rate dropped during recessions and picked up during recoveries and expansions, while the long-run trend value of real GDP growth moves around its long-run average rate of 2.63 percent for the period 1980 to 2011. Within the current business cycle, the ability to distinguish acceleration

---

[10]We provide detailed explanations of AIC and SIC in Chapter 5.
[11]We provide a detailed discussion about a structural break later in this chapter.

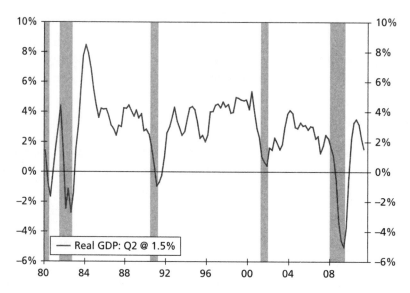

FIGURE 4.7   Real GDP (Year-over-Year Percentage Change)
Source: U.S. Bureau of Economic Analysis

and deceleration in economic growth has been highly beneficial to avoid the extreme forecasts of a recession or boom that many analysts have mistakenly, and frequently, made.

Identify the Cycle

How does SAS software help identify the cycle in an economic, financial, or business time series? It is important to recognize that many, but not all, macroeconomic time series follow a predictable pattern over the business cycle and as such can be characterized by certain statistical properties. Two techniques will be employed to identify and characterize the cycle: (1) autocorrelation and partial autocorrelation functions and (2) Q-statistics and white noise.[12]

One key benefit, among many others, of the SAS software is that just one SAS command will produce ACFs and PACFs. An ACF is basically the ratio between the autocovariance and variance (i.e., the autocovariance divided by the variance). Because we are interested in autocorrelations at different displacements, we will generate ACFs for a time series for different lags (i.e., we can postulate the ACFs for the rate of U.S. employment growth up to 24 lags). Therefore, the ACFs for up to 24 lags would be:

$$\text{ACFs}_{(\tau)} = \frac{auto\ covariance_{(\tau)}}{variance} \qquad \tau = 0, 1, 2 \ldots 24 \tag{4.4}$$

---

[12]For more detail, see William H. Greene (2011), *Econometric Analysis*, 7th ed. (Upper Saddle River, NJ: Prentice Hall).

The formula for the ACFs is just the usual correlation formula; the only difference in the ACFs is that we generate a series of correlations between a variable, y_t, and it lags at a later distance, y_τ. In correlation analysis, we generate a correlation coefficient between two different variables, let us say, x_t and y_t. The ACFs formula is:[13]

$$ACFs_{(\tau)} = \frac{cov\,(y_t,\, y_{t-\tau})}{\sqrt{var(\,y_t)}\,\sqrt{var(\,y_{t-\tau})}} \qquad (4.5)$$

Note: We consider ACFs from $\tau = 1$[14] because ACFs = 1 at $\tau = 0$ at the current value of a variable always has a perfect correlation (which is 1) with itself.

Essentially, both PACF and ACF represent an association between y_t and $y_{t-\tau}$, but the key difference is that the PACF represents a correlation between y_t and $y_{t-\tau}$ after controlling for the effects of $y_{t-1}, \ldots, y_{t-\tau+1}$. The ACF, however, indicates a simple correlation with y_t and $y_{t-\tau}$ and does not control the effects for $y_{t-1}, \ldots\ldots, y_{t-\tau+1}$.

Analyze the Output: What Do We Learn from ACFs and PACFs?

Now, how can an analyst produce the plots of the ACFs and PACFs to determine whether a time series has cyclical pattern? How can an analyst know whether the ACFs and PACFs are indicating a cyclical pattern in a time series? Several techniques in SAS can produce the ACFs and PACFs plotted against the τ and generate the ACF and PACF plots up to 24 lags. Three rules of thumb determine whether a series exhibits a pattern of cyclical behavior: (1) ACFs are large relative to their standard errors; (2) ACFs have a slow decay; and (3) PACFs have a spike and are large compared to their standard errors.

Here, we characterize the U.S. nonfarm payrolls growth year-to-year percentage change using ACFs and PACFs. A plot of the payrolls growth (see Figure 4.8) suggests that it does not contain an explicit (linear) time trend, but it does suggest cyclical behavior. During expansions, employment growth tends to stay well above zero (positive) and then turns negative during recessions.

To confirm the cyclical behavior of the payroll growth series, we display the ACFs (see Table 4.2) and PACFs (see Table 4.3) along with two standard error bands (Std Error) in the far right column of the table. The ACFs for non-farm payrolls growth are large compared to their standard errors and display slow one-sided decay. The PACFs show a spike at lag 1, and it is large, at least for the first four lags relative to their standard errors, but then values drop off

---

[13]We present this ACF formula only so the reader can understand only how to calculate ACFs; we expect the reader to generate ACFs by using the SAS software.

[14]Note: We use τ (tau) for lag order and t for time period.

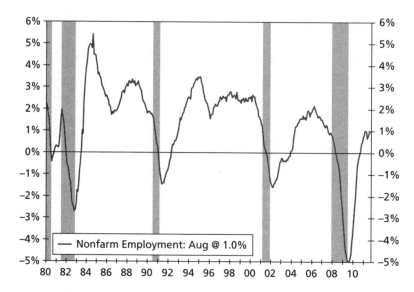

FIGURE 4.8 Nonfarm Employment Growth (Year-over-Year Percentage Change)
Source: U.S. Bureau of Labor Statistics

sharply. Both the ACFs and PACFs of employment growth are indicating cyclical behavior (i.e., ACFs are large relative to their standard errors; ACFs have a slow decay; and PACFs have a spike and are large compared to their standard errors). In sum, based on the ACFs and PACFs, nonfarm payroll growth has a strong cyclical behavior consistent with our expectations of its behavior in economic cycles.

The two standard errors band provide an initial good rule of thumb to judge whether ACFs and PACFs are large relative to the standard error, but the analysis can be strengthened by testing whether a series has white noise or no serial correlation.[15] If a series has white noise, it does not have a persistent behavior over time. If a series does not have white noise, also known as serial correlation or autocorrelation, we judge that the series follows a persistent pattern, in this case, a cyclical behavior for employment growth.

Two reliable statistical procedures can test the hypothesis whether the employment series displays white noise: Box-Pierce Q-statistic (Q_BP) and Ljung-Box Q-Statistic (Q_LB).[16] Essentially, the null hypothesis of both Q_BP and Q_LB

---

[15] White noise and autocorrelation are very important concepts. We provide a detailed discussion of both concepts in chapter 5.

[16] For more details, see Greene (2011).

[17] For more details, see Diebold (2007), Chapter 7.

TABLE 4.2 Employment Growth Autocorrelations (ACFs)

Lag	Covariance	Correlation	Correlation Visualization	Std Error
0	3.510987	1.00000	| |********************|	0
1	3.478113	0.99064	| . |*******************|	0.050965
2	3.412676	0.97200	| . |****************** |	0.087723
3	3.312945	0.94359	| . |****************** |	0.112265
4	3.183517	0.90673	| . |***************** |	0.131258
5	3.033285	0.86394	| . |***************** |	0.146627
6	2.864489	0.81586	| . |**************** |	0.159301
7	2.680619	0.76349	| . |*************** |	0.169808
8	2.485137	0.70782	| . |************** |	0.178502
9	2.277920	0.64880	| . |************* |.	0.185649
10	2.064523	0.58802	| . |************ |	0.191448
11	1.850694	0.52711	| . |*********** |	0.196083
12	1.639656	0.46701	| . |********* |	0.199729
13	1.448778	0.41264	| . |******** |	0.202546
14	1.266436	0.36071	| . |*******. |	0.204718
15	1.097225	0.31251	| . |****** . |	0.206362
16	0.941259	0.26809	| . |*****. |	0.207588
17	0.793754	0.22608	| . |*****. |	0.208485
18	0.655403	0.18667	| . |****. |	0.209121

The dots (".") before and after the asterisks "*" signal the results are within two standard errors band. Where no dot appears after of the asterisk then the series has a spike. In addition, the steady decline in the correlation as the lag order is increased is illustrated by fewer asterisks in column 4, the correlation visualization.

tests is H_0: The series is white noise. The alternative hypothesis is H_A: The series is not white noise. The consensus is that the Q_LB test, in small samples, performs better than the Q_BP.[17] If we reject the null hypothesis, then the series does not display white noise and hence possibly follows a cyclical pattern. SAS software produces both Q_BP and Q_LB tests along with ACFs and PACFs.

Testing for a Unit Root

One of the most important elements of time series analysis is to test whether a series is stationary or not, which is also known as testing for a unit root. A stationary time series implies the mean and variance of the series are constant over time. If the mean and/or the variance are not constant over time, then the series is characterized as nonstationary or as containing a unit root. Moreover, a

TABLE 4.3 Employment Growth Partial Autocorrelations (PACFs)

Lag	Correlation		
1	0.99064	| . |******************|
2	−0.50231	| *********| . |
3	−0.38539	| *******| . |
4	−0.19967	| ****| . |
5	0.02576	| . |*. |
6	−0.01864	| . | . |
7	−0.05064	| .*| . |
8	−0.04183	| .*| . |
9	−0.09280	| **| . |
10	0.01544	| . | . |
11	0.10687	| . |** |
12	0.07138	| . |*. |
13	0.37174	| . |******* |
14	−0.17462	| ***| . |
15	−0.14411	| ***| . |
16	−0.07886	| **| . |
17	−0.06201	| .*| . |
18	−0.02603	| .*| . |

"." The dots around the vertical line with the asterisks signal two standard errors band. Where no dot appears in front of the asterisk then the series has a spike,.

stationary series fluctuates around a constant, long-run mean with a finite (constant) variance that does not depend on time; it is therefore mean reverting. If a series is nonstationary, then it has no tendency to return to its long-run mean, and the variance of the series may be time dependent.[18] Furthermore, if one or more time series are non-stationary, the OLS method cannot be employed because it assumes the underlying data series are stationary. If the data series are nonstationary (often the case for many time series), then the OLS results will be spurious since the stationary assumption is violated and any perceived relationship between economic time series will not reflect the true relationship.

[18]For a detailed discussion about the unit root concept, see G. S. Maddala and In-Moo Kim (1998), *Unit Roots, Cointegration, and Structural Change* (Cambridge, UK: Cambridge University Press).

Dickey and Fuller (1979, 1981)[19] proposed a standard unit root testing procedure that was first known as DF (Dickey-Fuller) test. In 1981 they extended the DF test into the ADF (augmented Dickey-Fuller) test of a unit root. Unit root testing became popular in economics, especially among macroeconomists, after the publication of the seminal paper by Nelson and Plosser (1982).[20] They employed unit root methodology on 14 U.S. macroeconomic time series. They rejected the null hypothesis of a unit root for only one time series, which was the unemployment rate. Nelson and Plosser concluded that many macroeconomic series are nonstationary, which implies that many macroeconomic series exhibit trending behavior or a nonstationary mean and therefore are not mean reverting. Using such a series, often in level form, will produce unreliable results.

There are two major types of nonstationary behavior: difference stationary (DS) and trend stationary (TS).[21] It is important for an analyst to identify whether the series follows DS or TS patterns because both sources of nonstationarity have different implications and solutions. If a series follows the DS pattern, then the effect of any shock will be permanent. To convert the series into a stationary process, an analyst would have to generate the difference of the series.[22] A common source of nonstationarity is TS behavior, which implies that the series has a deterministic trend (upward or downward) over time. In this case, the analyst will regress the series on a time trend, using a time-dummy variable, in order to remove the trend. This is also known as detrending the series.

During the past 25 years, extensive research has been done in the area of unit root testing, and the results can be seen in the dozen of unit root tests available. Almost every unit root test has some advantages and some shortcomings. Dickey and Fuller (1979, 1981) introduced the eminent and first standard process for unit root testing, the ADF unit root test. Other unit root tests also have benefits. For instance, Phillips and Perron (1988)[23] proposed an alternative to the ADF test, called the PP test, while Kwiatkowski, Phillips, Schmidt,

---

[19]D. Dickey and W. Fuller (1979), "Distribution of the Estimators for Autoregressive Time Series with a Unit Root," *Journal of American Statistical Association* 74: 427–4311; D. Dickey and W. Fuller (1981), "Likelihood Ratio Tests for Autoregressive Time Series with a Unit Root," *Econometrica* 49: 1057–1072.
[20]Charles R. Nelson and Charles Plosser, (1982), "Trends and Random Walks in Macroeconomic Time Series: Some Evidence and Implications," *Journal of Monetary Economics* 10, no. 2, 139–162.
[21]It is important to note that if a series is DS, then it may contain a stochastic trend. A stochastic trend implies the trend is driven by random shocks and there is no particular trend to which it returns, see Maddala and Kim (1998) for more detail about stochastic trend.
[22]If the first difference of the series is stationary, then the series is called first-order stationary or the order of integration is 1. We can write first-order stationary as I(1), general form is I(d), where "I" stands for integration and "d" is order of integration.
[23]P. Phillips and P. Perron (1988), "Testing for Unit Roots in Time Series Regression." *Biometrika* 75, 335–346.

and Shin (1992) introduced the KPSS test.[24] The ADF and PP tests use the null hypothesis of a unit root (a time series contains a unit root) while the KPSS test has a stationary null hypothesis (i.e., a time series is stationary). ADF and PP tests are known as nonstationary tests; KPSS is known as a stationary test. We focus here on the ADF, PP, and the KPSS tests of unit root.

The Dickey-Fuller Tests

Let y_t be a time series and consider a simple autoregressive of order 1 (AR (1)) process

$$y_t = \rho y_{t-1} + \varepsilon_t$$
$$\varepsilon_t \sim wn(0, \sigma^2) \qquad (4.6)$$

where

ρ = parameter to be estimated

ε_t = error term and assumed to be white noise, which implies a zero mean and constant variance

Then the hypothesis of interest is

$$H_0: \rho = 1 \Rightarrow y_t \text{ is nonstationary (unit root)}$$

$$H_1: |\rho| < 1 \Rightarrow y_t \text{ is stationary}^{25}$$

The test statistic is

$$t_{\rho=1} = \frac{\hat{\rho} - 1}{SE(\hat{\rho})}$$

where

$\hat{\rho}$ = least square estimate

$SE(\hat{\rho})$ = usual standard error estimate

Dickey and Fuller (1979) showed that under the null hypothesis of a unit root ($\rho = 1$), this statistic, $t_{\rho=1}$, does not follow the conventional student's t-distribution.[26] They first considered the unit root tests and derived the asymptotic

---

[24]D. Kwiatkowski, P. Phillips, P. Schmidt, and Y. Shin (1992), "Testing the Null Hypothesis of Stationarity Against the Alternative of a Unit Root," *Journal of Econometrics* 54, 159–178.
[25]Here *stationary* means "weak stationary," also known as covariance stationary. For strict stationary, one must employ conditional probability on the series, which is not an easy task in applied econometrics. Therefore, we are following the weak stationary approach. We use the terms *stationary* and *mean reversion* interchangeably throughout the book.
[26]Since the time series under consideration does not have a constant mean and variance, the traditional student's t-distribution cannot be employed as the t-distribution assumes a constant mean and variance.

distribution of $t_{\rho=1}$, which is called a DF distribution. The standard DF test has the following form, after subtracting y_{t-1} from both side of Equation 4.6:

$$\Delta y_t = \alpha y_{t-1} + \varepsilon_t \tag{4.7}$$

where

$\alpha = \rho - 1$

The null and alternative hypothesis may be written as:

H_0: $\alpha = 0 \Rightarrow y_t$ is nonstationary (unit root)

H_1: $\alpha < 0 \Rightarrow y_t$ is stationary.

The key difference is that we will use the DF statistic, τ(tau) statistic, instead of the conventional t-distribution. In addition, the distribution of the corresponding DF statistic, $\hat{\tau}$, has been tabulated under the null hypothesis of $\alpha = 0$.[27]

As mentioned earlier, the two major sources of nonstationary are difference-stationary and trend stationary. Difference stationary is divided into two categories: random walk and random walk with drift. A random walk model implies that the current value of the y (y_t) is equal to the lag of y (y_{t-1}) plus an error term (ε_t). Equation 4.7 is an example of the random walk model. A random walk model is also known as a zero-mean model because it implies that a series has a mean of zero. But in practice, an economic series rarely has a zero mean. When we allow for a nonzero mean, it is known as a random walk with drift, and can be tested under Equation 4.8:

$$\Delta y_t = \gamma + \alpha y_{t-1} + \varepsilon_t \tag{4.8}$$

Random walk with drift and random walk (without drift) are both cases of difference stationary because the difference of the series must be generated in order to convert it into a stationary series. We can include a deterministic linear trend in the unit root test (Equation 4.8) such as:

$$\Delta y_t = \gamma + \alpha y_{t-1} + \beta \; time + \varepsilon_t \tag{4.9}$$

where

$time$ = dummy variable and artificially generated as $time = 1$ for the first sample observation, $time = 2$ for the second observation, and so on

Dickey and Fuller (1979) provided different tabulated values for all three cases: random walk, random walk with drift and deterministic trend and a constant.

One important issue related with the DF test of unit root is that it is valid only if the series y_t follows an AR(1) process. If the series is correlated at a higher-order lag and follows an AR (p) process, where AR (p) > AR (1), then

---

[27]Tables are available in Fuller (1976). The SAS software automatically produces the table value along with estimated $\hat{\tau}$ values.

the assumption of a white noise error term is violated. The ADF offers a parametric correction for higher-order correlation by assuming that y_t follows an AR(p) process and adding up to p lags differenced terms of the dependent variable, Δy_t in this case, to the right-hand side of the test regression where p is lag order.

$$\Delta y_t = \gamma + \alpha y_{t-1} + \beta \ time + \sum_{j=1}^{p} \phi_j \Delta y_{t-j} + \varepsilon_t \qquad (4.10)$$

The standard ADF unit root test contains three different equations to be tested: the random walk case, the random walk with drift case, and the linear deterministic trend and a constant. The ADF test is a useful tool to identify stationarity of the series as well as the source of nonstationarity, if the series is not stationary.

The Phillips-Perron Test

Phillips and Perron (1988) proposed an alternative test of the unit root, which is known as the PP (Phillips-Perron) test. The PP test also has the null hypothesis of a unit root (nonstationary) and the alternative of no unit root (stationary). The major difference between the ADF and PP tests is how they control for serial correlation when testing for a unit root. The PP test estimates Equation 4.7 (of course, we can include drift, Equation 4.8, and a linear time trend, Equation 4.9), and then the PP test modifies the t-ratio of the α coefficient so that serial correlation does not affect the asymptotic distribution of the test statistic. The PP test is based on the statistic

$$\tilde{t}_\alpha = t_\alpha \left(\frac{\gamma_0}{f_0} \right)^{\frac{1}{2}} - \frac{T(f_0 - \gamma_0)(SE(\hat{\alpha}))}{2f_0^{\frac{1}{2}} S} \qquad (4.11)$$

where

$t_\alpha = t$-ratio of the α

$\gamma_0 = $ consistent estimate of the error variance of Equation 4.7 and calculated as $\frac{(T-K)S^2}{T}$, where K is the number of regressors in the equation

$f_0 = $ estimator of the residual spectrum at zero frequency

$T = $ sample size

$SE(\hat{\alpha}) = $ coefficient's standard error

$\hat{\alpha} = $ estimate of the α (α is from Equation 4.7)

$S = $ standard error of the test regression

The standard DF test assumes that the error term is white noise, or no autocorrelation; if there is autocorrelation, then the ADF test will be used. The ADF test includes lag-dependent variables as a right-hand-side variable in the test equation to solve the autocorrelation issue. The greater the number of lags of the dependent variable, the fewer number of observations available for the estimation process, which is known as size distortion. The PP test, however, takes care of the autocorrelation issue through nonparametric statistics and does not include a lag-dependent variable as a right-hand-side variable.[28]

The Kwiatkowski, Phillips, Schmidt, and Shin Test

Kwiatkowski, Phillips, Schmidt, and Shin (1992) introduced the so-called KPSS test of a unit root. The KPSS test differs from the ADF and PP in that the null hypothesis is stationary (no unit root) and the alternative is nonstationary (unit root). The KPSS statistic is based on the residual from the OLS regression of y_t on the exogenous variables x_t' :

$$y_t = x_t' \delta + \varepsilon_t \tag{4.12}$$

where

x_t' = optional exogenous variables that may consist of constant, or a constant and a trend, and δ parameters to be estimated

ε_t error term = white noise

The Lagrange Multiplier (LM) statistic is defined as:

$$LM = \sum_{t=1}^{T} S(t)^2 / (T^2 f_0) \tag{4.13}$$

where

$S(t)$ = cumulative residual function and can be estimated using the following:

$$S(t) = \sum_{r=1}^{t} \hat{\varepsilon}_r \tag{4.14}$$

based on the residuals $\hat{\varepsilon}_t = y_t - x_t' \hat{\delta}$.

f_0 = estimator of the residual spectrum at zero frequency

One benefit of the KPSS test is that it can be used to confirm the conclusion from the ADF and PP tests since the KPSS test has a different null hypothesis. Overall, we recommend applying all three tests to statistically determine whether a series is stationary. Testing for a unit root in a series is a much better approach than simply assuming a series is stationary or nonstationary even when a visual interpretation of the data would suggest no unit root.

An analyst should know the concept of unit root testing. In Chapter 7 we show how to implement ADF, PP, and KPSS in SAS as well as how to determine whether a time series is stationary or nonstationary.

Structural Change: A New Normal?

Another important feature of applied econometric analysis is to identify whether a time series contains a structural break. The most important assumption of any

---

[28] The nonparametric statistics discussion is beyond the scope of this book, but interested readers can consult Maddala and Kim (1998).

time series model is that the underlying process is the same across all observations in the sample. All time series data, therefore, should be analyzed and tested for periods of an abrupt change in the time series pattern. Furthermore, if an economic, financial, or business data series contains a structural break, then the series acts differently during different time periods; therefore, any estimated relationship in one time period does not work in another time period—recall our discussion of Okun's law. As mentioned earlier in this chapter, the U.S. productivity growth rate between 1974 and 2011 had two different eras in terms of growth rates: the era of slow productivity growth from 1974 to 1995 and strong productivity growth from 1996 to 2011. The post–mid-1990s is known as the era of the productivity resurgence. Econometrically, the U.S. productivity growth rate experienced a structural break during the mid-1990s, "shifting" the growth rate of productivity upward.[29]

Why the break? One hypothesis is that it was caused by the information technology revolution. If a time series has a break in the trend growth rate—that is, if the trend growth shifted up or down and continued at this level for an extended period—then the time series will behave differently compared to the pre-break era. In the case of productivity growth, trend growth had shifted upward and stayed there for 15 to 20 years, signifying a break from the 1974 to 1995 period.

Why is it important for an analyst to identify a structural break in a time series? Typically, businesses and policy makers make decisions based on past behavior and currently available information and, as a result, simply extrapolate a time series. In reality, a time series may have a break in the trend and/or average growth rate. Therefore, decisions based on past rules of thumb can be misleading in the future. Consider again the breakdown in the money growth and inflation link after 1982.

Another example of a possible structural break is U.S. home prices. The S&P/Case-Shiller home price index, a measure for U.S. home prices, grew consistently during the period from 1997:Q1 to 2006:Q2 period (see Figure 4.9). This time period contained the 2001 recession, which did not appear to break the growth pattern of home prices. An analyst in 2005 who extrapolated home prices for the 2006 to 2010 time period would feel safe in not anticipating any structural break in the growth rate of home prices due to business cycles.

With the benefit of hindsight, this assumption proved to be disastrously wrong. Home prices fell continuously during the period from 2006:Q3 to 2009:Q1 throughout the United States. In addition, at least since 2009, the home price index had shifted downward. The average value for the S&P/

---

[29] See for a detailed discussion, Mark Vitner and Azhar Iqbal (2013), "Is Productivity Growth Too Strong for Our Own Good?" *Business Economics* 48, 29–41.

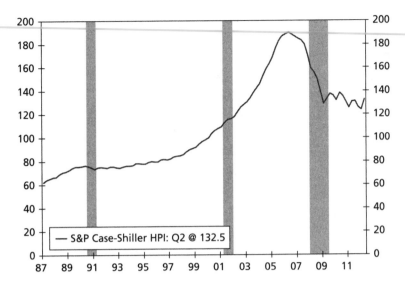

FIGURE 4.9 S&P Case-Shiller Home Price Index (not seasonally adjusted)
Source: S&P/Case-Shiller

Case-Shiller index for the 2009 to 2011 period is 132 compared to 167 for the 2004 to 2005 period, as can be seen in Figure 4.9.

Key factors behind the structural change in home prices and the housing boom/bust were a large number of foreclosures, credit tightening, significant job losses, and a fundamental change in the expectations of buyers that home prices would appreciate continuously. Moreover, legitimate buyers who assumed that home prices would not fall during the period from 2006 to 2010 faced serious financial challenges due to the structural change in the home prices.

As the two previous examples illustrate, an analyst should always test the possibility of a structural break in any time series in order to identify a change in the underlying pattern of economic fundamentals. In this section, we present three different ways to test for a structural break in an economic, financial, or business time series, all of which are made easy with the SAS software. First, we can run a regression against a dummy variable to test for a structural break where y_t is the variable of interest.

$$y_t = \beta_0 + \beta_1 Dummy_t + \varepsilon_t \qquad (4.15)$$

$$t = 1, 2, \ldots T$$

$$Dummy_t = \begin{cases} 0 & \text{if } t < TB \\ 1 & \text{if } t \geq TB \end{cases}$$

Dummy is a break dummy, and it is generated artificially by assuming that *TB* is the break date, values for the dummy variable before the break are zero and, after the break, they take a value of 1. For instance, say y_t is the U.S. home price index, and we are interested to test 2006:Q3 (the first quarter when home prices fell) as a break date. Then the *TB* is 2006:Q3 and the dummy equals 1 after 2006:Q2 and zero before and for 2006:Q2. If the coefficient, β_1, is statistically significant, its *t*-value will allow a test of significance, and then we can assume the series has a structural break. Moreover, if the sign of the β_1 coefficient is positive (negative), then the trend has shifted upward (downward).

Second, we can employ the Chow test,[30] which enlists an F-test criterion, to determine whether the series has a break or not. The null hypothesis of the Chow test is that the series does not contain a structural break; the alternative hypothesis is that the series does contain a structural break. SAS software offers the Chow test, so an analyst only needs to know how to use the SAS procedure and interpret the results.

Both the break dummy and the Chow test are standard ways to test for a structural break. However, one limitation is that both approaches assume that an analyst can identify a break date prior to running these tests. This is known as an exogenous break date. What happens if an analyst does not suspect a particular break date? An unknown break date is called an endogenous break date. The state space approach considers an endogenous break and is explained in Chapter 7.

Separating Cycle and Trend in a Time Series: The Hodrick-Prescott Filter

How can the components of trend growth and the cycles around that trend for any given time series be distinguished? The method we have adopted here is the Hodrick and Prescott (1997)[31] filter approach. This approach begins with the recognition that aggregate economic variables experience repeated fluctuations around their long-term growth path.[32] Moreover, we can hypothesize that the growth or trend component of any economic series itself varies smoothly over time. That is, the trend in most variables is not a constant number but varies over time, as would be noticeable, for example, with productivity and real interest rates.

The HP filter has two justifications, one theoretical and one statistical. The theoretical part of the HP filter is connected with real business cycle (RBC) literature. In the RBC world, the trend of a time series is not intrinsic to the data but reflects prior outcomes of the researcher and depends on the economic

---

[30]Gregory C. Chow (1960), "Tests of Equality between Sets of Coefficients in Two Linear Regressions," *Econometrica* 28, no. 3, 591–605.

[31]R. Hodrick and E. P. Prescott, (1997). "Postwar U.S. Business Cycles: An Empirical Investigation," *Journal of Money Credit and Banking* 29, 1–16.

[32]Robert E. Lucas Jr. (1981), *Studies in Business Cycle Theory* (Cambridge, MA: MIT Press).

question being investigated. The HP filter's popularity among applied macro-economists results from its flexibility to accommodate these priors since the implied trend line resembles what an analyst would draw by hand through the plot of the data (see Kydland and Prescott, 1990).[33]

The selection mechanism that economic theory imposes on the data via the HP filter can be justified using the statistical literature on curve fitting. The conceptual framework presented by Hodrick and Prescott (1997) can be summarized as follows, and our text closely follows their work:

$$y_t = g_t + c_t$$

$$\text{for } t = 1, 2, 3 \ldots T \tag{4.16}$$

where

T = sample size

A given series y_t is the sum of a growth component g_t and a cyclical component c_t. There is also a seasonal component, but as the data we often use are seasonally adjusted, this component has already been removed by those preparing the data series.

In this framework, the HP filter optimally extracts a trend (g_t), which is stochastic but moves smoothly over time and is uncorrelated with a cyclical component (c_t). The assumption that the trend is smooth is imposed by assuming that the sum of squares of the second differences of g_t is small.

An estimate of the growth component (g_t) is obtained by minimizing

$$\underset{[g_t]_{t=-1}^{T}}{Min} \left\{ \sum_{t=1}^{T} C_t^2 + \lambda \sum_{t=1}^{T} [(g_t - g_{t-1}) - (g_{t-1} - g_{t-2})]^2 \right\} \tag{4.17}$$

where $c_t = y_t - g_t$ is the cyclical component, which is the deviation from the long-run path (expected to be near zero, on average, over long a time period) and the smoothness of the growth component is measured by the sum of squares of its second difference:

$$\Delta^2 g_t = (1 - L)^2 g_t = [(g_t - g_{t-1}) - (g_{t-1} - g_{t-2})] \tag{4.18}$$

where L = lag operator (e.g., $Lx_t = x_{t-1}$)

The parameter λ (in Equation 4.17) is a positive number that penalizes the variability in the growth component (g_t). That is, the larger the value of λ, the smoother the solution to the series. The parameter λ helps us to reduce variability and smooth the series g_t and provides a deterministic trend. Note here the role of the prior knowledge of the researcher and the fact that those priors could be biased and therefore lead to biased results. For a sufficiently large λ, at the optimum all the $g_{t+1} - g_t$ must be arbitrarily near some constant β, and

---

[33] Finn E. Kydland and E. C. Prescott, (1990). "Business Cycles: Real Facts and a Monetary Myth," Federal Reserve Bank of Minneapolis *Quarterly Review* 14, no 2, pp. 3–18.

therefore the g_t is arbitrarily near $g_0 + \beta_t$. This implies that the limit of solutions to Equation 4.17 as λ approaches infinity is the least squares fit of a linear time trend model. In this context, the "optimal" value of λ is $\lambda = \delta_g^2 / \delta_c^2$ where δ_g and δ_c are the standard deviations of the innovations in the growth component (g_t) and in the cyclical component (c_t), respectively.

For an analyst, it is important to determine the value of the λ in order to apply the HP filter on any time series. Fortunately, past research has determined different values of λ for different types of data frequency. A low-frequency economic data series, such as an annual time series, is usually less volatile than a quarterly time series. For instance, Hodrick and Prescott (1997) suggested the value of $\lambda = 1,600$ for quarterly data and for annual observations; Baxter and King (1999) have used a λ value of 100.[34] For a monthly time series, Zarnowitz and Ozyildirim (2006) used a value of $\lambda = 14,400$.[35]

There are several issues related to the cyclical component (c_t). By definition, $c_t = y_t - g_t$, and y_t is the natural logarithm of a given time series. This is one advantage of using log form instead of level form, since the change in the growth component (g_t), $g_t - g_{t-1}$, corresponds to a growth rate. Nelson and Plosser (1982) concluded that many macroeconomics series contain a unit root in their level form. The y_t naturally may be one of them (nonstationary at level), and we can test this in our application. The growth component (g_t) should be nonstationary, as it is a trend (long-run trend growth) component of a given series and should be smooth, but this will also need to be tested.

Since the cyclical component (c_t) is a deviation from the growth component, and it is expected to be stationary, the economy's output should exhibit reversion to trend growth, and the effect of shocks, though they may persist over time, should decline and eventually die out. In other words, the stationarity of c_t implies that no matter what kind of fluctuations occur in the series, deviations from its long-run growth component (g_t) are temporary and the series will move, on average, smoothly over time toward trend.

One key advantage (among many others) of the HP filter is that once we estimate the g_t and c_t, we can identify, at any point of time, whether the current value of a series is below trend growth or above trend. This feature of the HP filter presents, therefore, a useful policy guideline that may help policy makers in their decision-making process. For instance, let y_t represent real GDP (log form) and g_t its long-run growth path if the economy continuously grew, but at a rate less than g_t for a period of three years (2010–2012). In this case, the economy is experiencing subpar growth, not in level terms, but in growth terms. That

[34] M. Baxter and R. G. King (1999), "Measuring Business Cycles: Approximate Band-Pass Filters for Economic Time Series," *Review of Economics and Statistics* 81, 573–593.

[35] V. Zarnowitz and A. Ozyildirim (2006), "Time Series Decomposition and Measurement of Business Cycles, Trends and Growth Cycles," *Journal of Monetary Economics* 53, 1717–1739.

will require an adjustment in the behavior of producers, consumers, and policy makers without adopting more radical policy changes associated with recessions since the economy continues to grow, just at a slower pace. It is certainly possible to conceive of a severe and long period of below-trend growth that causes more hardship on a cumulative basis than a mild and short recession, as persistent underperformance will alter, over time, incentives and expectations of economic agents. In fact, long slowdowns in employment and demand growth have occurred repeatedly in recent times (1992–1994, 2002–2004) even while output and supply growth held up well, supported by the process of technology and productivity (Zarnowitz and Ozyildirim, 2006). So, with the help of the HP filter, we can judge where the economy stands relative to trend and adjust our policies and objectives accordingly, rather than reverting to policies typically used to respond to a recession. An economic slowdown requires some serious considerations and adjustments by both public and private decision makers. Yet such adjustments must be made in the context of our assessment of the economic behavior relative to trend as we judge by using the HP filter.

APPLICATION: JUDGING ECONOMIC VOLATILITY

For many economic series, volatility is often cited but seldom quantified. Over the years, we have sought to provide a perspective on this concept in many investment decisions. One primary lesson we have learned is that when we provide a context for the concept of volatility, decision making is improved.

Look at the Data

A simple but important way to begin the analysis of any economic or financial variable is to plot the data against time. For instance, Figure 4.10 compares the year-over-year change in GDP growth against its long-run average.[36] A plot of a time series provides a visual look at the data. This should be the first step of any applied time series analysis because this step allows the analyst to identify any unusual aspects of the data series. A plot shows whether the series contains an outlier—one or more extreme values in the time series—which impacts calculations, such as the mean or standard deviation. An analyst should attempt to understand the reason for such an extreme value, such as an unusual event or simply a misprinted value that should be corrected in subsequent releases.

---

[36]We examine the real GDP series here since it is the primary measure of economic success and a benchmark. The series is seasonally adjusted and an annualized quarterly growth rate is employed here in the analysis. Shaded areas represent recessions declared by the National Bureau of Economic Research.

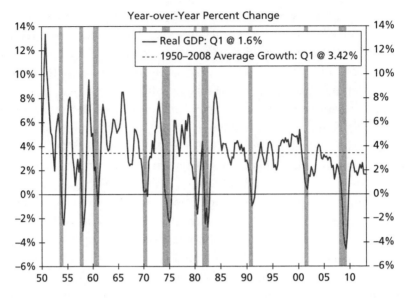

FIGURE 4.10 Real GDP
Source: U.S. Department of Commerce and Wells Fargo Securities, LLC

Second, a plot may also provide evidence to suggest whether the variable of interest contains an explicit time trend or a cyclical pattern. Third, a plot may also provide a visible indication of a structural break in the time series. A structural break suggests that the model defining the behavior of the variable of interest, such as the unemployment rate, is different before and after the break.

Figure 4.10 indicates that the real rate of U.S. economic growth does not contain a substantial outlier or an explicit time trend. However, a cyclical pattern is evident in the real GDP growth rate, as it tends to fall during recessions and rise during the early phase of recoveries. By adding the long-run average growth rate—3.4 percent during the period from 1950 to 2008—as a dotted line, it is clear that the pace of growth in this expansion has changed markedly. For instance, during the 1960s and 1970s, real growth during expansions tracks above the average long-run growth rate, while since the mid-1980s, growth has trended lower than the long-run average.

Putting Simple Statistical Measures to Work

Another way to characterize an economic or financial variable is to estimate its mean (the central tendency of a data series), standard deviation (how much deviation exits from the mean), and stability ratio—the standard deviation as a percentage of the mean. A time series can be divided into different periods when it appears that the series has changed. Then the mean, standard

TABLE 4.4 Real GDP (Annualized Rate)

Business Cycles*	Mean	S.D.	Stability Ratio
1949:Q4–1954:Q2	4.95	4.33	87.47
1954:Q2–1958:Q2	2.30	3.44	149.78
1958:Q2–1961:Q1	3.10	3.71	119.56
1961:Q1–1970:Q4	4.22	2.37	56.24
1970:Q4–1975:Q1	3.27	2.87	87.75
1975:Q1–1980:Q3	3.18	2.86	89.92
1980:Q3–1991:Q1	2.98	2.61	87.59
1991:Q1–2001:Q4	3.20	1.61	50.38
2001:Q4–2009:Q2	1.53	2.31	**150.95**
2009:Q2–2012:Q4†	2.17	1.21	55.85
1948:Q1–2012:Q4	3.22	2.72	84.41

S.D. = Standard deviation
*Trough to trough
†Not a complete business cycle
Source: U.S. Department of Commerce and Wells Fargo Securities, LLC

deviation, and stability ratio can be estimated for each subsample. We can also test if the mean is statistically different between periods. The data series can be divided between different business cycles, different decades, or even different eras, such as pre– and post–World War II.

Here we compare the real rate of GDP growth during different business cycles. We separate the data into the dates corresponding with those business cycles, as seen in Table 4.4. For real GDP, the mean (average) growth rate varies significantly over different business cycles, with fairly rapid growth in the 1958 to 1980 period and then a much more modest growth rate in the period since 2001. Yet the standard deviation, one measure of variability in the series, also moves quite a bit during these decades. One major benefit of dividing this data into different eras and then calculating the mean, standard deviation, and stability ratio for each era is that it reveals how differently the rate of economic growth behaved during each of these economic cycles. Thereby it assists us in putting growth into some context for assessing volatility.

As shown in Table 4.4, the mean growth rate for GDP between 1948 and 2012 period is 3.22 percent, with a standard deviation of 2.72 and a stability ratio of 84.41. (The standard deviation is 84 percent of the mean.) The stability ratio represents the volatility of real GDP growth in each era, where a higher value of the stability ratio is an indication of more volatility. One benefit of

TABLE 4.5 Real Final Sales (Year-over-Year Percentage Change)

Business Cycles*	Mean	S.D.	Stability Ratio
1949:Q4–1954:Q2	5.33	3.07	57.67
1954:Q2–1958:Q2	2.26	2.41	106.68
1958:Q2–1961:Q1	2.97	2.74	92.16
1961:Q1–1970:Q4	4.30	2.08	48.25
1970:Q4–1975:Q1	2.85	2.80	98.28
1975:Q1–1980:Q3	3.11	2.81	90.61
1980:Q3–1991:Q1	3.03	2.49	82.27
1991:Q1–2001:Q4	3.55	1.79	50.56
2001:Q4–2009:Q2	1.52	2.31	**152.86**
2009:Q2–2012:Q4†	1.14	1.57	137.88
1948:Q1–2012:Q4	3.26	2.48	75.95

S.D. = Standard deviation
*Trough to trough
†Not a complete business cycle
Source: U.S. Department of Commerce and Wells Fargo Securities, LLC

the stability ratio compared to the standard deviation is that it identifies the magnitude of the difference in volatility of real growth by era compared to a benchmark average growth rate. For instance, if we set the stability ratio as the volatility criterion, then the period from 2001:Q4 to 2009:Q2 stands out as a period of low but relatively volatile growth. In contrast, the decades of the 1960s through 1980s were a period of better growth and more stable economic performance. From our viewpoint, the standard deviation alone is not the best measure of volatility. We would prefer the stability ratio to give us a sense of balance between growth and its relative variability. The stability ratio includes the mean and standard deviation and gives us information about which subsample has a higher standard deviation relative to the mean for growth. Therefore, it better identifies which time series is more volatile.

Tables 4.5 and 4.6 provide detail on the behavior of two other aggregate economic series, real final sales and real personal consumption. In both cases, we find that the 2001 to 2009 business cycle is the most volatile, and the average growth rates of real final sales and real personal consumption were both below their long-run average. These results reinforce the view that households and businesses are less confident today than in prior economic periods. Unease at the household level is reinforced by the observations we can quantify with the data.

TABLE 4.6 Real Personal Consumption (Year-over-Year Percentage Change)

Business Cycles*	Mean	S.D.	Stability Ratio
1949:Q4–1954:Q2	3.60	3.16	87.84
1954:Q2–1958:Q2	3.50	2.61	74.44
1958:Q2–1961:Q1	3.21	2.10	65.19
1961:Q1–1970:Q4	4.40	1.72	39.15
1970:Q4–1975:Q1	3.42	2.98	87.14
1975:Q1–1980:Q3	3.22	2.14	66.42
1980:Q3–1991:Q1	3.24	1.96	60.56
1991:Q1–2001:Q4	3.57	1.49	41.77
2001:Q4–2009:Q2	1.95	1.97	**101.10**
2009:Q2–2012:Q4[†]	1.63	1.28	78.47
1948:Q1–2012:Q4	3.35	2.13	63.58

S.D. = Standard deviation
*Trough to trough
†Not a complete business cycle
Source: U.S. Department of Commerce and Wells Fargo Securities, LLC

Corporate Profits

Recent commentaries have noted corporate profits as recording outsize performance compared to the past, and the analysis here suggests that profits growth has indeed been stronger than the long-run average. However, note that the current cycle has not yet been completed, and profits growth tends to moderate further into the business cycle. As illustrated in Table 4.7, corporate profits growth in the 2001 to 2009 cycle averaged 6.40 percent, which was below the average of 7.95 percent in the period from 1948 to 2012. Moreover, the volatility of these profits, measured by the stability ratio, is above that of the average of the long-run average. The fastest pace of growth for profits appeared in the period of high inflation from 1975 to1980, while the most volatile period appeared to be the period from 1954 to 1958.

Focus on the Labor Market Using Monthly Data

Tables 4.8 and 4.9 provide details on the behavior of two measures of the labor market that are highlighted in private strategic planning and in public policy, employment growth, and the unemployment rate. For employment, the most recently completed business cycle of 2001 to 2009 has been the

TABLE 4.7 Corporate Profits (Year-over-Year Percentage Change)

Business Cycles*	Mean	S.D.	Stability Ratio
1949:Q4–1954:Q2	5.60	19.78	353.25
1954:Q2–1958:Q2	4.32	17.51	**405.85**
1958:Q2–1961:Q1	6.26	20.29	324.13
1961:Q1–1970:Q4	5.00	10.08	201.40
1970:Q4–1975:Q1	8.15	24.61	302.06
1975:Q1–1980:Q3	11.58	16.39	141.51
1980:Q3–1991:Q1	7.91	13.60	171.87
1991:Q1–2001:Q4	5.83	8.13	139.49
2001:Q4–2009:Q2	6.40	14.71	229.87
2009:Q2–2012:Q4†	16.40	15.76	96.11
1948:Q1–2012:Q4	7.95	14.13	177.80

S.D. = Standard deviation
*Trough to trough
†Not a complete business cycle
Source: U.S. Department of Commerce and Wells Fargo Securities, LLC

TABLE 4.8 Employment Growth (Year-over-Year Percentage Change)

Business Cycles*	Mean	S.D.	Stability Ratio
1949:Oct–1954:May	2.61	3.61	138.64
1954:May–1958:Apr	1.25	2.82	225.38
1958:Apr–1961:Feb	1.05	3.00	285.55
1961:Feb–1970:Nov	2.79	1.63	58.30
1970:Nov–1975:Mar	2.16	1.94	90.15
1975:Mar–1980:Jul	2.76	2.34	84.52
1980:Jul–1991:Mar	1.79	1.88	105.30
1991:Mar–2001:Nov	1.80	1.29	71.64
2001:Nov–2009:Jun	0.19	1.65	**890.09**
2009:Jun–2012:Dec†	−0.13	2.33	−1,761.43
1948:Jan–2012:Dec	1.75	2.27	129.73

S.D. = Standard deviation
*Trough to trough
†Not a complete business cycle
Source: U.S. Department of Labor and Wells Fargo Securities, LLC

TABLE 4.9 Unemployment Rate

Business Cycles*	Mean	S.D.	Stability Ratio
1949:Oct–1954:May	3.96	1.36	**34.44**
1954:May–1958:Apr	4.69	0.86	18.31
1958:Apr–1961:Feb	5.96	0.82	13.78
1961:Feb–1970:Nov	4.70	1.04	22.15
1970:Nov–1975:Mar	5.69	0.82	14.45
1975:Mar–1980:Jul	6.99	0.98	14.05
1980:Jul–1991:Mar	7.12	1.51	21.16
1991:Mar–2001:Nov	5.50	1.17	21.17
2001:Nov–2009:Jun	5.58	1.05	18.84
2009:Jun–2012:Dec†	9.02	0.70	7.73
1948:Jan–2012:Dec	5.80	1.67	28.75

S.D. = Standard deviation
*Trough to trough
†Not a complete business cycle
Source: U.S. Department of Labor and Wells Fargo Securities, LLC

weakest period of average job growth as well as the most volatile, based on the stability ratio. Moreover, by both labor market measures, we can appreciate the challenges to household confidence and public policy in that today's labor market is truly different from in the past. These results reinforce the view that careful analysis of the data provides value in our evaluation of the economy and helps explain the disappointing sentiment expressed by many in the current environment.

Financial Market Volatility: Assessing Risk

For financial markets, risk is often measured by volatility. Tables 4.10 and 4.11 show calculations for volatility in the S&P 500 Index and 10-year Treasury yield, two financial benchmarks. For the S&P 500, we find that the previously completed business cycle of 2001 to 2009 has been the worst period for average S&P performance since the early 1970s, when rising oil prices, rapid inflation, and high interest rates plagued the economy. Moreover, the volatility of the 2001 to 2009 period is also quite high. The 1970 to 1975 period, however, remains the most volatile period for the S&P 500 Index. The 1970 to 1975 and the 2001 to 2009 periods were characterized by disappointing performance relative to the average gain of 8.4 percent over the 1948 to 2012 period as well

TABLE 4.10 S&P 500 (Year-over-Year Percentage Change)

Business Cycles*	Mean	S.D.	Stability Ratio
1949:Oct–1954:May	12.13	9.83	81.01
1954:May–1958:Apr	16.26	18.30	112.53
1958:Apr–1961:Feb	10.30	15.38	149.31
1961:Feb–1970:Nov	4.95	13.15	265.43
1970:Nov–1975:Mar	−0.02	17.68	**−116,177.63**
1975:Mar–1980:Jul	6.66	11.41	171.38
1980:Jul–1991:Mar	12.45	16.26	130.60
1991:Mar–2001:Nov	13.55	14.12	104.22
2001:Nov–2009:Jun	−1.32	18.51	−1,398.82
2009:Jun–2012:Dec†	11.13	15.76	141.62
1948:Jan–2012:Dec	8.43	15.93	189.07

S.D. = Standard deviation
*Trough to trough
†Not a complete business cycle
Source: Standard & Poor's, Federal Reserve Board and Wells Fargo Securities, LLC

TABLE 4.11 10-Year Treasury Yield

Business Cycles*	Mean	S.D.	Stability Ratio
1954:May–1958:Apr	3.06	0.47	15.20
1958:Apr–1961:Feb	3.99	0.48	12.03
1961:Feb–1970:Nov	4.99	1.18	23.71
1970:Nov–1975:Mar	6.74	0.64	9.54
1975:Mar–1980:Jul	8.51	1.24	14.53
1980:Jul–1991:Mar	10.32	2.23	21.60
1991:Mar–2001:Nov	6.27	0.89	14.26
2001:Nov–2009:Jun	4.25	0.59	13.84
2009:Jun–2012:Dec†	2.75	0.77	**28.14**
1953:Apr–2012:Dec	6.17	2.75	44.65

S.D. = Standard deviation
*Trough to trough
†Not a complete business cycle
Source: Standard & Poor's, Federal Reserve Board and Wells Fargo Securities, LLC

as a much higher level of volatility. Both were periods of weak equity market performance and a difficult time for household wealth and confidence.

SUMMARY

These simple and easily applied techniques provide useful information and enable an analyst to observe the basic behavior of a time series over different periods or business cycles. An analyst can use SAS to plot the series and to calculate the mean, standard deviation, and stability ratio. SAS software can also help to estimate a mean, standard deviation, and stability ratio.

CHAPTER 5

Characterizing a Relationship between Time Series

Once an analyst characterizes a time series in terms of its cycle and trend, then he or she may wish to identify a possible statistical relationship between that series and another time series of interest by asking: Do the two time series have a statistical relationship between themselves? More fundamentally, if a statistical relationship exists between the variables, why is it of interest to decision makers? As mentioned previously, there are many relationships suggested by economic and financial theory, such as the relationship between: gross domestic product (GDP) and the unemployment rate (Okun's law); inflation and the unemployment rate (Phillips curve); financial development and economic growth;[1] and the money supply and inflation (money neutrality). For each theory, a decision maker will test a relationship to answer key questions, such as: If there is a link between GDP growth and employment, then how many new jobs would be associated with a certain pace of GDP growth? How much inflation do we get for a given increase in the money supply?

Many of these relationships are based on different economic theories of behavior. In practice, however, these theories must be confirmed in order to offer a real-world guideline for decision makers. For instance, one economic theory might suggest that an increase in a country's money supply may change its price level, all else being equal, yet not impact real growth. Such money

---

[1] Ronald I. McKinnon (1973), *Money and Capital in Economic Development* (Washington, DC: Brookings Institution).

neutrality would suggest particular outcomes to investors.[2] Typically, if money growth increases the real GDP growth rate, equity investors benefit; if money growth spurs inflation over time then bond investors suffer. For example, in the United States during the January 2010–March 2012 period, a measure of the money supply (M2) increased 16.3 percent, real GDP increased 4.3 percent, and the inflation rate (personal consumption expenditure [PCE] deflator as a proxy for inflation) was up 4.6 percent. During that time period, equity investors enjoyed a 23.6 percent gain in the Standard & Poor's (S&P) 500 index while bond investors experienced a 41.8 percent drop in the 10-year Treasury bond yield. In practice, several questions need to be answered before a policy maker operationalizes this economic theory in the real world. One question is whether a major assumption of money-neutrality theory—that other things remain constant—is true. This assumption may not be true because an economy is dynamic and its many elements are constantly changing. Another question would be: What is the magnitude of the relationship—that is, is a 1 percent increase in the money supply associated with a 1 percent change in the inflation rate, or is it more or less than 1 percent? Moreover, what is the lag effect between money growth and inflation? That is, would a change in the growth of the money supply affect inflation in the same quarter, the next quarter, or the next year? Finally, is a change in the growth of the money supply always associated with a change in the inflation rate?

Recently in the United States, during January 2009 to March 2012, a large increase in the money supply was associated with a small change in the inflation rate (see Figure 5.1). M2 expanded more than 18 percent, while

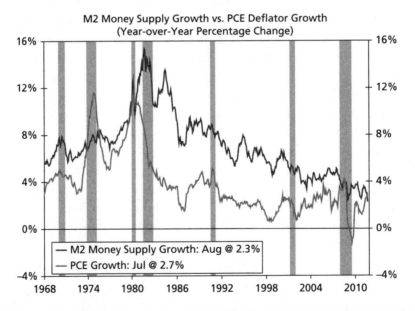

FIGURE 5.1 M2 Money Supply Growth versus PCE Deflator Growth (Year-over-Year Percentage Change)
Source: Federal Reserve Board and U.S. Bureau of Labor Statistics

[2]For more details about money neutrality, see N. Gregory Mankiw (2011), *Principles of Macroeconomics*, 6th ed. (Mason, OH: South-Western).

the PCE deflator, a measure of U.S. inflation, increased only by 5.2 percent during the same period. Why? Perhaps major economic factors including the aftereffects of the Great Recession created a large spare capacity of capital and labor and a low level of business and consumer confidence. These factors may have slowed the inflation growth rate relative to expectations, given the steep rise in the money supply. The question then becomes the reliability of the money-neutrality theory under current circumstances and the importance of testing economic relationships as they can possibly change over time.

The relationship between two (or more) variables of interest can be explored by starting an analysis with economic or financial theory and then conducting an econometric analysis to test that theory. For instance, in the case of money neutrality, we can start with an economic theory that suggests a direct relationship between the money supply and the inflation rate—that is, an increase in the money supply would raise the rate of inflation. Then we can collect data on the money supply and the inflation rate, plot the data, and employ various econometric techniques to quantify the relationship and identify the extent of money neutrality for a country. A final conclusion and set of policy recommendations could be developed based on the econometric results.

Several econometric techniques can characterize the statistical relationship between variables of interest.[3] We begin a statistical analysis with a simple correlation and regression analysis between the variables of interest. A correlation analysis indicates whether two variables are statistically associated. The correlation coefficient shows the magnitude of an association, and the p-value attached to the coefficient can be tested for statistical significance at any given level of significance.

A regression analysis more precisely identifies a statistical relationship compared to a correlation analysis. A regression analysis will specify a dependent variable as well as one or more independent variables. Furthermore, an R^2 statistic would quantify how much variation in the dependent variable is explained by the independent variable(s). The t-value would indicate whether an individual independent variable is statistically significant, and the F-test would show whether all (usually, more than one) independent variables, jointly, are statistically significant in a model.

Both correlation and regression analysis are reliable tools for a simple and quick econometric analysis; however, both assume that the underlying series are stationary. In reality, however, many time series, as suggested by Nelson and Plosser (1982), are nonstationary at level form and contain a unit root.[4]

---

[3]Later in this chapter we shed light on several major econometric techniques to quantify a statistical relationship.

[4]Nelson, R. Charles and Charles Plosser (1982),'Trends and random walks in macroeconomic time series: Some evidence and implications." *Journal of Monetary Economics* 10 issue 2, 139–162.

The unit root problem has very serious consequences, not only for modeling but also for forecasting. For example, when an analyst runs a regression in level form where all variables are nonstationary, he or she may face a number of issues. Granger and Newbold (1974) warn that with I(1) variables (the series is characterized by a first-order unit root), there is a possibility of spurious regression results.[5] That is, a very high R^2 can be obtained even though no meaningful relationship exists between the variables. According to Granger and Newbold, $R^2 > d(d =$ Durbin Watson statistic) is a good rule of thumb to judge whether the estimated regression is spurious. In the presence of a unit root in a time series, an analyst should not use the ordinary least squares (OLS) method (simple regression and correlation analysis).

The unit root problem may impact an economic or business forecaster as well. If an analyst employs the commonly used specification (level form of the variables instead of difference form), and the level form contains a unit root, then the forecast band (the upper and lower limit of the confidence) will be narrower than the true band because the assumption that the forecast variance is constant over time is not true (see Granger and Newbold [1974] for more detail). The forecaster might accept the relationship as significant when, in fact, it is not.

Engle and Granger (1987) solved the unit root problem and introduced the concept of cointegration and the error correction model (ECM).[6] Cointegration implies that the variables have a significant long-run relationship during the sample period. While this may be true over the entire sample period, a short-run deviation from that relationship may be possible. The ECM would show how much the deviation from the long-run relationship is possible in the short run.

Once an analyst identifies a statistical relationship between variables of interest, then he or she should determine the direction of the relationship. Which is the leading and which is the lagging variable? Which is the cause and which is the effect? The Granger causality test (Granger, 1969) helps an analyst to identify the direction of the relationship.[7] For instance, in the case of money neutrality, an analyst may want to test whether the money supply Granger-causes the inflation rate or not.[8] The causality idea is very important and useful for business leaders and policy makers. We want to know which variable is a leading and which one is lagging, whether X causes Y or Y causes X.

---

[5]C.W.J. Granger and P. Newbold (1974), "Spurious Regressions in Econometrics," *Journal of Econometrics* 2, 111–120.

[6]R. Engle and C.W.J. Granger (1987), "Co-Integration and Error Correction: Representation, Estimation, and Testing," *Econometrica* 55, no. 2, 251–276.

[7]C.W.J. Granger (1969), "Investigating Causal Relationships by Econometric Models and Cross-Spectral Methods," *Econometrica* 37, no. 3. 424–438.

[8]The Granger causality test identifies whether two (or more) variables statistically cause each other and thereby it is appropriate to say "Granger-causes" instead of "causes". The term "Granger-causes" implies quantifying statistical causality between the variables of interest. See Granger (1969) for more detail.

Financial data series are usually considered more volatile than real-sector economic variables (e.g., jobs, industrial production). That volatility may invalidate some fundamental statistical assumptions, such as the variance may not be constant over time and may be larger at some points or ranges of the data than for others. This problem is also known as heteroskedasticity. In this case, statistical results based on OLS are not valid. The solution to the problem is provided by Engle (1982) and it is known as the autoregressive conditional heteroskedasticity (ARCH) approach.[9] The benefits of the ARCH are numerous. For instance, if we find the ARCH effect in a time series, then that indicates the series has volatility clustering—the deviation from the mean is not constant over time and is smaller for some periods than others, and vice versa.

IMPORTANT TEST STATISTICS IN IDENTIFYING STATISTICALLY SIGNIFICANT RELATIONSHIPS

We discuss several useful test statistics here that are essential for any econometric analysis. The SAS software produces all these statistics, but it is important to first know their function and how to interpret them.

Level of Significance and p-value

In econometric analysis, whenever an analyst decides to reject or to not reject a null hypothesis, that decision should be based on a specific level of statistical significance. For instance, if a regression analysis concludes that the U.S. money supply is statistically associated with the inflation rate, this decision should be made at a specific level of significance. Typically we use a 5 percent (or $\alpha = 0.05$) level of significance; that is, we reject the null hypothesis that the estimated coefficient of the money supply is zero and that money growth does have a relationship with the rate of inflation during the sample period tested with a 5 percent probability of error in our decision. Moreover, $\alpha = 0.05$ also implies that our confidence level is 95 percent $(1 - \alpha)$; that is, we are 95 percent confident that the estimated coefficient is close to the true (but unknown) parameter linking money growth and inflation. The SAS software produces p-values. If a p-value is less than or equal to 0.05, then we will reject the null hypothesis at a 5 percent level of significance, implying that we are 95 percent confident in our results that money growth does influence inflation.

---

[9]Robert Engle (1982), "Autoregressive Conditional Heteroskedasticity with Estimates of the Variance of United Kingdom Inflation," *Econometrica* 50, 987–1008.

The t-Value or t-Test

In a regression model, a t-test (or t-value) indicates whether an independent variable is statistically associated with a dependent variable. For example, consider Equation 5.1:[10]

$$Y_t = \alpha + \beta X_t + \varepsilon_t \qquad (5.1)$$

where

Y_t = PCE deflator
$t = 1, 2, 3, \ldots, T$
X_t = M2
ε_t = error term

The t-value in Equation 5.1 has the null hypothesis H_0: $\beta = 0$; that is, X_t does not statistically explain the variation in Y_t, meaning the money supply is not statistically significantly associated with the inflation rate. A simple rule of thumb is that if a t-value is greater than or equal to 2 in absolute value, we reject the null hypothesis and conclude that X_t is statistically useful in explaining the variation in the Y_t. The SAS software produces a p-value for a t-test, and if the p-value is 0.05 (or less), then we can say that the null ($\beta = 0$) is rejected at 5 percent level of significance.

The F-Test

The F-test is a useful measure to test the model's overall goodness of fit. The F-test jointly examines whether the explanatory variables are statistically useful in explaining the variation in the dependent variable. For instance, we can add a third variable to Equation 5.1 and call it Z_t, with Z_t being the real GDP growth rate, capturing aggregate demand.

$$Y_t = \alpha + \beta_1 X_t + \beta_2 Z_t + \varepsilon_t \qquad (5.2)$$

The F-test, in the case of Equation 5.2, would test the null H_0: $\beta_1 = \beta_2 = 0$. That is, X_t and Z_t do not explain the variation in Y_t—money supply and GDP are not statistically associated with the inflation rate. The SAS software produces an F-test value as well as a p-value for that F-test value. If the p-value is less than or equal to 0.05, then we reject the null hypothesis and can say at a 5 percent level of significance that X_t and Z_t are statistically useful variables to explain movements in Y_t. It is important to note that in the case of the one-independent model (e.g., Equation 5.1), the t-value and F-test would be equal.

---

[10]Subscript t in Equation 5.1 indicates the variables are time series (i.e., a vector of values at different time).

R[2] and Adjusted R[2]

R^2 is another useful measure of a model's goodness of fit. If a regression model includes an intercept,[11] as in Equation 5.1, then the R^2 would range between 0 and 1. Furthermore, usually a higher R^2 is considered better than a lower R^2. This is because an R^2 indicates how much variation in the dependent variable is explained by the explanatory variable(s). An adjusted R^2 imposes a higher penalty to add a new variable in a regression model compared to an R^2. Typically, an R^2 increases by adding more variables in a regression, but the adjusted R^2 takes into account the fact that more variables are needed to account for the variation in the dependent variable. Therefore, it would be better to consider the adjusted R^2 in a multiple-variable regression model instead of R^2 alone. In the case of more than one explanatory variable in a regression analysis (e.g., Equation 5.2), the adjusted R^2 may be smaller than the R^2. That is, in the case of more than one explanatory variable in a regression model, an adjusted R^2 would provide a better insight about a model's goodness of fit. However, in a single explanatory variable regression model, the R^2 and adjusted R^2 may be equal. The SAS software produces both R^2 and adjusted R^2 values.

White Noise/Autocorrelation Detection Tests

One of the key assumptions of the OLS approach is that the errors are white noise; that is, there is no serial correlation in the errors. We rewrite Equation 5.1 as:

$$Y_t = \alpha + \beta X_t + \varepsilon_t$$

$$\varepsilon_t \sim N(0, \sigma^2) \qquad (5.3)$$

Error terms are assumed to be normally distributed with a mean of zero and a constant variance. If errors follow these properties, then we call the error term *white noise*. If the error term is white noise, there is no autocorrelation (or no serial correlation) among the error terms. In our economic/financial modeling and forecasting efforts, we want errors to be white noise. If errors are white noise, then they do not contain any useful information that may improve the forecast, so the errors are unforecastable. If, however, errors are forecastable, meaning they follow a deterministic pattern and are not white noise, then the errors contain some useful information that should be included in the regression model.

How would an analyst determine whether the errors are white noise or not? Two standard tests are useful: the Durbin-Watson "d" test and the Breusch-Godfrey test, alternatively known as a Breusch-Godfrey serial correlation LM

---

[11] α in Equation 5.1 is called the intercept term, and it is also known as a constant term of a model.

test (BG LM test).[12] The null hypothesis of a Durbin-Watson "d" test is that the errors are white noise. A simple rule of thumb is that if the value of the "d" test equals 2, then we fail to reject the null—suggesting the errors are white noise. If a regression model contains the lag of a dependent variable (if we include Y_{t-1} as a right-hand-side variable in case of Equation 5.3) as an explanatory variable, then the Durbin-Watson "d" test results would *not* be reliable.[13] Furthermore, the "d" test only indicates whether there is first-order autocorrelation and does not tell us about higher-order serial correlation.[14] Fortunately, both of these issues are addressed by the BG-LM test. The null hypothesis of the BG-LM test is the same as in the Durbin-Watson "d" test—the errors are white noise. The SAS software produces results of both tests along with p-values. If the p-value of the "d" test or BG-LM is 0.05 or less, then we reject the null hypothesis and conclude that the errors are not white noise and there is autocorrelation in the error terms. If these tests show conflicting results, then we suggest going with the BG-LM test conclusion since it includes the possibility of a higher-order autocorrelation and is reliable for those regression models that include a lag-dependent variable as an explanatory variable.

Model Selection Criteria: The AIC and SIC

In practice, more often than might be imagined, an analyst faces the issue of how to compare different models and decide which one is better. For instance, suppose the analyst has to decide between Equation 5.1 and Equation 5.2 for a model of the relationship between the money supply and inflation rate. Typically, the R^2 and adjusted R^2 of a regression model tends to move up, or increase, as the analyst includes more variables in that regression model. Usually the R^2 and adjusted R^2 would be higher for Equation 5.2 than Equation 5.1 because Equation 5.2 contains more independent variables than Equation 5.1. Therefore, the R^2 and adjusted R^2 may not be good model selection criteria. Two standard model selection criteria deal with this problem: the Akaike information criterion (AIC) and the Schwarz information criterion (SIC), also known as Bayesian information criterion (BIC).

Both AIC and SIC impose a harsher penalty for every additional variable compared to R^2 and adjusted R^2, which makes them more reliable model selection criteria. The model with a smaller SIC and AIC would be the best among

---

[12]For details about autocorrelation/white noise, the Durbin-Watson "d" test, and BG-LM test, see Chapter 6 of G. S. Maddala and Kajal Lahiri (2009), *Introduction to Econometrics*, 4th ed. (Hoboken, NJ: John Wiley & Sons).

[13]It is important to note that a Durbin "h" test addresses the lag-dependent variable as a regressor issue. SAS software also provides the "h" test. For more details, see note 12.

[14]Whether last-period, lag-1, error term ε_{t-1} in case of Equation 5.3, is correlated with current-period error term (ε_t).

competitors.[15] For instance, if Equation 5.1 has a smaller SIC and AIC compared to Equation 5.2, then Equation 5.1 would be the model for the money neutrality. Typically, AIC and SIC should pick the same model, but if there is some inconsistency, then we suggest choosing the model based on a smaller SIC, because the SIC penalty is harsher than the AIC. The good thing for an analyst is that SAS software produces both AIC and SIC, making the outcome easy to evaluate.

SIMPLE ECONOMETRIC TECHNIQUES TO DETERMINE A STATISTICAL RELATIONSHIP

This section discusses simple econometric techniques to quantify a statistical relationship between variables of interest. A graphical presentation of the variables shows the movements/pattern of the two (or more) variables over time, as shown in Figure 5.1. However, it does not indicate whether these variables are statistically associated or not. Correlation analysis and regression analysis quantify statistical relationships between variables of interest.

Correlation Analysis

The first step in an applied time series analysis is to determine whether two variables are statistically associated with each other before we model the relationship between them. The correlation coefficient is a measure of linear association between two variables. Values of the correlation coefficient are always between −1 and +1. A correlation coefficient of +1 indicates that two variables are perfectly related in a positive linear direction, a correlation coefficient of −1 indicates they are perfectly related in a negative linear direction, and a correlation coefficient of zero indicates that there is no linear relationship between the two variables. The SAS software reports a p-value for a correlation coefficient, and that p-value can be tested to determine if the two variables are statistically associated with each other or not.

A correlation analysis will reveal a linear association between two variables. A higher—in absolute terms—and statistically significant correlation coefficient is better than a lower one. The SAS software provides the PROC CORR to estimate the correlation coefficient.

Regression Analysis

A regression analysis indicates whether two (or more) variables have a statistically significant relationship. Correlation analysis and regression analysis are related in the sense that both deal with a linear relationship among variables.

---

[15]For details about SIC and AIC, see Maddala and Lahiri (2009).

In a regression analysis, an analyst specifies a dependent variable and one or more independent variables, and then examines whether the independent variable(s) explains any variation in the dependent variable. A simple linear regression helps describe a relationship between a single dependent variable, Y_t, and a single independent variable, X_t. Furthermore, with the help of an R^2, the analyst can estimate how much variation in Y_t is explained by X_t. If the analyst includes an intercept (or constant term) along with one or more explanatory variables in a regression equation, then the value of the R^2 will stay between zero and 1. Typically, a model with a higher R^2, along with a statistically significant t-value, is better than a model with a lower R^2.[16]

In regression analysis, R^2 and/or adjusted R^2 are commonly used as the model selection criterion. However, we suggest more emphasis be given to the AIC and SIC. That is, to select a regression model among its competitors, an analyst should use the AIC and SIC as a model selection criteria and pick a model that has the smallest AIC/SIC, as mentioned earlier in this chapter.

The PROC AUTOREG is a very useful tool offered by the SAS software to run a regression analysis. This procedure produces almost every important test statistic for the time series analysis, including a t-value, R^2, AIC, SIC, Durbin-Watson "d," and BG-LM. For the analyst, the emphasis is on the significance of the regression analysis and how to interpret key test statistics.

ADVANCED ECONOMETRIC TECHNIQUES TO DETERMINE A STATISTICAL RELATIONSHIP

In this section, we study some advanced econometric techniques to determine a reliable statistical relationship between variables of interest. The correlation analysis and regression analysis provide a measure of statistical association between two or more variables; however, both techniques assume the underlying dataset is stationary at level form. In addition, if the underlying dataset is nonstationary at level form, then the results based on the regression/correlation analysis are unreliable. Cointegration and ECM would provide reliable results in the case of a nonstationary dataset. The Granger causality test would indicate the direction of the relationship, and ARCH analysis is a useful tool to conduct statistical analysis using a financial data series.

Cointegration Analysis

Cointegration has become one of the most influential approaches in time series analysis. That is one reason why Robert Engle and Clive Granger, creators of

---

[16] A good source of application for the regression analysis is Maddala and Lahiri (2009).

the cointegration approach, won the 2003 Nobel Prize in Economics.[17] As mentioned earlier, if variables are nonstationary at level form, then the OLS results will be spurious. The solution to the spurious-results problem is cointegration. In other words, if two or more series are nonstationary at level form, then an analyst should apply a cointegration test on the variables of interest to obtain reliable econometric results.

Cointegration analysis indicates whether there is a long-run and statistically significant relationship between the variables of interest. Engle and Granger (1987) pointed out that a linear combination of two or more nonstationary series may be stationary.[18] If such a stationary, linear combination exists, the nonstationary time series are cointegrated. The stationary linear combination is called the cointegrating equation and may be interpreted as a long-run stable relationship among the variables.

Engle and Granger provided the first cointegration test. The null hypothesis of the Engle-Granger (E-G) test is H_0: no cointegration (the variables are not cointegrated). If the analyst rejects the null hypothesis, then the variables are assumed to have a stable, statistically significant relationship over time.

Johansen (1995) provides another notable approach to test cointegration.[19] The null hypothesis of the Johansen approach is also "no cointegration." Although both the E-G and Johansen approaches are useful tools to determine cointegration between variables of interest, the Johansen approach is more popular and widely used in practice.

One major reason behind this popularity is that the E-G approach only finds whether there is a linear relationship (just one cointegrating relationship) between variables of interest. It is a single-equation method and cannot determine/test if there is more than one cointegrating relationship, especially in the case of more than two variable models. For instance, in Equation 5.4, we are interested in testing the cointegrating relationship among the money supply, the inflation rate, and GDP (money neutrality).

$$Y_t = \alpha + \beta_1 X_t + \beta_2 Z_t + \varepsilon_t \tag{5.4}$$

where

Y_t = PCE deflator
X_t = M2
Z_t = real GDP growth rate
ε_t = error term

---

[17]The 2003 Nobel Prize was shared equally between Robert Engle "for methods of analyzing economic time series with time-varying volatility (ARCH)" and Clive Granger "for methods of analyzing economic time series with common trends (cointegration)."

[18]Robert Engle and Clive Granger (1987), "Co-Integration and Error Correction: Representation, Estimation and Testing," *Econometrica* 55, no. 2. 251–276.

[19]S. Johansen (1995). *Likelihood-Based Inference in Cointegrated Vector Autoregressive Models* (Oxford, U.K.: Oxford University Press).

The E-G approach indicates whether these three variables are cointegrated or not but does not tell how many cointegrating relationships exist. The Johansen approach, in contrast, is a multiple equation, or system approach, which is a vector autoregressive– (VAR-) based method. The Johansen approach tests for more than one cointegrating relationship. For instance, in the case of Equation 5.4, there is a possibility of two cointegrating vectors (which also means two cointegrating relationships).[20] The Johansen approach provides two test statistics for cointegration, the trace test and the maximum eigenvalue test. Essentially, both tests determine how many cointegrating vectors (or relationships) are in an underlying model. However, Johansen and Juselius (1990) suggest that the maximum eigenvalue test may be better.[21] The SAS software utilizes both the E-G test and the Johansen test, with both the trace and maximum eigenvalue test results.

Cointegration is an essential tool for applied time series analysis because it is a reliable tool to estimate a statistical relationship between variables of interest. Therefore, an analyst must learn what is it, how to apply it, and how to analyze the results. The first step would be to test for a unit root in the variables of interest. If they are nonstationary at level form—are I(1)—then *do not* use the OLS approach but instead employ cointegration tests. We suggest following both the E-G and Johansen approaches. If both approaches produce conflicting conclusions, then we suggest an analyst should go with the conclusion of the Johansen approach. As mentioned earlier, the Johansen approach is broader as it tests for as many cointegrating vectors as exist in a model, instead of just one cointegration relationship. Within the Johansen approach, an analyst should employ both the trace and maximum eigenvalue tests. In the case of conflicting conclusions between the two tests, we follow Johansen and Juselius (1990) and suggest going with the maximum eigenvalue test results.

The Error Correction Model

Once cointegration tests indicate that there is a long-run relationship between two or more variables, the analyst should determine how much deviation is possible from a long-run equilibrium relationship in the short run. The ECM shows the short-run dynamics of the relationship and identifies the degree of deviation. Essentially, cointegration and ECM analysis will determine a statistical relationship between variables of interest, with cointegration revealing the long-run properties and the ECM showing the short-run properties of the relationship.

---

[20] Usually, if there are n variables in a model, then the possibility of coinetgrating relationships would be $n - 1$ because we need two variables for a linear equilibrium relationship.

[21] For more details, see S. Johansen and K. Juselius (1990), "Maximum Likelihood Estimation and Inference on Cointegration—with Applications to the Demand for Money," *Oxford Bulletin of Economics and Statistics* 52. 169–210.

Engle and Granger (1987) also introduced the ECM approach. To develop a sense of the short-run dynamics process, we would suggest following the Engle and Granger approach. After determining cointegration, this approach first runs a regression by using the level form of the variable and saving the residuals. Basically, run Equation 5.4 by using OLS and save $\hat{\varepsilon}_t$ (estimated ε_t) the residuals. Since, by assumption, the analyst has already found a cointegrating relationship between the variables of interest, he or she can now use this series (the residuals) as an independent variable in the model (this is called Engle-Granger methodology). The analyst should use the lag of the residual[22] instead of the current-period residual[23] along with differenced form (first difference) of all other variables. The final equation would be as shown in Equation 5.5:

$$\Delta Y_t = c + \beta_3 \Delta X_t + \beta_4 \Delta Z_t + \beta_5 \hat{\varepsilon}_{t-1} + V_t \tag{5.5}$$

where

Δ = first difference form of the variable

$\hat{\varepsilon}_t$ (estimated ε_t) is used in level form

Since all variables, including the estimated error term, are stationary in Equation 5.5, OLS can be used to obtain estimated coefficients.

The ECM approach just discussed is based on a single equation and is another approach to analyzing the short-run properties of a relationship through a system of equations. That approach is based on VAR and is known as the vector error correction model (VECM). In simple words, the ECM is related to the E-G approach of cointegration as both are single equation methods. The VECM, however, is analogous to the Johansen cointegration approach as both are multiple equation methods. The SAS software does produce VECM, and the results based on the VECM are comprehensive in nature.

The Granger Causality Test

Neither regression nor correlation analyses can be interpreted as establishing cause-and-effect relationships; they can only indicate how, or to what extent, variables are associated with each other. The correlation coefficient measures only the degree of linear association between two variables. The regression coefficient indicates that the independent variable is statistically related with the dependent variable. Any conclusions about a cause-and-effect relationship must be based on the analyst's judgment. Furthermore, cointegration and ECM (or VECM) indicate whether there is a statistical relationship between the variables of interest. For business leaders and policy makers, there is an imperative

---

[22] The estimated $\varepsilon_t (\hat{\varepsilon}_t)$ may correlate with the current error term, which is now v_t (Equation 5.5), but the lag of the $\hat{\varepsilon}_t$ may not correlate with the error term (v_t) as lag of the $\hat{\varepsilon}_t$ occurred before the error term (v_t).

[23] One of the OLS assumptions is that independent variable(s) is not correlated with the error term.

to distinguish which is the leading variable and which is the lagging variable. That is, does money really cause inflation?

The Granger causality test is a better way to identify a causal relationship between two or more variables than simply assuming causality. Granger causality is a statistical concept of causality based on prediction. According to Granger causality, if a variable X_t "Granger-causes" a variable Y_t, then past values of X_t should contain information that helps predict Y_t above and beyond the information contained in past values of Y_t alone (Granger 1969).

The Granger causality test also indicates the direction of the causality, that is, whether it is one-way or two-way causality. For instance, if X_t "Granger-causes" Y_t but Y_t does not "Granger-cause" X_t then the relationship would be called one-way causality. If X_t "Granger-causes" Y_t and Y_t also "Granger-causes" X_t, then the test indicates two-way causality.

The SAS software produces Granger causality test results, and its null hypothesis of H_0: X_t does not "Granger-cause" Y_t (i.e., there is no causal relationship). The SAS software also produces an F-test along with a p-value for the F-test. If the p-value is less than or equal to 0.05, then at a 5 percent level of significance, the null hypothesis of no causality would be rejected.

The ARCH/GARCH Model

Financial data series are usually more volatile than economic time series. The volatility of financial data often violates some fundamental OLS assumptions, such as the variance is not constant and/or there is volatility clustering.[24] In either case, hypothesis testing based on OLS statistical results are not valid. For instance, the basic version of OLS assumes that the expected value of all error terms, when squared, is the same at any given point. This assumption is called homoskedasticity (i.e., the variance is constant over time). Sometimes, especially in financial data, the variance may not be constant over time and may be larger for some points or ranges of the data than for others. This heteroskedasticity issue has serious implications for a financial investor or planner. Typically a financial analyst uses the variance or standard deviation of returns as a proxy for a risk to the average return from a purchase of an asset or portfolio. The variance is assumed constant over time, implying that the level of risk does not vary over time, which seems a strong assumption. In practice, however, returns from a portfolio fluctuate, and some periods are more risky than others for an investment. Monthly changes in the S&P 500 index are, for example, larger in some periods than others, indicating that volatility can change over time (see Figure 5.2).

---

[24]Volatility cluster indicates that some periods are associated with higher variances than others. Moreover, the variance is forecastable, and both of these scenarios violate OLS assumptions.

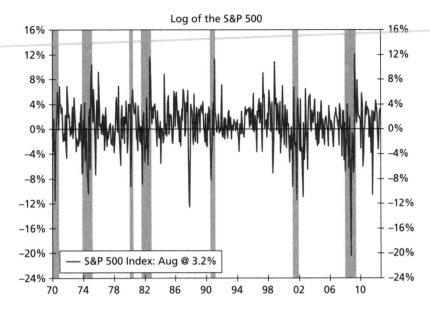

FIGURE 5.2 S&P 500 Index
Source: Standard & Poor's

Engle (1982) provided the solution to this issue—the ARCH approach.[25] A useful generalization of the ARCH model is provided by Bollerslev (1986) and is known as generalized autoregressive conditional heteroskedasticity (GARCH).[26] The ARCH and GARCH approaches are designed to deal with heteroskedasticity and volatility clustering issues. The goal of ARCH/GARCH modeling is to provide a volatility measure (like a standard deviation) that can be used in financial decisions concerning risk analysis, portfolio selection, and derivative pricing.

Traditionally researchers used to be concerned more about heteroskedasticity when they were dealing with a cross-section model of economic relationship and did not worry so much about the problem when conducting time series analysis. But now, due to the ARCH/GARCH approach, we strongly suggest that an analyst working with a financial data series, such as the return on an asset or portfolio, test for the ARCH effect.

Hamilton (2008) proposed use of the ARCH in macroeconomic applications and suggested that estimation of the conditional mean required an appropriate description of the conditional variance (volatility of the series), which is important for two reasons.[27] First, OLS results may lead to a spurious regression

---

[25] R. F. Engle (1982), "Autoregressive Conditional Heteroskedasticity with Estimates of the Variance of U.K. Inflation," *Econometrica* 50: 987–1008.

[26] T. Bollerslev (1986), "Generalized Autoregressive Conditional Heteroskedasticity," *Journal of Econometrics* 31: 307–327.

[27] James D. Hamilton (2008), "Macroeconomics and ARCH," prepared for the festschrift in honor of Robert F. Engle. Available at: http://dss.ucsd.edu/~jhamilto/JHamilton_Engle.pdf.

because of incorrect modeling of the conditional variance. Second, due to the possibility of outliers and high-variance episodes—the 2007–2008 time period for financial variables is a good example—the estimated coefficient may not be efficient (does not have a minimum variance). Consequently, if we incorporate the conditional variance directly into the estimation of the mean, then the estimates of the mean would be more efficient. Furthermore, Hamilton estimated the Taylor rule—the relationship among the federal funds target rate, inflation, and GDP—by using OLS as well as ARCH/GARCH. He concluded that the estimated coefficients of inflation and GDP from the GARCH approach were smaller than those based on the OLS approach. Therefore, a better way to conduct time series analysis, either using financial or economic variables, is to include the ARCH/GARCH approach.

One benefit for an analyst is that the SAS software has comprehensive tools to employ the ARCH/GARCH approach for financial data as well as economic variables. As discussed in Chapter 4, a time series can behave in many ways. Trends may be long term or cyclical over the sample period, contain a shock that breaks the trend, or be mean-reverting. It is important to identify the behavior of a time series in order to determine the most appropriate econometric technique to analyze the relationship of a series with other variables. Knowing the characteristics of a time series can help an analyst identify more accurate relationships, build better models, and more precisely determine the magnitude of a relationship. SAS software can help identify the characteristics most important to econometric analysis, and we show how to employ these techniques in SAS in Chapters 6 to 8.

SUMMARY

There are several different econometric techniques to quantify a statistical relationship between variables of interest. An analyst can start with simple correlation and regression analysis to determine the statistical relationship between the underlying variables. The next step would be to apply more sophisticated tests to obtain a reliable relationship. The reason to apply advanced techniques (e.g., cointegration and ECM) is that time series data usually contain a unit root at level form, and correlation/regression results are not valid in unit root problems. Therefore, cointegration and ECM are needed to determine a reliable statistical relationship between variables of interest.

The Granger causality test is a useful tool to determine the direction of the relationship—that is, which variable is leading and which one is lagging. In the case of a financial data series, due to volatility clustering, OLS results are not valid, and a better way to analyze financial data is the application of the ARCH test.

For an analyst, it is important to be familiar with these techniques and to know when and why a technique is needed to determine a reliable statistical relationship between variables of interest.

ADDITIONAL READING

As this is only a brief look at the key concepts in time series analysis, we offer some suggested readings for those who wish to go to the next level of econometric analysis.

For statistical foundations, Wonnacott and Wonnacott (1990) is a popular introductory statistics book.[28] The book is a good source for readers to refresh their knowledge of statistical distribution, estimation, and hypothesis testing. Maddala and Lahiri (2009) is a very useful book for basic econometric concepts and techniques, such as AIC, SIC, OLS, heteroskedasticity, and autocorrelation. Diebold (2007) provides an excellent discussion of important econometric concepts, such as trends, cycles, and unit roots.[29] Greene (2011) is a comprehensive econometric book and covers almost every major econometric concept and techniques for advanced (Ph.D.) students.[30] Maddala and Kim (1998) wrote one of the best specialized books on unit roots, cointegration, and structural change concepts.[31] A comprehensive and very advanced book (targeted more toward Ph.D. students) on time series analysis is Hamilton (1994), which provides detailed theory behind major econometric techniques.[32] Several econometric journals provide newly introduced econometric concepts and techniques. *Econometrica* and *Journal of Econometrics* are good source for theoretical econometrics. For applied econometric analysis, *Review of Economics and Statistics*, *Journal of Business and Economics Statistics*, and *Journal of Applied Econometrics* are useful journals. There are a few very good forecasting journals available as well, such as *Journal of Forecasting*, *International Journal of Forecasting*, and *Journal of Business Forecasting*.

---

[28]T. H. Wonnacott and R. J. Wonnacott (1990), *Introductory Statistics*, 5th ed. (New York: John Wiley & Sons).

[29]Francis X. Diebold (2007), *Elements of Forecasting*, 4th ed. (Mason, OH: Thomson).

[30]William H. Greene (2011), *Econometric Analysis*, 7th ed. (Upper Saddle River, NJ: Prentice Hall).

[31]G. S. Maddala and In-Moo Kim (1998), *Unit Roots, Cointegration, and Structural Change* (Cambridge, U.K.: Cambridge University Press).

[32]J. Hamilton (1994), *Time Series Analysis* (Princeton, NJ: Princeton University Press).

CHAPTER **6**

Characterizing a Time Series Using SAS Software

A ttempts to quantify the economic and financial relationships between variables with the help of econometric techniques extend back to the founding of the Econometric Society in 1930.[1] Over the past 20 years, the breadth of applications of time series analysis has expanded, with analysts relying extensively on real-world data and statistical software. These applications have extended far beyond the limited realm of traditional macroeconomics, and analysts who employ such methods extend far beyond the academic world. Much of the core economic and financial data utilized in applied econometric analysis is now available online and, in some cases, for a small cost. Furthermore, data often is available for use in a statistical analysis in a user-friendly format, such as Excel. Over the years, data collection methods have improved, increasing the scope of the data available.

Software that incorporates key econometric techniques has become an essential element of modern-day quantitative analysis. Such software produces statistical results in a few minutes, rather than hours, for routine techniques such as regression analysis. Until the late 1980s, it usually took researchers several days to estimate a regression. Researchers had to manually collect the data, format it to fit the needs of the statistical model, and finally calculate the results. While today's data processing is much quicker and relatively inexpensive, the

---

[1]The main objective of the Econometric Society is to utilize "theoretical-quantitative and empirical-quantitative approach" to analyze economic problem, see Econometric Society Web site for more details: http://www.econometricsociety.org.

risk is that researchers may be tempted to skip necessary steps in understanding the data, model, and results.

In this chapter, we specify the data (transform it if necessary) to properly test an economic hypothesis to illustrate key econometric techniques to test a hypothesis. We focus on using the econometric tools in SAS software and how to review SAS output.

TIPS FOR SAS USERS

One of the crucial elements of modern-day applied time series analysis, or any other applied quantitative analysis, is the econometric software. Statistical software is used at every level of applied research, from the basic level used by undergraduate students, to the advanced level used by policy makers, managers, and academics. Due to the flexibility of today's statistical software, an analyst may not need to learn the tedious math behind econometric techniques. However, the analyst still must be familiar with key econometric concepts, know how to employ econometric techniques in SAS software (or in any other statistical software), and know how to analyze the results produced by SAS.

SAS software is a powerful tool that offers a wide variety of econometric techniques. SAS is both a company and a widely known product around the world.[2] Originally, the acronym *SAS* stood for Statistical Analysis System; later SAS products became so diverse that the company officially dropped the full name and became simply SAS.

We employ SAS 9.3 in this book and in our workplace.[3] SAS software offers a wide variety of software products, and we use Base SAS and SAS/ETS (Econometric and Time Series Analysis) at work.[4] We further divide the SAS application processes into two broader steps: (1) the DATA step and (2) the econometric analysis, which we call the PROC step.[5] The Base SAS helps us in the DATA step, and the PROC step is heavily based on the SAS/ETS products.

Whether an analyst wants to characterize a time series (e.g., estimation of a time trend, unit root test, etc.) or determine a statistical relationship between variables of interest (e.g., correlation, regression analysis, or Granger causality

[2]According to the SAS Web site, SAS provides an integrated set of software products and services to more than 45,000 customers in 118 countries. http://www.sas.com/.
[3]One good thing about SAS software is that the price of the software is the same for all versions (i.e., SAS 9.1 and SAS 9.3). But because SAS 9.3 (the latest version) offers more options than the previous version, we suggest that the analyst should buy/use the most recent available version.
[4]For more details, see Lora D. Delwiche and Susan J. Slaughter (2008), *The Little SAS Book: A Primer*, 4th ed. (Cary, NC: SAS Institute). The SAS Web site, is also a very useful resource for Base SAS as well as SAS/ETS.
[5]SAS software provides many different procedures to perform several econometric concepts/techniques, and SAS uses *PROC* for a procedure. For instance, the procedure AUTOREG is known as *PROC AUTOREG*, and we use the *PROC AUTOREG* to perform regression analysis.

test), we follow this two-step process. The DATA step is similar to a foundation of a building, and the PROC step is the superstructure built up on this foundation.

Since data is the foundation of a time series analysis, we start with the DATA step. The first element of the DATA step is to import the dataset into the SAS system. Typically, an analyst has a dataset in an Excel spreadsheet, which needs to be brought into the SAS system to create a SAS dataset.[6] After creating a SAS dataset, we can modify the dataset according to the objective of the study. For instance, after importing a dataset into SAS, we can convert the variables of interest into log-difference form from the level form.

The PROC step consists of econometric analysis (i.e., it employs econometric techniques to test the underlying hypothesis). For instance, an analyst wants to test money neutrality using the U.S. data. The first step, the DATA step, is to import a dataset consisting of the money supply (M2) and inflation rate (personal consumption expenditure [PCE] deflator). Since M2 usually is reported in billions of dollars while the PCE deflator is an index, there are two different scales for these two variables. For that reason, it is better to use a log-difference form of the variables, which is the DATA step. After converting both variables into a log-difference form, we can apply regression analysis to estimate the relationship between the money supply and inflation rate. The estimation part is the PROC step. Put simply, the DATA step properly specifies the dataset, and the PROC step handles the estimation process of any applied study.

THE DATA STEP

SAS has specific naming conventions for files and variables. A SAS name is user defined; that is, an analyst can choose the names for variables of interest and for the dataset. Whenever an analyst creates a SAS dataset, he or she must import data into SAS from an Excel or CSV file and assign a SAS name to the file.

The analyst also needs to choose SAS names for variables in the dataset. Rules for choosing a SAS name are flexible. Many SAS names can be as long as 32 characters, although some have a maximum length of 8 characters. The first character of a SAS name must be an English letter (A, B,C, . . . , Z) or underscore (_). Subsequent characters can be upper- or lower-case letters, numeric digits (0,1,2, . . . ,9), or underscores. The few prohibitions on SAS names include spaces and special characters, such as the percent sign (%) or the at sign (@).[7]

---

[6]Most major economic and financial variables are available in Excel format from either public agencies for no cost or from private data providers for a small fee. Therefore, we assume the dataset is already in Excel format, and an analyst just needs to import that data into SAS. SAS software can also read data from other sources, other than Excel (i.e., Lotus, dBase, Microsoft Access, and other statistical software datasets—SPSS dataset, etc.).

[7]For more information about rules for SAS names, see Delwiche and Slaughter (2008) and SAS's Web site.

Suppose we import data on the money supply and the inflation rate in a file with the SAS name of money_inflation. In a next step, we choose "M2" for money supply and "PCE_deflator" for inflation rate. Now the data file contains the variables M2 and PCE_deflator, both of which are in level form. If we wish to generate the log-difference form of M2 and PCE_deflator, we instruct SAS to use the money_inflation data file and then to generate the log-difference form of the M2 and PCE_deflator using the commands discussed later in this chapter.

SAS names must be unique for all datasets. If we use the same SAS name for different datasets, SAS will replace the older dataset with the newer one, deleting the old dataset from the SAS system. We should attach easy and meaningful SAS names to variables as well as the dataset. For example, the title "money_inflation" includes variables that relate to money and inflation. Furthermore, the variables are named "M2" and "PCE_deflator" to remove doubt as to the data behind those variable names. Both SAS names are self-explanatory and easy to remember.

Finally, we want to highlight the SAS Macro variable, a tool used to facilitate SAS codes. It helps SAS users to dynamically modify the text in a SAS program through symbolic substitution. We can assign a large or small amount of text to a Macro variable and, after that, use that text simply by referring to the variable that contains it.[8]

Creating a SAS Macro variable is easy. We can start with %Let, which is a SAS keyword that commands SAS to perform a particular task; note that spelling must be correct but is not case sensitive. In SAS, whenever we write a SAS keyword, such as %Let, it will appear, by default, in blue font (note, we did not use blue color in this book, as the book is in black and white), indicating it is written correctly. User-defined SAS names, such as money_inflation, appear in black font, by default. The SAS code S6.1 provides the syntax and an actual example to write a SAS Macro variable.[9]

Syntax of a SAS Macro Variable

```
%Let A_SAS_name = Any text can be written here;
%Let data_dir = C:\My Documents\SAS\dataset; (S6.1)
```

We always start with %Let to create a SAS Macro variable in the SAS software. A_SAS_name is a SAS name of the analyst's choosing. After the equals sign, =, we can write any statement or provide a list of variables. Here is the most important element of SAS programming: Every line of SAS code must

---

[8] See SAS Web site or Delwiche and Slaughter (2008) for more details regarding SAS Macro variables.
[9] We use "S" to indicate a SAS code, such as S6.1, and we follow this tradition throughout this book.

end with a semicolon, ;, indicating a SAS code is done. Without a semicolon, SAS will not execute that code.

In S6.1, we created a SAS Macro variable and will use that variable in our data importing SAS code. We started with %Let and choose data_dir, a SAS name for our Macro variable that is short for "data directory." The Macro variable data_dir is equal to C:\My Documents\SAS\dataset. That is the data directory or location for our stored dataset, which we are interested in importing into the SAS system.

Why do we create data_dir, a Macro variable? One major benefit of a SAS Macro variable is that we can represent long statements with short ones. For instance, in this chapter we provide SAS code to import an Excel file into SAS system and use data_dir instead of spelling out the longer directory name. The SAS software reads &data_dir as C:\My Documents\SAS\dataset. Therefore, a SAS Macro variable makes a SAS code short and easy to use, while leaving less room for typographical errors. We must add an ampersand &, in front of the chosen SAS name of a Macro variable: For example, instead of data_dir, we use &data_dir. The ampersand is a SAS keyword that, when added in front of a SAS name, signals a SAS Macro variable.

Another useful tip for a SAS user is that if the SAS statement starts with an asterisk, *, and ends with a semicolon, ;, then that statement will not be part of the SAS program. Anything between an asterisk and ending with a semicolon can be used for personal notes or headlines, similar to a note pad within the SAS system, and will be written in green font. In practice, we write several different codes, and usually it is not easy to memorize every one of them. By adding a headline or memory note within a SAS program, an analyst is reminded of the purpose of that code. For instance, in S6.2, we add the headline SAS code to import an Excel dataset into SAS system. Adding a heading or making memory notes in every SAS program is a good habit.

```
*================================================;
*SAS code to import an excel dataset into SAS system;
*================================================;
PROC IMPORT Datafile="&data_dir\MI_data.xls"  (S6.2)
Out   =money_inflation Replace;
Sheet =sheet1;
Range ="A1:D650";
Getnames = yes;
Run;
```

SAS code 6.2 imports an Excel data file into SAS. The first three words—PROC IMPORT Datafile—are SAS keywords. PROC is short for "procedure," IMPORT is the name of the procedure, and Datafile represents the location and name of the file being imported.

Essentially, these three SAS keywords instruct SAS to import the Datafile into the SAS system. After Datafile, we provide the location (data directory) of the Excel file so that SAS can locate the file and bring it into the program. We use &data_dir, the SAS Macro variable we created earlier. SAS converts &data_dir into C:\My Documents\SAS\dataset, which is the location of the data file, and MI_data is the name of the Excel file.

In the second line, Out, which appears in blue font (indicating a SAS keyword) tells SAS to save the data file money_inflation in the SAS system. The word Replace is also a SAS keyword and replaces the Excel file name, if necessary. In this case, we replaced the Excel file name (MI_data) with money_inflation, the new name for the SAS data file. The next three lines represent specific details about the Excel file, including which sheet and how many columns and rows of that sheet are being imported. Sheet is telling SAS which specific sheet of the Excel file to import. In this example, we ask SAS to import sheet1 of the MI_data Excel file. The line Range distinguishes which columns and rows we are importing. "A1:D650" tells SAS to import columns A through D and rows 1 through 650. The line Getnames = yes instructs SAS to keep the variable names specified in the Excel file, in this case, M2 and PCE_inflation. Similar to always ending a line of code with a semicolon, we always end a SAS program with Run, which tells SAS the code is complete and ready to execute. SAS code must start with either PROC or DATA and end with Run.[10]

The SAS code to import an Excel file is a general instruction, and an analyst can import any Excel file with that code. The only changes the analyst needs to make are the location and name of an Excel file along with specific details, such as sheet name and number of columns and rows.

Once the Excel dataset is imported into SAS, then, if necessary, the data can be modified. SAS code S6.3 shows how to modify data within a file. Here the SAS code converts M2, money supply, into a log-difference form from level form.

```
*=========================================================;

*DATA modification;

*Converting a variable into log-difference from level form   ;

*=========================================================;

DATA money_inflation1; * New SAS name for data file;   (S6.3)

Set money_inflation; * Old SAS name for data file;

LM2 = Log (M2);   * Generating log of M2;

DLM2 = Dif1(LM2); *Generating difference of log_M2, basically
log-difference of M2;

Run;
```

---

[10]Sometimes, we end a SAS code with Quit and Quit is a SAS key word which instruct SAS to stop running the SAS code. We still need Run to complete a SAS code.

The first line of the code starts with the SAS keyword `Data`, and the second word is `money_inflation1`, the name we have assigned to the new dataset. The SAS keyword `Data` instructs the SAS system to create a data file and use `money_inflation1` as the SAS name for that file.

So why are we creating a new data file, money_inflation1 in this case? The second line of the code explains. Basically, in the two lines that follow, we ask SAS to use the money_inflation data file (the SAS keyword `Set` provides that instruction to the SAS system) and create another SAS dataset with the name money_inflation1 (the first line of the code `Data money_inflation1` asks SAS to do that). In the third line of the code, `LM2 = log (M2)`, we ask SAS to generate the log of M2 and title that new variable LM2. We have to write the variable's name, M2 in this case, in parentheses `(M2)` for SAS to generate the log of that variable.

In the next line, `DLM2 = Dif1(LM2)`, we request SAS to generate the difference of LM2. We added 1 after `Dif` to specify that we are looking at the first difference of the LM2. If we add 2 after `Dif` (`Dif2`), then SAS calculates the second difference, and so on. It is a general SAS format to generate the degree of difference of a variable by specifying `Dif1` at the end of the SAS code before we add `Run` to let SAS know that the code has concluded.

There is one major difference between the original data file, money_inflation, and the newly created one, money_inflation1. The new data file contains the log, LM2, as well as the log-difference, DLM2, of the money supply in addition to the level of the money supply, which is M2. It is good practice to create a new data file whenever you modify variables, so that the original data is kept in case it is needed later.

With this SAS code, a typical DATA step is complete. There are, however, two broader phases of the DATA step. In the first phase, the dataset is imported into the SAS system from Excel. The second phase of the DATA step involves data modification.

THE PROC STEP

Once you import data into the SAS system and modify it according to your needs, you need to employ econometric techniques to test the underlying hypothesis. This is known as the PROC step. As explained earlier, PROC is short for procedure. Several PROC commands in the SAS system perform different econometric analyses. Typically, the PROC step starts with the SAS keyword `PROC` followed by another keyword that identifies the actual function to be employed. For example, S6.4 is the SAS code to run a correlation analysis between the money supply and the inflation rate.

```
*=========================================================;

*Estimating Correlation Coefficient between DLM2 (Log-difference of
money supply) and DLPCE_deflator(Log-difference of inflation rate);

*=========================================================;
```

```
PROC CORR Data = money_inflation1;   (S6.4)
Var DLM2 DLPCE_Deflator;
Run;
```

The first three words, PROC CORR Data, are SAS keywords, where PROC CORR instructs SAS to use the correlation procedure and Data indicates what SAS dataset should be used in the correlation analysis. Note that the format of the first three words (PROC, PROC-name, and Data) of the PROC step remain the same, and only the name of the type of procedure needs to change; for example, CORR for correlation, Autoreg for regression analysis, and so on.[11]

The first line of the SAS code, PROC CORR, is asking the SAS system to run a correlation analysis using the money_inflation1 dataset. We specify the variables we wish to include in the correlation analysis in the second line, Var DLM2 DLPCE_Deflator, where Var is the SAS keyword for variable. Then we ask the SAS software to use DLM2 (log-difference of money supply) and DLPCE_Deflator (log-difference of inflation rate). As usual, we end our SAS code with Run.[12]

The PROC step also consists of two phases; the first phase indicates the name of the PROC and identifies the dataset to employ in the analysis, and the second phase specifies the variable list involved in the econometric analysis.

Seasonal Adjustment in SAS

Although many economic data releases are in a seasonally adjusted format, there are some areas where seasonally adjusted data is not available. One example is county-level unemployment rates, which are usually released in seasonally unadjusted format. Employment data provides an extensive history over time and at many levels (national, state, local for instance); it also is a very important variable for public and private sector decision makers. Removing the seasonal component from county-level unemployment rates allows an analyst to compare a time series between consecutive months or quarters. Furthermore, a plot of the seasonally adjusted series is more informative about trends or the stage of the business cycle than a plot of the unadjusted series, since unadjusted series usually show movements influenced by the season in addition to business cycle moves. The seasonally adjusted series remove this element and allow the analyst to focus on business cycle movements.

SAS software provides a procedure to seasonally adjust data, PROC X12. We provide SAS code to convert a seasonally unadjusted series into a seasonally

---

[11] See the SAS/ETS manual for more details about different PROC functions. The manual can be found at the SAS Web site http://www.sas.com.

[12] Note that in Chapter 8 we provide and discuss SAS results for correlation analysis based on PROC CORR. Here we are just introducing concepts of the PROC step.

adjusted series. For example, we can test Charlotte, North Carolina, MSA's unemployment rate, which is available in a nonseasonally adjusted format, and convert it into a seasonally adjusted series using the PROC X12 command. The SAS code consists of three major parts, shown in S6.5, S6.6, and S6.7, where "S" is short for SAS code.[13]

```
*=========================================================;
* Seasonal Adjustment using PROC X12;
* Seasonally adjusted Charlotte Unemployment rate        ;
*=========================================================;
PROC SORT Data = Charlotte_UR;          (S6.5)
By date;
Run;
PROC X12 data= Charlotte_UR Date = date;    (S6.6)
Var NSA_UR;
X11;
Output out = SA_UR A1 D11;
Run;
*=========================================================;
* Exporting and converting a SAS data file into an Excel dataset ;
*=========================================================;
PROC EXPORT Data= SA_UR  outfile="&data_dir\Charlotte_UR_SA.xls"
replace;
                        (S6.7)
Run;
```

One important note is that the underlying dataset must be in one particular interval—a monthly data series, for example—and that series should not have any missing values. This is because PROC X12 estimates seasonals for each time period, and if a value is missing the process will not work. The first part of the SAS code (S6.5) is used to sort the dataset, the Charlotte unemployment rate, which is sorted in an ascending order. We use PROC SORT, a useful PROC to arrange data in any order. In the next line of the SAS code, By date, indicates that SAS sorted the series by date, where date is a variable representing the time interval. The dataset Charlotte_UR consists of two variables, the unemployment rate

---

[13] Assuming that the dataset is already imported into the SAS system from Excel. We provided the SAS code to import an Excel data file into the SAS system earlier in this chapter; therefore, we skip the DATA step by assuming the required dataset is already in the SAS system. Throughout this chapter, we maintain the assumption that the required dataset is already in the SAS system.

(assigned the SAS name NSA_UR) and the time interval (assigned the SAS name date). In order to use PROC SORT, we must specify the variable we want to sort by—the ID variable—which in the present case is the date variable. Then SAS will use that ID variable to sort the rest of the dataset.

The next part, S6.6, seasonally adjusts the NSA_UR series. PROC X12 is used, and the variable to sort by must be specified. We use the date as our ID variable and identify Date = date, where Date (with capital D) is a SAS keyword and date (with a small d) represents the time interval. The first line of code S6.6 instructs SAS to employ PROC X12 and uses the Charlotte_UR dataset and date as an ID variable. The next line of the code, Var NSA_UR, specifies the variable of interest to seasonally adjust; here that variable is the Charlotte unemployment rate. The X11 term requests the seasonal adjustment process to be performed. In the line Output out = SA_UR a1 d11, Output is a SAS keyword and asks SAS to save the procedure's output in a separate file. We specify the file name as out = SA_UR, where out is a SAS keyword and SA_UR is the name we assigned to the new file of seasonally adjusted data. The next two items in the line are A1 and D11. The SAS software adds A1 at the end of the original variable that is not seasonally adjusted, in this case NSA_UR, and it appears NSA_UR_A1. The D11 term will be added at the end of the new series, the seasonally adjusted series, and shows up as NSA_UR_D11.

SAS code S6.7, known as PROC EXPORT, exports SAS output into user-friendly formats, such as Excel. The previous example exported the output based on the PROC X12 to the data file SA_UR. By converting the SAS dataset to an Excel file, we can plot both seasonally and not seasonally adjusted data series (see Figure 6.1) and also can share the output with other analysts who do not have SAS software.[14]

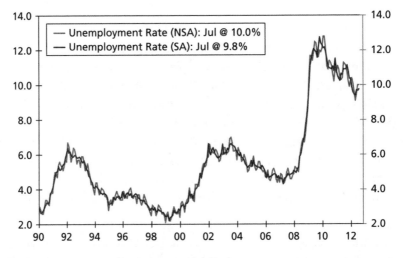

FIGURE 6.1 Charlotte Unemployment Rate, SA and NSA

---

[14]"It is important to note that SAS does offer options to plot variable(s) of interest and those options can be utilized to generate graph of variable(s)."

Calculating the Mean, Standard Deviation, and Stability Ratio of a Variable

To assess risk in financial markets, we are often interested in the volatility of a series. How do we quantify that volatility? Standard deviations are usually the first approximation of volatility in a series. However, we also advocate the calculation of the stability ratio, which is the standard deviation as a percentage of the mean.

SAS code S6.8 is employed to analyze the year-over-year percentage change in real gross domestic product (GDP), where PCHYA_GDPR_Q_ is the SAS variable name for real GDP. The first line of code S6.8 asks SAS to use the Means procedure and the dataset dataset. The second line, Var PCHYA_GDPR_Q_, specifies the variable, and we end the code with Run.

SAS software offers the PROC MEANS command that provides a complete description of the basic statistical properties of a variable, such as the mean, standard deviation, maximum and minimum values. In the example below, we show how to employ PROC MEANS for a single variable, the year-over-year percentage change of U.S real GDP.

```
*=========================================;
*PROC MEANS using single variable ;
*Real GDP, YoY percent change   ;
*=========================================;
PROC MEANS Data = dataset;
Var PCHYA_GDPR_Q_  ;  (S6.8)
Run;
```

Table 6.1 shows the SAS output for code S6.8. Notice that the title lines of the output provide information regarding the procedure and variables used as well as a timestamp. The table shows the descriptive statistics for the variable. The first statistic, labeled "N," indicates the total number of observations included in the analysis, which in this case is 150. The next two columns, labeled "Mean" and "Std Dev," provide the mean and standard deviation of

TABLE 6.1 SAS Output of PROC MEANS Using Single Variable (Real GDP)

The MEANS Procedure

Analysis Variable : PCHYA_GDPR_Q_ PCHYA(GDPR#Q)

N	Mean	Std Dev	Minimum	Maximum
150	2.7629	2.2878	−4.5790	8.4847

the variable, respectively. The last two columns, labeled "Minimum" and "Maximum," highlight the minimum and maximum values within the series, in this case −4.5790917 and 8.4847362. Together these two columns provide a range for the underlying data. In sum, the PROC MEANS imparts a complete statistical picture of a time series.

Important statistics can be added manually to the SAS output based on the PROC MEANS, including an estimation of a stability ratio, standard deviation as percentage of the mean, and the stability ratio of real GDP, which is 82.8 percent (2.2878/2.7629) × 100. The stability ratio allows for a better comparison of validity, especially if the analyst is comparing volatility between different time series or comparing one time series over different periods/business cycles.

Adding More Variables into PROC MEANS

Often analysts are interested in analyzing several variables and examining which series are more volatile than others. The PROC MEANS command can obtain the same information for several variables simultaneously. For instance, an analyst may wish to examine whether the average percentage change in real GDP is greater than the average percentage change in productivity.

The first line of SAS code S6.9 is identical to the first line in S6.8. The difference is in the second line occurs when we add corporate profits (PCHYA_ ZBECON_Q_ as SAS variable name) and productivity (PCHYA_JOMHNFM_Q_ as a SAS variable name) growth rates in the variable list, behind Var PCHYA_GDPR_Q. This now instructs the SAS software to run the PROC MEANS command on all three variables and estimate the basic statistics for each. We can add in as many variables as we wish to the analysis in the second line, which starts with Var, of SAS code S6.8 or S6.9.

```
*==================================================;
*PROC MEANS using many variables          ;
    *Real GDP, Corporate Profits and
Productivity, all in YoY percentage change form    ;
*==================================================;
PROC MEANS Data = dataset;            (S6.9)
Var PCHYA_GDPR_Q_  PCHYA_ZBECON_Q_  PCHYA_JOMHNFM_Q_;
Run;
```

Output based on code S6.9 is presented in Table 6.2. As with Table 6.1, the first two lines of Table 6.2 indicate the time and procedure employed. However, the third row of Table 6.1, which is "Analysis Variable: PCHYA_GDPR_Q_ PCHYA (GDPR#Q)," has disappeared from Table 6.2. Moreover, two additional

TABLE 6.2 SAS Output of PROC MEANS Using Many Variables

The MEANS Procedure

Variable	Label	N	Mean	Std Dev	Minimum	Maximum
PCHYA_ GDPR_Q_	PCHYA(GDPR#Q)	150	2.7629	2.2878	−4.57909	8.4847
PCHYA_ ZBECON_Q_	PCHYA(ZBECON#Q)	150	8.5973	13.5426	−33.51588	56.9707
PCHYA_ JOMHNFM_Q_	PCHYA(JOMHNFM#Q)	150	1.9075	1.5863	−2.3835	6.0851

TABLE 6.3 Stability Ratio

Variable Name	Stability Ratio
Real GDP	82.97%
Corporate Profits	157.44%
Productivity	83.25%

columns are added to Table 6.2 compared to Table 6.1, named "Variable" and "Label."

Tables 6.1 and 6.2 look slightly different since, after having added more variables to the procedure, the additional fields are needed to clearly show the statistical properties of each variable. The first column of Table 6.2 shows the SAS variable names, and the second column exhibits the original variable names as they appeared in the Excel file. All of the other columns portray the same information as a single-variable analysis.

If we set the standard deviation as a volatility measure, then the corporate profits growth rate is more volatile than GDP and productivity growth rates. Because the standard deviation for profits growth (13.54, rounded downward) is the highest and productivity growth is least volatile as it has the smallest standard deviation (1.59, rounded up) during the 1975:Q1 to 2012:Q2 time period. However, this conclusion would not be a fair one because profits growth has the highest mean (8.6, rounded up) and productivity growth the smallest mean (1.91, rounded up).

In Table 6.3, we provide stability ratios for these three variables. Now it would be a fair comparison of the volatility analysis as the stability ratio considers both mean and standard deviation. According to the stability analysis from Table 6.3, corporate profits have the highest stability ratio (157.44 percent) and real GDP has the smallest ratio (82.97 percent). Based on this analysis, it is more accurate to say that during the 1975:Q1 to 2012:Q2 time period, real

GDP growth rate experienced less volatility compared to corporate profits and productivity growth rates.

Data Division into Business Cycles

GDP growth was the least volatile compared to the profits and productivity growth during the 1975:Q1 to 2012:Q2 period. But does this conclusion hold true for all business cycles within that time period? Four business cycles occurred during that time period. We considered 1980 and 1981–1982 as one recession[15] because only 12 months separated the two recessions. The results of our volatility comparison are displayed in Table 6.4.

The first three business cycles show a consistent pattern. GDP growth is the least volatile compared to the profits and productivity growth during these business cycles since the smallest stability ratios during those business cycles are associated with the GDP growth. For the same time period, the profits growth turned out to be the most volatile, as the profits series contains the highest stability ratios. However, the 2001:Q4 to 2009:Q2 business cycle exhibits different behavior for these series as productivity growth has the smallest stability ratio during this business cycle. The highest stability ratio belongs to the profits series for the 2001:Q4 to 2009:Q2 business cycle. For the complete period, which is 1975:Q1 to 2009:Q2, GDP growth has the smallest stability ratio and profits growth has the highest stability ratio. Interestingly, for all four business cycles as well as for complete sample period, profits growth has the highest means, standard deviations, and stability ratios, which makes it the most volatile data series in our analysis.

Identifying a Time Trend in a Time Series

The baseline, the trend in any time series, is often the starting point for any strategic planning process for any branch of government or the private sector. Trend GDP growth sets the bar for any estimate of job and revenue growth rates at the federal or state government level.

The trend estimation process described here is divided into a first part that shows how to create a time trend variable and a second part that discusses the trend estimation process along with the SAS output. We will use the U.S. unemployment rate as a case study and assume that the unemployment rate data series is already imported into the SAS system. The SAS name of the dataset is unemployment_data. The dataset is sorted by the date variable using the PROC SORT.

---

[15]We identify a business cycle as the time period from trough to trough by using the dates defined by the National Bureau of Economic Research for a recession.

TABLE 6.4 Mean, Standard Deviation, Stability Ratio, and Business Cycles*

Period	Mean			Standard Deviation			Stability Ratio		
	GDP	Profits	Productivity	GDP	Profits	Productivity	GDP	Profits	Productivity
1975:Q1–1982:Q4	2.36	8.61	1.09	3.01	15.79	1.79	127.54	183.39	164.22
1982:Q4–1991:Q1	3.71	9.96	1.88	2.14	13.27	1.38	57.68	133.23	73.40
1991:Q1–2001:Q4	3.20	5.83	2.20	1.61	8.13	1.3	50.31	139.45	59.09
2001:Q4–2009:Q2	1.68	6.43	2.22	2.16	14.95	1.67	128.57	232.50	75.23
1975:Q1–2009:Q2	2.87	7.76	1.88	2.3	13.01	1.58	80.14	167.65	84.04

The SAS code S6.10 creates a time dummy variable. The first two lines of the code, `Data unemployment_data2` and `Set unemployment_data`, design a new dataset named `unemployment_data2` using the data file `unemployment_data`. The third line of S6.10, `Time =_n_`, indicates we created a new variable, the time dummy variable `Time`. `_n_` is a SAS keyword to generate a time dummy variable and it equals 1 for the first observation, 2 for the second observation and so on. The next line of S6.10, `Time_2=(Time)**2`, generates the square of the Time variable, which identifies the nonlinear trend in the unemployment rate. The `lunemployment = log (unemployment)` part of the code creates a variable for the log of the unemployment rate, which will also be used in the trend estimation process. The dataset `unemployment_data` contains only the unemployment rate and date; however, the dataset `unemployment_data2` includes the time dummy variable, `Time`; the square of the time dummy variable, `Time_2`; the log of the unemployment rate, `lunemployment`; in addition to the unemployment rate and the date. The dataset `unemployment_data2` has all of the variables needed in the estimation process. That data file is employed for the estimation process. The first part of a time trend estimation process is completely described in the S6.10 code. SAS code S6.11 shows the estimation part of the process.

```
*===============================;
*Creating a Time Dummy Variable ;
*===============================;
PROC SORT data = unemployment_data; by date; run;*dataset is
sorted by date;
DATA unemployment_data2;
Set unemployment_data;              (S6.10)
Time    =_n_ ;    * SAS code to create a Time Dummy ;
Time_2   = (Time)**2; *Squared of the Time Dummy ;
lunemployment = log (unemployment);*Log of the unemployment;
Run;

*=====================================================;
* Identify Time trend for unemployment rate      ;
* Estimation Process of a Linear Time Trend      ;
* PROC AUTOREG is employed              ;
*=====================================================;
 PROC  AUTOREG Data= unemployment_data2;
 Model unemployment =  Time ;      (S6.11)
 Run ;
```

Code S6.11 demonstrates the econometric method to estimate a linear time trend in a time series. The first line of the code indicates that the PROC AUTOREG is employed, and the SAS dataset unemployment_data2 is used in the econometric analysis. The next line of the code, Model unemployment = Time, shows that the time dummy variable, Time, is the independent variable and the variable unemployment is the dependent variable in the regression analysis. As always, we close the code with Run.

Table 6.5 shows the statistical output of S6.11. The results displayed are general in nature. That is, whenever we run a regression analysis using the PROC AUTOREG, the results outlook and interpretation will be similar to those shown in the table. Therefore, we explain the results in great detail, and the reader should get comfortable with these test statistics. The first line of Table 6.5 indicates that the SAS system is employed. The time, day, and date of the SAS code's execution is shown as well. The third line indicates that the variable "unemployment" is utilized as a dependent variable. The next line depicts that the OLS method is used as an estimation technique.

After that, several statistics are reported which are important measures to determine the model's goodness of fit. The sum of squared errors (SSE) is 1120.87227 and SSE is a key input to several important measures of a model's

TABLE 6.5 SAS Output Based on the PROC AUTOREG: A Linear Time Trend

The AUTOREG Procedure

Dependent Variable   Unemployment

Ordinary Least Squares Estimates

SSE	1120.87227	DFE	450
MSE	2.49083	Root MSE	1.57824
SBC	1705.44529	AIC	1697.21793
MAE	1.25422653	AICC	1697.24465
MAPE	19.9389712	HQC	1700.46004
Durbin-Watson	0.0123	Regress R-Square	0.0496
		Total R-Square	0.0496

Parameter Estimates

Variable	DF	Estimate	Standard Error	t Value	Approx Pr > |t|
Intercept	1	7.1276	0.1487	47.93	<.0001
Time	1	-0.002757	0.000569	-4.85	<.0001

goodness of fit, i.e., R^2, mean square error, etc. The DFE (DFE = 450) stands for degrees of freedom for error. In simple words, DFE indicates the number of observations (sample size) minus the number of parameters in the model. The mean square error (MSE = 2.49083) is the estimated variance of the error term. The root MSE (RMSE) is 1.57824 and it is the square root of the MSE. More simply, the MSE is the estimated variance and the RMSE is the estimated standard deviation of the error term. The RMSE shows the average deviation of the estimated unemployment rate (our dependent variable) from the actual unemployment rate.[16]

The Schwarz Bayesian criterion (SBC) = 1705.44529 and Akaike information criterion (AIC) = 1697.21793 are information criteria and are helpful tools to select a model among its competitors. The mean absolute error (MAE) = 1.25422652 and mean absolute percentage error (MAPE) = 19.9389712 are measures of errors. There are two R^2 statistics reported in Table 6.5, "Regress [Regression] R-Square" and "Total R-Square." The regression R^2 is a measure of the fit of the structural part of the model after transforming for the auto-correlation and thereby is the R^2 for the transformed regression. The total R^2 is also a measure of how well the next value of a dependent variable can be predicted using the structural part of the equation (right-hand-side variables including the intercept) and the past value of the residuals (estimated error term). Furthermore, if there is no correction for autocorrelation, then the values of the total R^2 and regression R^2 would be identical, as in our case, where both total and regression R^2 are equal to 0.0496. Another important statistic shown in Table 6.5 is the Durbin-Watson statistic, which is equal to 0.0123. A Durbin-Watson statistic close to 2 is an indication of no autocorrelation and a value close to zero, as in present case, is a strong evidence of autocorrelation—not a good sign.

The last part of Table 6.5 reports statistics to measure the statistical significance of the right-hand-side variables (independent variable[s] along with an intercept). The column under the name "Variable," shows the name of the intercept and independent variable, in this case "Time." The "DF" represents degrees of freedom; "1" indicates 1 degree of freedom for each parameter. The next column, "Estimate," shows the estimated coefficients for the intercept (7.1276) and for time (–0.002757). The next column exhibits the "Standard Error" of the estimated coefficient. This is a very important statistic for three reasons.

1. The standard error of a coefficient indicates the likely sampling variability of a coefficient and hence its reliability. A larger standard error relative to its coefficient value demonstrates higher variability and less reliability of the estimated coefficient.

---

[16]The RMSE is an estimate of the average difference between the actual and estimated unemployment rate.

2. The standard error is an important input to estimate a confidence interval for a coefficient. A larger standard error relative to its coefficient provides a wider confidence interval.

3. The coefficient relative to the standard error helps to determine the value of a t-statistic. An absolute t-value of 2 or more is an indication that the variable is more likely to be statistically useful to explain the variation in the dependent variable. In this case, both t-values, in absolute terms, are greater than 2 (47.93 for intercept and −4.85 for time), suggesting that both the intercept and time are statistically significant.

The last column, "Approx Pr > |t|," represents the probability level of significance of a t-value. Basically, this column indicates at what level of significance we can reject (or fail to reject) the null hypothesis that a variable is statistically significant. The standard level of significance is 5 percent; an "Approx Pr > |t|" value of 0.05 or less will be an indication of statistical significance. The values for both t-values are smaller than 0.05 (both are 0.0001); hence the intercept and time are statistically meaningful to explain variation in the unemployment rate. The negative sign of the time coefficient (−0.002757) demonstrates that the unemployment rate may have a downward time trend. It is statistically significant, as the t-value is greater than 2, which shows that the time trend may be linear.

SAS code S6.12 estimates a nonlinear (quadratic) trend for the unemployment rate. The first and the last lines of the code are identical to code S6.11. The difference is in the middle line. We added Time_2, which is square of the time dummy variable, and included it in the regression analysis to capture any nonlinearity of the time trend.

```
*=========================================================;

   *Estimation of a Nonlinear Trend;

*=========================================================;

PROC AUTOREG Data= unemployment_data2;

Model unemployment = Time Time_2 ;      (S6.12)

Run;
```

The results based on code S6.12 are reported in Table 6.6. Both SBC (1576.49193) and AIC (1564.15088) are smaller for the nonlinear model compared to the linear model. The t-values for the "Time", "Time_2," and the intercept are greater than 2, and the probability for the t-values is also smaller than 0.05, implying that these coefficients are statistically significant at the 5 percent level of significance. The negative sign of the "Time" and positive sign of "Time_2" imply that the unemployment rate may contain a nonlinear, U-shaped time trend.

Both SBC and AIC are smaller for the nonlinear trend model compared to the linear trend model and thereby we prefer a nonlinear trend model to estimate the unemployment rate.

TABLE 6.6 SAS Output Based on the PROC AUTOREG: A Nonlinear Time Trend

```
                    The AUTOREG Procedure

              Dependent Variable   Unemployment


                 Ordinary Least Squares Estimates

SSE                 831.34226    DFE                       449
MSE                    1.85154   Root MSE              1.36071
SBC                1576.49193    AIC                1564.15088
MAE                 1.09289712   AICC               1564.20445
MAPE                17.2903394   HQC                1569.01406
Durbin-Watson          0.0165    Regress R-Square      0.2951
                                 Total R-Square        0.2951


                       Parameter Estimates

                                Standard             Approx
Variable       DF    Estimate     Error    t Value   Pr > |t|

Intercept       1      8.9292    0.1929      46.30    <.0001
Time            1     -0.0266    0.001966   -13.51    <.0001
Time_2          1   0.0000526    4.203E-6    12.50    <.0001
```

SAS code S6.13A estimates a log-linear trend for the unemployment rate. The dependent variable is the log of the unemployment rate instead of its level.[17] The results based on the log-linear trend model are displayed in Table 6.7A. Both SBC and AIC are smallest for the log-linear trend model compared to the previous two models. The t-value indicates that the Time variable is statistically significant.

```
*======================================================;

*Estimation of a Log-linear Trend;

*======================================================;

PROC AUTOREG Data= unemployment_data2;

Model lunemployment =  Time ;       (S6.13A)

Run;
```

Although the log-linear trend model has smaller SBC and AIC values compared to the linear and nonlinear trend models, the log-linear model used the log of the unemployment rate. The other two models are based on the level

---

[17]As mentioned in Chapter 4, one method to estimate a log-linear trend is to use the log of the dependent variable and regress it on a time dummy variable. See Chapter 4 for more detail.

form of the unemployment rate. It may not be accurate to compare SBC and AIC among these three models because of different forms of the dependent variable. Because for the sake of comparison we need an identical dependent variable for all three models, which is the level form of the unemployment rate. Therefore, we run another model for the log-linear trend and that model uses the level form of the unemployment rate as a dependent variable and exponential form of the Time variable as a right-hand-side variable.

```
*=======================================;
*Log-linear Model Using the PROC MODEL ;
*=======================================;
PROC MODEL data = unemployment_data2;
unemployment = a0 + exp(a1*Time);  (S6.13B)
fit unemployment /fiml ;
Run;
```

Because it is more flexible, we employ the PROC MODEL to estimate the exponential trend model for the unemployment rate. Unfortunately, we could not estimate the above regression through the PROC AUTOREG although it produces SBC and AIC values automatically which the PROC MODEL can't do. Both procedures thus have some advantages and some limitations.

The first line of the S6.13B code is similar to the S6.13A code; the only difference is that we are using the PROC MODEL instead of the PROC AUTOREG. The second line shows the regression equation which we are interested in estimating. That is, unemployment = a0 + exp (a1*Time) where unemployment is the dependent variable and a0 is a user-defined SAS name for the intercept. exp is a SAS keyword that instructs SAS to use the exponential form of the variable in the estimation process. a1 is the slope coefficient, and Time is time dummy variable. exp (a1*Time) implies that the exponential form of the Time variable is used in the regression analysis. The next line of the code starts with fit, which is a SAS keyword that instructs SAS to fit the model for unemployment. fiml stands for "Full Information Maximum Likelihood"; it is an estimation method.[18] We employed FIML because it will estimate likelihood values, and that is an important input to calculate SBC and AIC.

Results based on the S6.13B are reported in Table 6.7B. Any time we employ the PROC MODEL, we obtain results similar to those displayed in that table.

The first row of Table 6.7B states that the PROC MODEL is employed, and second row indicates the FIML is the estimation method. The regression

---

[18]For more details about the FIML and PROC MODEL, see SAS/ETS 9.3 manual, available at the SAS Web site for no cost.

TABLE 6.7A SAS Output Based on the PROC AUTOREG: A Log-Linear Time Trend

The AUTOREG Procedure

Dependent Variable   lunemployment

Ordinary Least Squares Estimates

SSE	25.1060926	DFE	450
MSE	0.05579	Root MSE	0.23620
SBC	-11.590578	AIC	-19.817942
MAE	0.18886944	AICC	-19.791216
MAPE	10.4102402	HQC	-16.575825
Durbin-Watson	0.0129	Regress R-Square	0.0725
		Total R-Square	0.0725

Parameter Estimates

Variable	DF	Estimate	Standard Error	t Value	Approx Pr > |t|
Intercept	1	1.9565	0.0223	87.91	<.0001
Time	1	-0.000505	0.0000851	-5.93	<.0001

TABLE 6.7B SAS Output Based on the PROC MODEL: A Log-Linear Time Trend

The MODEL Procedure

Nonlinear FIML Summary of Residual Errors

Equation	DF Model	DF Error	SSE	MSE	R-Square	Adj R-Sq
unemployment	2	450	1079.8	2.3996	0.0844	0.0824

Nonlinear FIML Parameter Estimates

Parameter	Estimate	Approx Std Err	t Value	Approx Pr > |t|
a0	6.250254	0.1538	40.65	<.0001
a1	-0.00851	0.00568	-1.50	0.1349

Number of Observations		Statistics for System	
Used	452	Log Likelihood	-838.1754
Missing	0		

equation is fitted for the unemployment rate. "DF Model" stands for the model's degree of freedom; it is 2 because there are only two parameters, ao (the intercept) and a1 (the slope coefficient). "DF Error" is the degrees of freedom for the error, and it is 450. It is equal to total number of observations (which are 452) minus the DF model (which is 2). The next columns show SSE, MSE, and R^2 statistics. PROC MODEL also provides an adjusted R^2 (Adj R-Sq), which equals 0.0824. The next part of the table provides estimated coefficients and their measures of statistical significance. The a1 is attached to a t-value of -1.50, and probability for that t-value is 0.1349, which implies that the Time variable is statistically insignificant at the 5 percent level of statistical significance.

The last section of Table 6.7B shows the number of observations used in the regression analysis (452) and the log likelihood, which is -838.1754. PROC MODEL does not provide SBC and AIC, which are important inputs to select the appropriate trend model for the unemployment rate. However, SBC and AIC can be calculated by hand using these formulas:

$$\textbf{AIC} = -2\ln(L) + 2k \qquad = -2(-838.1754) + 2(2) \qquad = 1680.35$$

$$\textbf{SBC} = -2\ln(L) + \ln(N)\,k = -2(-838.1754) + \ln(452)\,2 = 1681.66$$

where
ln = Natural logarithm
L = value of the likelihood function (-838.1754)
N = number of observations (452)
k = number of estimated coefficients including the intercept (2)

The estimated value of the SBC is 1681.66 and for AIC is 1680.35.

Table 6.8 summarizes the SBC and AIC value for all three of the trend models we have discussed. The nonlinear model has the smallest SBC value as well as the smallest AIC value. We thus conclude that for the U.S. employment rate, a nonlinear trend model would be the most appropriate model.

Identifying Cyclical Behavior in a Time Series

Identifying cyclical behavior in a time series is vital for decision makers. A series that contains cyclical behavior is easier to analyze during a particular phase of a business cycle. We employ PROC ARIMA to identify cyclical behavior and use the U.S. unemployment rate as a case study.

The first line of code S6.14 shows that PROC ARIMA is employed and the unemployment_rate dataset is used in the analysis. In the second line of the code, Identify var = Unemployment, Identify and var are SAS keywords that instruct SAS to estimate autocorrelations and partial autocorrelation functions for the variable, in this case for unemployment rate.[19] Basically, the

TABLE 6.8 The SIC/AIC of All Three Models

	Linear	Nonlinear	Log-Linear
SIC/SBC	1705.45	1576.49	1681.66
AIC	1697.22	1564.15	1680.35

---

[19]"It is important to note that Identify statement has other functionalities in addition to produce ACF and PACF, see PROC ARIMA documents for more detail."

second line of the code asks SAS to provide autocorrelations and partial auto-correlation functions, which are important ingredients to determine whether a time series contains cyclical behavior.

```
*=========================================================;
*PROC ARIMA is employed                       ;
*Identify cyclical behavior in the Unemployment Rate   ;
*=========================================================;
PROC ARIMA Data = unemployment_data;
Identify var = Unemployment ;        (S6.14)
Run;
Quit;
```

The results based on the S6.14 code are displayed in Tables 6.9A to C. The first part of Table 6.9A shows basic statistics for the unemployment rate. That is, the mean and standard deviation of the unemployment rate are 6.5030 and 1.6153, respectively. A total of 452 observations are used in the analysis.

TABLE 6.9A SAS Output Based on the PROC ARIMA

The ARIMA Procedure

Name of Variable = Unemployment
Mean of Working Series   6.5030
Standard Deviation   1.6153
Number of Observations   452

Autocorrelations

Lag	Covariance	Correlation		Std Error
1	2.588375	0.99200	| . |********************|	0.047036
2	2.562314	0.98202	| . |********************|	0.081035
3	2.527517	0.96868	| . |*******************|	0.104085
4	2.484293	0.95211	| . |*******************|	0.122416
5	2.434453	0.93301	| . |******************|	0.137829
6	2.379193	0.91183	| . |*****************|	0.151158
7	2.318910	0.88873	| . |*****************|	0.162873
8	2.254643	0.86410	| . |****************|	0.173270
9	2.185666	0.83766	| . |****************|	0.182555
10	2.112596	0.80966	| . |***************|	0.190869
11	2.038112	0.78111	| . |***************|	0.198322
12	1.959424	0.75096	| . |**************|	0.205016
13	1.882106	0.72132	| . |*************|	0.211014
14	1.803725	0.69128	| . |*************|	0.216400
15	1.727334	0.66201	| . |************|	0.221232
16	1.650546	0.63258	| . |************|	0.225572
17	1.573644	0.60310	| . |***********|	0.229463
18	1.496765	0.57364	| . |**********|	0.232944

The dots (".") before and after the asterisks "*" signal the results are within two standard errors band. Where no dot appears after the asterisk then the series has a spike. In addition, the steady decline in the correlation as the lag order is increased is illustrated by fewer asterisks in column 4, the correlation visualization.

The second part of Table 6.9A shows a plot for the autocorrelation functions (ACFs). The ACFs plot indicates that the autocorrelations are larger relative to two standard-error bands (dotted line) at least for several lags. The ACFs also display a slow decay in the autocorrelations compared to the two standard-error bands. These are the first two conditions for identifying cyclical behavior. The ACFs also show that the unemployment rate contains cyclical behavior.[20] In Table 6.9B, the partial autocorrelations functions (PACFs) plot reveals a large spike at the first lag, confirming the ACFs' findings. Essentially, both ACFs and PACFs are providing strong evidence of cyclical behavior in the unemployment rate.

Table 6.9C provides results based on the autocorrelation test for various lag orders. The null hypothesis of the test is no autocorrelation and the alternative hypothesis is that autocorrelation is present. The first column of the table shows the lag order, how many lags of unemployment rate are used to estimate an autocorrelation. The second column provides "Chi-Square" test values and the third column indicates "DF," or degrees of freedom. The fourth column, "Pr > ChiSq" provides probabilities attached to the Chi-square test values. Since the probability values are significantly smaller than 0.05, we reject the null hypothesis of no autocorrelation at 5 percent level of significance, therefore concluding again that autocorrelation is present.

TABLE 6.9B SAS Output Based on PROC ARIMA

```
                          The ARIMA Procedure
                        Partial Autocorrelations
 Lag   Correlation   −1 9 8 7 6 5 4 3 2 1 0 1 2 3 4 5 6 7 8 9 1
  1      0.99200      |                      .  |********************|
  2     −0.12908      |                   ***|  .                    |
  3     −0.20311      |                  ****|  .                    |
  4     −0.17446      |                   ***|  .                    |
  5     −0.10603      |                    **|  .                    |
  6     −0.06197      |                    .*|  .                    |
  7     −0.05277      |                    .*|  .                    |
  8     −0.03378      |                    .*|  .                    |
  9     −0.06198      |                    .*|  .                    |
 10     −0.05383      |                    .*|  .                    |
 11      0.01684      |                    . |  .                    |
 12     −0.06284      |                    .*|  .                    |
 13      0.07145      |                    . |*  .                   |
 14     −0.00139      |                    . |  .                    |
 15      0.05690      |                    . |*  .                   |
 16     −0.02625      |                    .*|  .                    |
 17     −0.03473      |                    .*|  .                    |
 18     −0.02909      |                    .*|  .                    |
```

"." The dots around the vertical line with the asterisks signal two standard errors band. Where no dot appears in front of the asterisk then the series has a spike, .

---

[20] "It is important to note that a slow decay of ACFs may indicate the series is non-stationary. We suggest to test non-stationary behavior of a series using unit root tests. The chapter 7 of this book show how to test for a unit root using SAS."

TABLE 6.9C SAS Output Based on PROC ARIMA

```
                         The ARIMA Procedure
                  Autocorrelation Check for White Noise
   To    Chi-          Pr >
   Lag   Square   DF   ChiSq -------Autocorrelations ------------

   6     2513.80   6   <.0001 0.992   0.982 0.969   0.952 0.933   0.912
   12    4399.43  12   <.0001 0.889   0.864 0.838   0.810 0.781   0.751
   18    5587.85  18   <.0001 0.721   0.691 0.662   0.633 0.603   0.574
   24    6221.30  24   <.0001 0.544   0.514 0.483   0.453 0.422   0.392
```

Since the presence of autocorrelation indicates that the unemployment rate shows a persistent pattern, periods of relatively higher unemployment rates may be associated with other periods of relative higher unemployment rates. That is, during recessions and the early phases of a recovery, unemployment rates may stay at an elevated level for a while. A good example of this is the U.S. unemployment rate during the 2008 to 2012 period, when unemployment stayed elevated at around 9 percent plus. The last part of Table 6.9C provides autocorrelations functions values, which are identical to those provided in Table 6.9A.

Modeling Cyclical Behavior: Identify AR(p) and MA(q)

The ACFs, PACFs, and autocorrelation test findings provide strong evidence of cyclical behavior in the unemployment rate. The next step would be to model that cyclical behavior to predict the behavior of the unemployment rate. The modeling of cyclical behavior requires identification of autoregressive (AR) and moving average (MA) orders, in other words an ARMA (p, q).[21] Most time series data involve a non-stationary characteristic, so we need to identify the order of integration, also called I(d), to determine whether the series is nonstationary or not. We combine the process to identify the orders of AR (p), MA (q) and I(d), known as ARIMA, autoregressive integrated moving average.[22]

SAS software provides a user-friendly method to tentatively identify the order of candidate ARMA or ARIMA models, known as the SCAN method for the smallest canonical correlation approach.[23]

The SAS code in S6.15 identifies the orders of AR(p), MA(q) and I(d), using the U.S. unemployment rate as a case study. In the second line of the code, we

---

[21] Where *p* indicates order of autoregressive and *q* attaches to the moving averages order.

[22] For more details about ARMA/ARIMA models, see Francis X. Diebold (2007), *Elements of Forecasting*, 4th ed. (Mason, OH: South-Western, Thomson), Chapter 5.

[23] For more details about the SCAN, see SAS/ETS 9.3, PROC ARIMA.

added the SAS keyword SCAN, which instructs SAS to identify tentative ARMA/ARIMA order for unemployment rate using the SCAN method. We ended the S6.15 code with Run and Quit.[24]

```
*============================================================;

*The smallest Canonical (SCAN) Correlation Method;

*Identify Order of ARIMA (p,d,q) Models by Using the SCAN
Method;

*============================================================;

PROC ARIMA Data= unemployment_data;

Identify var = unemployment SCAN ;        (S6.15)

Run;

Quit;
```

Tables 6.10 and 6.11 are based on SAS code S6.15. The first part of Table 6.10 provides squared canonical correlation estimates; the second part shows the SCAN Chi-square probability value of the test. We highlighted the MA (1); and AR (2), and the corresponding value, 0.3708. The value 0.3708 is the first one that is greater than 0.05 and implies that, at a 5 percent level of significance, we failed to reject the hypothesis of no correlation. This indicates that the unemployment may be modeled using one of the following candidate models: ARMA(2,1), ARIMA(1,1,1) or ARIMA(0,2,1). Each of these three models can be estimated using PROC ARIMA and the AIC and/or SBC statistics can be

TABLE 6.10 SAS Output Based on PROC ARIMA: The SCAN Method

			Squared Canonical Correlation Estimates			
Lags	MA 0	MA 1	MA 2	MA 3	MA 4	MA 5
AR 0	0.9883	0.9733	0.9530	0.9271	0.8970	0.8628
AR 1	0.0229	0.0621	0.0715	0.0507	0.0464	0.0437
AR 2	0.0527	0.0028	0.0014	0.0004	<.0001	<.0001
AR 3	0.0487	0.0021	0.0009	0.0002	<.0001	<.0001
AR 4	0.0198	<.0001	<.0001	<.0001	<.0001	<.0001
AR 5	0.0089	<.0001	<.0001	<.0001	<.0001	<.0001

			SCAN Chi-Square[1] Probability Values			
Lags	MA 0	**MA 1**	MA 2	MA 3	MA 4	MA 5
AR 0	<.0001	<.0001	<.0001	<.0001	<.0001	<.0001
AR 1	0.0012	<.0001	<.0001	<.0001	0.0001	0.0004
AR 2	<.0001	**0.3708**	0.5371	0.7530	0.9770	0.9110
AR 3	<.0001	0.4317	0.6532	0.8044	0.9090	0.9644
AR 4	0.0028	0.9187	0.9264	0.9428	0.9679	0.9951
AR 5	0.0450	0.9413	0.9432	0.9878	0.9994	0.9663

---

[24]The Quit option tells the SAS system to stop running the code.

TABLE 6.11 Tentative Order Selection Tests

```
              The ARIMA Procedure

                  ARMA(p+d, q)
            Tentative Order Selection Tests

                   ----SCAN---
                   p+d      q

                    2       1

             (5% Significance Level)
```

compared to select the best-fitting model. The SCAN method summarizes the results and provides a tentative order of ARIMA in Table 6.11.

The PROC ARIMA and SCAN methods are powerful tools to identify the model for the cyclical behavior of a time series. By using these tools, we can conclude that the U.S. unemployment rate contains cyclical behavior. Furthermore, the SCAN method suggests a p + d order equal to 2 and MA (1). That is, in the modeling process of the unemployment rate, it would better to use lag-1 of the unemployment rate as right-hand-side variables and also lag-1 of the error term (as MA(1)) as a right-hand-side variable in the test equation.[25]

SUMMARY

This chapter provides useful tips for users to get started in SAS. By utilizing several econometric techniques, an analyst can characterize different time series through SAS. We wish to stress that the first step of an applied time series analysis is to understand the behavior of a time series, which helps during modeling and forecasting. An analyst should plot a variable over time for visual inspection (i.e., to determine whether the series has a trend, cyclical behavior, etc.). In a next step, calculation of the mean, standard deviation, and stability ratio over different business cycles will help the analyst to understand the series behavior over time.

Formal trend estimation of a time series is also essential, as it helps analysts to determine whether a series has an upward or downward trend over time. By characterizing the cyclical behavior of a series, an analyst can learn the series' behavior over different phases of a business cycle.

---

[25] "The SCAN method suggests p + d equals 2 and that may indicate that the unemployment rate is non-stationary. Furthermore, we suggest to test unemployment rate for non-stationary using the unit root tests (ADF for example). The unit root testing is discussed in chapter 7 of this book."

Testing for a Unit Root and Structural Break Using SAS Software

This chapter employs SAS software to test for a unit root and structural break in a time series. We demonstrate, using the U.S. consumer price index (CPI) as a case study, how to test for a unit root using the Dickey-Fuller test; the Phillips-Perron test; and the Kwiatkowski, Phillips, Schmidt, and Shin test. Testing for a unit root determines whether the data series is stationary and if the series has a constant mean and variance over time. A basic ordinary least squares (OLS) analysis assumes that data is stationary. If the data is nonstationary, the OLS results are not reliable.

Another important feature of applied econometric analysis is to identify whether a time series contains a structural break. Furthermore, if an economic, financial, or business data series contains a structural break, then the series acts differently during different periods. Therefore, any estimated relationship in one time period does not work in another time period. Three different approaches are utilized to identify a structural break in the U.S. home prices: (1) a dummy-variable method, (2) the Chow test, and (3) the state-space approach. Last, the application of the Hodrick-Prescott (HP) filter is shown using the U.S. corporate profits series.

TESTING A UNIT ROOT IN A TIME SERIES: A CASE STUDY OF THE U.S. CPI

Is there an underlying pattern to a time series that could mislead analysts when they attempt to identify the behavior of a series over several economic cycles? Testing unit root in a time series is one of the most important aspects of modern time series analysis because if one or more variables are nonstationary, then the OLS-based results for that model will be spurious. The SAS software provides traditional unit root tests, such as the augmented Dickey-Fuller (ADF), Phillips-Perron (PP), and Kwiatkowski-Phillips-Schmidt-Shin (KPSS). This section shows how to employ these tests as well as how to analyze the SAS output. We use the U.S. CPI data series as a case study and apply all three unit root tests to the CPI.

The SAS code S7.1 shows how to employ the ADF test. PROC Autoreg and CPI_data are used in the analysis. In the second line of the code, after Model, we specify the variable name, CPI. After = /, Stationarity is a SAS keyword that instructs SAS to employ the stationarity (or unit root) test on the CPI. In parentheses, (ADF) shows the name of the unit root test and asks SAS to apply the ADF unit root test. The code ends with Run and Quit.

```
*==============================================;
*The PROC Autoreg is employed                 ;
*Testing Unit Root for CPI, YoY % Change      ;
*==============================================;
*==============================================;
* The Augmented Dickey-Fuller (ADF) Test      ;
*==============================================;
PROC Autoreg Data=CPI_data;
Model CPI = /STATIONARITY=(ADF) ;    (S7.1)
Run;
Quit;
```

Table 7.1 indicates the output based on code S7.1. The first part of the table shows the model's measures of goodness of fit, and the last part discusses the intercept's statistical significance. Since we are interested in determining whether CPI contains a unit root at level form (which is in the present case is the year-over-year [YoY] change), the middle section of the table is where we identify the unit root. The first column, labeled "Type," describes the underlying regression model used. That is, "Zero Mean" implies the CPI is regressed on its own lag and an error term. In other words, there is no intercept or trend included in the test regression. This is also known as a random walk model. The "Single Mean" indicates that an intercept term is

TABLE 7.1 SAS Output Based on the ADF Unit Root Test

The AUTOREG Procedure

Dependent Variable   CPI

Ordinary Least Squares Estimates

SSE	3896.64562	DFE	451
MSE	8.64001	Root MSE	2.93939
SBC	2262.52763	AIC	2258.41395
MAE	2.11622732	AICC	2258.42283
MAPE	133.437081	HQC	2260.035
Durbin-Watson	0.0196	Regress R-Square	0.0000
		Total R-Square	0.0000

Augmented Dickey-Fuller Unit Root Tests

Type	Lags	Rho	Pr < Rho	Tau	Pr < Tau	F	Pr > F
Zero Mean	3	-4.9483	0.1260	-2.0187	0.0419		
Single Mean	3	-11.3979	0.0948	-2.5942	0.0953	3.5882	0.1518
Trend	3	-18.8073	0.0857	-3.0536	0.1192	4.8055	0.2117

Parameter Estimates

Variable	DF	Estimate	Standard Error	t Value	Approx Pr > |t|
Intercept	1	4.1922	0.1383	30.32	<.0001

included in that test regression. This is also known as a random walk with drift model.[1]

The "Lags" column shows up to three lags of the CPI are included as right-hand-side variables. The "Rho" shows the OLS t-value, and "Pr < Rho" column provides the probabilities attached to those t-values. The null hypothesis is the presence of a unit root (nonstationary), and the alternative is that there is no unit root (stationary). At the 5 percent level of significance, we fail to reject the null hypothesis of a unit root for CPI in all three cases. The next two columns provide values for the "Tau" test. Probabilities corresponding to those values are shown under the label "Pr < Tau." Interestingly, we can reject the null hypothesis of a unit root for the "Zero Mean" case at the 5 percent level of significance because "Pr < Tau" is 0.0419, which is smaller than 0.05. The next two columns provide values for the "F" test and "Pr > F" probabilities attached to those values, respectively. The F-test value shows that we failed to reject the null hypothesis. The null hypothesis of the F-test is that the coefficients of the underlying model are simultaneously zero; the alternative hypothesis is that the coefficients are not zero. In both the "Single Mean" and "Trend" cases we fail to reject the null hypothesis, implying that all estimated coefficients—intercept, slope, and trend—are simultaneously zero. In conclusion, based on the "Tau" test, we reject the null hypothesis. The ADF test indicates that CPI is stationary at 5 percent of significance.

---

[1] For more details about unit root tests, see Chapter 4.

TABLE 7.2 SAS Output Based on the PP Unit Root Test

```
                    The AUTOREG Procedure
                  Dependent Variable  CPI

              Ordinary Least Squares Estimates

  SSE           3896.64562      DFE                       451
  MSE              8.64001      Root MSE              2.93939
  SBC           2262.52763      AIC               2258.41395
  MAE           2.11622732      AICC              2258.42283
  MAPE          133.437081      HQC                  2260.035
  Durbin-Watson    0.0196       Regress R-Square       0.0000
                                Total R-Square         0.0000
```

			Phillips-Perron Unit Root Test		
Type	Lags	Rho	Pr < Rho	Tau	Pr < Tau
Zero Mean	4	−5.1968	0.1168	−2.2759	0.0223
Single Mean	4	−10.9534	0.1057	−2.7454	0.0678
Trend	4	−16.5832	0.1336	−3.0485	0.1205

			Parameter Estimates		
Variable	DF	Estimate	Standard Error	t Value	Approx Pr > |t|
Intercept	1	4.1922	0.1383	30.32	<.0001

SAS code S7.2 indicates the PP test is employed on the CPI. In this case we simply change the test option from ADF to PP; the rest of code S7.2 is identical to the S7.1 code. The output based on the S7.2 code is displayed in Table 7.2. The middle section of the table shows the PP test output; we focus on that part as the rest of the table is identical to Table 7.1. The null hypothesis of the PP test is also that there is a unit root, and the alternative is that there is no unit root. Furthermore, three different options are included in the test regression: "Zero Mean," "Single Mean," and "Trend." These three cases are identical to those discussed in the ADF test results. The test equation includes up to four lags. The PP test also reports two different test statistics, "Rho" and "Tau," and their corresponding p-values are reported under the labels "Pr < Rho" and "Pr < Tau," respectively.

At 5 percent level of significance, the Tau test rejects the null hypothesis of a unit root in the case of "Zero Mean," which is consistent with the ADF's findings. Both ADF and PP test results imply that the CPI is stationary and does not contain either an intercept term or a time trend in the final equation.

```
*==============================================;

* The Phillips-Perron (PP) Test               ;

*==============================================;

PROC Autoreg Data = CPI_data;
```

```
Model CPI = /STATIONARITY=(PHILLIPS) ;     (S7.2)
Run;
Quit;
```

The KPSS test, SAS code S7.3, is also employed on the CPI, and results are shown in Table 7.3. The middle section of the table shows the KPSS test output. The null hypothesis of the KPSS test is thus stationary, and the alternative is nonstationary. If we fail to reject the null hypothesis, then the underlying series would be stationary.

```
*=========================================================;
* The Kwiatkowski-Phillips-Schmidt-Shin (KPSS) Test        ;
*=========================================================;
PROC AUTOREG Data = CPI_data;
Model CPI = /STATIONARITY=(KPSS) ;     (S7.3)
Run;
Quit;
```

TABLE 7.3 SAS Output Based on the KPSS Unit Root Test

The AUTOREG Procedure

Dependent Variable   CPI

Ordinary Least Squares Estimates

SSE	3896.64562	DFE	451
MSE	8.64001	Root MSE	2.93939
SBC	2262.52763	AIC	2258.41395
MAE	2.11622732	AICC	2258.42283
MAPE	133.437081	HQC	2260.035
Durbin-Watson	0.0196	Regress R-Square	0.0000
		Total R-Square	0.0000

KPSS Stationarity Test

Type	Lags	Eta	Prob10pr	Prob5pr	Prob1pr
Single Mean	5	3.8796	0.3470	0.4630	0.7390
Trend	5	0.5163	0.1190	0.1460	0.2160

KERNEL = NW, SCHW = 4

Parameter Estimates

Variable	DF	Estimate	Standard Error	t Value	Approx Pr > |t|
Intercept	1	4.1922	0.1383	30.32	<.0001

If the KPSS test includes an intercept in the regression equation, then it does not provide results for the "Zero Mean" because the "Zero Mean" case implies there is no intercept term in the test equation. Table 7.3 shows results for the "Single Mean" and "Trend" cases, and up to five lags of the dependent variable are included as right-hand-side variables. Estimated values of the KPSS test are reported under the label "Eta," and the corresponding p-values of those test values are shown under the columns "Prob10pr," Prob5pr," and "Prob1pr." These columns indicate the p-value for a particular level of significance, which are 10 percent, 5 percent, and 1 percent. Since we used a 5 percent level of significance for ADF and PP tests, we will follow the same level of significance for the KPSS test. The second column from the right of the KPSS results section shows the p-value for 5 percent; for both the "Single Mean" and "Trend" cases, p-values are larger than 0.05. This implies that we fail to reject the null hypothesis, thereby concluding that CPI is stationary at 5 percent level of significance.

Results from all three of the unit root tests suggest that the CPI data series has stationary characteristics.

IDENTIFYING A STRUCTURAL CHANGE IN A TIME SERIES

In recent years, an active debate has ensued on whether the unemployment rate has shifted upward in relation to the pace of economic growth representing a structural break with the past. Similarly, another debate has centered on the possibility of a structural change caused by the home price boom and bust of the previous decade. The level of the U.S. home prices, using the Standard & Poor's (S&P)/Case-Shiller home price index (HPI) as a measure, has shifted downward since 2006, as shown in Figure 7.1.

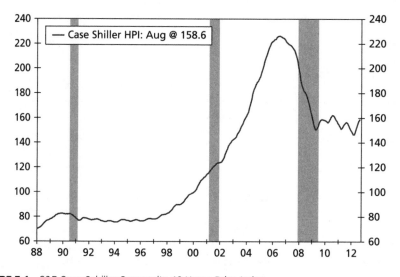

FIGURE 7.1 S&P Case-Schiller Composite-10 Home Price Index
Source: S&P Case-Shiller

In this section, we discuss three different methods to identify a structural break in a time series. The first method uses a dummy variable–based regression analysis. We show how to generate a dummy variable in the SAS software. The second method is known as the Chow test. We describe how an analyst can apply, as well as analyze, the output of the Chow test. The third method is employed through the PROC ARIMA. The benefit of this approach is that an analyst does not need to specify a specific break date. In contrast, for the first two methods, we have to choose a break date and then test whether that break date is statistically significant or not. Using these three methods, we identify the structural break(s) in the S&P/Case-Shiller HPI.

Testing for a Structural Break: The Dummy Variable Approach

The first method to identify a structural break in a time series is based on a dummy variable regression. We create a dummy variable: The dummy variable is equal to 1 on and after the break date and is equal to zero before the break date.[2] If the dummy variable is statistically significant, then it would be evidence of a structural break in a time series.

SAS code S7.4 shows how to create a dummy for a break date. Let us assume the HPI dataset is already imported in the SAS system and we have assigned the SAS name `HPI_data` to the data set. The HPI variable is a quarterly time series, and the data file `HPI_data` contains HPI and date variables. Furthermore, the HPI data file is sorted by date. The next step is to create another data file named `HPI_data2`, using the file `HPI_data`. This process is outlined in the first two lines of code S7.4. The next line provides details about the dummy variable. That is, the `if date >= '1apr2006'd then d_2006 = 1` code uses Q2 2006 as a break date and the dummy variable `d_2006` equal to 1 on and after that date. The `if` and `then` in the code are SAS keywords to create a conditional variable, which is the dummy variable in this case; the condition is `'1apr2006'd`, which is the break date. We select Q2 2006 as a break date for HPI because that is the peak date for S&P/Case-Shiller HPI. After six years, the HPI is still well below the peak, therefore potentially qualifying Q2 2006 as a structural break date. The next line of the code, `else d_2006 = 0`, indicates the d_2006 variable equal to zero for the pre–Q2 2006 time period and completes the process of creating a dummy variable for a particular break date.

```
*===========================================================;

*Creating a dummy variable for a structural break date       ;

*2006:Q2 as a break date,
It was the peak quarter for Case-Siller HPI                  ;

*===========================================================;
```

---

[2]That is, dummy = 1 for T > = TB and dummy = 0 for T < TB, where "TB" is a break time and "T" is sample time.

```
DATA HPI_data2;

Set HPI_data;

if date >= '1apr2006'd then d_2006=1;   (S7.4)

else d_2006=0;

Run;
```

TABLE 7.4 Testing for a Structural Break: The Dummy Variable Approach

The AUTOREG Procedure

Dependent Variable   HPI

Ordinary Least Squares Estimates

SSE	90220.7536	DFE	96
MSE	939.79952	Root MSE	30.65615
SBC	956.136521	AIC	950.966586
Regress R-Square	0.3416	Total R-Square	0.3416
Durbin-Watson	0.0403		

Parameter Estimates

Variable	DF	Estimate	Standard Error	t Value	Approx Pr > |t|
Intercept	1	99.1368	3.5880	27.63	<.0001
d_2006	1	50.1384	7.1039	7.06	<.0001

We run a simple regression using PROC AUTOREG (code S7.5), with d_2006, our dummy variable, as an independent variable and HPI is the dependent variable. The results based on code S7.5 are reported in Table 7.4. The t-value for the d_2006 variable is 7.06, and the p-value for that t-value is <0.0001. This implies that, at a 5 percent level of significance, d_2006 is statistically significant, suggesting that the HPI does indeed have a structural break at Q2 2006.

```
*===================================;

*The Dummy Variable Approach          ;

*The PROC AUTOREG is employed         ;

*===================================;

PROC AUTOREG Data= HPI_data2;

Model HPI = d_2006 ;   (S7.5)

Run;

Quit;
```

Testing for a Structural Break: The Chow Test

Another method to test for a structural break in a time series is known as the Chow test. One major benefit of the Chow test is that we do not need to create

TABLE 7.5 Testing for a Structural Break: The Chow Test

```
                    The AUTOREG Procedure
                  Dependent Variable   HPI

               Ordinary Least Squares Estimates

   SSE               137034.875     DFE                       97
   MSE                     1413     Root MSE            37.58631
   SBC               992.513199     AIC               989.928232
   Regress R-Square      0.0000     Total R-Square        0.0000
   Durbin-Watson         0.0091
```

		Structural Change Test			
Test	Break Point	Num DF	Den DF	F Value	Pr > F
Chow	74	1	96	49.81	<.0001

Variable	DF	Estimate	Standard Error	t Value	Approx Pr > |t|
Intercept	1	111.9272	3.7968	29.48	<.0001

a dummy variable for a break date; however, we still need to provide a break date. Code S7.6 shows how to run the Chow test, applying it to the HPI data. Using PROC AUTOREG we add the "Chow" option, instructing SAS to run the Chow test. The chow = 74 indicates the break date at the 74th observation of the HPI data; this corresponds to Q2 2006.

```
*=================================;
*The Chow Test                   ;
*The PROC AUTOREG is employed    ;
*=================================;
PROC AUTOREG Data= HPI_data2;
Model HPI = / chow=74; (S7.6)
Run;
Quit;
```

The results based on the Chow test are displayed in Table 7.5. The middle section of the table shows results specifically related to the Chow test. The first column, labeled "Test," indicates the Chow test is employed, and the second column, "Break Point," shows the break point at the 74th observation. The next column reports the number of breaks that are used in this case, 1, and "Den DF" identifies denominator degree of freedom for the Chow test. The F-test value is 49.81, and the p-value for the F-test is <.0001, suggesting rejection of the null hypothesis. The null hypothesis of the F-test is that there is no structural break, and the alternative is that there is a structural break. The results of the Chow test confirm the findings of the dummy variable approach—that is, the HPI data may contain a structural break with Q2 2006 as the corresponding break date.

Testing for a Structural Break: The State-Space Approach

The state-space approach is a convenient and powerful tool to estimate and forecast models. It uses available data to do the estimation process, and it can identify structural break(s) in a time series.[3] PROC ARIMA employs a state-space approach that offers an OUTLIER option which can identify a structural break in the variable of interest. The OUTLIER tool considers three types of changes: additive outliers (AO), level shifts (LS), and temporary changes (TC). Additive outliers indicate that one (or more) observations are very different (or far away) from the rest of the observations. The level shifts (also known as structural breaks) show that a variable has two or more different structures. That is, if we divide a time series into two subsamples, each will have very different means and/or standard deviation. The LS occurs usually due to a policy environment change, such as a shift from higher tax rates to lower tax rates. The TC exhibits a fixed duration of change in a variable before the variable returns to the previous level. For example, the gross domestic product (GDP) growth rate turns negative during recessions, but then returns to positive territory once the recession ends.

A two-step procedure is provided to identify a structural change (or an outlier) in a variable. In this case, we use the S&P/Case-Shiller HPI data series. Unlike the previous cases using the dummy variable approach and the Chow test, we will not specify a particular break date when using the state-space approach. In the state-space approach, every observation of the complete sample is utilized, and the possibility of a change (either AO/LS or TC) at every date is considered. Furthermore, based on a Chi-square test, this approach determines whether the HPI data series contains a change at any point of time. The null hypothesis of the Chi-square test is that the underlying variable does not contain a change; the alternative hypothesis is that it does have a change. Furthermore, PROC ARIMA will determine the break date as well as the nature of the change (i.e., whether the HPI data has a change, and, if so, whether the change can be defined as an additive outlier, a level shift, a temporary change, or a combination of the three.

---

[3]For more detail about the state space approach, see G. S. Maddala and In-Moo Kim, (1998), *Unit Root, Cointegration and Structural Change* (Cambridge, UK: Cambridge University Press).

TABLE 7.6A Identifying ARIMA (p, d, q) for the HPI

ARMA $(p + d, q)$
Tentative Order Selection Tests
----SCAN---

p + d	q
5	2

(5% Significance Level)

Step 1

The state-space approach first characterizes the time series, HPI in this case, and determines the order of ARIMA (p, d, q). Then the ARIMA (p, d, q) model for HPI is estimated, and either a structural change or an outlier is be identified based on the Chi-square test.

The SAS code for the first step of the state-space approach—identifying the ARIMA order (p,d,q) for the HPI series—is listed in SAS code S7.7A.

```
PROC ARIMA Data= HPI_data2;
Identify Var= HPI SCAN;  (S7.7A)
Run;
Quit;
```

Notice that we use the SCAN option with PROC ARIMA. The SAS output is displayed in Table 7.6A.

The SCAN options determines "p+d =5" and "q=2." Because the data is a time series, it would be appropriate to use the difference form of the series due to the possible presence of nonstationarity. In the first step of the state-space approach, the ARIMA (4, 1, 2) has been identified for the HPI series.

Step 2

The second step of the approach is to estimate the HPI data series using the ARIMA (4, 1, 2) model. SAS code S7.7B shows how to estimate the ARIMA (4, 1, 2) model for the HPI series. As previously noted, we want to use the first difference of the series. The variable HPI(1) (as displayed in the second line of coding) indicates that we are employing the first difference of the HPI series. The third line instructs SAS to Estimate the HPI (first difference) and uses p = 4, which is AR(4) (up to four lags of the dependent variable as right-hand-side variables), and q = 2, which is MA(2) (up to two lags of the error term as right-hand-side variables).

```
*===================================;
*The State Space Approach            ;
*The PROC ARIMA is employed          ;
*The break date is unknown           ;
*===================================;
PROC ARIMA Data= HPI_data2;
Identify Var= HPI(1) ;            (S7.7B)
Estimate p=4 q=2 noint method=ml;
Outlier maxnum= 3 alpha=0.05 id=date;
Run;
Quit;
```

The `noint` indicates the regression equation does not contain an intercept term, and `method=ml` implies that the maximum likelihood method for estimation is employed.[4] The fourth line of the code indicates that we will use the Outlier option to identify changes (structural break and/or outlier) in the HPI series. The `maxnum=3` specifies the maximum number of changes; we choose 3—in other words, we are interested in finding up to three changes in the HPI. This is an arbitrary number. A simple rule of thumb is not to select a large number (as it may create an over-fitting problem) and also to avoid selecting a smaller number (as it may create a problem of under-fitting). Furthermore, if we select three as the maximum number of changes and the Outlier option declares that there are less than three changes, we can reduce the number to the one suggested by the Outlier option. The `alpha=0.05` indicates the level of significance is 5 percent. The `id=date` shows the variable date is used as a date and SAS will identify the change date, if there is any.

The results based on code S7.7B are provided in Table 7.6B. The first part of the table shows the summary of the ARIMA procedure: the maximum number of possible changes searched (3), the number of changes found in the approach (3), and the level of significance used (5 percent). The bottom part of the table displays specific details about the nature of the changes (whether it is AO and/or LS) and the change dates. The first column, "Obs," indicates the specific value at which a change (whether AO or LS) occurred (i.e., at the 91st observation, the HPI data series experienced a level shift). Since we have provided the

---

[4]The maximum likelihood (ML) is a method to estimate the parameters of a statistical model, an alternative to the OLS and other methods. The ML method selects values of a model's parameters that produce a distribution which gives the data the highest probability. In other words, the ML estimates parameters that maximize the likelihood function. For more details about the ML method, see William H. Greene (2011), *Econometric Analysis*, 7th ed. (Upper Saddle River, NJ: Prentice Hall).

TABLE 7.6B Testing for a Structural Break: The State-Space Approach

The ARIMA Procedure

Outlier Detection Summary

Maximum number searched	3
Number found	3
Significance used	0.05

Outlier Details

Obs	Time ID	Type	Estimate	Chi-Square	Approx Prob> ChiSq
91	01-JUL-2010	Shift	-4.80696	110.73	<.0001
77	01-JAN-2007	Additive	1.76115	46.71	<.0001
75	01-JUL-2006	Additive	-1.42355	25.17	<.0001

date variable as the ID in the SAS code, the second column, labeled "Time ID," provides the change dates.

There are three change dates found in the HPI time series: July 2010 (Q3 2010), January 2007 (Q1 2007), and July 2006 (Q3 2006). The third column, "Type," indicates the types of changes. The state-space approach found one structural shift (Q3 2010) and two additive outliers (Q1 2007 and Q3 2006). The estimated values of the coefficients are provided under the label "Estimates," and the Chi-square test values are shown under the label of "Chi-Square." The p-values corresponding to the Chi-square test are provided in the column "Approx Prob > ChiSq."

Our results from the state-space approach validate the hypothesis of a structural break in the HPI data series. However, the break date identified in the state-space approach is different from those dates identified in the dummy variable approach and the Chow test. However, we can at least conclude that the HPI series contains a structural break and that, to some extent, the HPI series behaved differently during the post-2006 era compared to the pre-2006 era.

THE APPLICATION OF THE HP FILTER

Investors often calculate moving averages of stock or commodity prices to determine if prices are breaking out above the historical trend (a buy signal) or falling below trend (a sell signal). While a moving average can provide some useful information on the overall trend of a time series, a powerful and more appropriate method to identify whether a time series is deviating from its long-run trend growth is the Hodrick-Prescott (HP) filter. This section discusses how to employ the HP filter and uses PROC EXPAND to examine U.S. corporate profits.

The first step of the HP filter process is to generate a log of the corporate profit series, which can be seen in the steps of SAS code S7.8. We assume that the corporate profits data series is imported and sorted by date in the SAS system using the data file name `HP_data`. The data file `HP_data2` represents the data for corporate profits in log form. Notice that the second line of code, `set HP_data`, informs SAS to use the data from that file to create the new data set. The third line of data transforms the profits data into log form and places it in the HP_data2 dataset. This new variable is labeled `lProfits`.

```
*=====================================;
*Generating Log of Corporate Profits      ;
*=====================================;
Data HP_data2;
Set HP_data;
lProfits = log(Profits) ; (S7.8)
Run;
```

Code S**7.9** demonstrates the application of the HP filter process using the PROC EXPAND function. The line `out=filter_data_out` instructs SAS to create a new data file that will contain the output from code S7.9, and the name of the file, a user-defined name, is `filter_data_out`. The `method=none` indicates that no special estimated method is requested. The variable date is used as an Id. The next line of the SAS code, `Convert lprofts =lprofits_hpt / transformout= (hp_t 1600);`, asks SAS to convert `lProfits` (which is log of the profits series) to `lprofits_hpt`, a user-defined SAS name. The `transformout = (hp_t 1600)` part of the line shows the long-run trend growth (`hp_t` is standard for the long-run trend growth component) is estimated, and the λ=1600 is used. In other words, the SAS system will create a new variable, `lprofits_hpt`, which is the long-run trend growth component of the profits series. The next line of code indicates the deviation from long-run trend growth, also known as the cyclical component, is estimated (`hp_c` indicates the cyclical component is estimated), and the λ=1600 is employed. That is, another new variable, `lProfits_hpc`, is created, and it reflects the cyclical movements of the profits series.

```
*=================================;
*The SAS Code for HP Filter            ;
*=================================;
PROC EXPAND data= HP_data2 out=filter_data_out method=none;
id date;
Convert lProfts =lProfits_hpt / transformout= (hp_t 1600);
Convert lProfits = lProfits_hpc / transformout= (hp_c 1600); (S7.9)
Run;
```

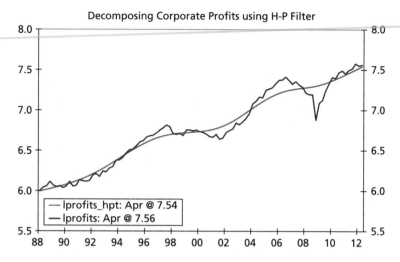

FIGURE 7.2 Decomposing Corporate Profits Using the HP Filter
Source: Bureau of Economic Analysis

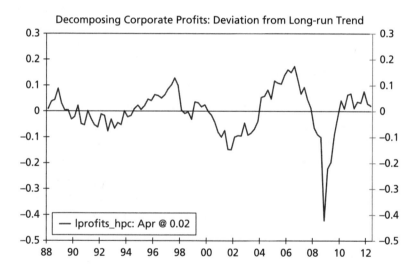

FIGURE 7.3 Cyclical Component of the Profits
Source: Bureau of Economic Analysis

The data file `filter_data_out` contains the actual profits series, log of the profits, `lProfits_hpt` (long-run trend growth component for profits), and `lProfits_hpc` (cyclical component of the profits data). The `filter_data_out` file can be exported using **PROC EXPORT** in an Excel format.[5]

Figure 7.2 shows the log of the profits (`lprofits`) and the long-run trend growth (`lProfits_hpt`).

Figure 7.3 plots the cyclical component of the profits (`lprofits_hpc`).

---

[5]Note, discussed in Chapter 6, SAS code S6.7, shows how to export a data file from the SAS system.

APPLICATION: BENCHMARKING THE HOUSING BUST, BEAR STEARNS, AND LEHMAN BROTHERS

In decision making, many rules of thumb are employed in understanding economics and finance[6]—for example, the relationship between gross domestic product (GDP) and the unemployment rate (Okun's law), the unemployment rate and the job vacancy rate (Beveridge curve), and the inflation rate and money supply (money neutrality).[7] In business, many decisions are made based on these economic and financial relationships, which incorporate not only the past but also the perceived current environment. But what happens if these relationships suddenly change? Beginning in the mid-2000s, a number of key economic and financial variables underwent a sudden change, deviating from their long-term trends in a way so dramatic as to suggest a structural shift. While it can be difficult to evaluate these turning points in the moment, these episodes are reminders that economic and financial relationships can change over time and also can change quite suddenly and must be tested. Therefore, policies or decisions based on previous experiences may not always work as expected.

2006: The Housing Bust

One example of a possible structural break, which is when a data series experiences a sudden and significant shift, is the trend in U.S. home prices. The S&P/Case-Shiller HPI grew consistently during the period from Q1 1997 to Q2 2006 (see Figure 7.4). Despite the 2001 recession, home prices continued to grow over that period, suggesting a long-run trend character to home prices. An analyst in 2005 who extrapolated home prices for the 2006 to 2010 time period would have felt safe not anticipating any change in the future trend of home prices and therefore would not have presumed a structural break in the growth rate of home prices was soon on the horizon.

With the benefit of hindsight, this assumption proved to be disastrously wrong. Home prices continuously fell during the Q3 2006 to Q1 2009 period throughout the United States. In addition, at least since 2009, the HPI has shifted downward. The average value for the S&P/Case-Shiller HPI for the 2009 to 2011 period was 156 compared to an average of 194 for 2004–2005.

So what did we find? The S&P/Case-Shiller HPI data series shows that there was indeed a structural shift in the growth of home prices. Using the state-space

---

[6]John E. Silvia, Azhar Iqbal, Sarah Watt, and Kaylyn Swankoski (2013), "When Is This Time Different: Benchmarking the Housing Bust, Bear Stearns and Lehman Brothers," February 4, Wells Fargo Securities, LLC. https://wellsfargoresearch.wachovia.net/Economics/Pages/default.aspx.
[7]For more details about these relationships, see Gregory N. Mankiw (2010), *Macroeconomics*, 7th ed. (New York: Worth).

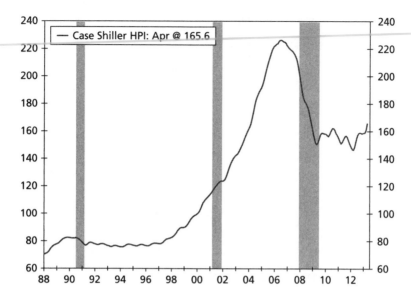

FIGURE 7.4 S&P/Case-Shiller Home Price Index
Source: S&P/Case-Shiller and Wells Fargo Securities, LLC

approach, we find that in March 2006, the growth rate in national home prices dropped 2 percentage points from the previous month and marked the beginning of a continuous slowdown in price growth, and eventual contraction, starting in January 2007.[8]

Key macroeconomic factors behind the structural change in home prices and the housing boom and bust were a large number of foreclosures, credit tightening, significant job losses, and a fundamental change in the expectations of buyers that home prices would appreciate continuously. Moreover, buyers who assumed that home prices would not fall during the 2006 to 2010 time period faced serious financial challenges due to the structural change in home prices relative to outstanding mortgage debt.

2007: Bear Stearns and the Overnight Market for Risk

The decline in home values that began in late 2006 had far-reaching effects, with one of the first manifesting itself in the financial markets as the underlying value of housing-related assets came into question. Risk in the overnight marketplace can be proxied by the TED spread, the spread between the three-month London Interbank Offered Rate (LIBOR) rate and the Treasury bill rate as expressed in basis points (see Figure 7.5). By late June 2007, Bear Stearns had pledged a collateralized loan to cover the positions of one of its funds.[9] In addition, Bear

---

[8]The econometric results can be found in the Table 7.7. All of the results are significant at the 0.01 level.

[9]For a more complete review of the Bear Stearns episode, see William D. Cohan (2009), *House of Cards: A Tale of Hubris and Wretched Excess on Wall Street* (New York: Doubleday).

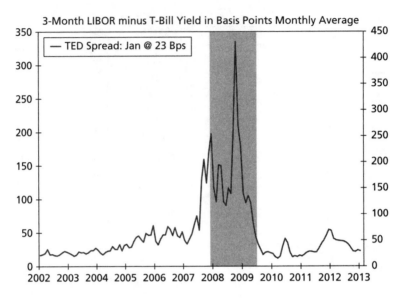

FIGURE 7.5 TED Spread
Source: Bloomberg LP and Wells Fargo Securities, LLC

Stearns was negotiating with other institutions to lend money against collateral to another fund. The funds traded collateralized debt obligations. By mid-July, Bear Stearns indicated that the funds had lost much of their value. Bear Stearns' losses from its mortgage securities business threatened confidence in the markets, and measures of risk, including the TED spread, jumped on the fear of contagion.

In fact, the fear of risky lending using subprime mortgage–backed bonds as collateral initiated unease concerning the ability to cover debt obligations, and a structural shift in pricing in the overnight marketplace ensued. When tested for a structural break, the TED spread experienced a structural shift in August 2007, jumping 140 basis points (bps) during the month, see Table 7.7 for results. The upward shift in the TED spread following Bear Stearns' collateralized debt obligation liquidation crisis in the summer of 2007 suggests an increased risk premium on bank lending that broke away from the long-run trend. While the TED spread did not peak until October 2008, a structural shift in the level had already occurred, making this period an outlier rather than a point of long-term change.

The structural shift in the TED spread was only temporary, due in large part, to the reaction of the Federal Reserve and U.S. Treasury Department to improve liquidity in the market. In January 2009, the TED spread experienced another structural shift, this time moving lower. The spread fell 50 bps over the month following the beginning of mortgage-backed security purchases by the Federal Reserve (quantitative easing, or QE1) and capital injections for banks under the U.S. Treasury's Capital Purchase Program. It is interesting that the approach taken here can identify both the break upward in the spread and the success in the Fed's actions to meet that disruption.

TABLE 7.7 Identifying a Structural Break Using the State-Space Approach

S&P/Case-Shiller HPI		
Break Date	Type of Break	Coefficient
Mar-06	Level Shift	−0.6147*
Jan-10	Additive Outlier	0.3368*
Jan-09	Additive Outlier	−0.3256*
Jun-04	Level Shift	0.5164*
TED Spread		
Break Date	Type of Break	Coefficient
Oct-08	Additive Outlier	134.41*
Oct-87	Additive Outlier	73.52*
Aug-07	Level Shift	76.66*
Jan-09	Level Shift	−77.31*
LIBOR–OIS Spread		
Break Date	Type of Break	Coefficient
Oct-08	Additive Outlier	145.26*
Sep-08	Level Shift	46.93*
Jan-09	Level Shift	−45.31*
Aug-07	Level Shift	36.40*
VIX Index		
Break Date	Type of Break	Coefficient
Oct-08	Level Shift	19.14*
Sep-08	Level Shift	18.85*
Aug-98	Level Shift	18.83*
Sep-11	Additive Outlier	12.11*

*Significant at the 0.01 level.

2008: Lehman and the Financial Crisis

Stress in financial markets was also evident by a structural shift in the LIBOR–overnight indexed swap (OIS) three-month spread in August 2007. Just when financial market participants were adjusting to the new level of financial market stress, a more sizable structural shift in the LIBOR–OIS spread occurred. In early June 2008, Lehman Brothers announced that it expected a significant

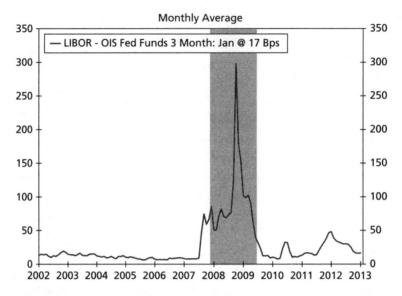

FIGURE 7.6 LIBOR–OIS Fed Funds Three-Month Spread
Source: Bloomberg LP and Wells Fargo Securities, LLC

loss ($2.8 billion) for the second quarter following a write-down in assets and trading losses. Investor confidence fell, and Lehman's market value declined. In August, the potential purchase of Lehman by the Korea Development Bank was halted by a lack of financing for the deal. On September 15, Lehman filed for bankruptcy.[10] However, the markets had already reacted, as illustrated by the dramatic move in the LIBOR–OIS spread (see Figure 7.6) and the gradual increase in the volatility index (VIX; see Figure 7.7) in late 2007, due, in part, to the events surrounding Bear Stearns and the liquidity crisis. The VIX index, the Chicago Board Options Exchange's measurement for future volatility in the stock market, experienced two major structural shifts following the collapse of Lehman. The first occurred in September 2008, when the VIX index rose 27 bps; the second occurred in October 2008, when it rose 41 bps.

However, the most significant shift in the LIBOR–OIS spread did not occur until September 2008, when Lehman collapsed and counterparty risk soared. A 200 bps increase in the LIBOR–OIS spread resulted from the fear that other financial institutions would soon follow. In January 2009, the LIBOR–OIS spread shifted again, this time falling 35 bps and coming in line with the previous trend following efforts by the Fed and the Treasury Department to increase liquidity and capital, results are reported in Table 7.7.

---

[10]Michael Lewis (2010), *The Big Short: Inside the Doomsday Machine* (New York: Norton).

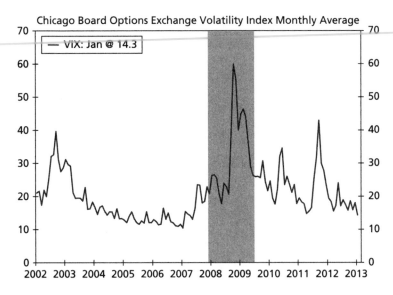

FIGURE 7.7 VIX Index
Source: Bloomberg LP and Wells Fargo Securities, LLC

SUMMARY

For decision makers, it is important to characterize the behavior of a time series before utilizing it in the decision-making process. Relying on general rules of thumb and past trends, and assuming that this time is not different, may lead to inaccurate expectations and inappropriate decisions. Our findings validate the hypothesis that home prices, the TED spread, the LIBOR–OIS spread, and the VIX index experienced structural shifts, reminding us that previous relationships can change, and do change, quite quickly. These findings should instill caution in decision makers and warn that the future may be distinctly different from the past. Therefore, intended public policy and private strategy should be flexible to accommodate the future uncertainty concerning the behavior of any particular variable.

CHAPTER 8

Characterizing a Relationship Using SAS

A question that is essential to analysts in the economic and financial world is: To what extent are certain variables related to each other? This chapter provides methods for using SAS software to determine the statistical relationship between economic and financial variables and to interpret the results. First we share useful tips for an applied time series analysis and then we examine how to estimate the statistical relationship between two (or more) variables.

USEFUL TIPS FOR AN APPLIED TIME SERIES ANALYSIS

Helpful hints are the reliable servant of any good work. An analyst needs to be familiar with a few key guidelines for applied research. The guidelines include using economic and financial theories as a benchmark and testing the theory with econometric techniques by employing time series data (or cross-section/ panel data).[1] Most applied econometric analysis is now done by statistical software, which produces results quickly. Such speed can be a trap, however, because the software does not care what kind of data is inputted and whether it is the best basis for the statistical results.

For example, using any statistical software, an analyst can produce correlation coefficients between the population in Gambia and the gross domestic

---

[1]The focus of this book is applied time series analysis. Therefore, examples of time series data are used throughout in the book.

product (GDP) of the United States.[2] The correlation coefficient may be statistically significant, yet any correlation is likely to reflect a third factor: a deterministic time trend (i.e., an upward or downward time trend over time). That is, both the U.S. GDP and the Gambian population are likely to have an upward trend over time, which also influences the correlation and produces a spurious relationship. Software uses whatever data is presented to it and produces results. An analyst's job is to ensure that the input data makes sense when examining a relationship. To conduct any effective applied time series (or any quantitative) analysis, an analyst should start with an economic or financial theory that suggests a hypothesis and then test that hypothesis with the help of data and relevant econometric techniques.

Next, an analyst must address several data issues: How long a time span should be included in the analysis? What functional form of the variables is appropriate? What is the number of observations to be tested? How will such a dataset match the statistical techniques and economic or financial perspectives of the study? For instance, is a monthly dataset of 10 years (120 observations) better than an annual dataset of 40 years (40 observations) for the relationship being tested? Statistical techniques require a large number of observations to preserve degrees of freedom,[3] which ensure that results will be reliable. From a statistical point of view, a longer history means more reliable results. From an economic theory perspective, more information provides a basis for a deeper and more comprehensive analysis.[4]

That said, variables can behave differently during recessions than during expansions. The longer the time period covered, the greater the opportunity to identify how a relationship behaves over an economic cycle, its volatility and the probability of a structural break. Additionally, recessions and recoveries, and even midcycle expansions over time, are not alike. For example, some recessions are deeper than others. Recoveries also differ, as seen in Figure 8.1, where employment is displayed following its cycle peak. An analyst should include at least several business cycles, if possible, to increase the credibility of the results for any time series analysis.

Another practical question arises: Over what functional form (e.g., level versus growth rate) of the variables should be used in a time series analysis. Although the answer depends on the objective of the study, the log-difference form of variables generally provides a better statistical outlook than the level

---

[2]Gambia is the smallest country on the African mainland, and the United States is the largest economy in the world. These two nations should not have a statistically significant correlation coefficient.

[3]The degrees of freedom indicate the number of observations included in the final estimation process.

[4]See G. S. Maddala and In-Moo Kim (1998), *Unit Roots, Cointegration, and Structural Change* (Cambridge, U.K.: Cambridge University Press).

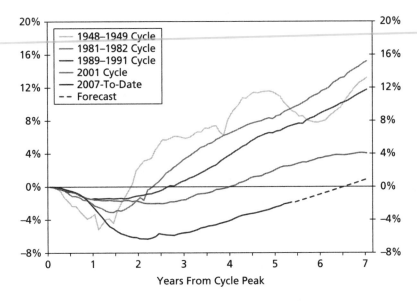

FIGURE 8.1 Employment Cycles: Percentage Change from Cycle Peak

form of the variables. Why? Usually the log-difference form of a variable solves nonstationary issues; therefore, statistical results can be interpreted outside of a deterministic time trend.[5]

For instance, in equation 8.1, Y_t is the Standard & Poor's (S&P) 500 index (indexed to 1941–1943), and X_t is the U.S. GDP (in billions of dollars). If an analyst used the level form of these variables, it would be difficult to interpret the estimated coefficient (β), because GDP is in billions of dollars and the S&P 500 index is an index. Let us assume $\beta = 0.67$ and is statistically significant. We can assert that a 1-unit increase in GDP, which is $1 billion, is associated with a 0.67-unit increase in the S&P 500 index. This is an odd assertion because each variable is in a different scale.

$$Y_t = \alpha + \beta X_t \qquad (8.1)$$

However, the log-difference form will convert these variables into growth rates, and then both variables will share the same scale: percent form. We can now explain $\beta = 0.67$ as a 1 percent increase in GDP growth rate associated with an 0.67 percent increase in the S&P 500 index. A similar point about the dataset would be to use a consistent form for dependent and independent variables in an analysis. That is, if the dependent variable is a month-over-month (MoM) percentage change, then it would be better to use a MoM percentage change in the independent variable instead of a year-over-year (YoY) percentage change.

---

[5] See William H.Greene, (2011), *Econometric Analysis*, 7th ed. (Upper Saddle River, NJ: Prentice Hall).

Next, the statistical properties of the dataset can be tested by utilizing the appropriate SAS techniques. Correlation, regressions, and cointegration tests determine statistical associations between two or more variables. It is very important to distinguish between statistical correlation and statistical causality.[6] Although a correlation tells us that two variables move together over time, it does not indicate which variable leads and which variable lags. The Granger causality test, however, does identify statistical causality between variables of interest, identifying which variable is a leading variable and which is a lagging.

Often an analyst has to select one model among several and determine which model is better among its competitors. We strongly recommend selecting a model based on criteria such as the Akaike information criterion (AIC) and the Schwarz information criterion (SIC), where a model with the lowest AIC/SIC would be better than others. Furthermore, an analyst should not choose a model based primarily on the R^2 value.[7]

Finally, an analyst should review the statistical results carefully and ask whether these results make economic sense. For example, are the signs and magnitudes of the estimated coefficients consistent with the theoretical views? In addition, the analyst always should plot the actual and fitted values of the dependent variable, along with the residuals, for visual inspection, and check whether they make sense with respect to economic theory.

CONVERTING A DATASET FROM ONE FREQUENCY TO ANOTHER

An important issue an analyst may face when estimating a statistical relationship between two or more variables is that the variables may not be available in the same frequency. For a statistical analysis, the data series must share the same frequency to run a correlation or regression analysis. If one series has monthly data points and another has quarterly data points, then there would be an uneven number of observations in the analysis, or the series would cover different time periods. SAS code S8.1 shows how to convert a time series from one frequency to another. In this example, monthly employment data is converted into a quarterly series using the PROC EXPAND command.

```
*=========================================================;
*Converting monthly dataset into quarterly frequency      ;
*The U.S. employment data as a case study                 ;
*=========================================================;
PROC EXPAND data = monthly_data
Out = qtr_data from = month to = qtr;   (S8.1)
```

---

[6] See Chapter 5 for more details about this issue.

[7] See Chapter 5 for more details about model selection criteria.

```
Convert employment /observed = average;
ID date;
```
Run;

Assume that the employment data is imported and sorted in the SAS system and the data file name is `monthly_data`. The second line of code S8.1 starts with `Out = qtr_data`, which creates a data file name `qtr_data` in the SAS system, and `from=month to = qtr` indicates a monthly data series is being converted into a quarterly series. The third line of the code indicates which series to covert (employment) and what values or calculations to use. In this case, we use `observed = average` to take the average of the three observations to create a quarterly series.[8] The `ID date` in the code shows the date variable is used as an ID variable to convert the employment data series. The code is ended with `Run`.

```
*=====================================;
* Merging two data files into one        ;
*=====================================;
```
Data combined_data;
Merge data_GDP qtr_data; **(S8.2)**
By date;
Run;

Monthly employment data has now been converted into a quarterly frequency and can be merged with quarterly GDP data to assess the relationship between employment and output. Let us assume that the data file "data_GDP" is already imported and sorted into the SAS system and that the file contains quarterly GDP data along with the date variable. SAS code S8.2 is an example of how to merge two data files into one.[9] The `combined_data` is the name of the newly created data file. The second line of code S8.2 is `Merge data_GDP qtr_data`, which indicates that these two data files are being merged into one file, `combined_data`. The `By date` part of the code specifies to merge the files by their date variable. Whenever we merge two or more data files, the files being merged must share a common variable that match the data together.

The Correlation Analysis

A first step of a quantitative analysis could be to run a correlation analysis between variables of interest and to test whether these variables are statistically associated with each other and the direction of the association (i.e., whether

---

[8]There are other options besides the average when converting monthly data into quarterly data, such as using the first (or last) monthly value for the quarter.
[9]It is possible to merge several different data files into one.

GDP is positively or negatively correlated with employment and the S&P 500 index). A correlation analysis is simple but more precise than a plot of two series over time because it quantifies to what extent, if any, two series are statistically related to each other. We use U.S. GDP, employment, and S&P 500 index as a case study and run a correlation analysis between these variables.

```
*=========================================;
* Correlation analysis using PROC CORR       ;
*=========================================;
*Using the level form of GDP, S&P500 index and employment;
PROC CORR data = correlation_data;
Var GDP employment SP500; (S8.3)
Run;
```

SAS code S8.3 shows the PROC CORR command utilizing the data file correlation_data to run a correlation analysis among GDP, employment, and the S&P 500 index. In the second line of the code, Var is a SAS keyword after which we provide the list of variables to be included in the correlation analysis: GDP, employment, and SP500 (S&P 500 index). The results based on code S8.3 are reported in Table 8.1. The dataset covers the Q1-1975 to Q2-2012 time period, using the level form of the variables.[10] Furthermore, the employment and S&P 500 index series are converted into a quarterly frequency using the S8.1 code and then the quarterly series are used in the correlation analysis.

The first part of Table 8.1 shows descriptive statistics, which are useful to characterize a time series. The mean, standard deviation (Std Dev), sum of the series (Sum), and minimum and maximum values of the three series are presented in the table. One quick check of the data reliability is that these series do not contain a negative or zero value, as the minimum value of each of these series is positive. This indicates that an unusual value (such as a zero or negative value) is not presented in the test variables. Because we use the level form of GDP, employment, and the S&P 500 index, there should not be any negative values. The standard deviations of all three series are smaller than the mean of that series, which indicates these series are generally stable over time.

The second part of Table 8.1 reports the correlation matrix based on the Pearson correlation coefficient. The Pearson correlation coefficient shows a linear statistical association between two variables.[11] The correlation coefficients range between −1 and 1, where 1 represents a perfect positive linear

---

[10]Interestingly, all three variables are in different measurement scales (GDP is in billions of dollars, employment is in thousands of persons, and the S&P 500 index is an index of value 10 = 1941–1943).

[11]For more details about the correlation and Pearson correlation coefficient, see Chapters 8 and 9 of D. Freedman, R. Pisani, and R. Purves (1998), *Statistics*, 3rd ed. (New York: Norton).

TABLE 8.1 The Correlation Analysis Using Level Form of the Variables

```
                        The CORR Procedure

               3 Variables:  GDP  Employment  SP500


                          Simple Statistics

 Variable      N     Mean    Std Dev      Sum    Minimum    Maximum

 GDP          150    9097     2793     1364487    4791       13549
 Employment   150  112241    18753    16836076   76536      137935
 SP500        150  638.91   485.21       95837   78.77        1497


              Pearson Correlation Coefficients, N = 150
                     Prob > |r| under H0: Rho=0


                            GDP      Employment      SP500

          GDP            1.0000       0.9741        0.9492
          GDP                         <.0001        <.0001

          Employment     0.9741       1.0000        0.9412
          Employment     <.0001                     <.0001

          SP50           0.9492       0.9412        1.0000
          SP500          <.0001       <.0001
```

association between the two variables (i.e., a rise in one variable is associated with a rise of the exact magnitude in the other variable). A coefficient of −1 shows a perfectly negative linear association (i.e., an increase in one variable is correlated with a decline in the other variable of the same magnitude). The correlation coefficient is also tested for statistical significance. The null hypothesis is H0: Rho=0, where Rho is the correlation coefficient and Rho=0 means the coefficient is not statistically significant. The alternative hypothesis is that the coefficient is statistically significant. The p-value attached to the correlation coefficient is also reported. The variables' names are listed both vertically and horizontally. The diagonal values are 1 because a variable always has a perfect correlation with itself.

The correlation coefficient between GDP and employment is 0.9741, indicating that GDP and employment are positively correlated. The p-value for that coefficient is less than 0.05; thus, at a 5 percent level of significance, we can reject the null hypothesis that the correlation coefficient between GDP and employment is not statistically significant. Therefore, we find that GDP and employment are statistically correlated. The correlation coefficient between GDP and the S&P 500 index is 0.9492 and is statistically significant. Employment and the S&P 500 index is also statistically positively correlated with a coefficient of 0.9412.

The correlation analysis found a very strong statistical association among GDP, employment, and the S&P 500 index. However, the strong statistical association among GDP, employment, and the S&P 500 index could be due to a third factor, such as a time trend. Because we use the level form of these variables and all have an upward trend over time, the correlation analysis likely captured an upward time trend. One possible solution to remove a potential time trend is to use a growth rate of these series, such as the year-over-year percentage change, and rerun the correlation analysis.

```
*==========================================================;
*The YoY % change of GDP, S&P500 index and employment is used ;
*==========================================================;
PROC CORR data=correlation_data;
Var GDP_yoy employment_yoy SP500_yoy; (S8.4)
Run;
```

Code S8.4 is used to run a correlation analysis using the growth rates of GDP, employment, and the S&P 500 index. The only difference between codes S8.4 and S8.3 is that in the second line of the S8.4 we listed GDP_yoy (year-over-year percentage change of GDP), employment_yoy (year-over-year percentage change of employment), and SP500_yoy (year-over-year percentage change of S&P500 index). The results based on code S8.4 are reported in Table 8.2.

From Table 8.2, the descriptive statistics based on the growth rates of the three series show that both employment and the S&P 500 index growth rates are more volatile than the GDP growth rate because the standard deviations of both series are higher than their respective means. The standard deviation of the GDP growth rate is smaller than the mean. The correlation coefficients are positive and statistically significant at the 5 percent level of significance. However, the magnitude of the coefficients is smaller compared to the ones based on the level form of the variables. That is, the correlation coefficient between GDP and employment growth is 0.8308 compared to a correlation coefficient of 0.9714 based on the level form. The coefficient between the growth rates of GDP and the S&P 500 index is 0.4139 compared to 0.9492 in level terms. The correlation coefficient between growth in employment and the S&P 500 index growth rate also dropped significantly to 0.2455 from 0.9412.

Summing up, we suggest using growth rates of the variables of interest in correlation analysis instead of the level form since many variables may contain a deterministic trend that affects the correlation analysis. The correlation coefficients based on the growth rates are smaller than those based on the level form; however, the smaller coefficients are more realistic. For instance,

TABLE 8.2 The Correlation Analysis Using Difference Form of the Variables

```
                         The CORR Procedure

         3 Variables: GDP_yoy  Employemnt_yoy SP500_yoy

                       Simple Statistics

Variable              N    Mean  Std Dev   Sum    Minimum   Maximum

GDP_yoy             150    2.76    2.28   414.43   -4.57      8.48
Employment_yoy      150    1.42    2.02   213.91   -4.95      5.40
SP500_yoy           150    8.96   16.07    1345   -40.08     45.86

            Pearson Correlation Coefficients, N = 150
                 Prob > |r| under H0: Rho=0


                        GDP_yoy    Employment_yoy   SP500_yoy

        GDP_yoy          1.0000        0.8308         0.4139
        GDP_yoy                        <.0001         <.0001

        Employment_yoy   0.8308        1.0000         0.2455
        Employment_yoy   <.0001                       0.0025

        SP500_yoy        0.4139        0.2455         1.0000
        SP500_yoy        <.0001        0.0025
```

the correlation coefficient between growth in employment and the S&P 500 index is 0.2455, indicating that 25 percent of the time, employment and the S&P 500 index growth rates move together. The level form of these variables has a correlation coefficient of 0.9412, meaning that 94 percent of time, these variables move in the same direction, which is overly strong. Because there are many determinants of the S&P 500 index other than employment, 94 percent seems too good to be true, and 25 percent co-movement is more believable. The objective should be to identify an *accurate* correlation, not a higher correlation. A higher correlation sometimes may be spurious because of a third factor, such as a deterministic time trend.

The Regression Analysis

A regression analysis is more precise than a correlation analysis. In regression analysis, we specify a dependent variable and one or more independent variables (also known as left-hand- or right-hand-side variables, respectively). With the help of different tests we can identify the individual variable's statistical significance along with overall goodness of fit of a model.

The PROC AUTOREG command is used to run a regression analysis in SAS. We use the U.S. money supply (M2) and inflation rate (CPI) data series as a case

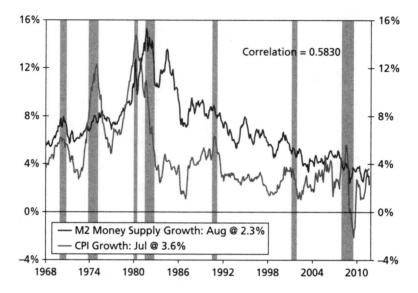

FIGURE 8.2 M2 Money Supply Growth versus CPI Growth (Year-over-Year Percentage Change)

study. The relationship between the money supply and inflation rate is also known as money neutrality. That is, inflation is often considered a product of excessive growth in the money supply relative to actual economic output. Put simply, an increase in the money supply may boost the general price level of a country. The question is: How might we quantify that?

```
*==============================================;
* Regression analysis using PROC AUTOREG       ;
* Using Level form of the M2 and CPI           ;
*==============================================;
PROC AUTOREG data=MI_data;
Model PCIU_M = MNY2_M; (S8.5)
Run;
```

SAS code S8.5 indicates how to run a regression analysis. The SAS data file MI_data contains the U.S. consumer price index (CPI), with the SAS name PCIU_M, and the money supply, measured by M2 and given the SAS name of MNY2_M. The second line of the code starts with Model, a SAS keyword that instructs SAS to run a regression using the listed variable. After Model we list the dependent variable (PCIU_M in the present case), an = (equals sign), and then the list of the independent variable (MNY2_M here). The results based on code S8.5 are reported in Table 8.3.

The first part of Table 8.3 reports several statistics that are important measures to determine a model's goodness of fit. The sum of square (SSE) is 91789.45896, and SSE is a key input to several important measures of a

TABLE 8.3 The Regression Analysis Using the Level Form of the M2 and CPI

```
                         The AUTOREG Procedure

                   Dependent Variable   PCIU_M

                  Ordinary Least Squares Estimates

    SSE                 91789.4586    DFE                       451
    MSE                  203.52430    Root MSE             14.26619
    SBC                3703.83645     AIC                3695.60467
    Regress R-Square        0.9211    Total R-Square         0.9211
    Durbin-Watson           0.0022
```

Variable	DF	Estimate	Standard Error	t Value	Approx Pr > |t|
Intercept	1	59.9083	1.3296	45.06	<.0001
MNY2_M	1	0.0202	0.0003	72.54	<.0001

model's goodness of fit (i.e., R^2, mean square error, etc.). "DFE" indicates the number of observations (sample size) minus the number of parameters in the model. The mean square error (MSE = 203.52430) is the estimated variance of the error term. The "Root MSE" is 14.26619, and it is the square root of the MSE. The MSE is the estimated variance, and the Root MSE is the estimated standard deviation of the error term. The Root MSE shows the average deviation of the estimated CPI from the actual CPI (our dependent variable).

The SBC and AIC values are helpful information criteria used to select a model among its competitors. There are two R^2 statistics reported in Table 8.3, which are "Total R-Square" and "Regress (Regression) R-Square." The total R^2 is a measure of how well the next value of a dependent variable can be predicted using the structural part (right-hand-side variables including the intercept) and the past value of the residuals (estimated error term). The regression R^2 is also a measure of the fit of the structural part of the model after transforming for the autocorrelation and thereby is the R^2 for the transformed regression. Furthermore, if no correction for autocorrelation is employed, then the values of the total R^2 and regression R^2 would be identical, as in our case. Another important statistic shown in Table 8.3 is the Durbin-Watson value. A Durbin-Watson statistic close to 2 is an indication of no autocorrelation; a value close to zero, as in the present case, is strong evidence of autocorrelation.

The last part of Table 8.3 reports measures of statistical significance for the right-hand-side variables, or the independent variables, along with an intercept. Column "DF" represents degrees of freedom, and shows one degree of freedom for each parameter. The next column, "Estimate," shows the estimated coefficients for the intercept (59.9083) and for "MNY2_M" (0.0202).

The next column exhibits the standard error of the estimated coefficient and is important for several reasons. First, the standard error of a coefficient shows the likely sampling variability of a coefficient and hence its reliability. A larger standard error relative to its coefficient value indicates higher variability and less reliability of the estimated coefficient. Second, the standard error is an important input in estimating a confidence interval for a coefficient. A larger standard error relative to its coefficient would provide a wider confidence interval. Last, a coefficient-to-standard error ratio helps to determine the value of a t-statistic. A t-value is an important test to determine the statistical level of significance of a variable including the intercept. An absolute t-value of 2 or greater is an indication that the variable is statistically useful to explain variation in the dependent variables. Both t-values, in absolute terms, are greater than 2 (45.06 for intercept and 72.54 for MNY2_M), suggesting that both the intercept and MNY2_M are statistically significant.

Finally, the last column, "Approx Pr > |t|," represents the probability level of significance of a t-value. Essentially, the last column indicates at what level of significance we can reject (or fail to reject) the null hypothesis that a variable is statistically significant. The standard level of significance is 5 percent; an Approx Pr > |t| value of 0.05 or less will be an indication of statistical significance. The values for both t-values are smaller than 0.05 (both are 0.0001); hence the intercept and MNY2_M are statistically meaningful to explain variation in the CPI. The positive sign of the MNY2_M coefficient indicates that an increase in the money supply is associated with a higher value of the CPI. As the t-value is greater than 2, the relationship between CPI and M2 is statistically significant.

The Spurious Regression

The results reported in Table 8.3 seem to indicate the CPI-M2 model is robust because the R^2 value is high (0.9211), the t-value is greater than 2, and the MNY2_M estimate has a positive sign, which is consistent with economic theory. The R^2 shows around 92 percent variation in the CPI is explained by M2, which seems too good to be true because there are several determinants of inflation other than the money supply. Furthermore, these results may be spurious because the Durbin-Watson statistic is very low, which is an indication of autocorrelation. The R^2 is significantly greater than the Durbin-Watson statistics ($R^2 = 0.9211$; Durbin-Watson = 0.0022), which also indicates possible spurious results.

One major reason for the spurious results is that we used the level form of the CPI and M2 series, which seem to have deterministic time trends. The regression analysis may have captured the time trend and shows higher R^2 and t-values. One possible solution is to use the growth rates of the CPI and M2

TABLE 8.4 Regression Analysis Using Difference Form of the Variables

```
                    The AUTOREG Procedure

             Dependent Variable   PCIU_yoy

             Ordinary Least Squares Estimates

      SSE              3608.67889  DFE                  451
      MSE                 8.00151  Root MSE         2.82869
      SBC              2237.85792  AIC           2229.62613
      Regress R-Square    0.0750  Total R-Square    0.0750
      Durbin-Watson       0.0263
```

Variable	DF	Estimate	Standard Error	t Value	Approx Pr > |t|
Intercept	1	2.4145	0.3218	7.50	<.0001
MNY2_yoy	1	0.2670	0.0441	6.05	<.0001

instead of the level form.[12] The next SAS code, S8.6, can be employed to run a regression analysis using the growth rates (YoY percentage change) of the CPI (PCIU_yoy) and money supply (MNY2_yoy). The results based on code S8.6 are reported in Table 8.4.

```
*=======================================================;
*Using Difference form(YoY % change)of the M2 and CPI    ;
*=======================================================;
PROC AUTOREG data=MI_data;
Model PCIU_yoy = MNY2_yoy ; (S8.6)
Run;
```

One noticeable change we observe is a significant reduction in the R^2, which dropped from 0.9211 to just 0.0750. In other words, the growth rate of the money supply only explains around 8 percent of the variation in the CPI growth rate, which is a more realistic number. The t-value shows the growth rate of the money supply is statistically significant in explaining variation in the CPI growth rate and both move in the same direction. The Durbin-Watson statistic is still close to zero (0.0263) and is a sign of

---

[12]A better solution is to employ cointegration and the ECM approach, which we discuss in the next section of this chapter. For now, we just explain a simple way to run a regression analysis, which is to use growth rates of the variables of interest instead of the level form.

autocorrelation in the error term. Therefore, the next step is to solve the autocorrelation problem.

Autocorrelation Test: The Durbin 'h' Test

The Durbin-Watson test detects first-order autocorrelation in the CPI–money supply model. A standard practice to solve a first-order autocorrelation issue is to include a lag of the dependent variable as a right-hand-side variable in the test equation.[13] In SAS code S8.7, we include a lag of the CPI growth data as a right-hand-side variable. We reestimate the equation and test for autocorrelation again for the possibility of higher-order autocorrelation. However, with the lag of the dependent variable included as a right-hand-side variable, the Durbin-Watson test would not be reliable because it assumes there is not a lag-dependent variable included as a regressor. The Durbin 'h' test is a better tool to detect autocorrelation in the current case. The null hypothesis of the Durbin 'h' test is that the errors are white noise (there is no autocorrelation) and the alternative is autocorrelation. SAS code S8.7 performs the Durbin 'h' test. The PCIU_yoy_1 is the first lag of the CPI growth rate, and the lagdep is the SAS keyword to perform the Durbin 'h' test. After lagdep, we specify the lag of the dependent variable, which is PCIU_yoy_1.

```
*=====================;
*Durbin 'h' test;
*=====================;
PROC AUTOREG data=MI_data;          (S8.7)
Model PCIU_yoy = MNY2_yoy PCIU_yoy_1 /lagdep = PCIU_yoy_1;
Run;
```

Results presented in **Table 8.5** indicate one noticeable change is the drop in both the SBC and AIC values. The drop indicates that this model is better than the previously estimated models, which are reported in **Tables 8.3** and **8.4**. The R^2 increases to 0.9805 when we include a lag-dependent variable as a regressor, which is expected. A variable usually is highly correlated with its lag. This is captured by a higher R^2. The t-value attached to the PCIU_yoy_1 is greater than 2, and, at a 5 percent level of significance, the lag of the CPI growth rate is statistically significant. An interesting observation is that the money supply growth rate is not statistically significant at a 5 percent level of significance, and it also has a negative sign, which is contrary to the economic theory.

The Durbin 'h' statistic is 9.3864 and the p-value ("Pr > h") is 0.0001, which indicates that, at a 5 percent level of significance, we reject the null

---

[13]For more details about autocorrelation issue and how to solve it, see Chapter 6 of G. S. Maddala and K. Lahiri (2010), *Introduction to Econometrics*, 4th ed. (Hoboken, NJ: John Wiley & Sons).

TABLE 8.5 Autocorrelation Test: The Durbin 'h' Test

```
                        The AUTOREG Procedure

                  Dependent Variable   PCIU_yoy


                    Ordinary Least Squares Estimates

        SSE                 74.9058345      DFE                    449
        MSE                    0.16683      Root MSE           0.40845
        SBC                488.613902       AIC            476.272855
        Regress R-Square        0.9805      Total R-Square      0.9805
        Durbin h                9.3864      Pr > h              0.0001


                                  Standard              Approx
        Variable      DF    Estimate    Error    t Value    Pr > |t|

        Intercept      1      0.0824     0.0492     1.68      0.0943
        MNY2_yoy       1     -0.0064     0.0067    -0.97      0.3346
        PCIU_yoy_1     1      0.9854     0.0068   144.25      <.0001
```

hypothesis of no autocorrelation. In other words, the Durbin 'h' test detects the presence of autocorrelation and that indicates there is higher-order autocorrelation because we have already included the lag of the dependent variable to solve first-order autocorrelation. That is, we need to find the order of autocorrelation and then solve that issue. Before we move to that phase, let us introduce another test of autocorrelation, which is known as the LM test.

Autocorrelation Test: The LM Test

Godfrey's test for serial correlation is known as the LM test of autocorrelation. The null hypothesis of the LM test is that the errors are white noise, or there is no autocorrelation, and the alternative is that there is autocorrelation. SAS code S8.8 is employed to perform the LM test. The term godfrey = 1 indicates the LM uses a lag of one period, where godfrey is the SAS keyword to perform the LM test of autocorrelation. The results based on code S8.8 are reported in Table 8.6.

```
*======================;
*The LM test           ;
*======================;
PROC AUTOREG data=MI_data; (S8.8)
Model PCIU_yoy = MNY2_yoy PCIU_yoy_1 /godfrey=1;
Run;
```

SAS codes S8.7 and S8.8 essentially estimate the same model. The only difference is that code S8.8 performs the LM test instead of the Durbin 'h' test, which was shown in code S8.7. Therefore, the R^2, SBC, AIC, and t-values reported in Table 8.6 are similar to those shown in Table 8.5. The Godfrey's LM test result is 88.8901 and the p-value ("Pr > LM") attached to the LM test result is 0.0001, indicating that the null hypothesis of no autocorrelation should be rejected and we suspect the errors are autocorrelated. Table 8.6 also shows the Durbin-Watson statistics, but due to the presence of the lag-dependent variable, that statistic is not reliable. The Durbin 'h' and the LM tests both agree on the presence of higher-order autocorrelation in the errors.

Autocorrelation Test: Finding the Appropriate Lag Order

Both the Durbin 'h' and LM tests found a higher-order autocorrelation for the CPI–money supply model. We next have to find the appropriate order of the autocorrelation and solve that issue. We suggest using the SBC and AIC information criteria to determine the appropriate autocorrelation order. That is, the model with the lowest SBC and AIC values is the best model. SAS code S8.9 performs the LM test by including up to three lags of the dependent variable as right-hand-side variables.

TABLE 8.6 Autocorrelation Test: The LM Test

```
                The AUTOREG Procedure

            Dependent Variable   PCIU_yoy


             Ordinary Least Squares Estimates

    SSE            74.9058345   DFE                    449
    MSE               0.16683   Root MSE           0.40845
    SBC            488.613902   AIC             476.272855
    Regress R-Square   0.9805   Total R-Square      0.9805
    Durbin-Watson      1.1229

            Godfrey's Serial Correlation Test

           Alternative    LM           Pr > LM

           AR(1)        88.8901        <.0001

                          Standard            Approx
    Variable    DF    Estimate    Error    t Value    Pr > |t|

    Intercept    1     0.0824    0.0492     1.68       0.0943
    MNY2_yoy     1    -0.0064    0.0067    -0.97       0.3346
    PCIU_yoy_1   1     0.9854    0.0068   144.25       <.0001
```

```
PROC AUTOREG data = MI_data; (S8.9)
Model PCIU_yoy = MNY2_yoy PCIU_yoy_1 PCIU_yoy_2 PCIU_yoy_3 /
godfrey=3;
Run;
```

We start by including the second lag of the dependent variable as a right-hand-side variable and run the regression. Then we add the third lag of the dependent variable and rerun the model. If the model with a fourth lag shows an uptick in both the SBC and AIC values, there is no need to test more lags since the model with the third lag of the dependent variable is the one with the lowest SBC and AIC values. The appropriate order of the autocorrelation suggested by SBC/AIC is three. We include up to three lags of the CPI growth rate (our dependent variable) as regressors and estimate the model. Furthermore, to confirm the appropriate order, we test for autocorrelation using the LM test. The results based on code S8.9 are reported in Table 8.7.

SBC and AIC values based on code S8.9 are smaller than those reported in Tables 8.3 to 8.6. The t-values of all three lag regressors are greater than 2, which suggests these variables are statistically significant. The money supply growth

TABLE 8.7 Finding the Appropriate Lag-Order Using the LM Test

Ordinary Least Squares Estimates

SSE	59.102039	DFE	445
MSE	0.13281	Root MSE	0.36444
SBC	394.098946	AIC	373.552708
Regress R-Square	0.9843	Total R-Square	0.9843
Durbin-Watson	1.9923		

Godfrey's Serial Correlation Test

Alternative	LM	Pr > LM
AR(1)	0.3527	0.5526
AR(2)	0.3824	0.8259
AR(3)	3.0039	0.3910

Variable	DF	Estimate	Standard Error	t Value	Approx Pr > |t|
Intercept	1	0.0553	0.0440	1.26	0.2097
MNY2_yoy	1	-0.0006	0.0061	-0.10	0.9214
PCIU_yoy_1	1	1.4750	0.0470	31.37	<.0001
PCIU_yoy_2	1	-0.6094	0.0792	-7.69	<.0001
PCIU_yoy_3	1	0.1194	0.0473	2.52	0.0120

rate is not statistically significant, indicating there is no statistical relationship between CPI growth and growth in the money supply over our sample period.

The LM test values are much smaller, and the p-values attached to those values are higher than 0.05, meaning we fail to reject the null hypothesis of white noise, or no autocorrelation. That suggests the appropriate lag order is three to address the autocorrelation issue.

This concludes our discussion of how to run a simple correlation and regression analysis. We expect that an analyst can use the SAS codes provided above to improve his or her skills. One way to do that would be to pick some variables as a case study and apply these tools.

The Cointegration and ECM Analysis

Regression analysis is a simple way to identify a statistical relationship between variables. In time series analysis, many variables are nonstationary at the level form, and the ordinary least squares (OLS) results using nonstationary variables would be spurious. That is, due to the nonstationary issue, a regression analysis using OLS may not provide reliable information about a statistical relationship between variables of interest. A better way to characterize a statistical relationship between time series variables is to employ cointegration and error correction model (ECM) techniques. A cointegration method identifies a long-run, statistically significant relationship between variables. The ECM determines how much deviation is possible in each period from the long-run relationship.[14]

The first step in an applied time series analysis is to test for a unit root in the variables of interest.[15] If the series are nonstationary, then the second step is to apply cointegration and ECM to determine a statistically significant relationship between the variables. This section discusses how to employ cointegration tests, both Engle-Granger and Johansen approaches, in the SAS system. We use the U.S. CPI and money supply (M2) variables as a case study and characterize the statistical relationship. The dataset is monthly and covers the January 1985 to June 2012 time period since inflation in the 1970s and early 1980s was very high and not reflective of today's environment. We apply the augmented Dickey-Fuller (ADF) unit root test on the CPI and money supply and find both series are nonstationary at their level form. The first difference of both series is stationary. It confirms we should not apply OLS but rather use cointegration and ECM techniques to determine the relationship between the CPI and money supply.

---

[14]For more details about nonstationary, spurious regression, cointegration, and ECM, see Maddala and Kim (1998).

[15]Chapter 6 of this book provides a detailed discussion about how to test for a unit root in a time series.

The Engle-Granger Cointegration Test

The first cointegration technique applied to the CPI and money supply data is the Engle-Granger (E-G) cointegration test. This is a single-equation approach, with one dependent variable and one or more independent variables. SAS code **S8.10** is performed to apply the E-G test on the CPI–money supply data. In the SAS software, when we include independent variable(s) in the equation, the "ADF" option performs the E-G cointegration test. For example, the second line of the code, Model dcpi = dm2 / STATIONARITY= (ADF), indicates that the dcpi (first difference of the CPI) is our dependent variable and dm2 (first difference of the money supply) is the independent variable. The SAS keyword STATIONARITY= (ADF), which usually performs the ADF unit root test, in this case will apply the E-G cointegration test on the data series because we have included dm2 as an independent variable. In the present case, the ADF option will follow the two-step estimation and testing procedure of the E-G approach. In the first step, the OLS residuals of the regression in the Model statement are estimated. The second step applies the ADF unit root test on these residual series. The null hypothesis of the E-G cointegration test is no cointegration (no statistically significant relationship between the CPI and money supply); the alternative hypothesis is cointegration. The results based on S8.10 code are reported in Table 8.8.

```
*================================;

*Engle-Granger Cointegration Test     ;

*================================;

PROC AUTOREG data=MI_data;

Model dcpi = dm2 / STATIONARITY= (ADF);  (S8.10)

Run;

Quit;
```

The first part of Table 8.8 shows the measures of a model's goodness of fit, such as the R^2 and the root mean square error. The last part exhibits the estimated coefficients and their measures of statistical significance, such as the t-value and its corresponding p-value. The middle section of Table 8.8 presents the results based on the E-G cointegration test.[16]

Two types of test equations are estimated for the E-G cointegration test, which are reported under the label "Type." The first type is "Single Mean," which indicates that an intercept term is included in the test equation. The second type is "Trend," which shows that the test equation contains an intercept

---

[16]The first and last parts of the Table 8.8 are similar to those of Table 8.3. We have discussed those parts in great detail in the regression analysis section of this chapter. See discussion under Table 8.3 for more details about measures of a model's goodness of fit as well as statistical significance measures of individual variables.

TABLE 8.8 Results Based on the Engle-Granger Cointegration Test

The AUTOREG Procedure

Dependent Variable dcpi

Ordinary Least Squares Estimates

SSE	78.920532	DFE	328
MSE	0.24061	Root MSE	0.49052
SBC	475.982711	AIC	468.384525
MAE	0.29627018	AICC	468.421222
MAPE	98.7835059	HQC	471.415331
Durbin-Watson	1.1627	Regress R-Square	0.0107
		Total R-Square	0.0107

Engle-Granger Cointegration Test

Type	Lags	Tau	Pr < Tau
Single Mean	3	-8.4164	<.0010
Trend	3	-8.5334	<.0010

Parameter Estimates

Variable	DF	Estimate	Standard Error	t Value	Approx Pr > |t|
Intercept	1	0.4195	0.0366	11.47	<.0001
dm2	1	-0.002010	0.001069	-1.88	0.0608

and a linear time trend. The concept behind the Single Mean and Trend types is similar to those of the unit root test (ADF).[17] That is, the E-G cointegration approach employs the ADF test to determine whether the two variables are cointegrated. The difference between the E-G approach and the ADF test is that we test for cointegration between *two or more* variables and, in the case of unit root testing, we characterize whether *one* variable is stationary or not. The "Lags" column indicates that up to three lags are included in the test equations. The "Tau" column represents the estimated statistics, and the "Pr < Tau" column provides p-values corresponding to the tau value. In both cases, the p-values are smaller than 0.05. Therefore, we reject the null hypothesis of no cointegration at a 5 percent level of significance—the CPI and money supply have a statistically significant relationship.

A cointegration test examines whether the CPI and money supply have a statistical relationship over the sample period. Furthermore, it is well known

---

[17]For more detail about the "Single Mean" and "Trend" types, see the unit root test section of the Chapter 7 of this book.

that the CPI and money supply have a long-run relationship. However, sometimes these series deviate from this long-run relationship. Therefore, the next step is to determine (1) whether the deviation from the long-run link is statistically significant and (2) what the magnitude of the deviation is. The ECM method provides answers of these questions.

The Error Correction Model

In applied time series analysis, the process to characterize a statistical relationship between variables consists of two steps. The first step is to decide whether the series have a statistical relationship over the entire sample period. That is determined by the cointegration test, which examines the series for a long-run relationship. If the two variables have a long-run relationship, then the second step is to quantify how much deviation from the long-run relationship is possible in each period. That is estimated by the ECM. If the series are not cointegrated then we will not apply the ECM method. Therefore, the existence of a long-run relationship between series of interest is the precondition for the ECM.

Application of the ECM consists of two steps. The first step is to run an OLS regression using the level form of the variables, which in this case is the level of the CPI (the dependent variable) and the money supply (the independent variable), and save the estimated residuals, or the error term, which we call error_ECM. In the next step, Equation 8.2 will be estimated using the OLS method. $DCPI_t$ and $DM2_t$ are the first difference forms of the CPI and money supply, respectively. The lerror_ECM$_t$ is the lag of the error_ECM. The first lag of the error_ECM, instead of the current form, is utilized because the current form of the error_ECM may be correlated with ε_t, which is the error term of Equation 8.2. One OLS assumption is that the value of the independent variable should not be correlated with the error term. If the assumption is violated, then the OLS results would not be reliable.[18]

$$DCPI_t = \alpha + \beta_1 DM2t + \beta_2 1error\_ECM_t + \varepsilon_t \qquad (8.2)$$

Step 1

```
*================;

*ECM Procedure   ;

*================;

*Step 1, Run a regression using the level form of the variables
and save residuals;
```

---

[18]For more details, see Chapter 3 of D. N. Gujarati and D. C. Porter (2009), *Basic Econometrics*, 5th ed. (New York: McGraw-Hill Irwin).

```
PROC AUTOREG data=MI_data;
Model PCIU_M = MNY2_M ; (S8.11)
Output out=ecm_data r=error_ECM;
Run;
Quit;
```

SAS code S8.11 is employed to perform the first step of the ECM procedure. A regression is estimated using the level form of the CPI and money supply, and the error term is saved. The third line of the code creates and saves the estimated residual from this regression, which is the objective of this step. Output is a SAS keyword to create and save a data file from the results. out = ecm_ data saves the newly created data file ecm_data; out is a SAS keyword used to assign the file name. The r = error_ECM saves the estimated residuals and assigns error_ECM as a SAS name to that series. The SAS keyword r indicates the estimated residuals of the test equation are being saved.

SAS code S8.12 creates the lag of the error_ECM, and we assign lerror_CM as a SAS name. The lag of the error_ECM will be used as an independent variable in step 2 of the ECM procedure.

```
*=======================================;
 Generating lag of the error-ECM series    ;
*=======================================;
DATA ecm_data;
Set ecm_data; (S8.12)
lerror_ECM=lag1 (error_ECM);
Run;
```

SAS code S8.13 completes the ECM procedure. The data file ecm_data is used to run the regression analysis. The results based on code S8.13 are reported in Table 8.9.

Step 2

```
*==============================================================;
*Step 2, first difference form of the CPI and M2 along with
lag-1 of the ECM is used in the regression analysis;
*==============================================================;
PROC AUTOREG data=ecm_data;
Model dcpi = dm2 lerror_ECM; (S8.13)
Run;
Quit;
```

TABLE 8.9   Results Based on Step 2 of ECM

```
                   The AUTOREG Procedure

                Dependent Variable   dcpi

              Ordinary Least Squares Estimates
```

SSE	78.8518335	DFE	326
MSE	0.24188	Root MSE	0.49181
SBC	481.077444	AIC	469.689271
MAE	0.29604983	AICC	469.763117
MAPE	99.3721836	HQC	474.232339
Durbin-Watson	1.1604	Regress R-Square	0.0112
		Total R-Square	0.0112

```
                    Parameter Estimates
```

Variable	DF	Estimate	Standard Error	t Value	Approx Pr > |t|
Intercept	1	0.4201	0.0367	11.45	<.0001
dm2	1	-0.002011	0.001071	-1.88	0.0614
lerror_ECM	1	-0.001179	0.002879	-0.41	0.6824

The R^2 values (both "Regress" and "Total") are 0.0112, which are too low; that is, the independent variables are explaining only 1 percent of variation in the dependent variable. Both "dm2" and "lerror_ECM" are statistically insignificant at the 5 percent level of significance.

We expect a negative and statistically significant estimated coefficient of the lerror_ECM. A negative value of the error_ECM's coefficient would adjust the co-movements of the CPI and money supply variables toward the long-run path. For instance, the error_ECM is the difference between the actual and estimated values of a dependent variable; hence it is the deviation from the long-run path of the CPI. Furthermore, the values of the error_ECM series can be negative, positive, or zero. If the value of the error_ECM is zero, then the actual and estimated values of the CPI are identical. A negative (positive) value of the error_ECM indicates that the actual value is higher (smaller) than the estimated value. In the case of smaller estimated values of the CPI, a negative coefficient value of the error_ECM will adjust the estimated values upward and toward the actual values, and vice versa.[19]

---

[19] If estimated values are smaller than actual values, the error-ECM will contain negative values and the negative coefficient will adjust the estimated CPI upward and toward the actual CPI because a negative value multiplied by a negative value produces a positive value: that is, $(-3) \times (-4) = 12$. Following the same logic, in the case of a positive error-ECM value, the coefficient will adjust the estimated CPI downward and toward the actual values.

A statistically significant coefficient of the lerror_ECM implies that the short-run deviation from the long-run path is statistically significant. In Table 8.9, the lerror_ECM coefficient is negative (–0.001179), but it is not statistically significant at the 5 percent level. Interestingly, the money supply coefficient has a negative sign, which is inconsistent with the theory of money neutrality, and it is statically insignificant at 5 percent significance level.

Summing up, the results are not in favor of a money supply–inflation link. This is because, in practice, several other factors influence the rate of inflation besides the money supply. Other useful variables to include in the money neutrality theory would be the GDP growth rate to capture overall economic growth and the unemployment rate or nonfarm employment data to capture the strength of labor market. The objective here has been to show how to employ the E-G cointegration test and ECM approach in SAS software.

One essential lesson is that whenever characterizing a statistical relationship between variables, an analyst's objective is to determine whether the relationship suggested by a prevailing theory is supported by the data during a particular sample period. That is, do the data and statistical techniques support the theoretical relationship? If we could not establish a statistical relationship between the CPI and money supply, it simply means the data during the period studied do not support the relationship. Then we look at why that might be. In the present case, we think it is necessary to include a few more variables to represent other factors in the economy to isolate the money/inflation link.

The Johansen Cointegration Approach: The Trace Test

E-G cointegration test and ECM are single-equation approaches—that is, one dependent variable with one or more right-hand-side variables. In contrast, the Johansen cointegration approach is a multivariate approach—more than one dependent variable and more than one right-hand-side variable. The Johansen approach can be more flexible than the E-G cointegration test.[20]

The Johansen cointegration test quantifies whether the variables contain a long-run relationship. The vector error correction model (VECM) determines the short-run dynamics. The VECM is also a multivariate approach where two or more dependent variables with two or more right-hand-side variables estimated through a system of equations.[21] SAS software provides the varmax procedure to employ the Johansen cointegration test as well as the VECM on variables of interest.

Using the same dataset as in the E-G and ECM approaches, both the Trace and Maximum tests of cointegration are applied to the relationship between the CPI and money supply. SAS code S8.14 shows how to employ the Trace test.

---

[20]For more details about the cointegration approach, see Maddala and Kim (1998).
[21]See Maddala and Kim (1998) for more detail about the multivariate and VECM approaches.

```
*=========================================;
*Johansen Cointegration Test: Trace Test      ;
*=========================================;
PROC VARMAX data=MI_data; (S8.14)
Model PCIU_M MNY2_M / P=2 cointtest=(Johansen=(normalize=
PCIU_M));
Run;
Quit;
```

PROC VARMAX is used to employ cointegration, VECM, the Granger causality test, and other techniques. After the Model statement, a list of variables is provided—in the present case, the CPI (PCIU_M) and money supply (MNY2_M). The term P=2 indicates the lag order of 2 is selected for the model. Since the Johansen cointegration approach employs a VAR (P) method, where P is standard for lag order, we must select a lag order. cointtest is a SAS keyword for a cointegration test, and we specify Johansen, for the Johansen cointegration test. If we do not specify the Johansen test, the SAS software will default to the Trace test. The normalize=PCIU_M instructs the SAS system to normalize the CPI-estimated coefficient to 1 because the CPI is our target variable and we are interested in finding the estimated coefficient of the money supply, which is our right-hand-side variable.

Results based on code S8.14 are reported in Table 8.10. The null hypothesis of both the Trace and Maximum tests is that there is no cointegration, and the alternative is that there is cointegration. If we reject the null hypothesis of no cointegration in favor of the alternative hypothesis of cointegration, then in the next step, we will estimate a VECM (P) model to quantify the short-run dynamics. Furthermore, it will be essential to determine whether to include a deterministic trend to capture the time trend in the series, a constant if a series follows a random walk with drift, or both.[22] We construct the VECM (P) based on the information provided by the VAR (P) model (i.e., the cointegration test will determine the VECM (P) functional form).

SAS provides five different functional form options for a VECM (P):

1. There is no separate drift in the VECM (P) form.

2. There is no separate drift in the VECM (P) form, but a constant enters only via the error correction term.

3. There is a separate drift and no separate linear trend in the VECM (P) form.

---

[22]We strongly suggest consulting with the SAS user manual of SAS/ETS 9.3, Chapter 35, the VARMAX Procedure, for technical details about the Johansen cointegration, Trace and Maximum tests, VAR(P), and five different options for a VECM(P). The manual is available at SAS web site: www.sas.com/.

TABLE 8.10 The Johansen Cointegration Approach: The Trace Test

HO: Rank=r	H1: Rank>r	Eigenvalue	Trace	5% Critical Value	Drift in ECM	Drift in Process
		Cointegration Rank Test Using Trace				
0	0	0.1278	45.3478	15.34	Constant	Linear
1	1	0.0016	0.5106	3.84		

HO: Rank=r	H1: Rank>r	Eigenvalue	Trace	5% Critical Value	Drift in ECM	Drift in Process
		Cointegration Rank Test Using Trace Under Restriction				
0	0	0.3125	131.0457	19.99	Constant	Constant
1	1	0.0245	8.1248	9.13		

Hypothesis of the Restriction

Hypothesis	Drift in ECM	Drift in Process
H0 (Case 2)	Constant	Constant
H1 (Case 3)	Constant	Linear

Hypothesis Test of the Restriction

Rank	Eigenvalue	Eigenvalue	DF	Chi-Square	Pr > ChiSq
0	0.1278	0.3125	2	85.70	<.0001
1	0.0016	0.0245	1	7.61	0.0058

4. There is a separate drift and no separate linear trend in the VECM (P) form, but a linear trend enters only via the error correction term.

5. There is a separate linear trend in the VECM (P) form.[23]

In Table 8.10 under the label "Cointegration Rank Test Using Trace," the column "H0: Rank=r" contains a value of "0," which indicates that the maximum cointegration rank is zero—that is, no cointegration. The "H1: Rank > r" is also "0"—that is, the cointegration rank is greater than zero, which implies cointegration. The "Eigenvalue" and "Trace" columns provide the values of the Eigenvalue and Trace test statistics, respectively. The level of significance is 5 percent. The last two columns, "Drift in ECM" and "Drift in Process," indicate the option (from 1 to 5) for the VECM (P). The first row indicates that the Trace test value (45.3478) is greater than the 5 percent critical value (15.34); that implies we reject the null hypothesis of a zero cointegration rank. From the second row, the Trace value 0.5106 is smaller than the critical value (3.84),

---

[23] See the VARMAX procedure for more details about these cases.

which indicates we reject the null hypothesis of cointegration rank of "1." That is, the results confirm that the CPI and money supply are cointegrated and the cointegration rank is 1. The last two columns show the "Constant" in the "Drift in ECM" and a "Linear" in the "Drift in Process." This implies that there is no separate drift in the error correction model, and the column "Drift in Process" means the process has a constant drift before differencing.

The second part of table reports the "Cointegration Rank Test Using Trace Under Restriction." The results also favor a cointegration Rank 1 between the CPI and money supply. Because the value of the Trace test (131.0457) in the first row is greater than the 5 percent critical value (19.99) and thereby we reject the null hypothesis of cointegration rank is 0 in favor of the alternative hypothesis which is the rank is greater than 0. However, we fail to reject the null hypothesis that the rank is greater than 1 at the 5 percent level of significance. Therefore, the cointegration rank is 1. The last two columns show option 2 for the VECM (P) as a "Constant" in the "Drift in ECM" and "Drift in Process" is identified. That is, there is no separate drift in the VECM (P) form, but a constant enters via the error correction model.

In sum, the results based on the cointegration Trace test suggest that the CPI and money supply are cointegrated—have a statistically significant relationship. Furthermore, two options, Case 2 and Case 3, are identified for the VECM (P), to quantify the short-run dynamics. The next step is to decide which case is more appropriate. The last part of Table 8.10 shows the results and the null hypothesis (H0) in Case 2 is more appropriate; the alternative is that Case 3 is a better form of the VECM (P). The cointegration rank 1 is selected from the first two parts of the table; therefore, we look at the last row, and under the label "Pr > ChiSq" (p-value of the Chi-square test), which is 0.054 and greater than 0.05. Therefore, at the 5 percent level of significance, we fail to reject the null hypothesis and suggest that Case 2 is a better form for the VECM (P).

The Johansen Cointegration Approach: The Maximum Test

SAS code S8.15 explains how to employ the Maximum test of cointegration. The only difference between code S8.14 (the Trace test) and S8.15 is that S8.15 specifies the Maximum test under the Type = Max.

```
*===========================================;
*Johansen Cointegration Test: Maximum Test        ;
*===========================================;
PROC VARMAX data=MI_data; (S8.15)
Model PCIU_M MNY2_M / p=2 COINTTEST=(JOHANSEN=(Type = Max
normalize=PCIU_M));
Run;
Quit;
```

TABLE 8.11 Johansen Cointegration Approach: Maximum Test

Cointegration Rank Test Using Maximum Eigenvalue				
H0: Rank=r	H1: Rank=r+1	Eigenvalue	Maximum	5% Critical Value
0	1	0.1278	44.8373	14.07
1	2	0.0016	0.5106	3.76

The results based on code S8.15 are displayed in Table 8.11. The "H0: Rank=r" explains cointegration rank of zero (in the first row), no cointegration. The second row indicates the cointegration rank is 1 (under "H0"), and "H1" suggests a rank of 2. At a 5 percent level of significance, we reject the null hypothesis of zero cointegration in favor of the rank of 1. That is, the Maximum test results also suggest a cointegration rank of 1 for the CPI and money supply.

The Vector Error Correction Model

The Johansen tests results indicate a cointegration rank of 1 for the CPI and money series, and Case 2 is selected for the VECM (P) form. SAS code S8.16 is employed to run a VECM of order 2—that is, VECM (2) and P=2 shows the lag order is 2. ECM is a SAS keyword for the error correction model and rank=1 specifies a cointegration rank of 1. The keyword ectrend means Case 2 is followed for the fitted model. The option Print=(estimates) asks SAS to print the results. The results based on code S8.16 are displayed in Table 8.12.

```
*======================================;
*Vector Error Correction Model (VECM)    ;
*======================================;
*case 2;
PROC VARMAX data=MI_data;  (S8.16)
Model PCIU_M MNY2_M / P=2 ECM=(rank=1 normalize=PCIU_M ectrend)
Print=(estimates);
Run;
Quit;
```

The first part of Table 8.12 presents the summary of the estimation process—that is, the model type is VECM (2) and restriction on the deterministic term indicates that Case 2 is estimated. The estimation method is Maximum Likelihood, and a cointegration rank of 1 is included in the estimation process.

TABLE 8.12 Results Based on VECM: Case 2

Type of Model	VECM(2)
	with a Restriction on the Deterministic Term
Estimation Method	Maximum Likelihood Estimation
Cointegrated Rank 1	

Parameter Alpha * Beta'Estimates

Variable	PCIU_M	MNY2_M	1
PCIU_M	-0.00003	0.00004	0.02365
MNY2_M	-0.00312	0.00379	2.51039

AR Coefficients of Differenced Lag

DIF Lag	Variable	PCIU_M	MNY2_M
1	PCIU_M	0.46272	-0.00080
	MNY2_M	-11.44204	0.29722

Model Parameter Estimates

Equation	Parameter	Estimate	Standard Error	t Value	Pr>|t|	Variable
D_PCIU_M	CONST1	0.02365	0.00496			1, EC
	AR1_1_1	-0.00003	0.00001			PCIU_M(t-1)
	AR1_1_2	0.00004	0.00001			MNY2_M(t-1)
	AR2_1_1	0.46272	0.04945	9.36	0.0001	D_PCIU_M(t-1)
	AR2_1_2	-0.00080	0.00112	-0.71	0.4784	D_MNY2_M(t-1)
D_MNY2_M	CONST2	2.51039	0.22467			1, EC
	AR1_2_1	-0.00312	0.00028			PCIU_M(t-1)
	AR1_2_2	0.00379	0.00034			MNY2_M(t-1)
	AR2_2_1	-11.44204	2.24127	-5.11	0.0001	D_PCIU_M(t-1)
	AR2_2_2	0.29722	0.05092	5.84	0.0001	D_MNY2_M(t-1)

Before we discuss the rest of Table 8.12, we explain the estimation process behind the VECM (2), which will help readers to interpret the estimated coefficients in the table. The VECM (2) estimates this set of equations:

$$D\_PCIU\_M_t = const1 + \beta_1 PCIU\_M_{(t-1)} + \beta_2 MNY2\_M_{(t-1)} + \beta_3 D\_PCIU\_M_{(t-1)} + \beta_4 D\_MNY2\_M_{(t-1)} + \varepsilon_t \tag{8.3}$$

$$D\_MNY2\_M_t = const2 + \gamma_1 PCIU\_M_{(t-1)} + \gamma_2 MNY2\_M_{(t-1)} + \gamma_3 D\_PCIU\_M_{(t-1)} + \gamma_4 D\_MNY2\_M_{(t-1)} + v_t \tag{8.4}$$

where

D = the first difference of a series (i.e., D_PCIU_M$_t$ represents the first difference form of the CPI)

t−1 = a lag of one period is used (i.e., MNY2_Y$_{(t-1)}$ is the lag-1 of the money supply).

In equation 8.3, we use the first difference of the CPI as a dependent variable. The independent variables include a lag of the dependent variable. Equation 8.4 contains the same right-hand-side variables, and the difference is the dependent variable, which is the first difference of money supply, D_MNY2_M$_t$. The error terms of the equation are ε_t and ν_t. Both equations include level and difference forms of the variables because the level form captures short-run dynamics and the difference form represents long-run fluctuations.

The second part of Table 8.12 shows the estimated coefficients of the CPI and money supply along with the intercept under the label "Parameter Alpha * Beta'Estimates." The "Variable" represents variable names included in the estimated process, which are "PCIU_M" and "MNY2_M." The estimated coefficients under "PCIU_M" are attached to the lag-1 of "PCIU_M" (which is the one-period lag of the CPI) in both equations. Since "MNY2_M$_{(t-1)}$," which is the lag-1 of the level form of money supply, is also present in both equations, two estimated coefficients are reported under the label "MNY2_M." The "1" shows constants (const1 and const2) of both equations.

The third part of Table 8.12 provides estimated coefficients corresponding to the lag of the dependent variables, which are the difference forms of the CPI and money supply. The last part of the table reports the estimated coefficients, standard error, t-value, and p-value. The first column on the right labeled "Variable" provides the names of the variables included in the equations. "EC" represents the ECTREND option, which is employed in Case 2. The "Equation" label names the dependent variables, and the SAS names of the right hand-side variables are reported under "Parameter." The columns "Estimates" and "Standard Error" display estimated coefficients and their standard errors. The "t Value" and "Pr > |t|" columns provide t-values and p-values of estimated parameters.

An important note here is that the t-values and p-values are missing for the level form of the variables as well as for the constants. The reason is that the level form of the CPI and money supply are nonstationary; thus, their t-values are not reliable. However, the first differences of both series are stationary, hence t-values are reliable. The p-value of D_PCIU_M$_{(t-1)}$ is smaller than 0.05, which implies that, at a 5 percent level of significance, D_PCIU_M$_{(t-1)}$ is statistically significant and may help explain variation in the D_PCIU_M$_t$. The p-value attached to the D_MNY2_M$_{(t-1)}$ is greater than 0.05; that is, D_MNY2_M$_{(t-1)}$ is not statistically significant in explaining variation in the D_PCIU_M$_t$.

In Case 2, where D_MNY2_M is the dependent variable, both $D\_PCIU\_M_{(t-1)}$ and $D\_MNY2\_M_{(t-1)}$ are statistically associated with the dependent variable, evidenced by the p-values for both variables being smaller than 0.05.

The Granger Causality Test

Both the cointegration and ECM tests determine whether two (or more) variables are statistically associated with each other. Still, neither technique shows the direction of the relationship. That is, which is the leading variable and which is the lagging variable? For instance, the cointegration tests reveal that the U.S. CPI and money supply are cointegrated. In other words, the tests show that the CPI and money supply have a statistically significant relationship, but they do not indicate whether changes in the money supply lead changes in consumer prices. The Granger causality test, however, determines which variable leads and which variable lags; in other words, it shows whether changes in money supply Granger-causes changes in the CPI.

Although the level form of the CPI and money supply are nonstationary, the first difference forms of both series are stationary, as we discussed earlier in this chapter. Furthermore, a nonstationary dataset may produce spurious results. So we may need to test Granger causality analysis using the difference form of the variables because the first difference form is stationary and may provide reliable results. SAS code S8.17 is employed to run Granger causality analysis for money supply and CPI using the first difference form of both variables; dcpi represents the first difference of CPI and dm2 shows the difference form of the money supply. The two Causal statements are employed to test bidirectional Granger-causality. We use the same CPI and money supply dataset that we used for the cointegration and ECM models to identify whether the money supply Granger-causes CPI.

```
*===========================;
*Granger Causality Test      ;
*===========================;
*Difference form of the variables;
PROC VARMAX data=MI_data;
Model dcpi dm2 / p=2 noprint;  (S8.17)
Causal group1=(dcpi) group2=(dm2);
Causal group1=(dm2) group2=(dcpi);
Run;
Quit;
```

PROC VARMAX also provides a Granger causality test option. The Model statement fits the regression equations for the listed variables, dcpi and dm2

TABLE 8.13 The Granger Causality Test Results, Using Difference Form of the Variables

```
                 The VARMAX Procedure
                Granger-Causality Test
      Test    DF   Chi-Square   Pr > ChiSq
       1       2      0.99         0.6094
       2       2     15.45         0.0004
        Test 1: Group 1 Variables: dcpi
                Group 2 Variables: dm2
        Test 2: Group 1 Variables: dm2
                Group 2 Variables: dcpi
```

in the present case. The `P=2` option indicates a lag order of 2 is utilized in the regression equations. The VARMAX procedure runs a VAR(P) model to test Granger causality between the variables of interest, and the `p=2` indicates a VAR(2) model is estimated for the CPI and money supply data.[24] The NOPRINT option suppresses output from the MODEL statement so no estimation results are printed and only results from the CAUSAL statement are printed.

Causal is a SAS keyword to run the Granger causality test. The term group1 specifies the dependent variable, and the right-hand-side variable(s) can be listed in the group2 option. Moreover, we state two Causal statements. The first considers the CPI (dcpi) as a dependent variable and money supply (dm2) as an independent variable. The second Causal statement treats money supply as dependent variable and the CPI as the independent variable. The null hypothesis of the test is that group2 does not Granger-cause the group1. In the present case, the first Causal statement, money supply, does *not* Granger-cause CPI. The alternative hypothesis is that money supply *does* Granger-cause CPI. It is important to note that we can assign more than one independent variable in the group2 option, in case we are interested in testing the causality of more than one variable.

The results based on code S8.17 are summarized in Table 8.13. Since we stated two Causal statements in the SAS code, two tests are performed. "Test1" determines whether money supply Granger-causes CPI, and "Test2" examines whether CPI Granger-causes money supply. In other words, a bidirectional Granger causality is tested between money supply and CPI.

The "Test1" results are reported in the first row, and the second row shows results for "Test2." The column labeled "DF" provides information about the degrees of freedom. The Chi-square test results are shown under the label "Chi-Square," and p-value for the Chi-Square test are presented in the column

---

[24] Since we select p=2 for Johansen cointegration tests as well as for the VECM model, for consistency, we keep the same "p" for the Granger causality test.

"Pr > ChiSq." The first row provides the results for the null hypothesis, money supply does not Granger-cause CPI, and the p-value for the Chi-Square test is 0.6094, which is larger than 0.05. Therefore, at the 5 percent level of significance, we fail to reject the null hypothesis and suggest that money supply does not Granger-cause CPI.

As mentioned earlier, "Test 2" determines whether CPI Granger-causes money supply. The p-value for the Chi-square is 0.0004, which is smaller than 0.05. This indicates that, at a 5 percent level of significance, we reject the null hypothesis and conclude that CPI Granger-causes money supply.

Granger causality test results are sometimes sensitive to the lag orders. That is, different lag orders may produce different concluding results. That raises the question: Which lag order should be used? We suggest choosing the lag order using AIC and SIC criteria. The model with the smallest SIC/AIC would be the most appropriate.[25]

The ARCH/GARCH Model

Volatility in a time series may create challenges for decision makers. A volatile series can generate issues in the modeling and estimation process that lead to a spurious analysis; that is, we may find a statistical relationship between variables of interest due to volatility when, in fact, there is no relationship. What issues are created by the volatility of a series? Typically, financial data series are more volatile than economic time series, and the volatility often violates some fundamental OLS assumptions (i.e., variance is not constant and/or there is volatility clustering, known as heteroskedasticity). In either case, hypothesis testing based on OLS statistical results are not valid.[26] In addition, in the presence of heteroskedasticity, the upper and lower limit of the forecast band based on the OLS would not be accurate.

Volatility has serious implications for a financial investor or planner. Typically a financial analyst would use the variance or standard deviation of returns as a proxy for risk to the average return from a purchase of an asset or portfolio. The variance is assumed constant, implying that the level of risk does not vary over time, which seems to be a strong assumption. In practice, however, returns from a portfolio fluctuate, and some periods are more risky than others for an investment. Yearly changes in the S&P 500 index are, for example, larger in some periods than others, indicating volatility (see Figure 8.3).

---

[25] For more details about the lag selection in a model, see Chapter 14 of James H. Stock and Mark Watson (2007), *Introduction to Econometrics*, 2nd ed. (New York: Pearson, Addison Wesley).
[26] See Chapter 5 of this book for more details about the volatility issue and ARCH/GARCH.

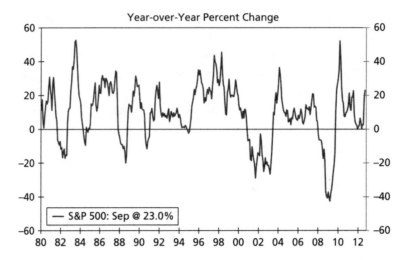

FIGURE 8.3 The S&P 500 Index (YoY)

```
*===========================================;
*Testing ARCH effect in the S&P 500 Index     ;
*===========================================;
PROC AUTOREG data = SP_data;
Model SP500_YoY = /ARCHtest;  (S8.18)
Run;
Quit;
```

The detection and correction of the volatility of a time series is important, and that is the focus of this section. The ARCH/GARCH approach helps to solve the volatility issue. SAS software offers options to estimate the ARCH/GARCH effect through the PROC AUTOREG command.

SAS code S8.18 is employed to test whether the S&P 500 (year-over-year percent change) has an ARCH effect; that is, whether the variance of the S&P 500 series is constant or not—whether the series has a volatility cluster. The ARCHtest option instructs SAS to perform the ARCH test on the series. The results based on code S8.18 are displayed in Table 8.14. The first part of the table shows statistics such as the sum of squared errors (SSE), mean square error (MSE), and Schwarz Bayesian Criterion (SBC), and the last part of the table provides estimated coefficients of the S&P 500 series.[27] The ARCH test results are presented in the middle part of Table 8.14. Two different test results are presented: the LM test proposed by Engle (1982) and the Q test of Mcleod and Li (1983). The null hypothesis of both the LM and Q tests is that there is no ARCH

---

[27] We have discussed these statistics in detail earlier in this chapter; see "The Regression Analysis."

TABLE 8.14 Testing an ARCH Effect for the S&P 500 Index

```
                    The AUTOREG Procedure
              Dependent Variable   SP500_YoY
              Ordinary Least Squares Estimates

    SSE            112445.404   DFE                      389
    MSE             289.06273   Root MSE            17.00185
    SBC            3321.72798   AIC               3317.76183
    MAE            13.0310639   AICC              3317.77214
    MAPE           416.746764   HQC               3319.33403
    Durbin-Watson      0.1122   Regress R-Square    0.0000
                                Total R-Square      0.0000
```

```
        Tests for ARCH Disturbances Based on OLS Residuals

    Order      Q         Pr > Q        LM        Pr > LM

    1       311.3220    <.0001      309.5869     <.0001
    2       528.6380    <.0001      314.2451     <.0001
    3       679.0621    <.0001      314.5042     <.0001
    4       780.6914    <.0001      314.6539     <.0001
    5       847.2200    <.0001      314.6611     <.0001
    6       887.7421    <.0001      314.8296     <.0001
    7       913.9318    <.0001      315.2551     <.0001
    8       932.5913    <.0001      315.2841     <.0001
    9       947.6502    <.0001      315.4514     <.0001
    10      959.7673    <.0001      315.5161     <.0001
    11      970.0790    <.0001      315.6081     <.0001
    12      978.7154    <.0001      315.6538     <.0001
```

```
                    Parameter Estimates

                                Standard          Approx
    Variable     DF   Estimate   Error    t Value  Pr > |t|
    Intercept    1     9.5207    0.8609    11.06    <.0001
```

effect (the variance is constant over time); the alternative is the presence of the ARCH effect (variance is not constant over time). SAS by default produces statistics for LM and Q tests. The p-values of both tests indicate that we reject the null hypothesis of no ARCH effect at the 5 percent level of significance. Put differently, the LM and Q tests support the idea that the S&P 500 series contains the ARCH effect. Implying that the variance is not constant over time and OLS results may provide a spurious conclusion about a statistical analysis using the S&P 500 series.

The results presented in Table 8.14 suggest that the SP500_YoY series has an ARCH effect. In this section we show how the ARCH effect will influence the OLS results. We run a regression equation between the S&P 500 (YoY) and nonfarm employment (YoY) using SAS code S8.19. The results are summarized in Table 8.15.

TABLE 8.15 Testing Employment–S&P500 Relationship Using ARCH/GARCH

Dependent Variable   SP500_YoY

Ordinary Least Squares Estimates

SSE	99698.9562	DFE	388
MSE	256.95607	Root MSE	16.02985
SBC	3280.77221	AIC	3272.83992
MAE	12.6464653	AICC	3272.87093
MAPE	654.080161	HQC	3275.98432
Durbin-Watson	0.1306	Regress R-Square	0.1134
		Total R-Square	0.1134

Parameter Estimates

Variable	DF	Estimate	Standard Error	t Value	Approx Pr > |t|
Intercept	1	5.7989	0.9686	5.99	<.0001
Employment_YoY	1	3.0705	0.4360	7.04	<.0001

Algorithm converged.

GARCH Estimates

SSE	105797.408	Observations	390
MSE	271.27540	Uncond Var	.
Log Likelihood	–1498.8241	Total R-Square	0.0591
SBC	3021.51276	AIC	3005.64817
MAE	12.7508241	AICC	3005.75206
MAPE	529.204607	HQC	3011.93698
		Normality Test	8.7051
		Pr > ChiSq	0.0129

Parameter Estimates

Variable	DF	Estimate	Standard Error	t Value	Approx Pr > |t|
Intercept	1	9.2393	0.5249	17.60	<.0001
Employment_YoY	1	1.0075	0.2420	4.16	<.0001
ARCH0	1	18.2306	2.5391	7.18	<.0001
ARCH1	1	1.0139	0.1974	5.14	<.0001

```
*=======================================================;
*Testing ARCH/GARCH effect for S&P500-employment relationship ;
*=======================================================;
PROC AUTOREG data=SP_data; (S8.19)
Model SP500_YoY = Employment_YoY /garch=(q=1);
Run;
Quit;
```

The first half of Table 8.15 shows results based on OLS not correcting for the ARCH effect. The estimated coefficient for "Employment_YoY" is 3.0705, the "Standard Error" is 0.4360, and the "t-value" is 7.04. The last part of the table provides results corrected for the ARCH effect and thereby more reliable results. The estimated coefficient for the employment series dropped to 1.0075, and the "Standard Error" and t-value are also smaller at 0.2420 and 4.16, respectively.

One key difference is that the magnitude of the relationship between the S&P 500 and the employment data series is smaller when we corrected the estimates for ARCH effect compared to the standard OLS results. For instance, in the case of the OLS results (first half of Table 8.15), the estimated coefficient for employment is 3.0705. That is statistically significant and implies that a 1 percent increase in employment growth may boost the S&P 500 index by 3.0705 percent.[28] When we corrected estimates for the ARCH effect, the employment coefficient (1.0075) is much smaller and indicates that a 1 percent increase in the employment growth rate is associated with 1 percent growth in the S&P 500 index. The basic idea here is that in the presence of the ARCH effect, the estimated coefficients, and their standard errors/t-values tend to get larger than those that are corrected for an ARCH effect.

APPLICATION: DID THE GREAT RECESSION ALTER CREDIT BENCHMARKS?

Despite the Federal Reserve's efforts to spur economic growth through extensive monetary policy, the current recovery has proceeded at a sluggish pace.[29] Reviewing previous recoveries, the pattern of credit and lending has been an essential node in the transmission process of monetary policy. Here we take a statistical approach to review the patterns of bank loan delinquencies, charge-offs, and the loan-to-deposit ratio. We find that in some instances, the pattern of these credit benchmarks has been altered, explaining some of the weakness in monetary policy transmission.

Delinquency Rates: Identifying Change Post-Great Recession

The ability to repay loans is influenced by the economic environment and therefore, as illustrated in Figure 8.4, loan delinquencies follow a predictable

---

[28] Since both series are in growth rate (i.e., year-over-year percentage change), and that why we can interpret results, estimated coefficient, in term of growth rates. That is, a one percentage change in the employment growth is associated with a 1.0075 percentage change in the S&P 500 growth
[29] This section is adapted with permission from John E. Silvia, Azhar Iqbal, and Sarah Watt, "Identifying Change: Did the Great Recession Alter Credit Benchmarks?" Wells Fargo Securities, LLC, March 25, 2013. https://wellsfargoresearch.wachovia.net/Economics/Pages/default.aspx.

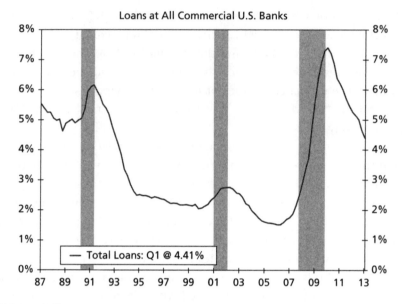

FIGURE 8.4 Delinquecy Rates
Source: Federal Reserve Board and Wells Fargo Securities, LLC

pattern over the business cycle. As would be expected, there is a sharp rise in delinquencies at commercial banks associated with the recessions of 1990–1991, 2000–2001, and 2008–2009. Yet, beyond the typical cyclical pattern, there is a question about the sharp rise in delinquencies through the Great Recession. Was the change in delinquency rates across loan types significantly different? To anticipate, the answer is yes.

Broken down by loan category, data begins in 1987. We split the data sample into two periods: first, the period from 1987 to 2007, and then the entire sample period of 1987 to 2012 to see if the Great Recession had a significant effect on credit patterns. We can test whether there is a behavioral difference between credit categories—such as the degree to which delinquencies rise due to a recession or whether loan delinquencies vary by category in their reaction timing to recessions—by running a regression of the delinquency rates of varying loan types.

Our analysis shows that there was no statistically significant difference in the trends between loan categories from 1987 to 2007, see Table 8.16 for results. However, outcomes differ dramatically when 2007 to 2012 is included in the sample period. The past recession was driven by an imbalance in real estate markets, the residential market in particular. Therefore, the pattern between real estate and other loan types has been significantly altered and suggests that credit in these sectors may now function differently. Real estate delinquencies are now statistically different from consumer and commercial and industrial (C&I) loan delinquencies.

TABLE 8.16 Testing Delinquency Rates Behavior over Two Different Time Periods

Delinquency Trends			
Relationship	Mean Estimate	t-Value	Pr > t
1987–2007			
Consumer - Real Estate	0.12	0.65	0.5186
C&I - Real Estate	−0.13	−1.24	0.2193
C&I - Consumer	−0.25	−1.53	0.1288
1987–2012			
Consumer - Real Estate	−0.71	−3.02	0.0032
C&I - Real Estate	−1.15	−4.93	<.0001
C&I - Consumer	−0.44	−3.13	0.0023

It is a simple regression analysis and an earlier part of this chapter discusses about a regression analysis.

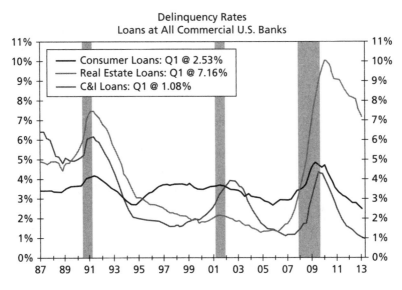

FIGURE 8.5 Delinquency and Charge-Offs
Source: Federal Reserve Board and Wells Fargo Securities, LLC

In addition, the relationship between C&I and consumer loan delinquencies has changed over time as C&I delinquency rates have tracked lower than consumer loans since the mid-2000s (see Figure 8.5). This difference is statistically significant and would support the view that C&I portfolios are stronger at this stage of the business cycle.

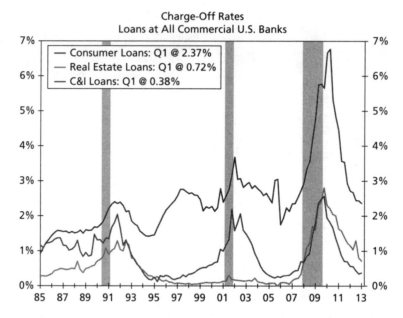

FIGURE 8.6 Charge-Off Rates
Source: Federal Reserve Board and Wells Fargo Securities, LLC

For the credit officer as well as the investor, there is a new playing field here in credit—at least for the time being. This would be a good time to evaluate our credit benchmarks in recognition of the difference in delinquency rates and perhaps adjust our credit criteria.

Patterns in Charge-Off Rates: Identifying Differences in the Character of Trends

Similarly, some patterns in charge-off rates have also changed. While charge-offs also exhibit a distinct cyclical pattern, charge-offs for consumer loans appear to also have a gentle upward slope over time (see Figure 8.6). Are these patterns statistically significant and, if so, should we incorporate this information in our credit modeling? Yes, on both counts, see Table 8.17 for results.

For details about a time trend estimation, see Chapter 6.

The uptrend in consumer loan charge-offs through the past three business cycles is consistent with the impression that over the past 30 years, credit availability has improved for many households (see Figure 8.7). However, with that availability, credit quality appears to have declined, therefore leading to higher charge-offs—particularly for consumer loans.

Breakdown of the Monetary Policy Transmission Mechanism

Recent years have brought forth a debate on the effectiveness of monetary policy. This debate focuses on the substantial increase in the Federal Reserve's

TABLE 8.17 Identifying a Time Trend in Charge-off Rates

Time Trends in Loan Charge-Off Rates			
	Mean Estimate	t-Value	P > t	Trend Type
Real Estate				Nonlinear/U-shaped
Intercept	1.15	8.09	0.001	
Time	−0.04	−7.15	0.001	
Time-square	0.00	8.46	0.001	
C&I				Nonlinear/U-shaped
Intercept	1.27	7.38	0.001	
Time	−0.02	−2.93	0.0042	
Time-square	0.00	3.06	0.0028	
Consumer				Linear
Intercept	1.31	8.32	0.001	
Time	0.02	9.51	0.001	

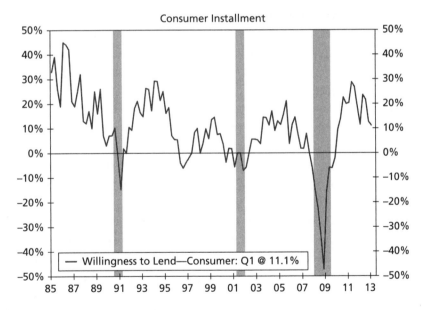

FIGURE 8.7 Banks' Willingness to Make Loans
Source: Federal Reserve Board and Wells Fargo Securities, LLC

balance sheet, the commensurate increase in excess bank reserves and yet only a modest rise in bank lending (see Figure 8.8). Bank lending has indeed risen since the recession ended—up 11 percent at commercial banks since bottoming three years ago. Yet the extent of the rise compared to the rise in bank

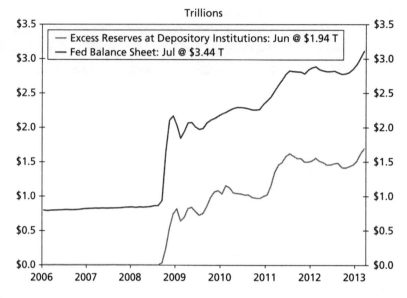

FIGURE 8.8   Federal Reserve Balance Sheet
Source: Federal Reserve Board and Wells Fargo Securities, LLC

reserves appears modest. This reflects a greater degree of caution on the part of many banks, evidenced by still tight credit standards, as well as regulatory uncertainty with respect to future capital requirements. This is not unusual as this reflects the pattern of the money multiplier concept. This multiplier varies over the business cycle as lenders and borrowers alternate between periods of caution and exuberance.[30]

Figure 8.9 provides an illustration of the breakdown in the money multiplier process associated with the Great Recession of 2008–2009. Here the banking system witnessed a sharp drop in the ratio of loans to deposits, thereby reducing the money multiplier as banks are not turning over deposits into loans at a pace that was associated with the 1985 to 2007 period. Is this latest period a statistical break with the past?

It is clear from Figure 8.9 that the loan-to-deposit ratio in the current economic expansion is distinct from previous expansionary periods. Testing for a structural break confirms that this period is indeed different, see Table 8.18 for results. The loan-to-deposit ratio experienced a significant shift downward between the second and fourth quarter of 2009. This change has likely diminished the effectiveness of monetary policy since 2010 and would help explain the simultaneous existence of a very large Fed balance sheet, a large pool of bank excess reserves, and yet only a modest increase in bank loans. Such is the price of uncertainty in a post–Great Recession economy.

---

[30]See N. Gregory Mankiw (2010), *Macroeconomics*, 7th ed. (New York: Worth), pp. 551–553, and especially his discussion on the money multiplier experience during the 1930s.

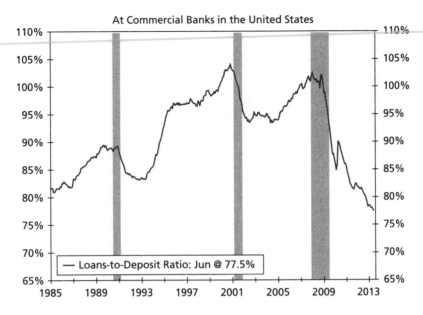

FIGURE 8.9 Loan-to-Deposit Ratio
Source: Federal Reserve Board and Wells Fargo Securities, LLC

TABLE 8.18 Identifying Structural Break(s) in the Loan-to-Ratio

Structural Break in the Loan-to-Deposit Ratio			
Break Date	Break Type	Coefficient	Pr > ChiSq
Q2 2010	Level Shift	5.8486	<.0001
Q4 2008	Add, Outlier	1.756	<.0002
Q3 2009	Level Shift	−1.7427	0.0033
Q2 2009	Level Shift	−1.4849	0.0123
Q4 2009	Level Shift	−1.4729	0.013

Note, we employ the state-space approach to test structural breaks in the Loan-to-Deposit Ratio. See Chapter 7 for details about the state-space approach.

SUMMARY

This chapter provides applications of several econometric techniques, including useful tips for an applied time series analysis and econometric techniques to determine a statistical relationship between variables of interest.

An analyst can start with a simple econometric analysis by estimating correlation and regression analysis for the underlying variables. In the next step, cointegration and ECM tests should be utilized to determine a statistical relationship between variables of interest. One reason is that most time series data are nonstationary at level form and regression and correlation results are not reliable in the case of nonstationary. Cointegration and ECM provide reliable results. For decision makers, it is important to determine the direction of the relationship, particularly which variable is leading and which one is lagging. Financial data series mostly suffer with the volatility cluster. To obtain meaningful results, we suggest utilizing the ARCH approach.

The final point we stress here is that the decision of what econometric techniques to utilize is dependent on the objective of the study. Therefore, familiarity with all of these techniques would be helpful in determining which technique is more suitable to fulfill the requirement.

CHAPTER 9

The 10 Commandments of Applied Time Series Forecasting for Business and Economics

One of the most important elements of today's decision-making world, in both the public and the private sectors, is the forecasting of macroeconomic and financial variables. For instance, the key driver of borrowing costs is short-term interest rates. The Federal Reserve Board's federal funds target rate, the primary short-term interest rate, has been around 0 to 0.25 percent for more than four years (December 2008 to the time of this writing, July 2013). Decision makers thus ask: How much longer will the Fed leave rates low? Although several factors influence the Fed's decisions on rates, the two main economic factors are inflation and unemployment.[1] The Fed may begin to raise the federal funds target rate if (a) inflation expectations for the next one and two years continuously stay above its inflation target of 2 percent and/ or (b) the unemployment rate falls below 6.5 percent.[2] Accurate forecasts of

---

[1]For more details, see John Taylor, (1994), "The Inflation/Output Variability Trade-off Revisited," Conference series, Federal Reserve Bank of Boston.

[2]Janet Yellen, (2013), "A Painfully Slow Recovery for America's Workers: Causes, Implications, and the Federal Reserve's Response," February 11, Washington, DC.

inflation and unemployment can help a decision maker predict the likelihood of a rate hike by the Fed.

During the past few decades, econometric model-based forecasting has become very popular in the private and the public decision-making process. In this chapter, we present 10 commandments of applied time series forecasting that an analyst should learn. These commandments, in our opinion, help produce accurate forecasts. The commandments are:

1. Know What You Are Forecasting

2. Understand the Purpose of Forecasting

3. Acknowledge the Cost of the Forecast Error

4. Rationalize the Forecast Horizon

5. Understand the Choice of Variables

6. Rationalize the Forecasting Model Used

7. Know How to Present the Results

8. Know How to Decipher the Forecast Results

9. Understand the Importance of Recursive Methods

10. Understand Forecasting Models Evolve over Time

Our discussion is based on "Six Considerations Basic to Successful Forecasting" in *Elements of Forecasting* by Francis Diebold and *A Companion to Economic Forecasting* by M. P. Clements and David F. Hendry.[3]

COMMANDMENT 1: KNOW WHAT YOU ARE FORECASTING

> If one does not know to which port one is sailing, no wind is favorable.
> —Seneca

An analyst must know what he or she is going to forecast, because everything depends on it: the appropriate forecast method and the potential cost to forecasting (the forecast error). We divide a forecast objective into four broad groups:

1. Event's Uncertain Outcome Forecast, Certain Timing
   The first category of forecasting is the event's outcome forecast when timing is known. For instance, the U.S. Bureau of Labor Statistics (BLS) releases every month the nation's employment report containing the change to nonfarm payrolls and the unemployment rate. The change in the nonfarm payroll number is a key driver of the financial market.

---

[3]Francis Diebold (2007), *Elements of Forecasting* (Mason, OH: Thomson South-Western); and M. P. Clements and David F. Hendry (2001), *A Companion to Economic Forecasting* (Malden, MA: Wiley-Blackwell).

A forecaster knows the timing of the event and the release of nonfarm payroll numbers, but he or she doesn't know the outcome of the event— have payrolls stayed the same, have they increased or decreased, and by how much? This category of forecast objective is common in economic and business forecasting.

2. Timing of the Event Uncertain, Outcome Known

The second category of forecasting objective is to forecast the timing of the event when the outcome is known. For instance, in business cycle analysis, a forecaster knows the next phase of the event but does not know when it will begin. This type of forecasting is less frequent than the first category of forecasting but is very important. Policy makers and business leaders give considerable weight to business cycle analysis in their decision-making process. For example, government spending usually increases during a recession as they try to fill the gap left by the private sector. In addition, the Fed cuts its target rate.[4] Another example is the behavior of the Standard & Poor's (S&P) 500 index. During a recession, the S&P 500 index usually trends down, but at some point the S&P 500 index will come back. The timing of such a reversal, however, is unknown. A forecaster may want to forecast the timing of the bull or bear market or the next recession.

3. Bubble Forecast

The third forecast objective, and the one that we believe is the hardest part of forecasting, is to forecast asset bubbles.[5] Because of the negative implications, we want to forecast most bubbles and know when (the timing of the event) and where (in which sector) the bubble will take place. We do not know when we will experience the next bubble or in which sector it will occur. Therefore, the timing, the location and the outcome of the event are all unknown.

4. Time Series Forecast

A common objective in economics and business is to forecast for a particular time period, such as predicting gross domestic product (GDP) over the next eight quarters. Often we know the timing of the event. In this case, we know when the Bureau of Economic Analysis (BEA) will release the next quarterly GDP data and wish to forecast the outcome of the event—the expectations of GDP values for the next eight quarters.

---

[4] It is not a necessary condition, but most of the time it happens. The point we want to make here is that the Fed and the government work differently during the phases of the business cycle.

[5] Stiglitz (1990) defined a bubble in this way: "If the reason that the price is high today only because investors believe that the selling price will be high tomorrow and fundamental factors do not seem to justify such a price then a bubble exits." For more details, see Joseph Stiglitz, (1990), "Symposium on Bubbles," *Journal of Economics Perspectives* 4, no. 2. 13–18.

COMMANDMENT 2: UNDERSTAND THE PURPOSE OF FORECASTING

Once we know our forecast objective (what we are going to forecast), then the natural question would be: What is the cost of getting it wrong? What is the forecast loss function? We believe that there is a bridge between forecast objective and forecast error, and the bridge is: Why forecast? Forecast loss functions depend on two elements: the forecast objective and the reasons for forecasting.[6]

Let's pretend there are two forecasters, A and B. Both have the same objective, which is to identify when the recovery phase of a recession will begin. It is an event timing forecast, with the event outcome, the beginning of the recovery phase, known. Let us assume forecaster A is a firm manager. His firm produces consumer goods that have the pro-cyclical behavior of higher demand in a recovery and expansion and less demand in a recession. The firm forecasts for an economic recovery and produces a large number of products, assuming higher-than-normal demand this season. The economy, however, does not recover, and the firm cannot sell all its products, thereby incurring a loss. Forecaster B, in contrast, is an independent forecaster and forecasts frequently. She believes that once she predicts a recovery correctly, she will receive recognition from the media and forecasting peers; if wrong, there will be no tangible consequences. As a result, she will continue to forecast, even if previous forecasts missed the timing. Forecaster A, compared to the Forecaster B, does not have the luxury of missing the forecast often.

COMMANDMENT 3: ACKNOWLEDGE THE COST OF THE FORECAST ERROR

The third commandment stresses that a forecaster must know the cost of forecast error. Forecasters rarely predict the actual number, so there are forecast errors. For example, Forecaster A projects next quarter's real GDP growth rate as 3.5 percent and Forecaster B sees a rate of 1.5 percent. The BEA releases the real GDP growth rate, which is 2.5 percent. Both forecasters are wrong. However, Forecaster A's 3.5 percent growth rate is higher than the actual growth rate; he has over-forecasted. Forecaster B, who predicted a 1.5 percent growth rate, under-forecasted the rate of real GDP growth. These are the two types of forecast errors (the difference between the actual and the forecasted) we may face. Every forecast error is associated with a cost. The question is whether the cost of over-forecasting is the same as the cost of under-forecasting.

---

[6]See the next section for more details about a loss function.

Set Y as the actual value of the target variable, GDP growth rate for example, and $\hat{Y}$ as the forecast of Y.[7]

$$e = Y - \hat{Y} \tag{9.1}$$

where

e = forecast error

$e = 0$ means that the forecast is equal to the actual

$e \neq 0$ indicates the forecast is different from the actual

If both Y and $\hat{Y}$ are greater than 0, then $e > 0$ implies under-forecasting and $e < 0$ implies over-forecasting.

Over time an analyst would produce several forecasts for a variable; that is, one-quarter-ahead GDP growth rate forecasting during the 2006:Q1 to 2012:Q4 period implies 28 forecasts.[8] The e_t is the forecast error for each period and if we aggregate errors from each period then we can call it $L(e_t)$ which indicates the total cost associated with the forecast errors, e_t, and is known as the loss function.

$$e_t = Y_t - \hat{Y}_t$$
$$L(e_t) = \text{Total cost associated with forecast errors} \tag{9.2}$$

where

e_t = forecast error for each quarter time series

Y_t = actual values of the GDP growth rate during the 2006:Q1 to 2012:Q4 period time series

$\hat{Y}_t$ = forecasts for the Y_t during that time period

Symmetric versus Asymmetric Loss Function

The loss function, $L(e_t)$, indicates the cost of being wrong. If we rephrase our previous question in terms of a loss function, then if the loss function is identical, it is a symmetrical loss function. A symmetric loss function implies that $e_t > 0$ (under-forecasting) and $e_t < 0$ (over-forecasting) are both associated with an identical total loss. A simple example of a symmetric loss function would be forecasting the experience of a small firm that produces consumer goods. In a regular season, the firm sells 100,000 units, with a per-unit profit of $2.00. Unsold units would have to be stored at the cost of $2.00 per unit. We generate two scenarios to show a symmetric loss.

Scenario 1: The firm forecasts for a regular season demand and expects to sell 100,000 units. The economy experienced a strong recovery increasing

[7]Here a forecast implies out-of-sample forecast of the target variable. We use forecast/forecasted and predicted throughout this chapter; both represent out-of-sample forecasts.

[8]There are 28 quarters during that time period. The forecast for each of the 28 quarters indicates a time series of forecast $\hat{Y}_t$.

demand for an additional 25,000 units, thus creating a total demand of 125,000 units (100,000 + 25,000). The firm has thus under-forecasted demand and missing the opportunity to profit an additional $50,000 (25,000 units × $2.00 per unit).

Scenario 2: The firm forecasts for a strong economic recovery and produces an additional 25,000 units for a total of 125,000 units. The season turned out to be a normal year, and the firm sells only 100,000 units, with 25,000 units stored at a total cost of $50,000 ($2.00 per unit). The firm over-forecasted the demand, producing a loss of $50,000.[9]

Net, the firm suffers a $50,000 loss in both cases.

The symmetric loss function is not the only possibility. The loss function can be asymmetric, implying that the loss from under-forecasting, $e_t > 0$, is not identical to the loss from over-forecasting, $e_t < 0$. In reality, loss functions are most often asymmetric. We again follow the above example but this time assume that the loss function is asymmetric. Suppose another storage facility opens in the town and charges only $1.00 per unit. Assuming the same scenarios as above, in the first scenario the firm expects to sell 100,000 units when the actual demand is 125,000 units, missing out on $50,000 in additional profits.

In the second scenario, the firm forecasts for demand of 125,000 units but can sell only 100,000 units. However, with the new storage facility that costs only $1.00 per unit, the firm's over-forecasting cost is only $25,000. Therefore, the cost of under-forecasting (a lost opportunity of additional profit of $50,000) is higher than the cost to over-forecasting (storage cost of $25,000).

Here is another example of an asymmetric loss function. In the leisure and hospitality industry, it is important to forecast the number of visitors. Let us assume the number of visitors a hotel expects to host over the next month is 2,000. The hotel's manager makes arrangements for 2,000 visitors. If the number of visitors exceeds that number, the arrangements will not be enough. The hotel may lose some business, and many visitors may be unhappy with their stay. Under-forecasting may lead to customer dissatisfaction. But over-forecasting will lead to monetary loss as the firm makes unnecessary arrangements. This hotel places greater importance on customer satisfaction than on monetary loss; therefore, the loss function is not symmetric.

Linear versus Nonlinear Loss Function

Up to this point we have discussed the cost associated with being wrong in forecasting. Another important issue would be whether the loss function is

---

[9]It is important to note that there are other consequences of both under- and over-forecasting, such as reputation loss; for example, if customers could not buy the firm's product, they may not come back the next time. But, for simplicity's sake, we assume monetary cost only. Furthermore, in case of a perfect forecast, the firm would not lose potential profit or pay storage costs.

linear (the cost of each unit of forecast error is the same) or nonlinear (the cost varies between forecast errors). For instance, from the last example, the hotel predicts that 2,000 people will visit next month, but 500 more people arrive than expected. Now the question is: Among those additional 500 people, does each impose the same loss to the firm? To answer this question, we generate two scenarios. First let us assume that each additional family costs $100. The hotel's loss is thus $50,000 (500 × $100). Since the cost of each forecast error is identical, the loss function illustrates a linear cost function. Now let us assume that the first additional family costs $100, the second family costs $102, the third family $105, and so on, and each unit of forecast error has a higher cost than the previous error. This is an example of a nonlinear cost function.

A further nuance is that we may want to determine if the linearity of the loss function is the same for under-forecasting and over-forecasting, or if the two scenarios have two different forms of a loss function. The simple cases are (1) a linear loss function for both under-forecast and over-forecast and (2) a nonlinear loss function for both under-forecast and over-forecast. The complex case would be, for example, a linear loss function for under-forecast but a nonlinear loss function for over-forecast, and vice versa. For example, the hotel forecasts 2,000 visitors, but only 1,500 visitors show, leading to an over-forecast of 500 families. Each missing visitor costs $50 to the hotel with a total loss of $25,000: a linear loss function. If the hotel forecasts 2,000 visitors but actually there were 2,500, there is an under-forecast of 500 visitors. Each extra visitor costs $100 with a total loss of $50,000, again a linear loss function. Overall, the hotel has an asymmetric loss, where the loss from over-forecasting is different from the loss of under-forecasting.

Another possibility of loss function would be an asymmetric nonlinear loss function. A simple example: The forecast for visitors was 2,000, and only 1,500 families showed (over-forecasting). Each missing family costs $50 for a total loss of $25,000. In the case of under-forecast, 2,500 families visit while the forecast was 2,000 families, and each family costs more than the prior family. This would be a nonlinear asymmetric loss function scenario.

To sum up this section, a forecaster must know whether their loss function is (1) symmetric or asymmetric, (2) linear or nonlinear, (3) symmetric and linear or nonlinear, or (4) asymmetric and linear or nonlinear.

COMMANDMENT 4: RATIONALIZE THE FORECAST HORIZON

The fourth commandment of the economic and business forecasting states that a forecaster must consider the forecast horizon and realize that accuracy depends on that horizon. Simply put, the forecast horizon is how far out we are looking to forecast. Do we want a daily forecast of the S&P 500 index? A weekly forecast of initial jobless claims? Or a monthly forecast of the unemployment rate? The forecast horizon can be one day or up to several years. We can divide the forecast horizon into short-term forecasting (usually up to two years in most macroeconomics applications) and long-term forecasting (typically for utility and energy development application). The reason for this division is that short-term forecasting requires different treatments from long-term forecasting.

Short-Term Forecasting

Broadly speaking, short-term forecasting is for a short time period in which the chance of a big change (structural change, regime shift, policy change, etc.) is very low. For instance, a one-month-ahead forecast of the S&P 500 index or a firm's forecast for next quarter's earnings would not likely be subject to a significant structural change in the model. During short-term forecasting we may see some significant change—a natural disaster, for instance—but chances are less likely when compared to a long-term forecast.

Long-Term Forecasting

When forecasting for a long time period (at least a couple of years ahead), the chances of significant changes are very high. For instance, the forecast of the S&P 500 index beyond the next two years is not easy because of the high probability of a significant change in the model for equity returns. During January 2008, the U.S. economy was in recession and the S&P 500 index remained in bearish territory. Let us assume we were sitting in January 2008 and making a two-year-out forecast for the S&P 500 index. This forecast would be difficult because if the recession not only ended in 2008 but was followed by a strong recovery, then the S&P 500 index may quickly turn bullish.[10] One thing is clear: Longer-term forecasting is associated with higher uncertainty than a shorter-term forecast horizon is.

The challenge for forecasters is that the longer the forecast horizon, the degree of confidence in that forecast declines and the range of possible outcomes rises. The magnitude of the forecast error tends to increase as we lengthen the forecast horizon. A forecaster thus must know about the forecast horizon and whether it is short term or long term. He or she also must be aware that the definition of short-term and long-term is subjective and varies with respect to the subject.

An important point an analyst should keep in mind during the modeling for long-term forecasting is that many macroeconomic variables behave differently during different phases of a business cycle. The U.S. unemployment rate tends to rise during recessions and fall during expansions. A forecaster interested in

---

[10]The recovery from the 2007 to 2009 recession turned out to be weaker than the historical standard. The S&P 500 index was 1,242 on December 2010, which was lower than the January 2008 level of 1,379.

forecasting the unemployment rate for the next six to eight years should consider business cycle movements because the average business cycle duration, defined as trough to trough post–World War II, is around 70 months. Another important consideration is policy change. Political parties have different tax and spending preferences, and which party is in power can affect long-term forecasting. The possibility of a structural change, due to internal or external shocks, is higher during long-term forecasting than during short-term prediction.[11]

COMMANDMENT 5: UNDERSTAND THE CHOICE OF VARIABLES

Once a forecaster has determined his or her forecast objective, loss function, and forecast horizon, the next step is the choice of the variables or available information set to build a forecasting model. For instance, what are the appropriate datasets and econometric tools for forecasting? In this section we discuss the data choice and issues related to the dataset. In the next section we focus on the methodology.

The dataset can be divided into two categories: (1) the variable we want to forecast—the dependent variable, and (2) the variables that help us to forecast—the independent variables (the predictors).

First, a forecaster must have a comprehensive understanding about the dependent variable. For instance, what is the source of the data—are you compiling external datasets or internal sources (like revenue and sales)? What is the frequency of the data: weekly, monthly, quarterly, or annual? You should also know the history of the dependent variable and how far the data collection goes back. The longer the history, the better. The next step is to find out what sort of independent variables are available. There are issues related with the choice of independent variables as well. The choice of independent variables depends on the forecast horizon (whether long term or short term), release date, frequency of the variables, and history of the variables.

Some examples show how the choice of the dataset varies with the objective of forecasting. The first example involves a small firm that produces consumer products and sells them only in North Carolina. The firm's manager wants to build a forecasting model to predict next season's demand, a short-term forecast for one period ahead. In addition, the market area consists of only one state, so the chance of economic shocks and uncertainty is small. The forecasting model thus would rely heavily on North Carolina–specific variables, such as state employment and state personal income, which are potential predictors for consumers demand.

---

[11] The section "Commandment 7: Know How to Present the Results" discusses a measure of calculating the forecast interval that can be used to present forecast results for long-term forecasting.

Another example involves economists at the Federal Reserve Board interested in building an econometric model to predict the overall U.S. economic performance for the next five years, a long-term forecast. During such a lengthy period, the probability of shocks is high, increasing the forecast uncertainty. This model would contain information from major sectors of the economy (i.e., variables representing consumers, investors, government, housing, and labor). The United States is an open economy, and international trade is also an essential element of the economy. Some measures of the world economy would need to be included in the model. In sum, in long-term forecasting, we often need to include more information in the models and consider the possibility of shocks and uncertainty.

An analyst must also consider how many predictors should be included in a forecast model. The answer, to some extent, depends on the forecasting objective. In short-term forecasting, the most recent information of predictors is a key to successful forecasting. Typically, five to seven variables are included as predictors.[12] In long-term forecasting, however, an analyst may want to include more variables to ensure the model captures the wide range of factors that may influence the target variable(s) over an extended period.

There is a balance. We want to include important information in the model, but, at the same time, we should not include too many variables in a traditional econometric modeling framework because that creates over-fitting and/or degree-of-freedom issues. But excluding essential predictors would lead to under-fitting, which reduces the predictive power of the model.[13]

COMMANDMENT 6: RATIONALIZE THE FORECASTING MODEL USED

The sixth commandment emphasizes selecting an econometric method for the forecasting. There are a number of econometric tools commonly used in today's time series forecasting world. Each econometric method has some advantages and some limitations. We suggest selecting an econometric method consistent with the forecasting objective.[14] Here are a few examples that show different forecasting techniques that can be used for different forecasting objectives.

Suppose an analyst is interested in forecasting the daily closing value of the S&P 500 index. There is not much economic information available with a daily frequency that can be included in a forecasting model, and it is not clear that much of this economic information has an impact on equity prices. One standard

---

[12]For a detailed discussion about the role of predictors in forecasting, see Chapter 11.

[13]It is known as the specification error. For a detailed discussion of this error, see R. Pindyck and Daniel Rubinfeld (2000), *Econometric Models and Economic Forecasts*, 4th ed. (New York: McGraw-Hill), pp. 128–133.

[14]For details about the econometric techniques, see Chapters 4 and 5.

econometric tool used in these kinds of scenarios is the ARIMA model.[15] In contrast, to predict a monthly data series, such as a one-month-forward forecast for unemployment, an analyst could use the econometric technique known as the vector autoregressive (VAR) approach, which uses economic variables as potential predictors (e.g., interest rates and inflation).[16] Forecasting the daily close of the S&P and the monthly unemployment rate represent a short-term forecasting approach that uses two different models. The difference between the approaches, however, is that in case of the unemployment rate forecasting, the model includes economic predictors, and the forecast is based on these predictors.

A final example represents the long-term forecasting experience: a five-year-ahead forecast of the U.S. GDP growth rate. Two econometric methods are commonly used for long-term forecasting. First, a macroeconometric model, also known as a structural model, includes hundreds of variables. This model is purely based on economic relationships that reflect economic theory. A system of equations is built based on economic theory and then estimated simultaneously with the help of econometric techniques, such as two-stage least square (2SLS).[17] A benefit of this approach is that much information can be included in the model, but one limitation is that we have to estimate sometimes hundreds of equations. The alternative to the large-scale macroeconometric model is the VAR.[18] Typically in a VAR model, we include eight or more variables representing major sectors of an economy, implicitly assuming that everything depends on everything.[19] VAR modeling, relative to the macroeconometric models, is easy to estimate; that is one reason why it is commonly used in forecasting.

Summing up, there are number of econometric techniques commonly used to forecast economic and financial variables. We suggest selecting a technique that is consistent with the forecasting objective. The approach, in our view, should not be too technical/heavily mathematical and ignores economic theory or practical realities, or too simple and ignores the econometric principles. The appropriate approach is nicely summarized by Diebold (2007) and is known as the KISS principle: "Keep it sophisticatedly simple."[20]

---

[15]The autoregressive integrated moving average (ARIMA) model usually does not need predictors to forecast a time series. This approach characterizes a time series and then forecasts the series without including additional variables/predictors. The ARIMA approach is also known as an atheoretical model because it is not based on an economic or financial theory. For more details about the ARIMA model, see Chapters 4 and 10 (for a forecasting application).

[16]For a detailed discussion and forecasting application of the VAR approach, see Chapter 11.

[17]One template for the macroeconometric model is Ray Fair, (2004), *Estimating How the Macroeconomy Works* (Cambridge, MA: Harvard University Press).

[18]The VAR approach can be used for both long-term and short-term forecasting. For more details, see Christopher Sims (1980), "Macroeconomics and Reality," *Econometrica* 48, no. 1: 1–48.

[19]It is important to note that we can include more/less than eight variables; it depends on a researcher's objective.

[20]Diebold (2007).

COMMANDMENT 7: KNOW HOW TO PRESENT THE RESULTS

An analyst can summarize and present forecasting results in different ways and which way is better depends on the objective of the forecast. That is, the results can be summarized into a single number (known as point forecast), a range of numbers (an interval forecast), probability distribution of the number (density forecast), probability of an event (probability forecast), and conditional forecasting (scenario-based analysis).

A point forecast is a widely used approach in both the private and the public sectors. An example of a point forecast is when analysts predict a 2 percent (a single number) GDP growth rate for the next quarter. The major benefit of this approach is that it is easy to present, understand, and digest. However, it would be better to provide a range of the forecast—in the 1.5 to 2.5 percent range (an interval forecast) since a point forecast suggests a degree of preciseness seldom achieved in forecasting. Typically, a specific level of confidence is attached with the forecast interval, that is, a forecaster is 95 percent confident that the actual GDP growth rate would fall in the 1.5 to 2.5 percent range. There are greater chances that the actual number would fall in the range than that the point forecast would match the actual number. So the interval forecast provides more information than the point forecast, but the interval forecast also requires more calculation (i.e., estimation of the 95 percent confidence interval).

Another way to present forecast results is to provide the entire probability distribution of the forecast, termed a density forecast. We assume that the forecast is normally distributed with a mean μ and standard deviation σ. The 95 percent confidence interval (a forecast interval) can be calculated as $\mu \pm 1.96\sigma$, and the entire probability distribution (different confidence levels, 90 or 99 percent, etc.) of the forecast is called the density forecast.[21] The difference between an interval forecast and a density forecast is that an interval forecast attaches with one confidence level (in the present case, 95 percent) and a density forecast indicates any desired confidence level. Put differently, the 2 percent GDP growth rate is a point forecast, 2 ± 0.5 (the 1.5–2.5 percent range) is interval forecast (we attach 95 percent confidence interval to that range), and the complete probability distribution (any desired confidence level) of the forecast is the density forecast. The density forecast provides more detail than the point and interval forecast, but it also requires a lot of simulation, which is one reason the density forecast is not commonly used in the forecasting world.

There are a couple of other ways to present forecast results, and one is the probability forecast (i.e., the probability of an event's occurrence). A common example of the probability forecast is the recession probability—for example, the six-month forward probability of a recession is 20 percent. One way to predict a recession is to build a Probit model and produce a recession

---

[21] For more details about the interval and density forecast, see Chapter 3 of note 20.

probability.[22] The probability forecast is different from a point forecast in the sense that the probability forecast states the probability of an event's occurrence (the probability of a recession) and the point forecast is a single number (forecast for a GDP growth rate).[23]

An increasingly popular way to present forecast results is known as scenario-based analysis—for example, different possible paths of the GDP growth rate for the next three years would be (1) mild growth rates scenario (e.g., less than 1 percent growth rate); (2) possibility of *normal* growth rates in the range of 2 to 3 percent; and (3) a path of strong (over 3.5 percent) growth rates. Scenario-based forecasting is gaining attention because of its flexibility and ability to provide opportunities for decision makers to consider different possible outcomes of economic growth. Remember, scenario-based forecasting is different from interval forecasts in the sense that scenarios are conditioned on the predictors and represent different paths of the target variable. Interval forecasts, however, state a range of forecasts, which usually represent just one possible path because it conditioned on only one set of predictors' values.

Summing up, point forecasting is good for short-term (one period ahead) forecasting and for medium-term forecasting (one year ahead), while interval and density forecasting provide a wider range of outcomes and better represent the possible range of real-world outcomes. At the same time, point forecasting is relatively easier to estimate than interval forecasting, and interval forecasting is easier to calculate than density forecasting. In the case of an event's timing (we know the outcome but the timing of the event is unknown) or event's outcome (we know the timing of the event but outcome is unknown) forecasting, probability forecasting is a better option. For long-term forecasting (more than a few years ahead) and policy making, scenario-based forecasting is a better approach.

COMMANDMENT 8: KNOW HOW TO DECIPHER THE FORECAST RESULTS

As mentioned, it is extremely difficult to predict the point outcome perfectly every time, and the possibility of a nonzero forecast error is often high. In the case of a time series forecast, where an analyst produces a forecast on a regular basis, forecast errors can be represented by a time series. For example, from 2008 to 2012, we submitted forecasts for the unemployment rate to Bloomberg for every month. If we calculate our forecast errors for that time period, we get

---

[22]In the case of a Probit model, the dependent variable is a dummy variable that has a value of either zero or one. Typically, if the economy is in recession, then the dummy equals one; otherwise it equals zero. For more details, see J. Silvia, S. Bullard, and L. Huiwen (2008), "Forecasting U.S. Recessions with Probit Stepwise Regression Models," *Business Economics* 43, no. 1.7–18.

[23]In some ways, both a point forecast and a probability forecast provide a single number, but the interpretation and ideas behind the numbers make these two approaches different from each other (i.e., a forecast of 2 percent GDP growth rate versus the 20 percent probability of a recession).

a time series that consists of our forecast errors, which we will call e_t. The e_t contains 60 observations (60 months of forecast). Some are zero (in the case of a perfect forecast), positive (under-forecasting), and negative (over-forecasting). Given the fact that we do not perfectly forecast the unemployment rate every time, what we need is to estimate two measures of the forecast error: (1) What is the average forecast error? (2) On average, how many times did we predict the direction of the change correctly (directional accuracy)?

There are several benefits to calculating these two statistics. One major benefit is that the average forecast error indicates the average deviation of the forecast from the actual reported outcome and can be utilized to calculate the forecast interval. For instance, the average forecast error for the unemployment rate model is 0.2 percent. If the model predicts an 8.0 percent unemployment rate for the next month, the forecast interval would be 7.8 to 8.2 percent (forecast ± average forecast error). The average forecast error can also be employed as a benchmark to select or compare different models or two or more subsamples for the model. From the example of the unemployment rate model, at the end of 2009, we can calculate the average forecast error for 2009 and compare it with the average forecast error for 2008. If the model for 2009 produces a smaller average forecast error than the model for 2008, we can say the model performs better in 2009 than it does in 2008, all else being equal. If we want to select one model among competitors, the model with the smallest average forecast error would be our choice.

Directional accuracy provides several benefits as well. Let us assume that the directional accuracy of the unemployment rate model is 80 percent (80 percent of the time, the model correctly predicted the direction of the actual number), and the model predicts an 8.1 percent unemployment rate for the next month, assuming that the current month's unemployment rate is 8.0 percent. The 80 percent directional accuracy shows that there is an 80 percent probability that the unemployment rate would increase during the next month.

So a better way to select a model is to consider both the average forecast error and the directional accuracy measures. A model with the smallest average forecast error and the highest average directional accuracy will be the best among its competitors.

How does an analyst estimate the average forecast error and the average directional accuracy? There are several ways. The out-of-sample root mean square error (RMSE) is utilized as a measure of average forecast error.[24] Equation 9.3 is employed to calculate the RMSE:

$$\text{RMSE} = \sqrt{\frac{1}{t} \sum (Y_{t+1} - \hat{Y}_{t+1})^2} \tag{9.3}$$

---

[24]There are some other ways to calculate forecast error, such as mean absolute error. For a detailed discussion about the forecast error, see Chapter 14 of James Stock and Mark Watson (2007), *Introduction to Econometrics*, 2nd ed. (Boston, MA: Pearson Education).

where

$\hat{Y}_{t+1}$ = one-period-ahead forecast

Y_{t+1} = actual value of the target variable

The magnitude of this statistic indicates the average forecast error over time. Furthermore, a model with a smaller RMSE is the better model among its competitors for a particular variable.

The out-of-sample RMSE is a very good measure of forecast evaluation. However, in practice, and in the financial sector in particular, the direction of the actual variable is also very important since most hedged positions are based on a directional change rather than just the magnitude of the change. To make a financial profit and/or to reduce financial losses, it is imperative to predict the direction of the variable. Since many macroeconomic variables are reported either in percentage change or net change, the sign (positive or negative) of the actual variable is also crucial. Equation 9.4 is used to estimate the directional accuracy:

$$\text{Sign of } Y_{t+1} \equiv \text{Sign of } \hat{Y}_{t+1} \qquad (9.4)$$

where

$\hat{Y}_{t+1}$ = a forecast

Y_{t+1} = actual value of the variable

In addition, if the forecast shares an identical sign (plus or minus) with the actual variable, then the direction is correct. For average directional accuracy, the following equation can be used:

$$(X/N) \times 100$$

where

X = number of forecasts that have the right direction

N = total number of forecasts

We convert the ratio into a percentage by multiplying by 100.[25]

There are a few variables that are alternatively reported in level form such as the unemployment rate, and ISM (the Institure for Supply Management) manufacturing index, and so on. We can use equation 9.5 to compute the directional accuracy of the forecast for those variables:

$$\text{Sign of } (Y_t - Y_{t+1}) \equiv \text{Sign of } (Y_t - \hat{Y}_{t+1}) \qquad (9.5)$$

If the difference between the actual current month and the prior month values $(Y_t - Y_{t+1})$ has the same sign as the difference between the forecast and the actual prior month value of the time series $(Y_t - \hat{Y}_{t+1})$, then the direction

[25] For more details about the importance of the directional accuracy, see John Silvia and Azhar Iqbal (2012), "A Comparison of Consensus and BVAR Macroeconomic Forecasts," *Business Economics* 47, no. 4: 250–261.

of the forecast is correct. From the previous example, if the forecast was 8.1 percent and the actual unemployment rate came in at 8.2 percent, then the model was accurate in terms of direction.

In sum, a forecasting approach just based on the RMSE may not provide the most opportunity for a firm to generate financial gains. The first step to a more accurate forecasting approach would be that the forecast should be close to the actual or have a minimum average forecast error (RMSE). The second step should be that the direction of the forecast would also be accurate (directional accuracy), on average.

COMMANDMENT 9: UNDERSTAND THE IMPORTANCE OF RECURSIVE METHODS

At the end of the eighth commandment, a forecaster would know his or her forecasting objective and loss function, have selected variables of interest and econometric methods, and would be familiar with the forecast evaluation measures. While it seems that he or she is ready to forecast the target variable, we propose one more step in the process of building a forecasting model, especially in time series forecasting. The forecaster should conduct a controlled forecasting experiment, also known as the recursive method, before finalizing a forecasting model. For instance, consider an analyst interested in building a forecasting model for the unemployment rate. He or she has selected the potential predictors as well as an econometric methodology. Let us assume that, for the time series model, the analyst has picked a monthly dataset for the 1980 to 2012 time period. The objective is a one-month-ahead forecast for the unemployment rate.

In a controlled forecasting experiment, we suggest running a regression analysis using the dataset for the January 1980 to December 2005 period and generating a forecast for January 2006.[26] Then we suggest repeating the regression analysis to include January 2006 values; the forecast will be generated for February 2006. Then the regression analysis is repeated to include February 2006 values, and prediction will be made for March 2006, and so on. This recursive method will be repeated until the analyst reaches the sample end point. In this case, November 2012 will be the end point for regression analysis, and the last forecast will be made for December 2012.

The key benefit of this controlled forecasting experiment is that, at the end of the experiment, the analyst will have seven years (January 2006–December 2012) of out-of-sample forecast data and the corresponding actual unemployment rate for that time period. The analyst can then estimate the out-of-sample

---

[26]The important point here is that the analyst will assume that the dataset is only available up to December 2005 and does not know the value of the January 2006 unemployment rate. That way the analyst will produce out-of-sample forecast for unemployment rate.

RMSE and average directional accuracy from that dataset, figures that can be utilized for several purposes. The RMSE and directional accuracy can be employed to select the final model specification, if that is needed. That is, for instance, there are 10 potential predictors, and the analyst is only interested in including 5 predictors in the final model. The set of 5 predictors that produce the smallest RMSE and the highest directional accuracy would be the best model among competitors. The RMSE and directional accuracy would also shed light on the likely average forecast error as well as directional accuracy for the future time period.

The most important choice is the selection of the time period for the controlled forecasting experiment. In the present case, that would be January 2006 to December 2012. Typically, macroeconomic and financial variables perform differently during different phases of a business cycle. A good model should perform accurately during different phases of a business cycle. In the present example, the unemployment rate tends to rise during recessions and falls during expansions, and we want a model that predicts unemployment rates accurately during recessions as well as expansions. The selected time period (January 2006–December 2012) for the experiment represents different phases of a business cycle. January 2006 to November 2007 indicates the pre-recession era, the December 2007 to June 2009 period is associated with the Great Recession, and the post–June 2009 period shows a recovery/expansionary time period. If the model performed accurately during the 2006 to 2012 time period, then an analyst can expect that the model would perform accurately in the future as well.

In sum, we suggest that the final step of a time series forecasting model should include a controlled forecasting experiment. The time period selected for the controlled experiment should include different phases of a business cycle and be able to forecast accurately during different phases of a business cycle.

COMMANDMENT 10: UNDERSTAND FORECASTING MODELS EVOLVE OVER TIME

The last commandment implies that there is no silver bullet in applied time series forecasting. This is a point that is often neglected in traditional forecasting literature. Once a forecasting model is built, all too often a forecaster assumes mission accomplished. Based on personal experience, the actual job is just beginning: The need to evaluate and maintain accuracy of the forecast model continues over time. If a model has been built and is performing accurately, should a forecaster relax and assume it will always remain accurate? The simple answer is *no*. Forecasting models are like sailing a boat; they require constant adjustments to the financial and economic winds and the currents. Many analysts look for a best forecasting model, and once it is found they stop searching. This is wrong. The world changes constantly. A finalized model will almost certainly break down over time, as the economy and the relationships among economic variables evolve. One well-known example is that of the Phillips curve, which found that higher wage inflation was associated with a lower unemployment rate. Although the relationship appeared to work very well during in the 1960s, the model fell apart in the 1970s.[27]

A useful tip to a forecaster, especially in short-term forecasting, is that once a time series forecasting model is finalized, the next procedure should be used to evaluate and maintain its performance. If the forecast missed the direction or the forecast errors are larger than the RMSE for a certain period of time (say, three consecutive months in a monthly dataset), the forecaster should consider revising the model. A best practice is to evaluate all of the models at the end of every year and compare the current year's performance with the previous year's using the real-time out-of-sample RMSE as well as directional accuracy criteria. If a model has a higher RMSE along with a lower directional accuracy compared to the previous year, then the analyst should reconstruct the model using the procedure for controlled forecasting.[28] In practice, analysts must build forecasting models then continuously evaluate their performance and, if necessary, revise the models.

The 2007 to 2010 time period was very tough for time series forecasting. There are several reasons for this: the Great Recession, the oil price spike, the housing market crash, the financial crisis/credit crunch, and different types of stimulus packages. These factors made real-time, short-term forecasting harder, and the life span of many models became shorter than normal.[29]

SUMMARY

In summary, we suggest that time series forecasting has two phases: In the first phase, a forecaster needs to know the forecasting objective and loss function, select the dataset (dependent and independent variables), econometric methodology, and then finalize a model based on the controlled forecasting experiment. In the second phase, a forecaster should continuously monitor and maintain forecasting performance of the models. When the model breaks down, as it eventually will, the forecaster must construct a new model following the approach adopted in the first phase. Because one model specification will not remain accurate forever, and even the best model specification may need to be revised at some point, time series forecasting is an evolving process.

---

[27] During the 1970s, high inflation accompanied by high unemployment was seen to invalidate the Phillips curve. For more details, see David Romer (2006), *Advanced Macroeconomics*, 2nd ed. (New York: McGraw-Hill), pp. 252–258.

[28] The forecaster should first reselect the predictors and, if necessary, the econometric methods, and then finalize the model based on the controlled forecasting experiment.

[29] In a normal time period, a model may produce accurate forecast for a couple of years, but since the 2007 to 2009 recession, we have revised many models.

CHAPTER 10

A Single-Equation Approach to Model-Based Forecasting

Model-based forecasting approaches are essential elements in the process of effective decision making. One major benefit of using these forecasting approaches is that the model can serve as a baseline for adjusting economic guidance for risk assessment, and a model's forecasting performance can be monitored over time to compare expected versus actual outcomes. In addition, a model that is not performing as expected can be revised and rebuilt to improve guidance to decision makers. Decision makers utilize models to generate both long-term and short-term forecasts. The focus of this chapter, however, is on short-term forecasting.[1] We discuss different methods to build forecasting models and describe which method may be appropriate for a forecaster depending on the forecasting objective and on the available data set.

This chapter focuses on single-equation, univariate, forecasting. A univariate model contains one dependent variable and one or more predictors (independent variables). Within a univariate forecasting framework, we discuss two approaches: unconditional and conditional forecasting. With the unconditional forecasting model, we do not need out-of-sample values of predictors to generate an out-of-sample forecast. Conditional forecasting, in contrast, implies that the forecasted values of the dependent variable are conditioned on the predictors' values. Another major difference between unconditional and conditional forecasting is that sometimes unconditional forecasting includes only lags of the dependent variable and error terms as right-hand-side variables.

---

[1] Chapter 12 discusses the long-term forecasting approach.

The conditional forecasting models, however, include additional variables as predictors.

The conditional forecasting approach is divided into two broader categories: (1) when a dependent variable is traditional in form (i.e., the dependent variable can contain any numerical value), and (2) when a dependent variable is nontraditional in the sense that it is a dummy variable (binary variable) and contains only two values, zero and one. The division between these two conditional forecasting approaches reflects different estimation techniques. A model with a dummy-dependent variable is sometimes referred to as a logit or probit model and these models are commonly used to predict the probability of an economic event.

In this chapter, we provide a detailed discussion of unconditional, conditional, and Probit forecasting approaches. We suggest guidelines for the analyst when choosing between the unconditional and the conditional forecasting approach as well provide SAS codes to help generate forecasts.

THE UNCONDITIONAL (ATHEORETICAL) APPROACH

Typically, a forecaster can utilize economic/financial theory to build a model. However, sometimes economic/financial theory is unable to provide guidelines for forecasting for two main reasons: (1) the reliability of an economic theory is questionable (at least in the short-run) and (2) the potential predictors (based on the economic theory) are not available at the desired frequency.

Recently, the Great Recession rendered less reliable several economic theories (at least in the short-run), with one example being Okun's law.[2] Okun's law posits a relationship between the gross domestic product (GDP) growth rate and the unemployment rate. However, the recovery period from the Great Recession does not replicate this relationship, as GDP entered into expansionary territory, surpassing its pre-recession level while the unemployment rate remained stuck at elevated levels for a significant amount of time. This scenario makes a forecaster wonder whether he or she should utilize the GDP growth rate to forecast unemployment rates over the short-run.

Economic/financial theory is also unable to help a forecaster when the desired forecasting frequency of the dependent variable is different from the potential predictors that economic/financial theory suggests are the most appropriate variables. For example, if we wanted to forecast the daily closing price of the Standard & Poor's (S&P) 500 index, it will be hard to find an explanatory variable that is also reported at a daily frequency. Therefore, we may not be able to include valuable predictors in our forecasting model. In this case, the unconditional forecasting approach is a useful tool.

---

[2]For more details on Okun's law, see Gregory Mankiw (2012), *Macroeconomics*, 8th ed. (New York: Worth).

The unconditional forecasting approach includes both the lags of the dependent variable and stochastic error terms as right-hand-side variables. Since there is no economic/financial theory behind the unconditional forecasting approach, it is also known as an atheoretical forecasting approach. The lags of the dependent variable that are used as right-hand-side variables are called autoregressive (AR), and the number of lags is denoted by p. Hence, the notation AR (p) shows the number of lagged dependent variables that are used as right-hand-side variables. Let us assume that y_t is our target variable. If we include two lags of y_t (y_{t-1} and y_{t-2}) as right-hand-side variables, then we say y_t follows AR (2) process, as shown in equation 10.1.

$$y_t = \alpha + \beta_1 y_{t-1} + \beta_2 y_{t-2} + \varepsilon_t \tag{10.1}$$

where

ε_t = white noise error term

β = parameters to be estimated

The general form of an AR (p) process, which includes up to p lags of the y_t as right-hand-side variables, is shown in equation 10.2.

$$y_t = \alpha + \beta_1 y_{t-1} + \beta_2 y_{t-2} + \ldots + \beta_p y_{t-p} + \varepsilon_t \tag{10.2}$$

Put simply, if y_t follows an AR (p) process, it implies that only the p lags of y_t are needed to generate a forecasted value of the y_t series.

The second possibility when forecasting is to use the stochastic error terms as the only right-hand-side variables. In this case, y_t follows a moving average (MA) process. The number of lag values of the error terms are defined by q, and MA (q) states the y_t series follows the MA process using up to q lags of the error term. Equation 10.3 implies that y_t is generated by the MA (q) process, and ϑ is a constant term.

$$y_t = \vartheta + \gamma_0 \varepsilon_t + \gamma_1 \varepsilon_{t-1} + \gamma_2 \varepsilon_{t-2} + \ldots\ldots + \gamma_q \varepsilon_{t-q} \tag{10.3}$$

The third possibility is that both AR and MA processes are used in predicting y_t. In this case, an ARMA (p, q) model is needed to forecast y_t.[3] Equation 10.4 is an example of an ARMA (1, 1) model where the first lagged value of y_t as well as lag-1 of error term (ε_t) are utilized to predict y_t, where θ is a constant.

$$y_t = \theta + \beta_1 y_{t-1} + \gamma_0 \varepsilon_t + \gamma_1 \varepsilon_{t-1} \tag{10.4}$$

Most time series data involve a nonstationary characteristic so we need to identify the order of integration, I (d), whether the series is nonstationary or not. We combine the process to identify the orders of AR (p), MA (q), and I (d), which is known as ARIMA (autoregressive integrated moving average).[4] An ARIMA (p, d, q) model can be built to forecast y_t.

---

[3]Where p indicates order of autoregressive and q is associated with the moving averages order.

[4]For a more extensive review of ARIMA models, see William Greene (2011), *Econometric Analysis*, 7th ed. (Upper Saddle River, NJ: Prentice Hall).

The Box-Jenkins Forecasting Methodology

How do we determine the order of an ARIMA (p, d, q) model? What are the appropriate values for p, d, and q? The answer to this question is provided by Box and Jenkins (1976) and is known as the Box-Jenkins (B-J) methodology.[5] The technical name of the B-J methodology is ARIMA modeling. The B-J approach consists of four steps: (1) identification, (2) estimation, (3) diagnostic checking, and (4) forecasting.

Step 1: Identification

The first step in the B-J methodology is to identify the order of the ARIMA model—the values for the p, d, and q. Traditionally, the plots of autocorrelation functions (ACFs) and partial autocorrelation functions (PACFs) were utilized to determine the value of p, d, and q.[6] But SAS software provides a user-friendly method to identify the order of ARIMA (p, d, q), known as the SCAN method, for the smallest canonical correlation approach. SAS identifies the appropriate order of ARMA/ARIMA for a given time series.[7] We suggest using the SCAN approach because it uses a broader range of p, d, and q to determine the appropriate values of ARIMA (p, d, q) model.

Step 2: Estimation

Once an analyst identifies the order of the ARIMA (p, d, q) model, the next step is to estimate the identified model. Statistical software can be used to estimate the model, which we demonstrate in coming sections.

Step 3: Diagnostic Checking

The next step is to check the model's goodness of fit. One standard way to do so is to examine whether the estimated residuals from the chosen model are white noise. The idea behind the white-noise testing is that if the estimated residuals are white noise, then no additional information outside of the model should be included. If the estimated residuals are white noise, then the estimated model can be used to forecast the target variable. However, if the estimated residuals are *not* white noise, it implies that there is a residual presence of autocorrelation, and we will have to return to the first step and again identify the ARIMA (p, d, q) model to eliminate the autocorrelation, repeating steps 2 and 3 as well.

---

[5]The original Box-Jenkins methodology was presented in the first edition of their book; the most recent edition was published in 2008: George Box, Gwilym Jenkins, and Gregory Reinsel (2008), *Time Series Analysis: Forecasting and Control* (Hoboken, NJ: John Wiley & Sons).

[6]For more details on ACFs and PACFs, see Chapter 6 of this book.

[7]For more details on the SCAN, see SAS/ETS 9.3, PROC ARIMA. The SAS/ETS manual is available at www.sas.com/. See Chapter 6 of this book for an application of the SCAN method.

Step 4: Forecasting

The last step of the B-J approach is forecasting of the target variable. That is, after estimating the chosen model, we utilize the estimated coefficients to generate forecast values for the target variable.

Overall, the B-J approach is very useful *for short-term forecasting* (up to a few months ahead), not long-term forecasting. Because the economy contains several moving elements over time, the analyst will find it useful to include predictors to capture the state of the economy in a forecasting model, especially for medium- and long-term forecasting.

Application of the Box-Jenkins Methodology

As an example, we will apply B-J methodology on a data series of the number of initial claims filed for unemployment, released as a weekly series by the U.S. Department of Labor (DoL).[8] The initial jobless claims series provides an early look at the state of the labor market because other labor market indicators such as nonfarm payrolls and the unemployment rate are released on a monthly basis. While initial jobless claims data can be used to predict labor market indicators, forecasting the initial claims series itself is not easy. One major reason for that is that there are not many economic indicators available on a weekly basis that can be utilized in the forecasting model. The B-J forecasting approach, therefore, would be a practical option given the weekly frequency of the initial jobless claims data series.

Figure 10.1 shows the number of initial unemployment insurance claims (in thousands) filed in a given week. In analyzing this data, the first step is to

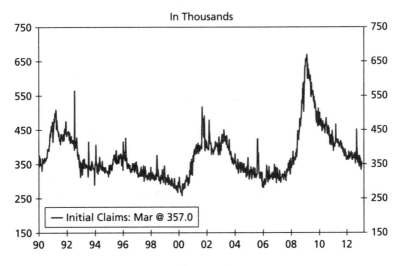

FIGURE 10.1 Number of Initial Claims Filed for Unemployment Insurance

---

[8]For more details on the DoL's Unemployment Insurance Weekly Claims report, see www.dol.gov /dol/topic/unemployment-insurance/.

apply a unit root test, such as the augmented Dickey-Fuller (ADF) test, on the target series to determine whether the series is stationary. In other words, find the order of 'd' for the initial claims series. The analyst can then utilize the SCAN approach to determine the order of ARMA (p, q).[9]

```
*===================================================================;
*The Smallest Canonical (SCAN) Correlation Method;
*Identify Order of ARIMA (p, d, q) Model for Initial Claims
series;

*===================================================================;
*Identification;
*Identifying order of integration (d)using the ADF Test;
*level form ;
PROC AUTOREG Data=Claims_data;
Model Initial_claims = / STATIONARITY=(ADF) ;  (S10.1A)
Run;
Quit;
```

TABLE 10.1A   ADF Test Results Using Level Form of Initial Claims

Dependent Variable: Initial Claims (level)

Ordinary Least Squares Estimates

SSE	5646956.93	DFE	1211
MSE	4663	Root MSE	68.28655
SBC	13683.8865	AIC	13678.7864
MAE	52.0875105	AICC	13678.7897
MAPE	13.6352096	HQC	13680.7066
Durbin-Watson	0.0620	Regress R-Square	0.0000
		Total R-Square	0.0000

Augmented Dickey-Fuller Unit Root Tests

Type	Lags	Rho	Pr < Rho	Tau	Pr < Tau	F	Pr > F
Zero Mean	3	-0.3533	0.6026	-0.4293	0.5277		
Single Mean	3	-10.9128	0.1082	-2.3170	0.1667	2.6844	0.3818
Trend	3	-11.1991	0.3598	-2.3178	0.4234	2.7173	0.6312

Parameter Estimates

Variable	DF	Estimate	Standard Error	t Value	Approx Pr > |t|
Intercept	1	374.6221	1.9615	190.99	<.0001

---

[9]For more details about the unit root test as well as ADF test, see Chapters 4 and 7 of this book.

```
* 1st difference form;

PROC AUTOREG Data= Claims_data;

Model D_Initial_claims = / STATIONARITY=(ADF) ;  (S10.1B)


Run;

Quit;
```

SAS code S10.1A is used to perform the ADF test on the level form of the initial claims data series and the results based on the code are reported in Table 10.1A. The middle part of the table shows the ADF test results. The null hypothesis of the ADF test is that the series is nonstationary, and the alternative hypothesis is that the series is stationary. If a series is stationary at level form, the 'd' for that series is zero (d=0). If the first difference of a series is stationary, then the 'd' would be 1 (d=1). From Table 10.1A, we cannot reject the null hypothesis of nonstationary for initial claims at a 5 percent level of significance because the p-values (Pr < Rho, Pr < Tau, and Pr > F) are greater than 0.05.

The first difference form of the initial claims data is tested for stationary behavior using SAS code S10.1B and the results are reported in Table 10.1B. At a 5 percent level of significance, we reject the null hypothesis of nonstationary behavior and suggest that the first difference of the initial claims data series is stationary, and 'd=1.' We will utilize the first difference form of the initial claims data in the SCAN approach.

Using SAS code S10.2, the SCAN approach is performed on the initial claims series (first difference). The results are reported in Table 10.2.[10] In the second line of the SAS code, Initial_claims(1), (1) indicates the first difference of the initial claims series. It is important to note that since we already selected the order of 'd' through ADF testing, the label 'p+d' in Table 10.2 will provide order for 'p' only, not for 'd.' The SCAN option provides three tentative and different orders for 'p' and 'q,' which are MA (2), ARMA (2, 1) and AR (4). The question arises: Which ARMA order an analyst should select for forecasting? A simple answer is that we estimate three different models using these three orders and test the estimated residuals for autocorrelations from each model. Then we then select the one that produces white noise–estimated residuals. Interestingly, in the present case, all three orders produced white noise residuals.[11] In these kinds of scenarios, an analyst should utilize other available tools to select a model. The information criteria can be used to choose a model among its competitors. We employ the Schwarz information criterion (SIC) to select the model. We run three different ARIMA models using three different orders and the MA (2) model produces the smallest SIC values; therefore, that is our preferred model for forecasting.[12]

TABLE 10.1B ADF Test Results Using Difference Form of Initial Claims

Dependent Variable: Initial Claims (Difference)

Ordinary Least Squares Estimates

SSE	349907.997	DFE	1210
MSE	289.18016	Root MSE	17.00530
SBC	10305.5653	AIC	10300.4661
MAE	11.5442997	AICC	10300.4694
MAPE	100.001939	HQC	10302.3861
Durbin-Watson	2.4497	Regress R-Square	0.0000
		Total R-Square	0.0000

Augmented Dickey-Fuller Unit Root Tests

Type	Lags	Rho	Pr < Rho	Tau	Pr < Tau	F	Pr > F
Zero Mean	3	-14657.19	<.0001	-23.57	<.0001		
Single Mean	3	-14659.25	<.0001	-23.56	<.0001	277.58	<.0010
Trend	3	-14688.32	<.0001	-23.55	<.0001	277.38	<.0010

Parameter Estimates

Variable	DF	Estimate	Standard Error	t Value	Approx Pr > |t|
Intercept	1	0.001652	0.4887	0.00	0.9973

*Identifying order of ARMA (p, q) using the SCAN approach:

PROC ARIMA Data= Claims_data;

Identify var = Initial_claims**(1) scan** ; **(S10.2)**

Run;

Quit;

TABLE 10.2 SCAN Results Finding Tentative Order of ARMA (p, q)

ARMA(p+d, q)

Tentative Order Selection Tests

----SCAN---

p+d	q
0	2
2	1
4	0

---

[10]It is important to note that the SCAN option produces lots of output. We are reporting only the relevant part, which is information about the ARMA (p, q) order. See SAS/ETS 9.3 manual, PROC ARIMA chapter, for more detail about the SCAN option: www.sas.com/.

[11]We estimate three models for initial claims using the ARMA orders suggested by the SCAN approach, and all three models produced white noise estimated residuals. We do not include the results in this book, but they are available upon request.

[12]The MA (2) model produces SIC = 10145. It is smaller than the ARMA (2, 1)'s SIC value of 10149 and the AR (4)'s SIC value of 10156.

Once an analyst has selected a particular ARIMA order for a given series—in this case we select p=0, d=1 and q=2—the next step is to test the reliability of the selected model. The standard approach is to estimate the model and test the estimated residuals for autocorrelation. If the estimated residuals show no autocorrelation, we will use the selected model for forecasting.

SAS code S10.3 performs an autocorrelation test (Chi-square) on the estimated residuals, and the results are reported in Table 10.3. The null hypothesis of the Chi-square test is that there is no autocorrelation (or white noise) and the alternative hypothesis is that there is autocorrelation. The first column, labeled "Lag," indicates how many lags we include in the test equation (up to 18 lags in this test).[13] The Chi-square statistic and the degrees of freedom (DF) are presented in the second and third columns, respectively. The p-values (under the label "Pr > ChiSq") are greater than 0.05 for all lag order, implying that we cannot reject the null hypothesis of white noise and the estimated residuals are white noise. Put simply, the identified model for initial claims (p=0, d=1, and q=2) passed the diagnostic test. The next step is forecasting initial claims using the identified model.

```
*Diagnostic Check;

PROC ARIMA Data=Claims_data;

Identify var=Initial_claims(1) ;  (S10.3)

estimate q=2;

Run;

Quit;
```

TABLE 10.3 Autocorrelation Check of Estimated Residuals

Autocorrelation Check of Residuals

Lag	Chi-Square	DF	Pr > ChiSq
6	4.31	4	0.3657
12	16.88	10	0.0770
18	22.72	16	0.1216

[13] How many lags should be included in a test equation is an empirical question. The basic idea is that lag order should not be too small because there is a possibility of higher-order autocorrelation that needs to be tested. At the same time, a lag order should not be too large because it may present a degree-of-freedom issue. We select lag order 18, which captures higher-order autocorrelation as well as limits any degree-of-freedom issues since we have over 1,200 observations.

SAS code S10.4 estimates and generates forecasts for the initial claims series. The fourth line of the code starts with Forecast, which is a SAS keyword to generate the forecast for the dependent variable. The option, lead=8, is asking SAS to provide forecasts for the next eight periods. interval=weekly indicates the weekly frequency of the dataset, and id=date shows that the date-variable is utilized as ID. The output is saved in the file name forecast_Claims. We plot the actual values and forecasted values for the initial claims series in Figure 10.2. From the figure, upper and lower lines represent the 95 percent confidence interval (the upper and lower forecast bands). Overall, the fitted values are consistent with the actual values. Note that the model accurately predicted the spikes in claims in 2011 and 2012.

```
* Forecasting;
PROC ARIMA Data= Claims_data;
Identify var = Initial_claims(1) ;    (S10.4)
Estimate q=2;
Forecast lead=8 interval=weekly id=date out=forecast_Claims;
Run;
Quit;
```

In conclusion, the B-J procedure and SAS codes provided in this chapter can be utilized to forecast financial and economic variables. At this point, we expect an analyst to be familiar with the notion behind the B-J approach as well as its application in SAS.

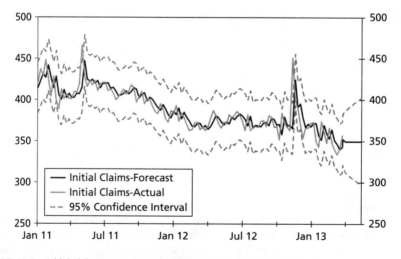

FIGURE 10.2   Initial Claims Forecast and 95 Percent Confidence Interval

THE CONDITIONAL (THEORETICAL) APPROACH

Several economic and financial theories provide guidelines that can be utilized to build a forecasting model. One example, the Taylor rule, suggests inflation expectations, and the output gap would describe the likely path of short-term interest rates, in particular the federal funds rate.[14] Therefore, the analyst can build a forecasting model for the short-term interest rate using guidelines from the Taylor rule. The idea here is that with the help of an economic/financial theory, we can build an econometric model and forecast the dependent variable based on predictors. While a forecasting model can contain two or more dependent variables with two or more predictors, the focus of this chapter is on single-equation forecasting. Chapter 11 discusses forecasting models with two or more dependent variables.[15]

The fundamental idea behind a single-equation forecasting approach is the utilization of economic and financial theory to identify the dependent variable and its predictors. Econometric techniques can then be utilized to estimate coefficients of the model, and an out-of-sample forecast can be generated with the help of the estimated coefficients and out-of-sample values of predictors.

One requirement of the single-equation approach, however, is that we must insert out-of-sample values of the predictor(s) for the desired forecast horizon in the model. Because of this, the approach is also known as conditional forecasting since out-of-sample forecasts of a dependent variable are conditioned on the predictors' future values. For example, an analyst can build a forecasting model using the Taylor rule with the model containing the Fed funds target rate as the dependent variable and the consumer price index (CPI) and GDP as predictors. The analyst must have future (out-of-sample) values for the CPI and GDP to generate an out-of-sample forecast for the Fed funds target rate. There are different ways to obtain future values of the predictors. ARIMA models can be utilized to generate out-of-sample forecasts of predictors, for example.[16] Another way to obtain out-of-sample values of predictors is to assume different economic scenarios for both series. Using CPI and GDP as an example, these difference scenarios might include (1) higher inflation with lower GDP growth rates, (2) subpar inflation and GDP growth rates, and (3) stronger GDP and inflation rates. This approach, which is also known as scenario-based analysis, is widely used in both public and private decision making.

---

[14] For more details on the Taylor rule see, Mankiw (2012).

[15] A model consisting of two or more dependent variables is also known as a system of equations. The vector autoregression (VAR) method is a common example of a system of equations. Chapter 11 provides a detailed discussion about the VAR approach.

[16] In the present example, ARIMA approach can be utilized to generate out-of-sample forecasts for CPI and GDP. The likely path of the Fed funds target rate, however, will depend on the forecasted values of the CPI and GDP.

The major benefit of scenario-based analysis is that, in the present case, different economic scenarios of inflation and GDP growth rates would provide corresponding different paths of the Fed funds rate. These varying scenarios will help decision makers in budget planning and investment decisions.

A Case Study of the Taylor Rule

We forecast the Fed funds target rate using the conditional (single-equation) forecasting approach. The original Taylor rule suggests that the nominal, short-term interest rate should respond to changes in inflation and output. Therefore, by utilizing future values of inflation and output growth rates, an analyst can forecast the Fed funds rate. One modification of the Taylor rule is that the future values of the Fed funds target rate also depends on the current level of the Fed funds rate.[17] That said, we estimate a modified Taylor rule to forecast the Fed funds target rate, using CPI as a proxy for inflation and the GDP growth rate as a proxy for output. We estimate equation 10.5:

$$\text{Fedfunds}_t = \alpha + \beta_1 CPI_t + \beta_2 GDP_t + \beta_3 \text{Fedfunds}_{t-1} + \varepsilon_t \qquad (10.5)$$

The ε_t is an error term. The level of the Fed funds rate, the compound annualized quarterly growth rate of the real GDP, and the year-over-year (YoY) percentage change of the CPI is included in the regression equation. Since inflation expectations are a key determinant of short-term interest rates, we use the YoY form of the CPI with the current level of Fed funds to capture the inflation expectations effect. The 1984:Q1 to 2012:Q4 period is used for estimation purposes, and Fed funds is forecasted for the 2013:Q1 to 2014:Q4 period (eight quarters ahead).

```
*=====================================================;
*Regression analysis is based on PROC MODEL            ;
*=====================================================;
PROC MODEL data=FF_data;
fedfunds  = ao + a1*CPI + a2*GDP + a3*lag(fedfunds)   ;
Fit   fedfunds;
                        (S10.5)
Solve fedfunds/ out=FF_Forecast forecast;
Outvars date;
Run;
```

---

[17]For more details on modifications of the Taylor rule, see Richard Clarida, Jordi Gali, and Mark Gertler (1999), "The Science of Monetary Policy: A New Keynesian Perspective," *Journal of Economic Literature* 37, no. 2.1661–1707.

SAS code S10.5 is utilized to estimate equation 10.5. PROC MODEL is employed because it is a useful procedure for conditional forecasting.[18] The second line of the code shows the estimation equation, where the Fed funds is the dependent variable and CPI, GDP, and the lag of the Fed funds are right-hand-side variables. The `ao` is an intercept and `a1` to `a3` are the coefficients to be estimated. In the third line, `Fit` is a SAS keyword that instructs SAS to estimate the equation for the Fed funds rate. `Solve` is a SAS keyword to generate forecasts for the variable of interest. The option out=FF_Forecast will save forecasted values of Fed funds rate in the data file named `FF_Forecast`, and the `forecast` option instructs SAS to generate a forecast for the Fed funds rate. `Outvars` is a SAS keyword that instructs SAS to include a specified variable in the output. That is, we ask SAS through the Outvars option to include variable `date` in the output file, which is `FF_Forecast`. The reason to include `date` variable in the output file is that the output file does not have a date variable, and we cannot tell which value is for what time period.

The results based on code S10.5 are reported in Table 10.4. The first part of the table shows summary statistics. The R^2 is very high and may suggest that the model fit is very good. The bottom part of the table exhibits individual variable statistics, such as the estimated coefficients and their corresponding t-values. The last column provides p-values for each estimated coefficient including the intercept. Based on the p-values, at 5 percent level of significant, all right-hand-side variables except CPI are statistically significant. Since we built equation 10.5 (our regression equation to generate the forecast) on economic theory, we will keep CPI in the final equation. One possible reason for the statistically insignificant coefficient of the CPI is that during the last couple of decades, inflation was not a significant factor in determining interest rate because inflation rates stayed around the target rate set by the Federal Open Market Committee (FOMC).

After estimating the regression equation for the Fed funds rate, we want to generate a forecast. Two key components to generating a forecast are the estimated coefficients and the out-of-sample values of the predictors (CPI and GDP). From Table 10.4, we do have an estimated coefficient for the CPI and GDP, but we still need the out-of-sample values of the predictors. One option is to use a forecast from a reliable source (either public or private sector) as out-of-sample values for GDP and CPI.[19] We utilize Wells Fargo Economics Group's

---

[18]PROC MODEL is a flexible procedure and allows including future values of predictors to generate forecast values for the dependent variable.

[19]A number of forecasts for several years are available from both public (Congressional Budget Office and Federal Reserve Board, e.g.) and private (e.g., Wells Fargo Securities, LLC) sectors at no cost.

TABLE 10.4 PROC MODEL Results for the Estimated Taylor Rule

The MODEL Procedure

Nonlinear OLS Summary of Residual Errors

Equation	DF Model	DF Error	SSE	MSE	Root-MSE	R-Square	Adj R-Sq
Fed funds	4	111	23.89	0.215	0.464	0.9731	0.9723

Nonlinear OLS Parameter Estimates

Var	Parameter	Estimate	Approx Std Err	t Value	Approx Pr > |t|
Intercept	ao	−0.27785	0.1189	−2.34	0.0213
CPI	a1	0.066769	0.0428	1.56	0.1220
GDP	a2	0.090453	0.0175	5.17	<.0001
Lag_FF	a3	0.945806	0.0194	48.72	<.0001

Lag_FF = Lagged value of fed funds rate (dependent variable)

forecasts for GDP and CPI and as out-of-sample values to generate the forecast for Fed funds rate for the 2013:Q1 to 2014:Q4 period.

Table 10.5 provides conditional out-of-sample forecasts of the Fed funds rate with the out-of-sample values of GDP and CPI. The Fed funds forecasts are conditional because if we change values of GDP and/or CPI then the forecasted Fed funds rate will also change. In this case, the out-of-sample values of the CPI are around the FOMC inflation target of 2 percent and GDP shows trend growth rates around 2 to 2.5 percent. Therefore, both predictors exhibit normal or trend growth. For that reason, we will choose this case to be the base-case scenario for path of the Fed funds rate.

The plot of the actual and forecasted Fed funds rate is shown in Figure 10.3. Given that the CPI values are around the FOMC inflation target and GDP growth is weak, the Fed funds rate moves upward very slowly, at 0.63 percent by the end of 2014. In a scenario of low inflation and low GDP growth rate, the FOMC is likely to keep the fed funds rate lower, with the intention of stimulating the economy.

TABLE 10.5 Base-Case Scenario: Forecast for Federal Funds Rate Conditioned on CPI and GDP Growth

Date	Federal Funds Rate	CPI (YoY)	GDP
1/1/2012	0.13	2.82	2
4/1/2012	0.13	1.90	1.3
7/1/2012	0.13	1.7	3.1
10/1/2012	0.13	1.9	0.1
1/1/2013	0.18	1.7	2.5
4/1/2013	0.23	2.1	2.1
7/1/2013	0.28	2	2.3
10/1/2013	0.32	2	2.2
1/1/2014	0.39	2.2	2.4
4/1/2014	0.46	2.1	2.6
7/1/2014	0.53	2.1	2.5
10/1/2014	0.63	2.2	2.9

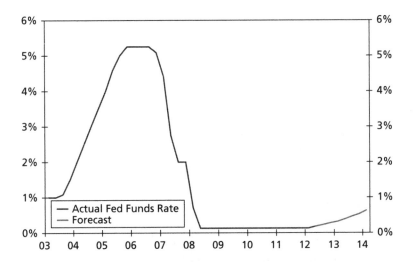

FIGURE 10.3 Base-Case Scenario: Forecast for Federal Funds Rate Conditioned on CPI and GDP Growth

The major benefit of the conditional forecasting approach is that the analyst can generate different paths (scenarios) of the conditioned on different paths of the predictors. In the scenario just given, the Fed funds target rate forecast is conditioned on normal, or perhaps subpar, growth rates of GDP and CPI. However, what would be a likely path for Fed funds rate if the economy experiences a different scenario?

TABLE 10.6 Strong GDP Growth Rate Scenario: Forecast for Federal Funds Rate Conditioned on CPI and GDP Growth

Date	Federal Funds Rate	CPI (YoY)	GDP
1/1/2012	0.13	2.82	2
4/1/2012	0.13	1.90	1.3
7/1/2012	0.13	1.7	3.1
10/1/2012	0.13	1.9	0.1
1/1/2013	0.37	1.70	4.50
4/1/2013	0.58	2.10	4.10
7/1/2013	0.79	2.00	4.30
10/1/2013	0.98	2.00	4.20
1/1/2014	1.20	2.20	4.40
4/1/2014	1.41	2.10	4.60
7/1/2014	1.60	2.10	4.50
10/1/2014	1.83	2.20	4.90

What About Strong Growth?

We explore the possibility of stronger GDP growth rates in Table 10.6.[20] In addition, we added 2 percent into the base-case GDP growth rates (out-of-sample values) and kept the CPI values the same. We stress here the important question: What would be the likely move of the FOMC (in terms of Fed funds decisions) if the economy shows a stronger GDP growth rate? From Table 10.6, we see that the Fed funds rate increases at a much faster rate, being about three times higher than the base-case scenario by the end of 2014. The plot of actual and forecasted Fed funds rates is exhibited in Figure 10.4. The plot shows the forecasted Fed funds rate as a steep curve and reaches around 2 percent (1.83 percent) by the end of 2014. That said, private sector borrowing costs may increase at a faster rate during a stronger GDP growth rate environment compared to the subpar economic growth scenario illustrated in Table 10.5.

In conclusion, the single-equation conditional forecasting approach is very useful for decision makers to generate different likely paths of economic and financial variables and to make budget/investment planning decisions.

---

[20]The stronger growth is possible due to several reasons, such as the housing sector (as of July 2013) showing signs of a stronger recovery, which may boost GDP growth, given that the housing sector was the major cause of the Great Recession.

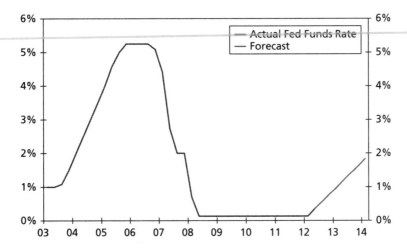

FIGURE 10.4 Strong GDP Growth Rate Scenario: Forecast for Federal Funds Rate Conditioned on CPI and GDP Growth

RECESSION FORECAST USING A PROBIT MODEL

In the previous two sections, we discussed unconditional (atheoretical) and conditional (theoretical) forecasting approaches within a single-equation regression framework. The major difference between the two approaches is that the unconditional forecasting approach does not include any additional predictors and uses statistical tools to characterize and forecast the variable of interest. Conditional forecasting, in contrast, utilizes predictors, usually identified with the help of economic/financial theory, in a regression analysis. Furthermore, out-of-sample forecasts of the target variable are conditioned on the predictors' values.

Common, however, between the two approaches is the functional form of the target variable. Sometimes a dependent variable may be nontraditional, in the sense that it contains a specific set of values, such as zero or one. This is known as a dummy-dependent variable model.[21] A regression analysis involving a dummy-dependent variable is known as a binary dependent variable regression. In the case of a binary regression, traditional econometric techniques, such as ordinary least squares (OLS), do not provide reliable results. This is because a binary regression is required to predict outcomes in a specific range such that the predicted values of the dependent variable stay in the zero to one range. The Probit model provides reliable results in the case of a dummy dependent variable regression analysis.[22]

---

[21]If a categorical variable takes only two values, it is known as binary variable. A variable with more than two categories is called multinomial or ordered variable.

[22]There is another approach to estimate a logistic regression known as Logit. For more details about categorical variables, logistic regression, and Probit/Logit models see Greene (2011), *Econometric Analysis*.

Probit models are used in both public and private decision making to predict the probability of an event. One application of a Probit model is to predict the probability of a recession. Several studies have employed the Probit approach to predict recession probability for the U.S. economy; see Silvia, Bullard, and Lai (2008) for more details.[23] Recently, a study by Vitner et al. (2012) proposed Probit models for all 50 states.[24] It is important to note that whether we are interested in predicting the recession probability for the U.S. (or any other country) economy or for a state, the fundamentals of a Probit model are the same. First, we need to create a dummy variable that is equal to one if the underlying economy is in recession and zero otherwise. Silvia et al. (2008) provided a detailed methodology to identify predictors for a Probit model to predict recession probability for the U.S. economy. This methodology can be replicated in the application to any other economy. We follow the Silvia et al. (2008) Probit model as a case study.

Application of the Probit Model

The first step to build a Probit model to predict the probability of a recession is to generate a dummy variable, which will be the dependent variable of the model. The dummy variable in our model equals one if the U.S. economy is in recession and zero otherwise. The National Bureau of Economic Research (NBER) provides official dates of peaks (the beginning of a recession) and troughs (the end of a recession) for the U.S. economy, which can be employed to create a dummy variable.[25] Specifically, the dummy variable will be equal to one for the months between peaks and troughs, and therefore in recession, and zero for the other months in the sample period.

The next step is to find predictors for the Probit model. Using the Silvia et al. (2008) model, we employ these three predictors: (1) the S&P 500 index; (2) the index of leading indicators, also known as LEI; and (3) the Chicago PMI employment index.

Once we generate the dummy variable and identify predictors for the Probit model, the final step is to determine the forecast horizon. How far in the future do we want to forecast? For instance, Silvia et al. (2008) forecasted the probability of a recession during the next six months. We follow that same forecast horizon. The forecast horizon would indicate the functional form (current

[23]John Silvia, Sam Bullard, and Huiwen Lai (2008), "Forecasting U.S. Recessions with Probit Stepwise Regression Models," *Business Economics* 43, no. 1: 7–18.
[24]Mark Vitner, Jay Bryson, Anika Khan, Azhar Iqbal, and Sarah Watt (2012), "The State of States: A Probit Approach," presented at the 2012 Annual Meeting of the American Economic Association, January 6–8, Chicago, Illinois.
[25]For recession definitions and dates, see the NBER website, www.nber.org/.

versus lags) of the dependent variable and the predictors. A six-month lag of the dummy variable instead of the current value is included in the test equation. In addition, the current form of the predictors is used in the model. There are two major reasons we use a six-month lag of the dependent variable with current values of the predictors. First, the regression output from the Probit model allows an analyst to measure the historical strength of the predictors to forecast six-month-out recession probability. Silvia at el. (2008) utilized a pseudo R^2 to judge the in-sample fit of the model. The second benefit of including six-month lags of the dependent variable is that to make a six-month-ahead forecast, we can utilize the current-month values of the predictors, which are available at the time of forecasting. The logistic equation 10.6 is estimated:

$$Y_{t+6} = \alpha + \beta_1 LEI_t + \beta_2 SP500_t + \beta_3 PMI\_Emp_t + \varepsilon_t \qquad (10.6)$$

where

Y_{t+6} = dummy dependent variable (six-month lead) that equals 1 if the U.S. economy is in recession and zero otherwise

$\alpha, \beta_1, \beta_2, \beta_3$ = parameters to be estimated

LEI, SP500, and PMI_EMP (Chicago PMI employment index) = predictors

ε_t = error term

Since the dependent variable is a dummy (1, 0) and the predicted probabilities must stay between the zero and one range, equation 10.7 would keep predicted probabilities in the required range. Equation 10.7 is a typical Probit model estimation equation. The left side of the equation indicates the probability of a recession is given on the values of predictors, which are LEI, SP500, and PMI_Emp. The right-hand side of the equation consists of estimated coefficients along with the predictors.[26]

$$Pr(Y_{t+hlt} = 1 | LEI, SP500, PMI\_Emp) = \Phi(\hat{\alpha} + \hat{\beta}_1 LEI_t + \hat{\beta}_2 SP_{500t} + \hat{\beta}_3 PMI\_Emp_t) \qquad (10.7)$$

where

Y = 1 implies recession

LEI, SP500, and PMI_Emp = predictors

Φ = cumulative standard normal distribution function that keeps the predicted probability in the zero to 1 range

So far we have discussed Probit modeling and key elements of a Probit model, such as the requirement to create a dummy dependent variable, the need to identify predictors of the model, and the identification of the forecast horizon. The next step is for SAS to generate a recession probability for next six months.

---

[26]For more details about Probit modeling and the cumulative standard normal distribution function, see Greene (2011).

SAS code S10.6 is employed to estimate the six-month-ahead recession probability for the U.S. economy.[27] The PROC LOGISTIC command is utilized, and the data file data_Probit contains all variables of interest. The SAS keyword descending orders the dependent variable according to the objective of the study. That is, in a binary choice model such as ours where nonevent (no recession) equals zero and event (recession) has a value of 1, PROC LOGISTIC, by default, estimates the probability for a lower value, which is a nonevent (no recession). However, we are interested in the probability of a recession (probability of an event's occurrence), and the keyword descending instructs SAS to generate the probability of a recession conditioned on the predictors. The dependent variable, NBER_6M, and predictors, LEI, SP500, and PMI_EMP, are listed in the second line of the code.

```
*===================================;
*SAS Codes for a Probit Model     ;
*===================================;
PROC LOGISTIC data=data_Probit descending;
Model NBER_6M = LEI SP500 PMI_Emp /link=Probit;
Output out=Probit_output Pred=probability_value;   (S10.6)
Run;
Quit;
```

We utilized month-over-month percentage changes of all the predictors instead of the level form because the level form often shows nonstationary characteristics. The growth rate (difference) form usually follows stationary path. link=Probit is another SAS keyword, which instructs SAS to fit a Probit model. The third line of the code saves the model's output in a desired file; we created the Probit_output data file, which contains actual values of the predictors and the dependent variable. The keyword Pred=probability_value produces a recession probabilities series, and that series is also saved in the data file Probit_output.

In Figure 10.5, we plot the probability of a recession. Shaded areas in the figure are recessions determined by the NBER. We generate a graph for the quarterly series, using three-month averages as a quarterly value because there is a lot of noise in the monthly series (see Figure 10.6). The quarterly graph for recession probability is much smoother and shows that the model produced a significantly higher probability during all recessions since 1980. That is, the Probit model successfully predicted all recessions since 1980.

---

[27]It is important to note that the procedure PROC LOGISTIC is offered by SAS/STAT. Therefore, an analyst must have SAS/STAT software to run code S10.6.

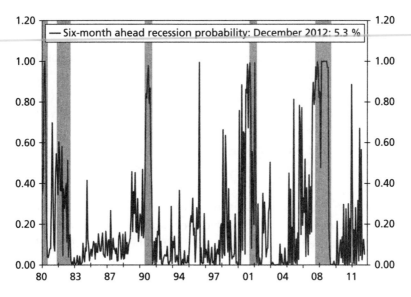

FIGURE 10.5 Recession Probability Using Monthly Data

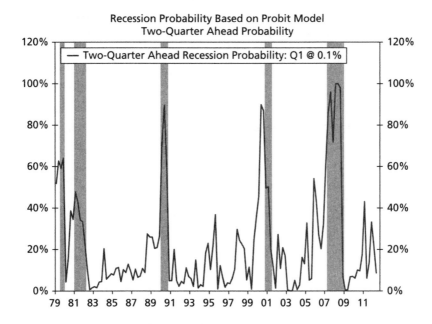

FIGURE 10.6 Recession Probability: Quarterly Average

SUMMARY

In this chapter we provided different methods of forecasting within a single-equation framework. The first method, the ARIMA model, is a very useful forecasting tool for high-frequency variables, such as the S&P 500 index's daily closing price or weekly initial claims data. When there are not many predictors available to include in such a model, the ARIMA approach is useful because it does not require additional variables to build a forecasting model.

The second forecasting method discussed was the conditional/theoretical approach. In this case, there are several predictors available to include in a forecasting model. The benefit of this approach is that a forecaster can generate different forecasts of the target variable conditioned on different values of the predictors.

The third method the analyst can use to predict the probability of a recession is a Probit model. This approach is widely used in both public and private decision making.

The question arises: What method is more beneficial for an analyst? All three methods are useful, and the choice depends on the forecasting objective. For instance, because it would be very difficult to build a conditional forecasting model to predict the daily closing price of the S&P 500 index, and the practical approach is to utilize ARIMA models. Similarly, conditional forecasts of the Fed funds target rate for the next couple of years, using different economic growth and inflation scenarios, would be more useful than a forecast from an ARIMA model (since ARIMA model would provide just one likely path of the Fed funds target rate). Predicting recession probability conditioned on predictors is more appropriate than an ARIMA model because predictors will capture the underlying state of an economy, which would increase reliability of the Probit model.

In short, all three methods are useful at different times and in different circumstances. An analyst must be familiar with all of these forecasting approaches.

CHAPTER 11

A Multiple-Equations Approach to Model-Based Forecasting

This chapter discusses the multiple-equations forecasting approach, which has more than one dependent variable along with several right-hand-side variables. Within the multiple-equations forecasting framework, we discuss vector autoregressions (VARs) and Bayesian vector autoregressions (BAVRs). The VAR/BVAR approaches can be utilized for short-term as well as long-term forecasting. Short-term forecasting is the focus of this chapter; we look at long-term forecasting in Chapter 12.

A specific forecasting approach in short-term forecasting is known as real-time forecasting of macroeconomic and financial variables. A real-time forecast implies forecasting before the actual release of a variable.[1] Silvia and Iqbal (2012) developed an accurate real-time short-term, one-month-ahead, macroeconomic forecasting framework that accounts for the real-time challenge of data availability but also provides a more accurate forecast, on average, than those of the Bloomberg real-time consensus forecast.[2] They compared their real-time forecasts with the Bloomberg real-time consensus for 20 major macroeconomic variables, including nonfarm payrolls, unemployment rate, Institute for Supply Management manufacturing index, consumer price index

---

This chapter draws heavily on John Silvia and Azhar Iqbal (2012), "A Comparison of Consensus and BVAR Macroeconomic Forecasts," *Business Economics* 47, no. 4.250–261.

[1] For a detailed discussion about real-time data, see Dean Croushore and Tom Stark (2001), "A Real-Time Data Set for Macroeconomists," *Journal of Econometrics* 105 (November): 111–130.

[2] John Silvia and Azhar Iqbal (2012), "A Comparison of Consensus and BVAR Macroeconomic Forecasts," *Business Economics* 47, no. 4.250–261.

(CPI), industrial production, and housing starts. In this chapter, we follow the approach developed by Silvia and Iqbal (2012).

This chapter sheds light on four important areas of real-time macroeconomic short-term forecasting.

1. Why do we care about short-term forecasting?
2. Why is an individual forecast approach that is better than consensus valuable?
3. Why is the timing of the release of the target (dependent) variable and predictor (independent) variable important to forecasting methods?
4. Why are traditional forecast evaluation methods not enough?

First, new macroeconomic data, especially when the values are different than consensus anticipated, alter asset prices in the equity, bond, and foreign exchange (FX) markets. Therefore, accurate forecasts of key macroeconomic variables, prior to their release announcements, will provide more opportunities to a firm and its clients to profit, or to at least minimize losses (see next section for details). The second question about individual versus consensus forecasts follows a vast amount of literature studying macroeconomic data releases and the financial market response to those announcements.[3] Yet most of this literature focuses only on the difference between the actual and consensus forecast. It does not focus on what determines the individual forecast accuracy and how that accuracy may change over time relative to the consensus. As Rigobon and Sack (2008) and Bartolini et al. (2008) concluded, the effect of the macroeconomic news announcements on the financial markets (e.g., equity and bond markets) is most significant when the actual release is different from market expectations.

Moreover, Bartolini et al. (2008) suggested that a stronger-than-expected news announcement may increase interest rates, strengthen the dollar, and raise equity prices. Because the release of macroeconomic data affects market response, the importance of an individual forecast approach that is better than consensus is increased. The first phase of this chapter establishes the importance of short-term macroeconomic forecasting and the individual forecast approach using BVAR. In other words, why do we care about short-term forecasting and an individual forecast approach? Why should we seek value in forecasts outside the consensus forecast?

The next part of the chapter discusses how to produce accurate as well as better-than-consensus forecasts of key macroeconomic variables. In addition, we compare Silvia and Iqbal's (2012) real-time forecasts with the Bloomberg real-time consensus. We also address a few very important issues to short-term

---

[3]See the next section, "The Importance of the Real-Time Short-Term Forecasting," for details.

macroeconomic forecasting. For example, the release timing of the target (dependent) variable as well as predictors is very important and often overlooked in conventional forecasting evaluations. Because data is released at different points in time and at different frequencies, release timing is an essential (yet the most neglected) issue to short-term forecasting and must be considered in the model specification.

For instance, nonfarm payrolls and unemployment data have a one-month time lag (e.g., on September 3, 2010, employment data was released for August 2010). In contrast, data on construction spending has a two-month lag. Additionally, employment data is released at the beginning of the month (most often on the first Friday of every month), before many other data macroeconomic data points. Due to the lagged nature of the data and the early release of employment data relative to other variables, there are truly a limited number of predictors available to model and predict nonfarm payrolls. Personal income and spending data is released at the end of the month (typically during the last week of the month). By the end of the month, we have likely already received updated data on a number of macroeconomic variables that can be used as predictors to model personal income and spending. Thus, forecasting personal income and spending may be considered easier and safer than predicting employment. In conclusion, the release timing of a target variable and its predictors is very important, and we discuss the topic in greater detail later in the chapter.

The final aspect of short-term forecasting is forecast evaluation. The commonly used forecast evaluation criteria are R^2 and root mean square error (RMSE), both in sample and out of sample. RMSE is the most frequently used method, but we believe that, in the financial sector, directional accuracy must be considered along with RMSE, as market positions often are taken on a directional basis rather than on specific numerical bet.

THE IMPORTANCE OF THE REAL-TIME SHORT-TERM FORECASTING

More accurate forecasts of macroeconomic variables prior to their release announcements will provide more opportunities to a firm and its clients to profit, or to at least minimize losses. This section discusses the importance of short-term macroeconomic forecasting in precisely those opportunities. Why short-term forecasting? Because scheduled macroeconomic variable announcements, especially when different from the consensus, affect asset price movements and volatility in the equity, bond, and FX markets. Consequently, accurate forecasts of key macroeconomic variables prior to their release announcements will enhance profit opportunities to a firm and its clients. There is a vast literature studying macroeconomic data releases and the response of financial market to those announcements.

The empirical evidence of the relationship between financial market volatility and macroeconomic news announcements dates back to the 1980s. For instance, Schwert (1981), Pearce and Roley (1985), and Jain (1988) provided evidence of financial market response to macroeconomic news announcements.[4] More recently, Anderson et al. (2007) and Bartolini et al. (2008) concluded that there would be a strong financial market response as a result of macroeconomic variables release announcements.[5] Furthermore, Huang (2007) suggested that the release of the U.S. employment situation report (nonfarm payrolls and unemployment rate) is the most influential news to the financial market.[6] Faust et al. (2007) found release announcements of inflation data moves exchange rates and interest rates.[7] Gilbert et al. (2007) suggested that release announcements of the U.S. Leading Economic Index (LEI) affect aggregate stock returns, return volatility, and trading volume.[8]

In addition, studies have found that macroeconomic data announcements of U.S. variables affect not only U.S. financial markets but foreign financial markets as well. Anderson et al. (2007) characterized the response of the U.S., German, and British equity, bond, and FX markets to real-time U.S. macroeconomic news announcements while Nikkinen and Sahlstran (2001) suggested that Finnish and U.S. financial markets respond to the announcements of the U.S. employment, CPI, and producer price index (PPI) data.[9]

In summary, macroeconomic news announcements do move equity, bond, and FX markets. Therefore, better forecasting can create strategic opportunities for firms and their clients.

THE INDIVIDUAL FORECAST VERSUS CONSENSUS FORECAST: IS THERE AN ADVANTAGE?

As demonstrated in the previous section, academic literature suggests a connection between macroeconomic data announcements and financial market

---

[4]G. W. Schwert (1981), "The Adjustment of Stock Prices to Information About Inflation," *Journal of Finance* 36: 15–29; D. Pearce and V. Roley (1985), "Stock Prices and Economic News," *Journal of Business* 58: 49–67; P. C. Jain (1988), "Response of Hourly Stock Prices and Trading Volume to Economic News," *Journal of Business* 61: 219–231.

[5]T. Andersen, Tim Bollerslev, Francis Diebold, and Clara Vega (2007), "Real-Time Price Discovery in Global Stock, Bond, and Foreign Exchange Markets." *Journal of International Economics* 73, no. 2 (November): 251–277.

[6]Xin Huang (2007), "Macroeconomic News Announcements, Financial Market Volatility and Jumps," working paper, Duke University, Durham, NC.

[7]Jon Faust, John Rogers, Shing-Yi Wang, and Jonathan Wright (2007), "The High-Frequency Response of Exchange Rates and Interest Rates to Macroeconomic Announcements," *Journal of Monetary Economics* 54, no. 4 (May): 1051–1068.

[8]Thomas Gilbert, K. Shimon, and L. Lars (2007), "Investor Inattention and the Market Impact of Summary Statistics," available at: http://papers.ssrn.com/sol3/papers.cfm?abstract_id = 1108050.

[9]J. Nikkinen and S. Petri (2001), "Impact of Scheduled U.S. Macroeconomic News on Stock Market Uncertainty: A Multivariate Perspective," *Multinational Finance Journal* 5, no. 2.129–148.

volatility. However, over the past decade and a half, the effect of macroeconomic news on asset prices may have changed. During the past decade, market consensus estimates have been better publicized, with more estimates being publicly available for every major macroeconomic variable. When the actual release is markedly different from the market consensus, financial markets move more significantly to the economic news (see Bartolini et al. [2008] for more details). The most widely used market consensus is provided by Bloomberg L.P.[10] The Bloomberg consensus is based on the median response from financial market participants.[11] Therefore, it is a reliable measure of market expectations for the upcoming release of a macroeconomic variable.

Rigobon and Sack (2008) and Bartolini et al. (2008) suggested that key macroeconomic variable release announcements do affect asset prices; however, the effect is more significant when the actual news is different from market expectations. Both studies used the median response of the survey taken by Bloomberg[12] as a proxy for the market expectations prior to the release announcements and found that if the actual release is different (stronger than expected or less than expected) than the market consensus, the market response to the news is more significant. In addition, Bartolini et al. (2008) suggested that the stronger-than-expected news announcement may increase interest rates, strengthen the dollar, and raise equity prices. Boyd et al. (2005) showed that stock prices respond differently to changes in the unemployment rate during recessions and expansions because the dividend and discount rate effects have different weights at different points of the business cycle.[13] Therefore, based on empirical evidence, we do recognize the macroeconomic variable release announcements effect.[14]

There are two implications for real-time short-term macroeconomic forecasting.

1. Reliable forecasts of macroeconomic variables prior to their release announcements provide more opportunities to a firm to generate profits (or reduce losses for itself and its clients).

---

[10]There are some other surveys too (e.g., Blue Chips and *Wall Street Journal*). But these surveys are for long-term forecasts (up to eight quarters ahead of major macroeconomic variables). The focus of this chapter is short-term forecasting, and the Bloomberg consensus is the best option for that purpose.

[11]The survey polls a group of economists, the number vary with the degree of interest in the indicator at issue. Surveys of highly watched indicators, such as nonfarm payrolls and unemployment rate, often have more than 70 respondents. The lag between the participants' response and the date of the indicator release also varies, from a few days to two weeks.

[12]Rigobon and Sack (2008) used the Money Market Services survey's consensus as proxy for market consensus before September 2004 and Bloomberg consensus after that.

[13]J. Boyd, Hu Jian, and J. Ravi (2005), "The Stock Market's Reaction to Unemployment News: Why Bad News Is Usually Good for Stocks," *Journal of Finance* 60, no. 2 (April): 649–672.

[14]Silvia and Iqbal (2012) noted that in their own experience sitting on a trading floor, markets do respond to the releases of macroeconomic data, sometimes sharply. A number of releases, such as nonfarm payrolls and inflation measures, can produce large effects.

2. The importance of an individual forecast approach that is better than the market consensus is increased, given that the markets move significantly when the actual release is different from the market consensus.

Key macroeconomic variable release announcements do affect financial markets; however, the effect is much more significant when the actual release is different from the market consensus. Thus, the importance of an individual forecaster and his or her better-than-consensus findings are thereby increased. An individual forecast approach can provide more opportunities to a firm and its clients to make money (or reduce losses). Moreover, because using the market consensus as a forecast will not add value to a firm, individual analysts have an incentive to develop their own, more accurate forecasts.

THE ECONOMETRICS OF REAL-TIME SHORT-TERM FORECASTING: THE BVAR APPROACH

This section provides the econometric methodology and forecast evaluation for real-time short-term forecasting. As mentioned earlier, Silvia and Iqbal (2012) employed the BVAR approach, an extension of the VAR model, to generate real-time forecasts. After the seminal work of Sims (1980), VAR became a major tool for macroeconomic forecasting.[15] Despite its success, however, there is a technical problem with VAR: The approach can utilize only a small subset of available information due to the degree-of-freedom problem, also known as the curse of dimensionality. To address this problem, Litterman (1980, 1986) presented the BVAR approach.[16] The BVAR approach is more flexible because it allows more variables as inputs than the VAR approach, permitting the inclusion of more information about the relationship than the traditional VAR model. Litterman (1986) showed that his approach is as accurate, on average, as those used by the best-known commercial forecasting services (DRI, Chase, and Wharton Econometrics at that time). Theoretically, recent literature shows significant development in BVAR modeling (see Sims and Zha [1998] for more details).[17] Empirically, however, improvement on Litterman's original methodology does not seem particularly significant (for more details, see Robertson and Tallman [1999]).[18]

The performance of Litterman's method is at least partially determined by the choice of several parameters—popularly referred to as the Minnesota prior.

---

[15] C. A. Sims (1980), "Macroeconomics and Reality," *Econometrica* 48, no. 1: 1–48.

[16] R. Litterman (1980), "Techniques for Forecasting with Vector Autoregressions," PhD dissertation, University of Minnesota. Litterman(1986), "Forecasting with Bayesian Vector Autoregressions—5 Years of Experience," *Journal of Business and Economic Statistics* 4: 25–38.

[17] C. A. Sims and T. Zha (1998), "Bayesian Methods for Dynamic Multivariate Models," *International Economic Review* 39, no. 4: 949–968.

[18] J. C. Robertson and Ellis W. Tallman (1999), "Vector Autoregressions: Forecasting and Reality," *Federal Reserve Bank of Atlanta Economic Review* 84, no. 1: 4–18.

Litterman was able to implement only a small number of the possible parameter combinations due to limited and expensive computer power at the time of his research. With the programming flexibility and speed available with today's advanced econometric software, an analyst can run Litterman's regression using many parameter combinations.

The Bayesian Vector Autoregression Model

As the BVAR model is an extension of the VAR model, we start our discussion with the VAR approach. In addition, we highlight issues related with the Sims VAR approach and benefits of Litterman's BVAR model. Let $Y_t = (Y_{1t}, Y_{2t}, Y_{3t}, \ldots, Y_{nt})$ be a set of time series data. The VAR (p) representation of the time series can be presented as shown in equation 11.1:

$$Y_t = \alpha + \beta_1 Y_{t-1} + \ldots + \beta_p Y_{t-p} + \varepsilon_t \qquad (11.1)$$

$$\varepsilon_t \sim N(0, \sigma_\varepsilon)$$

where

$\alpha = (\alpha_1, \alpha_2, \ldots, \alpha_n)$ is an n-dimensional vector of constants

$\beta_1, \beta_2, \ldots, \beta_p$ are $n \times n$ autoregressive matrices

$\varepsilon_t = n$-dimensional white noise process with covariance matrix $E(\varepsilon_t \varepsilon_t)' = \Psi$

The traditional VAR model has some limitations. The first issue is known as overparameterization; that is, an analyst has to estimate too many parameters, and some of them may be statistically insignificant. For example, a VAR model with five variables and four lags and a constant in each equation will contain a total of 105 (($1 + 5 \times 4$) $\times$ 5 = 105) coefficients. The second problem is that overparameterization will cause multicollinearity as well as a reduction in the degrees of freedom, which may result in a very good in-sample fit but a possibility of a large out-of-sample forecast error. This is sometimes referred to as over-fitting the model.

Litterman (1980) described an approach to overcome these problems. Litterman (1980, 1986) introduced the Bayesian VAR approach and used a prior, popularly referred to as Minnesota prior, and solved the issue of overparameterization (see Litterman [1986] for more details). Litterman's prior is based on three assumptions.

1. All equations contain a random walk with drift model. This essentially shrinks the diagonal elements β_1 toward 1 and the other coefficients (β_2, $\beta_3, \ldots, \beta_p$) toward zero.

2. More recent lags provide more useful information (have greater predictive power) than more distant ones.

3. A variable's own lags explain more than the lags of the other variables in the model.

The Litterman prior is imposed by the (mean and variance) moments for the prior distribution of the coefficients shown in equation 11.2.

$$E\left[(\beta)_{ij}\right] = \begin{cases} \delta_i, & j = i,\ k = 1 \\ 0 & otherwise \end{cases} \quad \text{and} \quad V\left[(\beta)_{ij}\right] = \vartheta \frac{\lambda^2}{k^2} \frac{\sigma_i^2}{\sigma_j^2} \qquad (11.2)$$

The coefficients $\beta_1, \beta_2, \ldots, \beta_p$ are assumed to be independent and normally distributed. The covariance matrix of the residuals is assumed to be diagonal, fixed and known, that is, $\Psi = \Sigma$, where $\Sigma = \text{diag}\,(\sigma_1^2, \ldots \sigma_n^2)$, and the prior on the intercept is diffuse. The random walk prior (δ_i) has some intuitive implication, such as $\delta_i = 1$ for all i, indicating that all variables are highly persistent. However, the researcher may believe that some of the variables in the model are following a mean reversion or at least not characterized by a random walk. This does not pose a problem for this framework, because a white noise prior can be set for some or all of the variables in the VAR model by imposing $\delta_i = 0$ where appropriate. The hyperparameter λ controls for the overall tightness of the prior distribution around δ_i. This hyperparameter governs the importance of prior beliefs relative to the information contained in the data; $\lambda = 0$ imposes the prior exactly so that the data does not inform the parameter estimate, and $\lambda = \infty$ removes the influence of the prior altogether so that the parameter estimates are equivalent to ordinary least squares (OLS) estimates. The factor $1/k^2$ is the rate at which the prior variance decreases with the lag length of the VAR, and σ_i^2/σ_j^2 accounts for the different scale and variability of the data. The coefficient $\vartheta\varepsilon(0,\ 1)$ governs the extent to which the lags of other variables are less important than own lags.[19]

Litterman's method is a good solution to many of the problems associated with the traditional VAR model. Another issue, however, is the presence of the unit root in any series of the model. What happened to the BVAR's estimate and to the forecasting in a nonstationary framework and possible cointegration relationships between the components of the BVAR model? There are two popular answers to this question. One group of economists, especially Lütkepohl (1991) and Phillips (1991), suggested that when the BVAR analysis unfolds in context of a nonstationary process and there is potential for cointegration relationships, the estimate would be biased.[20]

In contrast, a group of economists are in favor of using the BVAR model at the level form of the series. For example, Sims, Stock, and Watson (1990)

---

[19]Sims and Zha (1998) have modified the original Litterman's prior by imposing a normal prior distribution for the coefficient and an inverse Wishart prior distribution for the covariance matrix of the residuals Ψ.

[20]H. Lütkepohl (1991), *Introduction to Multiple Time Series Analysis* (New York: Springer). P.C.B. Phillips (1991), "Bayesian Routes and Unit Roots: de Rebus Prioribus Semper Est Disputandum," *Journal of Applied Econometrics* 6: 435–473.

showed that if the potential cointegration restrictions existing are not taken into account and the model is estimated in levels, this estimation is consistent.[21] Sims (1991) said that these critiques were poorly grounded and argued that, owing to the superconvergence property of the estimators in the presence of a cointegration relationship, these aspects tend to manifest themselves with clarity, irrespective of the type of the prior information used.[22] Alvarez and Ballabriga (1994) furnished evidence on this matter and performed a Monte Carlo simulation with a cointegrated process that allows consideration of the power of different estimation methods for capturing the long-run relationship.[23] The results obtained sustain Sims's proposition, rather than those of the critics, provided that the prior distribution has been selected in keeping with a goodness-of-fit criterion.

In addition to the Alvarez-Ballabriga evidence in support of Sims's views, the nonstationary issue also depends on what the target variable is, especially in forecasting. For instance, in the marketplace, and particularly in the financial sector, investors pay more attention either to the percentage change (e.g., month-to-month and/or year-to-year percentage change in CPI or retail sales) or net change (e.g., net monthly change in nonfarm payrolls) than to the level form of many variables since the level form is not the headline number that is reported.[24] Since major macroeconomic variables, such as employment and the CPI, are reported either in percentage form (growth rate) or net change, the nonstationarity issue may not be a problem in many cases. As a result—because of two reasons (a) based on Sims's and the Alvarez-Ballabriga suggestions and (b) most forecasts are a growth rate/net change of a variable instead of the level form of a variable—nonstationary and/or potential cointegration are less likely to affect the forecasting framework.

Forecast Evaluation: Real-Time Measures

This chapter presents an accurate real-time short-term (one-month-forward) macroeconomic forecasting framework. Furthermore, we are not just looking for accuracy per se but also for a better real-time forecasting approach that is more accurate than those of the Bloomberg real-time consensus forecast, on average, for major macroeconomic variables. The BVAR's real-time forecasts are compared with the Bloomberg real-time consensus. For comparison purposes, we use these

---

[21]C. A. Sims, J. Stock, and M. Watson (1990), "Inference in Linear Time Series Models with Some Unit Roots," *Econometrica* 58: 113–144.

[22]C. A. Sims (1991), "Comment on 'Empirical Analysis of Macroeconomic Time Series: VAR and Structural Models,' by Clements and Mizon," *European Economic Review* 35: 922–932.

[23]L. J. Álvarez and F. C. Ballabriga (1994), "BVAR Models in the Context of Cointegration: A Monte Carlo Experiment," *Documento de Trabajo*, no. 9405, Banco de España, Servicio de Estudios.

[24]The level form of a few variables is also important in some selected circumstances—for example, the ISM Manufacturing Index. However, these types of variables are very few.

two criteria: the real-time out-of-sample RMSE as the forecast evaluation criterion for the BVAR approach's real-time forecasts and the Bloomberg real-time consensus forecasts for each of the 20 macroeconomic variables. Equation 11.3 is employed to calculate the real-time out-of-sample RMSE:

$$\text{RMSE} = \sqrt{\frac{1}{t} \sum (Y_{t+1} - \hat{Y}_{t+1})^2} \tag{11.3}$$

where

$\hat{Y}_{t+1}$ = real-time one-month-ahead forecast, prior to the variable release

Y_{t+1} = actual release announcement of a macroeconomic variable

The magnitude of this statistic is used to compare the real-time out-of-sample performance of the BVAR approach and the consensus for all 20 variables. Furthermore, a model with a smaller RMSE is the best model among its competitors for a particular variable. For example, if the BVAR's CPI model has a smaller real-time out-of-sample RMSE than Bloomberg, the BVAR approach is the better model.

The real-time out-of-sample RMSE is a very good measure of forecast evaluation. However, in practice, and in the financial sector specifically, the direction of the release announcement is also very important since most hedged positions are based on a directional change rather than the magnitude of the change. As Bartolini et al. (2008) suggested, stronger-than-expected news announcements may increase interest rates, strengthen the dollar, and raise equity prices. Moreover, Boyd et al. (2005) showed that stock prices respond differently to changes in unemployment rate during recessions and expansions because the dividend and discount rate effects have different weights at different points of the business cycle. Therefore, it is very important to predict in real time the direction of the variable to make profits and/or minimize losses.

For instance, the average forecast error, RMSE, for the net change in the nonfarm payrolls model is, let us say, 75K (in forecasting, it may be a very reasonable number, given the volatility of the series), and the real-time one-month-forward forecast is +25K (a net gain of 25,000 jobs). Furthermore, if the actual release comes in as −45K (a net loss of 45,000 jobs), then this would imply that the actual payrolls stayed within the forecast +/− RMSE (25 +/−75; +100K and −50K) range. One would think the model is good; in fact, the model is still useful (in terms of the RMSE). However, it may not produce positive opportunities for the firm. Let us assume that the market consensus was a positive number, say +35K (net gain of 35,000 jobs) and the actual number comes in as a negative number, −45K. The response of the financial sector to the announcement would be significant as the news suggests weaker-than-expected job growth. If payrolls data came in weaker than expected, then equity prices may plunge since a negative payrolls number is generally associated with a weak labor market and thus a downshift in economic growth and corporate profit expectations.

A forecasting approach just based on the RMSE may not provide a firm with the most opportunity to generate financial gains. The first step to a more accurate forecasting approach would be that the forecast value should be close to the actual value or have the minimum average forecast error. Second, the direction of the forecast would also be accurate, on average. Since many macroeconomic variables are reported either in percentage change or net change, the sign (positive or negative) of the release announcement is also important. In the example—(forecast +25K versus actual −45K)—actual data stayed within the forecast +/− RMSE range, but the direction of the forecast was not correct, with a net gain of 25K jobs forecast but an actual net loss of 45K jobs. A better model evaluation must consider the directional accuracy along with the minimum forecast error, on average. Equation 11.4 is used to calculate the direction accuracy:

$$\text{Sign of } Y_{t+1} \equiv \text{Sign of } \hat{Y}_{t+1} \tag{11.4}$$

where
$\hat{Y}_{t+1}$ = a forecast
Y_{t+1} = actual release of a time series

It is important to note that there are a few variables that are reported on level terms or as an index, such as ISM Manufacturing and Non-Manufacturing surveys, the unemployment rate, and consumer confidence. We use equation 11.5 to calculate the directional accuracy of the forecast for those variables:

$$\text{Sign of } (Y_t - Y_{t+1}) \equiv \text{Sign of } (Y_t - \hat{Y}_{t+1}) \tag{11.5}$$

where
Y_t = prior-month value of the time series

If the difference between the actual release and prior-month value $(Y_t - Y_{t+1})$ has the same sign as the difference between forecast and the prior-month value of the time series $(Y_t - \hat{Y}_{t+1})$, then the direction of the forecast is correct.

For average directional accuracy, this equation is used:

$$(X/N) \times 100$$

where
X = number of forecasts that have the right direction
N = total number of forecasts

We convert the ratio into a percentage by multiplying by 100. If the forecast shares an identical sign with the actual release, then the direction is correct. For instance, from the previous example, if the forecast was −25K and actual release came in as −45K then the model was accurate in terms of RMSE as well as directionally accurate.

In conclusion, we suggest that a better forecasting approach must have a smaller real-time out-of-sample RMSE as well as a higher directional accuracy, on average, than the consensus forecast.

A SAS Application of the BVAR Approach: A Case Study of the Employment Forecast

In this section we discuss the SAS code for forecasting a macroeconomic or financial variable using the BVAR approach. We have selected nonfarm payrolls data series as a case study. As mentioned previously, we follow Silvia and Iqbal's (2012) proposed forecasting model for the nonfarm payrolls series. Their suggested model performed better in-sample and out-of-sample forecasting measures compared to its competitors and also performed better than the Bloomberg consensus in a real-time forecasting comparison (see the next section of this chapter for more details). SAS code S11.1 is utilized to generate a one-month-ahead forecast for nonfarm payrolls.[25] The procedure PROC VARMAX offers the BVAR option. In the second line of the code, after the SAS keyword Model, we list the variables of interest. Employment is our target variable (month-to-month change in nonfarm payrolls), and the other variables of the model are: help_wanted (help wanted index), Lay_off (number of job losers), ISM_M (ISM manufacturing employment index), ISM_NM (ISM non-manufacturing employment index), and claims (number of unemployment insurance claims filed).

```
PROC VARMAX data=payroll ;
Model Employment  Help_wanted Lay_off ISM_M ISM_NM Claims
/p=6 prior=(lambda=.4 theta=.3);    (S11.1)
Id date interval=month;
Output lead=1 out=forecast_payroll;
Run;
Quit;
```

The next step is to provide the number of lags (p=6), Silvia and Iqbal (2012) suggested to use lag order 6 (i.e., up to six lags of each variable). The lambda=.4 and theta=.3 are parameters of the Litterman's prior, as discussed earlier in this chapter. The third line of code instructs SAS to use the date

---

[25]It is important to note that SAS code S11.1 can be utilized to forecast any macroeconomic or financial time series. An analyst just needs to replace the listed variables with the desired variables to generate forecast for the variable of interest.

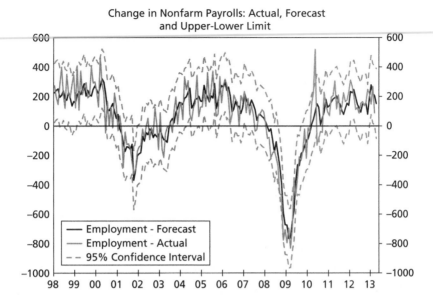

FIGURE 11.1 Nonfarm Payrolls: Actual, Forecast, and 95 Percent Confidence Interval

variable as ID, and the frequency of the dataset is month. In the next line, Output specifies a one-month-ahead forecast (as lead=1,) and the forecast along with actual and 95 confidence interval are saved in the newly created data file forecast_payroll.

In Figure 11.1, we plotted the actual employment data series along with the forecast and forecast interval. The forecast and actual values stay within the 95 percent forecast interval.[26] Overall, the model successfully predicted the turning points of the nonfarm payrolls series and produced consistent results.

FORECASTING IN REAL TIME: ISSUES RELATED TO THE DATA AND THE MODEL SELECTION

In addition to econometric modeling, there are several important issues that need to be considered in real-time (short-term) forecasting. For example, the functional form of a dependent variable and release timing of dependent/predictors are vital to an accurate real-time forecasting approach. This section discusses the functional form of variables and why the form is important. Furthermore, we present a procedure to select a predictor of a model.

---

[26] Except in May 2010, where the actual value (521K) is much larger than the upper limit (297K). This miss is a result of the 2010 Census. The U.S. Census Bureau hired hundreds of thousands of temporary workers that the model was unable to incorporate. Since we were aware of the census and could expect this census effect, we incorporated add-factors to the model's forecasted values, boosting the forecast number. For more details about add-factors, see Chapter 13 of this book.

The Functional Form of the Variables

This section discusses issues related to dependent/target variables and their predictors. First, the dependent variables forecasted typically include many macroeconomic and financial variables. Silvia and Iqbal (2012) selected 20 major macroeconomic variables for their study (a complete list of the variables is available in Appendix 11A). Most of these variables are reported either in percentage change or net change but not in level form. For instance, measures of inflation (CPI, Personal Consumption Expenditures deflator, and PPI), industrial production, retail sales, and durable goods orders are reported as month-to-month (MoM) and year-to-year (YoY) percentage changes while the nonfarm payrolls data is reported as a net monthly change. There are a few variables that are reported as level/index value, such as ISM Manufacturing/Nonmanufacturing indices and consumer confidence.

There are a few important points that we want to stress here. First, in the financial sector, the level form of many variables may not be relevant; instead, a specific form of a particular variable is meaningful to the market (e.g., a MoM percentage change in retail sales is more important than the level of the retail sales since the MoM percentage change suggests momentum/growth in the economy). Therefore, it is necessary to determine what form of the variable is meaningful to markets and what form the analyst is going to forecast.

Second, once an analyst determines the functional form of the target variable, then he or she seeks the best predictors for that variable. A final point is that the functional form of the predictors should be consistent with the functional form of the dependent variable (e.g., if the dependent variable is a MoM percentage change, it would be better to use a MoM percentage change of the predictors). Here we present a practical example of a retail sales model; see Silvia and Iqbal (2012) for more details. One of the predictors of the retail sales (MoM percentage change) is the ICSC Chain Store Index (chain-store sales). The chain-store sales is reported as a YoY percentage change. The retail sales model (we predict MoM percentage change in the sales) with chain-store sales (YoY percentage change) has a simulated out-of-sample RMSE of $24,201 million. If, however, the model uses the MoM percentage change of chain-store sales, then the simulated out-of-sample RMSE drops significantly to $3,042 million. One major reason for the two significantly different RMSEs from the same set of variables and same sample period is that the YoY percentage change represents a change that occurs over a different time period from the MoM change. Moreover, our objective is to forecast MoM percentage change in retail sales, and that suggests we should use the MoM percentage change in chain-store sales as a predictor, along with other predictors. This conclusion is true for many other variables as well.[27]

---

[27]The conclusion of this example is that we should at least include a functional form of the predictors, which is consistent with the target variable in the model specification process. If the same functional form is not a best option, then we can use the form that is consistent with the forecasting objective.

Consequently, the analysis suggests that during the model selection process, a forecaster should include the functional form of the predictor that is consistent with the functional form of the dependent variable.

It always has been difficult for researchers to filter through masses of data and find the most useful and best predictors. A small number of variables is essential, however, as including too many variables in a traditional econometric modeling framework creates over-fitting and/or degree of freedom issues—the curse of dimensionality problem.[28] However, due to advances in computer and database capabilities, combined with econometric/statistical software like SAS, a researcher can analyze each variable from a large dataset and select a reasonable number of variables based on some statistical criteria. This chapter suggests a step-wise procedure and selects a handful of predictors, mostly 5 to 7 variables, from a dataset of more than 300 variables.

Silvia and Iqbal (2012) propose a three-step procedure to select predictors for each of the 20 models from a database of over 300 variables. Four transformations of these 300 variables are utilized: (1) the level percentage change (MoM/YoY percentage change); (2) the lag of the variable; (3) the first-difference form; and (4) the lag of the first-difference form. In total, over 1,000 variables are created as potential predictors. The objective here is to include as many predictors as possible in the first step. In contrast to typical econometric modeling where a modeler already has a model specification guided by an economic theory, here the assumption is that an analyst does not know much about the model specification. The analyst must rely on data variation and statistical principles (basically, the data-mining technique) to indicate the choice of model specifications instead of utilizing previously employed models. The key advantage, among others, is that date-mining technique would allow each variable at least a chance to enter the final model and allows us to explore the usefulness in forecasting of all predictors to a greater extent.

The Selection of the Best Model Specification

To select predictors for all short-term forecasting models, Silvia and Iqbal (2012) utilize this three-step procedure.

1. We start by taking the regression of the dependent variable against each of these 1,000 variables, and retain those with significant predictive power. With a much smaller dataset, we then find the best model specifications with one predictor, two predictors, and so on, up to six predictors. The R^2 is used as the selection criterion in choosing these specifications. Ten variables are selected from this step.

2. We use the Granger causality test between the dependent variable against each of these 1,000 variables to come up with the top 10 variables based

---

[28]See Litterman (1986) for more details.

on the Chi-square test. We have now narrowed down our choice list to 20 variables, 10 from the regression and 10 from the Granger causality test.[29] These 20 variables, so far, came from an in-sample statistical procedure.

3. We use a simulated out-of-sample RMSE as a statistical measure to find the final model specification. Silvia and Iqbal set a 6-variable BVAR framework, which provides an opportunity for each of these 20 variables to audition as a predictor.[30] For most variables, we assume that the data is available, let us say, until 1999:M12, and we forecast for one month ahead. We then move one month forward, using data until 2000:M1, and again forecast for one month ahead. We repeat this process until the dataset reaches 2008:M11. At the end, we have 108 simulated out-of-sample one-month-ahead forecasted data points, which we use to calculate the RMSE. Six variables are thus selected based on the lowest RMSE value.

With the help of SAS, we increased the predictive power of the final model specification. As mentioned earlier, the BVAR method used a prior, referred to as the Minnesota prior. The efficacy of the BVAR model depends, to some extent, on the prior and selection of lag orders. A more flexible procedure is applied to select the prior and the lag orders, which involves the above-mentioned recursive method to calculate the out-of-sample RMSE, but this time we did not fix the lag orders or the value of Litterman's prior. We fixed a maximum lag order of 9 since the data series of many variables do not have a long history. As the Litterman's prior ranges between zero and one, with the flexibility and speed of the SAS system, we can get a better combination of the lags and the prior. For a six-variable model, for example, we choose a lag parameter, P, that ranges from 1 to 9, and the Litterman's prior, ϑ, that ranges from 0.1 to 0.9 with 0.1 increments, and follow the same procedure for λ. Altogether there will be 729 ($9 \times 9 \times 9 = 729$) models, consisting of a unique combination of P, ϑ, and λ, and 729 sets of RMSE. We select a combination that has the minimum RMSE and select the combination (values of P, ϑ, and λ,) as a final model specification. This model has the best overall simulated out-of-sample forecast performance based on the RMSE across multiple equations.

Timing of the Release: A Dependent Variable and Predictors

This section highlights a very important, and the most neglected, issue of the release timing of a dependent variable/predictors, an issue that must be

---

[29] In the second step, we included all variables and selected the top 10 variables other than those already selected in the first step. That way, we increased our choice list to 20 variables.

[30] Most of their models have five to eight predictors, and usually they start with a six-variable framework and then include/exclude variable(s) based on simulated out-of-sample RMSE.

considered in any practical model specification process for market forecasts. ~~Many macroeconomic variables are released with a time lag, such as a one-~~ month or two-month lag. For instance, the ISM manufacturing index is released on the first business day of the month for the previous month, with a one-month lag (on September 1, 2010, ISM manufacturing index was released for August 2010). Construction spending is released with a two-month lag, usually during the first week of the month (on September 1, 2010, construction spending data was released for July 2010). Indeed, during model specification, a researcher must consider these issues, as conventional forecasting procedure does not appear to recognize the data availability issues.

In real-time short-term macroeconomic forecasting, the most recent information about the predictors and dependent variable is crucial to a successful forecast. Here is an example of a nonfarm payrolls model. The model uses ISM manufacturing and nonmanufacturing employment indices as predictors, along with other predictors. If the model uses the lag form of the indices, instead of the current form, then the model has a simulated real-time one-month-ahead RMSE of 124K. With the current form of the employment indices, along with the same set of variables and same sample period, the model's RMSE drops significantly to 75K. This improvement in real-time forecasting using most recent values of predictors is true for many other models. As a result, having the most recent month's information regarding the predictors is an integral part of a good forecasting approach, and data availability is essential to having a realistic and useful model.

Another vital issue is the release timing of a dependent variable. For instance, ISM manufacturing, nonfarm payrolls, CPI, retail sales, industrial production, and personal income and spending data are released with a one-month lag, but the precise release timing is different for all these variables. Furthermore, the ISM manufacturing index is released on the first business day of every month; nonfarm payrolls is released on the first Friday of every month; CPI, retail sales, and industrial production usually are released toward the middle of every month; and personal income and spending data is released at the end of every month. Thus, although all these variables are released with a one-month lag, the precise release timing is different. Consequently, a forecaster cannot use current-month information of CPI, retail sales, and industrial production to predict nonfarm payrolls, the unemployment rate, or the ISM manufacturing index because the former are released after the latter. However, the researcher can use current-month information of the ISM manufacturing index and payrolls to predict the CPI, retail sales and/or industrial production. Similarly, current-month personal income and spending data cannot be used to predict CPI, retail sales, or industrial production. This issue is very important because, based on practical needs, many times when we need most recent values of predictors to generate forecast not all independent variables' recent values are available to include in the forecasting. That said, very often, at the end of the final step of a model specification, we end up with a handful of potential predictors (based on simulated out-of-sample RMSE) but have to drop some because they are released after the dependent variable. Moreover, if we use the lag form of those potential predictors (instead of the current values), the model's accuracy, based on simulated out-of-sample RMSE, deteriorates significantly.

Nonfarm payrolls data, for instance, is released on the first Friday of the month, and there are few independent predictors available for the model. ISM manufacturing and nonmanufacturing employment indices are very good predictors of the employment model and normally are released before the employment data's release. Therefore, the current month's information for these predictors can be used to forecast nonfarm payrolls. However, the use of the lag form of these predictors, instead of the current value, makes a significant difference, especially in terms of the simulated out-of-sample RMSE. From the previous example, if the nonfarm payrolls model uses the lag form of the ISM manufacturing and nonmanufacturing employment indices instead of the current form, then the model has a simulated real-time one-month-ahead RMSE of 124K. With the current form of the employment indices, along with the same set of variables and same sample period, the model's RMSE drops significantly to 75K. This is a major change in the RMSE, and this conclusion is true for many other models. The release timing of the dependent variable and predictors is very important and needs to be considered during the model specification process, especially in real-time short-term macroeconomic forecasting.

CASE STUDY: WFC VERSUS BLOOMBERG

In this section we compare real-time forecasts of Silvia and Iqbal (2012) using the BVAR approach with those of the Bloomberg real-time consensus for 20 key macroeconomic variables over the period of 2009:M01 to 2010:M08; 20 observations for each variable and total 400 (20 × 20). According to Silvia and Iqbal, every Friday morning, they submit the forecasts using the BVAR approach to Bloomberg and other media (and to their clients) for those variables that will be released during the next week. Therefore, the traders have enough time to make their investment decisions based on economic projections. Often they have almost a week to make their decisions (e.g., employment data releases on Friday; therefore, they submit their forecast usually one week before the actual release). The results appear in Tables 11.1 to 11.5.

Table 11.1 provides detailed information about the nonfarm payrolls forecasts.[31] Column 1 shows the date—when the forecast was submitted to the

---

[31] As an example, we present detailed results for nonfarm payrolls. For rest of the 19 variables, we provide a summary of the results in Tables 11.3 through 11.5.

TABLE 11.1 Net Change in the Nonfarm Payrolls: BVAR VS. Bloomberg Consensus

Date	WFC	Bloomberg Consensus	Prior Month	Revision	Actual Release	WFC	Bloomberg
29-01-2010	−68	20	−85	−150	−20	2304	1600
26-02-2010	−29	−67	−20	−26	−36	49	961
26-03-2010	177	195	−36	−14	162	225	1089
30-04-2010	200	180	162	230	290	8100	12100
28-05-2010	511	520	290		431	6400	7921
25-06-2010	−130	−110	431	433	−125	25	225
30-07-2010	−45	−60	−125	−221	−131	7396	5041
27-08-2010	−107	−15	−131	−54	−54	2809	1521
01-10-2010	7	5	−54	−57	−95	10404	10000
29-10-2010	40	64	−95	−41	151	12321	7569
24-11-2010	130	145	151	172	39	8281	11236
31-12-2010	156	135	39	71	103	2809	1024
28-01-2011	160	165	103	121	36	15576	16641
25-02-2011	200	180	36	63	192	64	144
25-03-2011	220	180	192	194	216	16	1296

(Continued)

TABLE 11.1 Net Change in the Nonfarm Payrolls: BVAR VS. Bloomberg Consensus (Continued)

Date	WFC	Bloomberg Consensus	Prior Month	Revision	Actual Release	WFC	Bloomberg
29-04-2011	165	180	216	221	244	6241	4096
27-05-2011	130	200	244	232	54	5776	21316
01-07-2011	88	100	54	25	18	4900	6724
29-07-2011	78	85	18	46	117	1521	1024
25-08-2011	30	95	117	85	0	900	9025
30-09-2011	35	50	0	57	103	4624	2809
28-10-2011	85	105	103	158	80	25	625
23-11-2011	133	112	80	100	120	169	64
30-12-2011	160	150	120	100	200	1600	2500
					MSE	4263.958333	5272.958333
					RMSE	65.30	72.62

media, Bloomberg and others. Column 2 indicates real-time forecasts using the BVAR approach and column 3 provides Bloomberg's real-time consensus for nonfarm payrolls. Column 4 contains the prior month's value and revisions to the prior month are shown in the column 5. Column 6 depicts the actual release of the nonfarm payrolls. The last two columns show real-time out-of-sample forecast error for the BVAR forecasts as well as the Bloomberg consensus.

It is worth mentioning that the nonfarm payrolls data is notorious for revisions, sometimes huge ones; in our analysis, 17 of the 20 months of nonfarm payrolls data were revised. Moreover, sometimes data is revised from a negative number (net job loss) to a positive (net job gain) and vice versa (e.g., on January 2010, the estimate for December 2009 nonfarm payrolls data was revised to +4K from −11K). That makes real-time one-month-ahead forecasting process for nonfarm payrolls harder. As mentioned earlier, we have set real-time out-of-sample RMSE along with real-time out-of-sample average directional accuracy as forecast evaluation criteria. Therefore, a model with a smaller RMSE and a higher average directional accuracy would be the most accurate.

As can be seen from Table 11.1, for the net change in nonfarm payrolls, the BVAR approach has a real-time out-of-sample RMSE of about 65K, and it is smaller than those of Bloomberg's real-time consensus, which is about 73K. Therefore, based on the RMSE, the BVAR model is more accurate than Bloomberg. The RMSE as a measure of forecast evaluation is necessary but not sufficient to adopt as a forecast procedure. The average directional accuracy would also be important. Markets move more when the actual announcement is different from the market expectations (stronger than expected or vice versa) because the direction of the release variable suggests momentum or loss of momentum in the economy. For instance, from Table 11.1, the BVAR's real-time forecast for January 2010 (released on February 5, 2010) was −68K (a net loss of 68,000 jobs) and the Bloomberg real-time consensus was +20K and the prior-month value was −85K. The actual release came in as −20K. The range for the BVAR forecast (forecast +/− RMSE) was between −3K and −133K (−68K +/− 65K); and between +93K and −53K (20K +/− 73K) for Bloomberg. Since the actual release stayed within one standard deviation within the range, the BVAR model and the Bloomberg consensus may be useful.

The implication of the actual release, however, is very different from those of the Bloomberg consensus. For instance, let us analyze the situation in real time. In February 2010, the U.S. economy was still in recession, as the National Bureau of Economic Research (NBER) had not yet declared the end of the 2007 to 2009 recession.[32] Moreover, the monthly net change in nonfarm payrolls

---

[32]The NBER, however, declared on September 20, 2010, that June 2009 was the end of the recession of 2007 to 2009.

TABLE 11.2 Summary of the Results: Net Change in Nonfarm Payrolls

	WFC	Bloomberg
Direction Right	19	16
Direction Wrong	5	8
Perfect Forecast	0	0
Both Missed	5	
Directional	0.79	0.67
Accuracy	79%	67%

was continuously showing net job losses since January 2008.[33] A market consensus of +20K indicated that people were expecting marginal improvement in the labor market. The BVAR model, however, still forecasted a net job loss of 68K. In addition, the investment decisions would be different based on these two outlooks for the labor market since the labor market is a key indicator of the U.S. economy. The actual release of a negative number (−20K) was consistent with the BVAR but also with the signal that the economy remained weak. Furthermore, as Rigobon-Sack (2008) and Bartolini et al. (2008) suggest, markets move significantly when the actual release is different from market expectations. Therefore, had the trader acted on and accurately forecast the direction of the actual release, it was a perfect opportunity for the trader to make money, given that the actual release was weaker than expected. That is just one example of the importance of the directional accuracy. From Table 11.2, the BVAR nonfarm payrolls model has an average directional accuracy of 79 percent (79 percent of the time the direction of the forecast was right), which is higher than Bloomberg consensus (of 67 percent). Therefore, the nonfarm payrolls model using the BVAR approach is more accurate, on average, than Bloomberg, in terms of the real-time out-of-sample RMSE and average directional accuracy.

In Table 11.3, we provide real-time out-of-sample RMSE and directional accuracy of each of the 20 macroeconomic variables for the BVAR and the Bloomberg consensus. The results indicate that BVAR has smaller RMSEs for 18 of the 20 variables than those of the Bloomberg consensus, which reflects the median forecast likely derived from a number of forecasting approaches. Only for 2 variables (durable goods orders and trade balance) does the BVAR have a slightly higher RMSE than Bloomberg; however, these variables have a higher directional accuracy than those of Bloomberg. In terms of real-time

---

[33]The actual release of nonfarm payrolls indicates a negative number (a net job loss) during the time period from January 2008 to February 2010. However, the November 2009 data was revised to a positive number (a net job gain), the first positive number since January 2008.

TABLE 11.3 Summary of the Results for 20 Variables

Indicators	WFC		Bloomberg Consensus	
	Accuracy	RMSE	Accuracy	RMSE
Consumer Confidence	73%	4.28	62%	4.6
Existing Home Sales	74%	0.26	74%	0.29
Durable Goods Orders	71%	2.45	61%	2.27
New Home Sales	62%	34.65	46%	39.72
Personal Income	83%	0.33	73%	0.42
Personal Spending	93%	0.21	77%	0.25
ISM Manufacturing	92%	1.99	69%	2.01
ISM Non-Manufacturing	77%	1.16	62%	1.615
Factory Orders	84%	0.92	74%	0.98
Employment	79%	65.3	67%	72.62
Unemployment Rate	92%	0.17	83%	0.18
Trade Balance	72%	4.17	52%	3.97
PPI	90%	0.52	86%	0.53
Retail Sales	72%	0.85	62%	1.20
Business Inventories	96%	0.28	89%	0.32
Industrial Production	79%	0.34	76%	0.42
CPI	86%	0.1	79%	0.12
Housing Starts	75%	44.23	42%	56.66
Leading Indicators	97%	0.1	90%	0.23
PCE Deflator	97%	0.11	94%	0.18
Average	82%	8.12	71%	9.43

average directional accuracy, 19 of the 20 models have a higher accuracy than those of Bloomberg. Only one model (existing home sales) has accuracy equal to Bloomberg. Nevertheless, this model has smaller RMSE than that of Bloomberg. From Table 11.4, for 17 of the 20 variables, the BVAR has a smaller RMSE as well as a higher (one has equal accuracy) average directional accuracy than that of Bloomberg. In addition, none of the BVAR model has a lower average directional accuracy than Bloomberg. As a result, the BVAR real-time forecasts are more accurate than those of the Bloomberg consensus, on average.

TABLE 11.4 Summary of the Results

	WFC			Bloomberg Consensus		
	Accuracy	RMSE	Combined	Accuracy	RMSE	Combined
Better	19	18	17	0	2	0
Equal	1	0		1		
Total	20					

TABLE 11.5 Summary of the Results

	WFC	% of Total	Consensus	% of Total
100	0	0	0	0.0
90–99	7	35.0	2	10.0
80–89	3	15.0	3	15.0
70–79	9	45.0	6	30.0
60–69	1	5.0	6	30.0
50–59	0	0.0	1	5.0
40–49	0	0.0	2	10.0
Total	20	100.0	20	100
80+	10	50.0	5	25.00
70+	19	95.0	11	55.00

A summary of results are in Table 11.5. It can be seen that 7 of the 20 models have real-time out-of-sample average directional accuracy of 90 percent or more compared to Bloomberg, which has only 2. Moreover, 50 percent of the models (10 of the 20) have a directional accuracy of 80 percent or more compared to 25 percent (5 of the 20) for Bloomberg. If we set, for example, 70 percent directional accuracy as a benchmark for a best model, then 19 of the 20 models (95 percent) passed that test compared to 55 percent (11 variables) for Bloomberg. Overall, average directional accuracy for BVAR models is 82 percent; for Bloomberg, 71 percent. In conclusion, clearly, the BVAR's forecasts are more accurate than those of the Bloomberg consensus, on average. It is worth mentioning that over the past year, we have been cited by Bloomberg in the top-five forecasters for major macroeconomic variables such as nonfarm payrolls, unemployment rate, and housing starts.

There is another essential question: Do markets respond differently to the macroeconomic variable release announcements in different stages of the business cycle? The answer to this question, based on empirical evidence and personal experience, is yes. For instance, Anderson et al. (2007) suggested that the equity market reacts differently to the macroeconomic news announcements depending on the stage of business cycle. Moreover, Boyd et al. (2005) concluded that stock prices respond differently to changes in the unemployment rate during recessions and expansions because the dividend and discount rate effects have different weights at different points of business cycle.[34] The vital points are: (1) the financial markets react differently to the news announcements depending on the stages of the business cycle—whether it is a recession or expansion, and (2) some variables may have a significant effect on the markets at some stage of the business cycle, during recession (or early phase of a recovery) rather than at a normal or steady stage of the economic expansion. For example, during the 2007 to 2010 recession and early phase of the recovery, the data release announcements regarding the housing sector received more financial market attention and thereby generated significant market volatility and reaction than in earlier cycles.[35] The housing sector boom-bust was a major cause of the 2007 to 2009 recession, and a solid economic recovery without a housing sector recovery was considered unlikely. Therefore, the housing-related data announcements were very important to the financial market at least during the 2007 to 2010 time period and continue to be so at the time of this writing. As a result, accurate forecasts of housing-related data are more important during this cycle than in earlier cycles.

Housing-related data announcements were very important to the markets. From Table 11.3, the BVAR's forecasts for those variables were better than those of the Bloomberg consensus, on average. For instance, BVAR forecasts for housing starts, a key representative of the housing sector, had a real-time out-of-sample RMSE of 44K (44,000 units) compared to 57K for the Bloomberg consensus. The housing starts model has a higher (75 percent) real-time average directional accuracy than Bloomberg (42 percent); see the table for details. Another important variable is new home sales. The BVAR model has a lower RMSE (35K) and higher directional accuracy (62 percent) compared to those of Bloomberg (RMSE = 40K and 46 percent directional accuracy). In addition, forecasts for existing home sales were more accurate than those of the Bloomberg consensus, on average (see the table for details). In conclusion, the essential point is that there could be a few macroeconomic variables which become vital to the markets because of their relation to the causes of recession/recovery (e.g., the housing sector became a key to the 2007 to 2009 recession and recovery).

A crucial issue is that many macroeconomic variables are notorious for revisions, which makes short-term forecasting accuracy difficult. For example,

---

[34]J. Boyd, Jian Hu, and J. Ravi (2005), "The Stock Market's Reaction to Unemployment News: Why Bad News Is Usually Good for Stocks," *Journal of Finance* 60, no. 2 (April): 649–672.

[35]It is worth mentioning that it is our anecdotal observation; we leave an empirical proof for future research.

in this analysis, housing starts, retail sales, and durable goods orders have been revised for all 20 months; employment was revised for 17 months; and industrial production was revised for 18 of the 20 months. This is a warning for researchers/forecasters often the fact using revised, not real-time, data in the short-term forecasting and that reduces forecast accuracy.

Summing up, first, the BVAR forecasts are more accurate than those of the Bloomberg consensus, on average. Second, some variables may get more financial sector attention due to their relation to the stages of business cycle. This implies that an analyst should be aware of the changing importance of these variables, and it is better to attempt to forecast all major macroeconomic variables accurately to build up some experience with real-time forecasts for each series. Finally, many macroeconomic variables are notorious for revisions, a fact that must be considered when using revised data to mimic real-time responses.[36]

SUMMARY

This chapter provides a real-time real short-term macroeconomic forecasting approach. Furthermore, we shed light on four important areas of macroeconomic forecasting:

1. The macroeconomic variable release impacts financial market volatility and direction; moreover, the impact is most significant when the actual release is different from the market expectation.

2. The economic value of a forecast methodology that is better than consensus is increased, provided that the markets move when the actual release values are significantly different from market consensus. An individual forecast approach that is better than consensus will provide more opportunities to make a profit or reduce losses.

3. In short-term forecasting (one month ahead), the actual release timing of the target variable (dependent variable) as well as the predictors is very important and needs to be considered in model specification.

4. Traditional forecast evaluation methods, such as R^2, adjusted R^2, RMSE, and so on, are necessary, but we recommend an additional step: directional accuracy.

Using the Silvia and Iqbal forecasting approach, we compared the BVAR's real-time forecasts with the Bloomberg real-time consensus and concluded that the BVAR forecasts are more accurate than those of the Bloomberg consensus, on average, for key macroeconomic variables.

---

[36] See Croushore and Stark (2001) for more details.

APPENDIX 11A: LIST OF VARIABLES

Silvia and Iqbal (2012) included 20 variables in their forecasting comparison of the BVAR model and the Bloomberg consensus. The first column provides the name of a variable. The second column shows the specific form of the forecasted variable. For example, a month-over-month (MoM) percentage change of the business inventories is forecasted. All variables are monthly series.

TABLE 11.A Forecast Evaluation 2010

Indicators	Functional Form
Business Inventories	MoM % Change
Consumer Confidence	Level of the Index
CPI	MoM % Change
Durable Goods Orders	MoM % Change
Existing Home Sales	Level (Millions of Unit)
Industrial Production	MoM % Change
Factory Orders	MoM % Change
Housing Starts	Level (Thousands of Unit)
ISM Manufacturing	Level of the Index
ISM Non-Manufacturing	Level of the Index
Leading Indicators	MoM % Change
New Home Sales	Level (Thousands of Unit)
Nonfarm Payrolls	MoM Net Change
PCE Deflator	MoM % Change
Personal Income	MoM % Change
Personal Spending	MoM % Change
PPI	MoM % Change
Retail Sales	MoM % Change
Unemployment Rate	% Form
Trade Balance	Level (Billions of Dollars)

CHAPTER **12**

A Multiple-Equations Approach to Long-Term Forecasting

Short-term forecasting is not the only important element of decision making. Several important decisions consider the longer-term economic outlook.[1] For instance, a firm's budget, investment, and employment decisions often incorporate the economic outlook for the next five to seven years. Long-term forecasting of key economic and financial variables, therefore, plays a crucial role in public and private sector decision making. This chapter presents procedures useful to develop models for long-term economic and business forecasting, which differ in several ways from the steps of short-run forecasting.[2]

When building forecasting models for a longer time period, an analyst should keep a few important points in mind. First, the chances of significant changes in the economic environment are very high. Forecasting the value of the Standard & Poor's (S&P) 500 index a few years out is not easy because there is a high probability of significant changes in the model for equity returns. In January 2008, for example, the U.S. economy was in recession and the S&P 500 index was in bearish territory. If an analyst was trying to make a forecast for the S&P 500 index two years ahead, he or she would struggle with the assumptions. If the recession ended in 2008 and was followed by a strong recovery, the S&P 500 index would have quickly turned bullish. However, that

---

[1]This chapter considers long-term forecasting as forcasts for at least two years out.
[2]Chapters 10 and 11 developed useful procedures for short-term forecasting.

was not the case.[3] So longer-term forecasting is associated with higher uncertainty when compared to a shorter-term forecast horizon.

Second, many macroeconomic variables behave differently during different phases of the business cycle. The average business cycle duration, defined as trough to trough since World War II, is around 70 months. The U.S. unemployment rate tends to rise during recessions and fall during expansions. An analyst interested in forecasting the unemployment rate for the next six to eight years would always need to consider business cycle movements.

Third, analysts need to consider policy changes. The two major political parties have very different tax and spending preferences. Elections thus may also affect the accuracy of long-term forecasting. Hence, the possibility of a structural change due to internal policy change or external shocks is higher during long-term forecasting compared to short-term prediction.

The last factor analysts need to think about is that the variables and model selection procedures are different for long-term forecasting from those for short-term forecasting. As mentioned in Chapters 10 and 11, in short-term forecasting, the predictors and final model specification are selected based on simulated out-of-sample root mean square error (RMSE), where the model with the smallest simulated out-of-sample RMSE is chosen. In long-term forecasting, large-scale macroeconometric models that utilize hundreds of variables and dozens of regression equations are all built on the basis of an economic theory.[4] There are at least two major reasons for this approach. The first reason is that the chance of a significant change in the behavior of a macroeconomic variable is higher in the long run, which can influence other sectors of the economy. For instance, the boom and subsequent bust in the U.S. housing sector was one of the major causes of the Great Recession and financial crisis of 2007 to 2009. Changes in the behavior of the housing sector therefore influenced changes in many other sectors of the U.S. economy. Forecasters often do not know ahead of time which sector of the economy will lead to changes in other sectors. Therefore, it is important to include as much information as possible in the long-term forecasting model. Typically, a forecaster wants to include key predictors representing major sectors of the economy in the model.

The second reason to rely on theory instead of statistical measures to create a long-term forecasting model is that most economic and financial data series do not have a long history—an essential element to calculate simulated out-of-sample RMSE. For instance, in Chapter 11, we mentioned that we finalize

---

[3]The recovery from the 2007 to 2009 recession turned out to be weaker than the historical standard, and the S&P 500 index was 1,242 on December 2010, which was lower than the January 2008 level of 1,379.

[4]For more details about macro-models, see Ray Fair (2004), *Estimating How the Macroeconomy Works* (Cambridge, MA: Harvard University Press).

short-term forecasting models based on the simulated out-of-sample RMSE. That is, we calculate simulated out-of-sample RMSEs for different model specifications and select the model that produces the smallest RMSE. In the case of long-term forecasting, due to a lack of a longer history of the dataset, it would be difficult to estimate simulated out-of-sample RMSE for different models and then compare those with each other to select the best model based on RMSE.[5]

Once an analyst selects the variables for the long-term forecast model, the next step is to estimate the model. There are two major categories of estimation methods: unconditional forecasting models and conditional forecasting models.

The unconditional forecasting approach utilizes Bayesian vector autoregression (BVAR) models. The BVAR approach is termed unconditional because it does not require future values of the right-hand-side variables to generate out-of-sample forecasts for target variables (this is covered in depth in the next section of this chapter). The conditional forecasting approach extends the single-equation approach (explained in Chapter 10) into a multiple equation system. The out-of-sample forecasts of the target variables are conditioned on the future values of the right-hand-side variables.

While both the conditional and unconditional long-term forecasting approaches identify variables of interest with the help of economic and financial theory, the unconditional approach forecasts based on the current and past values of the dataset while the conditional approach develops different scenarios for the target variables based on conditional future values of the right-hand-side variables. For instance, later in this chapter we look at what happens to U.S. economic growth if oil prices suddenly rise to $150 per barrel from $95 per barrel. This chapter discusses both the unconditional and conditional forecasting approaches and provides SAS codes helpful in generating these forecasts.

THE UNCONDITIONAL LONG-TERM FORECASTING: THE BVAR MODEL

In this section we explore the unconditional long-term forecasting approach, utilizing BVAR models. Before we discuss the BVAR approach, we look at the limitations of large-scale macro models, which were the major tools for long-term forecasting before the introduction of VAR/BVAR. For long-term forecasting, the traditional Keynesian models known as large-scale macro models seem to have been the natural tools from the 1950s to the 1970s.[6] In the late 1970s, however, a

---

[5]There a large number of series that go back only a couple of decades. Retail sales, existing home sales, and ISM nonmanufacturing data, for instance, go back only to the early 1990s. That is a short history to calculate two-year-ahead out-of-sample RMSEs.
[6]See Fair (2004) for more details about Keynesian models.

few prominent economists criticized the theoretical foundation of these models.[7] They thought that the traditional models consisting of dozens, if not hundreds, of econometric regressions were usually too large for the individual analyst to use effectively. They also recognized that forecasting with the traditional models requires the future values of the models' exogenous variables, which are often hard to predict. In addition, in practice, it is difficult to determine which variables are endogenous and which are exogenous. This is also known as the identification problem. (See Sims [1980] for more detail.) For these reasons, traditional large-scale macro models may not be easy to build in practice.

Sims (1980) provided a new framework for macroeconomic forecasting known as vector autoregressions (VAR). A VAR is an n-equation, n-variable model in which each variable is a linear function of its own lagged values, plus the lagged values of the other $n-1$ variables. In a VAR there are no exogenous variables. In other words, all variables are treated equally and the n variables are endogenous; future values of these variables can easily be forecasted due to the VAR approach's dynamic setup. The VAR approach has proven to be a powerful and reliable forecasting method in everyday use.[8] However, there is a technical problem despite its success. Macroeconomic time series usually have short sample sizes (e.g., quarterly gross domestic product [GDP] or monthly unemployment rate) while the number of VAR parameters increases rapidly with the increase in the number of variables and lags. This many parameters creates an over-fitting problem that leads to a good in-sample fit but poor out-of-sample forecasting performance. To avoid the over-fitting problem, a typical VAR has to be relatively small.

Litterman (1980) presented the BVAR approach to address this problem.[9] As mentioned in Chapter 11, Litterman's method imposes prior restrictions, also known as Minnesota Prior, on the VAR parameters. The prior allows the inclusion of a larger number of variables and their lags in the BVAR model compared to the traditional VAR model. Litterman (1986) showed that his approach is as accurate, on average, as those utilized by the best-known commercial forecasting services (DRI, Chase, and Wharton at that time).[10]

Variable selection is an important aspect of the BVAR (and VAR) forecasting approach. The variables should represent key sectors of the economy, but, at the same time, the analyst should not include too many variables, as that would create an over-fitting problem.

---

[7]Robert Lucas (1976), "Econometric Policy Evaluation: A Critique," *Carnegie-Rochester Conference Series on Public Policy*, no. 1. Christopher Sims (1980), "Macroeconomics and Reality," *Econometrica* 48, no. 1: 1–48.

[8]For more details, see James H. Stock and Mark W. Watson (2001), "Vector Autoregressions," *Journal of Economic Perspectives* 15, no. 4. 101–115

[9]Robert B. Litterman (1980), "A Bayesian Procedure for Forecasting with Vector Autoregressions," working Paper, Massachusetts Institute of Technology, Department of Economics.

[10]Robert B. Litterman (1986), "Forecasting with Bayesian Vector Autoregressions—Five Years of Experience," *Journal of Business and Economic Statistics* 4: 25–38.

For example, if the goal is to create a BAVR model of the U.S. economy, the analyst would be able to create an accurate forecast using an eight-variable BVAR model. The variables are: real GDP, 10-year Treasury yields, industrial production, unemployment rate, consumer price index, S&P 500 index, trade-weighted dollar, and the Commodity Futures Price index. Essentially we try to include variables from major sectors of the economy. In this case, real GDP (GDP) represents the broad economy, while 10-year Treasury yields (Ten_year) capture the effects of interest rates and borrowing costs on the economy. The unemployment rate (RUC) is a good labor market indicator, and CPI is a proxy for the inflation rate. Industrial production (IP) represents the production side of the economy, and the S&P 500 index (SP500) is utilized to represent the financial sector and the services sector, as major companies are closely related with the S&P 500 index. The U.S. economy is an open economy in which the exchange rate plays a key role in international trade. Trade-weighted index (Dollar) is included to capture the exchange rate effect on the economy. Commodities prices also affect the inflation rate and overall economy; that is why we include the CRB index (CRB) in the BVAR model.

Once an analyst decides to employ the BVAR approach for long-term forecasting and selects the variables for the model, the next step is to utilize SAS to estimate the model and generate forecasts. SAS code S12.1 estimates the eight-variables BVAR model.

```
*The Eight-variables BVAR Model ;
PROC VARMAX data=bvar_data ;                    (S12.1)
Model gdp Ten_year ruc  CPI  IP  SP500 Dollar CRB
/p=6 prior=(lambda=.4 theta=.3);
ID date interval=qtr;
output lead=8 out=forecast_bvar;
Run;
Quit;
```

PROC VARMAX offers the BVAR option. The data file `bvar_data` contains all eight variables. After the SAS keyword `Model`, we listed the variables of interests. The lag order (denoted by p) is 6, meaning that up to six lags of each variable are included in the BVAR model. The prior values `lambda=.4` and `theta=.3` are used.[11] The SAS keyword `ID` instructs SAS to utilize the variable name `date` as ID, and the interval is quarterly. The term `output` is another SAS keyword that generates and saves out-of-sample forecasts

---

[11] In Chapter 11 of this book, we explained the process to choose a lag order (p) and values for the prior (lambda and theta). We selected the values for p, lambda, and theta based on the Chapter 11 criteria.

for all eight variables. The output is saved in a data file named forecast_bvar, and lead=8 shows that eight quarters ahead is to be forecasted. We employ a quarterly dataset for the 1986:Q1 = 2013:Q1 period.

The forecasts based on SAS code S12.1 are presented in Table 12.1. The model predicted a GDP growth rate around 3 percent over the next eight quarters, peaking at 3.38 percent in 2014:Q3. The CPI shows an inflation rate of below 2 percent for the 2013–2014 periods. Both the industrial production and S&P 500 show strong growth rates. The dollar index is weakening, and the CRB index shows a moderate growth rate compared to historical standards. The 10-year Treasury yield stays below 2 percent, and the unemployment rate has a decreasing trend. Overall, the BVAR model predicts a moderate growth scenario for the U.S. economy.

For a visual look, the actual GDP growth, GDP forecasts, and the upper and lower forecast limits for a 95 percent interval are plotted in Figure 12.1.[12] The forecast seems accurate because the actual values and the forecasted values stay mostly within the forecast band, although, in Q4-2008 the actual GDP value crossed the lower limit of the forecast. One reason this may have happened is because the depth of the Great Recession was a surprise to many economists and analysts. However, the model did correctly predict the direction. Overall, the chart suggests that the BVAR model's forecasting performance is reliable.

THE BVAR MODEL WITH HOUSING STARTS

Given the importance of the housing sector on the performance of the U.S. economy, we look at another BVAR model, which includes housing starts data to capture housing sector activity. In this model we did not include the trade-weighted dollar. Therefore, the BVAR model still contains eight variables. SAS code S12.2 estimates the BVAR model with housing starts (HS_YoY), using the same lag and prior values as in S12.1.

```
*The BVAR Model with Housing Starts ;

PROC VARMAX data=bvar_data ;                    (S12.2)

Model gdp Ten_year ruc  CPI  IP  SP500 HS_YoY CRB

/p=6 prior=(lambda=.4 theta=.3);

ID date interval=qtr;

Output lead=8 out=forecast_housingbvar;

Run;

Quit;
```

---

[12]To save the space, we just plotted GDP (actual and forecast), but SAS produces the similar output for all eight variables.

TABLE 12.1 Forecasts Based on the Eight-Variable BVAR Model

									The Eight-Variables BVAR Model							
Date	Annualized Real GDP	Forecasted Annualized Real GDP	CPI (YOY)	Forecasted CPI (YOY)	IP (YOY)	Forecasted IP (YOY)	SP 500 (YOY)	Forecasted SP 500 (YOY)	Trade Weight $ (YOY)	Forecasted Trade Weight $ (YOY)	CRB Index (YOY)	Forecasted CRB (YOY)	Ten Years Treasury	Forecasted Ten Years Treasury	Unemployment Rate	Forecasted Unemployment Rate
1/1/2011	0.09	2.45	2.13	1.63	4.79	4.50	15.98	10.41	-4.21	-3.14	24.36	22.98	3.46	3.10	9.00	9.29
4/1/2011	2.47	2.39	3.35	2.87	2.86	3.43	16.22	20.42	-8.00	-5.37	24.54	23.28	3.21	3.42	9.03	8.79
7/1/2011	1.27	1.90	3.75	3.53	2.55	2.42	12.10	19.12	-6.36	-5.50	16.14	18.51	2.43	3.01	9.00	8.85
10/1/2011	4.09	1.64	3.33	3.21	3.30	2.47	1.79	8.72	0.40	-1.23	-4.99	1.31	2.05	2.19	8.67	8.84
1/1/2012	1.96	1.19	2.81	2.48	3.97	3.39	3.47	-1.42	1.13	3.89	-11.22	-14.40	2.04	1.82	8.27	8.47
4/1/2012	1.25	2.14	1.90	2.26	4.50	4.14	2.35	3.62	5.63	2.90	-14.26	-10.24	1.83	2.04	8.17	8.05
7/1/2012	3.11	2.00	1.70	1.55	3.32	4.08	14.08	3.58	4.93	5.50	-11.31	-10.92	1.64	1.79	8.04	8.01
10/1/2012	0.38	2.89	1.90	1.68	2.71	3.03	15.73	18.23	-0.44	3.03	-2.38	-3.74	1.71	1.76	7.83	7.81
1/1/2013	2.50	2.95	1.67	1.88	2.62	2.70	12.41	17.05	0.92	-0.39	-0.51	0.93	1.95	1.78	7.73	7.63
4/1/2013		2.62		1.57		2.91		12.76		0.46		-0.18		1.85		7.53
7/1/2013		3.17		1.34		3.67		10.68		0.54		-0.27		1.82		7.32
10/1/2013		2.95		1.11		4.49		9.71		1.16		0.04		1.84		7.08
1/1/2014		3.26		1.14		5.00		10.00		-0.09		2.35		1.83		6.83
4/1/2014		3.29		1.25		5.25		10.58		-1.17		5.30		1.82		6.58
7/1/2014		3.38		1.41		5.23		11.51		-1.99		7.21		1.83		6.31
10/1/2014		3.27		1.52		5.00		11.83		-2.52		7.61		1.82		6.06

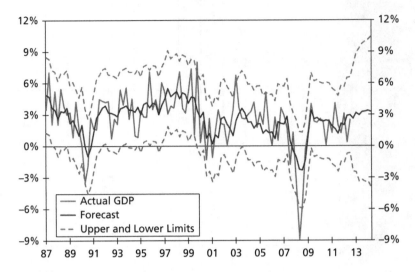

FIGURE 12.1 GDP Forecasts Based on the Eight-Variable BVAR Model

Table 12.2 reports forecasts based on code S12.2. The forecasts point toward relatively stronger growth rates for the U.S. economy compared to the one presented in Table 12.1. One major reason for this relatively stronger forecast is that the housing sector was a major cause of the Great Recession. Without a solid recovery in the housing sector, the overall economy may not experience a fast and strong recovery. The BVAR model predicts stronger growth rates for housing starts (a solid recovery), boosting the overall economy's growth rates.

Figure 12.2 plots actual GDP growth, the forecast with housing starts and the 95 percent interval based on the BVAR model with housing starts. The forecasts seem relatively accurate as the actual and forecast figures stay mostly within the forecast band.

Figure 12.3 shows actual GDP growth along with the forecast based on the original eight-variable BVAR model and the modified model with housing starts.

In summary, an analyst can generate forecasts for key economic and financial variables using the BVAR model. The SAS codes we used in S12.1 and S12.2 can be used to forecast any variable by replacing the listed variables with others of interest.

THE MODEL WITHOUT OIL PRICE SHOCK

The BVAR model's use of past and current values to forecast defines the approach as unconditional. However, sometimes it may be essential for decision makers to predict the future paths of key economic and financial variables under different policy environments or in the face of an external shock, such as an oil price shock.

TABLE 12.2 Forecasts Based on the Modified Model with Housing Starts

							The BVAR Model with Housing Starts									
Date	Annualized Real GDP	Forecasted Annualized Real GDP	CPI (YOY)	Forecasted CPI (YOY)	IP (YOY)	Forecasted IP (YOY)	SP 500	Forecasted SP 500	Housing Starts (YOY)	Forecasted Housing Starts (YOY)	CRB Index (YOY)	Forecasted CRB (YOY)	Ten Years Treasury	Forecasted Ten Years Treasury	Unemployment Rate	Forecasted Unemployment Rated
1/1/2011	0.09	2.41	2.13	1.69	4.79	4.51	15.98	11.09	-5.33	-7.00	24.36	23.43	3.46	3.12	9.00	9.28
4/1/2011	2.47	2.28	3.35	2.89	2.86	3.32	16.22	20.21	-4.88	-0.77	24.54	23.51	3.21	3.40	9.03	8.79
7/1/2011	1.27	1.84	3.75	3.48	2.55	2.35	12.10	18.27	5.89	6.96	16.14	18.56	2.43	2.98	9.00	8.85
10/1/2011	4.09	1.73	3.33	3.15	3.30	2.46	1.79	7.71	25.02	13.28	-4.99	0.96	2.05	2.18	8.67	8.83
1/1/2012	1.96	1.36	2.81	2.50	3.97	3.46	3.47	-1.88	22.05	26.28	-11.22	-14.72	2.04	1.82	8.27	8.47
4/1/2012	1.25	1.93	1.90	2.26	4.50	4.02	2.35	3.56	28.46	27.79	-14.26	-10.32	1.83	2.01	8.17	8.08
7/1/2012	3.11	2.01	1.70	1.57	3.32	4.17	14.08	4.49	25.96	27.87	-11.31	-10.68	1.64	1.83	8.04	8.03
10/1/2012	0.38	2.76	1.90	1.73	2.71	3.09	15.73	19.47	33.43	26.43	-2.38	-3.30	1.71	1.78	7.83	7.82
1/1/2013	2.50	3.35	1.67	1.71	2.62	2.68	12.41	14.87	35.56	34.14	-0.51	-0.14	1.95	1.76	7.73	7.61
4/1/2013		3.30		1.41		3.00		11.01		33.84		-0.95		1.83		7.48
7/1/2013		3.98		1.12		4.00		8.08		34.01		-0.84		1.82		7.19
10/1/2013		3.95		0.92		5.19		7.23		32.24		0.75		1.86		6.84
1/1/2014		4.14		1.04		6.15		8.68		31.23		4.85		1.89		6.47
4/1/2014		4.13		1.29		6.78		10.37		31.17		9.18		1.91		6.09
7/1/2014		4.19		1.52		6.92		11.64		29.69		11.42		1.93		5.69
10/1/2014		4.06		1.65		6.60		11.76		27.49		11.22		1.93		5.32

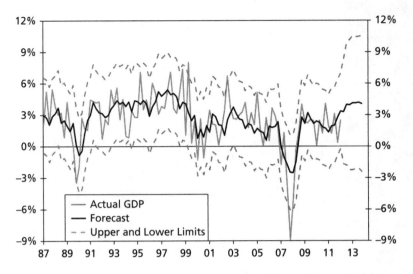

FIGURE 12.2 GDP Forecasts Based on the Modified Model with Housing Starts

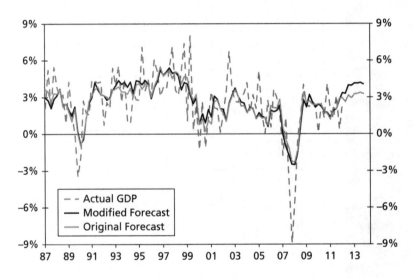

FIGURE 12.3 GDP Forecasts Based on the Original and Modified BVAR Model

What would happen to the economy if oil prices suddenly increased? The price for West Texas Intermediate crude oil (WTI) peaked at $133.88 per barrel on June 2008, a 98.4 percent increase from $67.49 per barrel just one year earlier. This swift price increase shocked consumers and squeezed their wallets as retail gasoline prices hit $4.00 per gallon for the first time. Such a shock to consumers and on their confidence and their willingness to spend could have large negative effects on economic activity. For this reason, decision makers might want to forecast economic growth under various scenarios, specifically oil price shocks. In this case study, we utilize the conditional forecasting approach and generate forecasts conditioned on a scenario with and without an oil price shock.

As mentioned previously, building a large-scale macro model to forecast the outcome of economic shocks is difficult. A more practical approach is to develop a small-scale multiple-equation model to generate conditional forecasts. For our case study, we create an eight-equation, eight-variable model. We utilize the same variables used in the BVAR model in the previous section. Because these variables represent major sectors of the U.S. economy, they can help build a small but effective macro model.

In this approach we build eight equations: one for each variable (equation 12.1). Each equation includes a lag of the dependent variable along with seven other variables as right-hand-side variables. The WTI crude oil price, our measure for oil prices, is also included in each equation as an exogenous variable.

Essentially, we are following the VAR logic and treating all variables as equal by building an equation for each variable; this implies that all of the variables are interconnected and dependent on each other. This solves the identification problem. The variable for oil prices, WTI, is left as the only exogenous variable that is not given its own model.

A Small-Scale Macro Model: Equation 12.1

```
GDP   = ao + a1*WTI + a2*lag(GDP)+ a3*Ten_Yr + a4*UR + a5*CPI +
a6*IP + a7*SP500 + a8*Dollar + a9*CRB +ε1

Ten_Yr = bo + b1*WTI + b2*lag(Ten_Yr)+ b3*GDP + b4*UR + b5*CPI +
b6*IP + b7*SP500 + b8*Dollar + b9*CRB +ε2

UR    = co + c1*WTI + c2*lag(UR)+ c3*GDP + c4*Ten_yr + c5*CPI +
c6*IP + c7*SP500 + c8*Dollar + c9*CRB +ε3

CPI   = do + d1*WTI + d2*lag(CPI)+ d3*GDP + d4*Ten_yr + d5*UR +
d6*IP + d7*SP500 + d8*Dollar + d9*CRB +ε4

IP    = eo + e1*WTI + e2*lag(IP) + e3*GDP + e4*Ten_yr + e5*UR +
e6*CPI + e7*SP500 + e8*Dollar + e9*CRB + ε5

SP500 = fo + f1*WTI + f2*lag(SP500)+ f3*GDP + f4*Ten_yr + f5*UR +
f6*CPI + f7*IP + f8*Dollar + f9*CRB +ε6

Dollar = go + g1*WTI + g2*lag(Dollar)+ g3*GDP + g4*Ten_yr +
g5*UR + g6*CPI + g7*IP + g8*SP500 + g9*CRB +ε7

CRB   = ho + h1*WTI + h2*lag(CRB)+ h3*GDP + h4*Ten_yr + h5*UR +
h6*CPI + h7*IP + h8*SP500 + h9*Dollar +ε8
```

In equation 12.1, GDP is the real GDP growth rate, Ten_Yr is the 10-year Treasury yield, UR is the unemployment rate, CPI is our proxy for inflation and IP stands for industrial production, the S&P500 index is denoted by SP500, the trade-weighted dollar is dollar, commodity prices are indicated by CRB, and WTI is our measure for oil prices. ε1 to ε8 are error terms of the model, and ao to h9 are the parameters to be estimated. SAS code S12.3 is employed to estimate the small-scale macro model described in Equation 12.1. The dataset covers the 1986:Q1 to 2013:Q1 time period for estimation, and conditional forecasts are generated for the 2013:Q2 to 2014:Q4 period.

```
Proc model data=Macro_data;                              (S12.3)

GDP   = ao + a1*WTI + a2*lag(GDP)+ a3*Ten_Yr + a4*UR + a5*CPI +
a6*IP + a7*SP500 + a8*Dollar + a9*CRB ;

Ten_Yr = bo + b1*WTI + b2*lag(Ten_Yr)+ b3*GDP + b4*UR + b5*CPI +
b6*IP + b7*SP500 + b8*Dollar + b9*CRB ;

UR   = co + c1*WTI + c2*lag(UR)+ c3*GDP + c4*Ten_yr + c5*CPI +
c6*IP + c7*SP500 + c8*Dollar + c9*CRB ;

CPI   = do + d1*WTI + d2*lag(CPI)+ d3*GDP + d4*Ten_yr + d5*UR +
d6*IP + d7*SP500 + d8*Dollar + d9*CRB ;

IP   = eo + e1*WTI + e2*lag(IP) + e3*GDP + e4*Ten_yr + e5*UR +
e6*CPI + e7*SP500 + e8*Dollar + e9*CRB ;

SP500  = fo + f1*WTI + f2*lag(SP500)+ f3*GDP + f4*Ten_yr +
f5*UR + f6*CPI + f7*IP + f8*Dollar + f9*CRB ;

Dollar = go + g1*WTI + g2*lag(Dollar)+ g3*GDP + g4*Ten_yr +
g5*UR + g6*CPI + g7*IP + g8*SP500 + g9*CRB ;

CRB   = ho + h1*WTI + h2*lag(CRB)+ h3*GDP + h4*Ten_yr + h5*UR +
h6*CPI + h7*IP + h8*SP500 + h9*Dollar ;

fit  GDP Ten_Yr UR CPI IP SP500 Dollar CRB;

solve GDP Ten_Yr UR CPI IP SP500 Dollar CRB / out=Forecast_WTI
forecast;

outvars date;

Run;

Quit;
```

As mentioned in Chapter 10, PROC MODEL is a flexible procedure to estimate multiple equation models, also known as large- and small-scale macro models. The SAS keyword fit instructs SAS to consider listed variables (in this case the eight variables) as dependent variables. The solve option will generate forecasts for each of the eight variables. The output is saved in the data file named Forecast_WTI.

As stated earlier, the forecasts are conditioned on the future values of exogenous variables and, in the present case, WTI. Note that there may be more than one exogenous variable. In the first example, our base case, we assume that there is no price shock. However, even though we forecast no shock, we still need to generate future values for our model. We decide to use the average price of the last five years (2008–2012) of $86.32 per barrel as our forecasted values. That is, we believe the price of oil will remain near its average over the forecast horizon. The forecasts are reported in Table 12.3. The GDP growth rates stay

TABLE 12.3 Forecasts Conditioned on the Average WTI Price Model: Without an Oil Price Shock Scenario

Date	Annualized Real GDP	Forecasted Annualized Real GDP	CPI (YOY)	Forecasted CPI (YOY)	IP (YOY)	Forecasted IP (YOY)	SP 500 (YOY)	Forecasted SP 500 (YOY)	WTI Price	Trade Weight $ (YOY)	Forecasted Trade Weight $ (YOY)	CRB Index (YOY)	Forecasted CRB (YOY)	Ten Years Treasury	Forecasted Ten Years Treasury	Unemployment Rate	Forecasted Unemployment Rate
								The Model Conditioned on the Average (WTI) Oil Price									
1/1/2011	0.09	2.60	2.13	2.07	4.79	6.96	15.98	12.97	93.54	−4.21	−3.40	24.36	22.83	3.46	2.84	9.00	9.28
4/1/2011	2.47	1.60	3.35	2.72	2.86	5.39	16.22	16.46	102.23	−8.00	−5.23	24.54	23.79	3.21	3.37	9.03	8.86
7/1/2011	1.27	1.24	3.75	2.97	2.55	3.24	12.10	15.52	89.72	−6.36	−6.67	16.14	19.44	2.43	3.18	9.00	8.92
10/1/2011	4.09	0.88	3.33	2.95	3.30	1.44	1.79	6.96	94.01	0.40	−2.89	−4.99	9.69	2.05	2.30	8.67	8.93
1/1/2012	1.96	1.12	2.81	2.83	3.97	1.72	3.47	−3.69	102.88	1.13	2.30	−11.22	−4.13	2.04	1.82	8.27	8.60
4/1/2012	1.25	1.65	1.90	2.22	4.50	2.38	2.35	−1.78	93.43	5.63	3.11	−14.26	−10.30	1.83	1.83	8.17	8.18
7/1/2012	3.11	2.00	1.70	1.61	3.32	3.50	14.08	−1.60	92.18	4.93	5.34	−11.31	−11.97	1.64	1.70	8.04	8.09
10/1/2012	0.38	2.05	1.90	1.58	2.71	2.99	15.73	10.80	87.96	−0.44	3.71	−2.38	−7.63	1.71	1.60	7.83	7.96
1/1/2013	2.50	1.93	1.67	1.86	2.62	2.43	12.41	12.09	94.34	0.92	−0.25	−0.51	−0.87	1.95	1.64	7.73	7.79
4/1/2013		1.93		1.58		2.38		10.14	86.32		0.66		−0.04		1.82		7.70
7/1/2013		1.84		1.51		2.14		8.42	86.32		0.40		0.36		1.77		7.67
10/1/2013		1.77		1.45		1.91		7.16	86.32		0.15		0.71		1.72		7.67
1/1/2014		1.71		1.39		1.71		6.27	86.32		−0.10		1.03		1.67		7.67
4/1/2014		1.67		1.35		1.55		5.70	86.32		−0.33		1.34		1.63		7.68
7/1/2014		1.65		1.31		1.43		5.38	86.32		−0.56		1.64		1.59		7.69
10/1/2014		1.64		1.28		1.34		5.26	86.32		−0.78		1.96		1.55		7.71

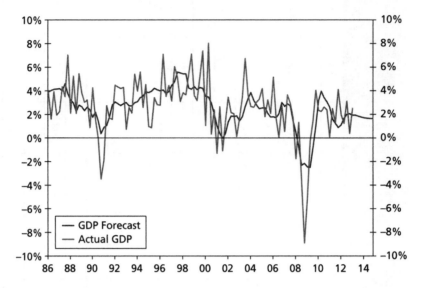

FIGURE 12.4 GDP Forecasts Conditioned on the Average WTI Prices: Without an Oil Price Shock Scenario

around 1.6 to 1.9 percent with the unemployment rate remaining at elevated levels. Overall, the forecast postulates a slower growth scenario.

In Figure 12.4 we plot the actual and forecasted GDP growth rates. The forecast appears to be consistent with movements in the actual GDP growth rates, although the decline in GDP growth during 2008 was much larger than forecasted.

THE MODEL WITH OIL PRICE SHOCK

In this section, we create long-term forecasts under the assumption that the price of oil rises. We used the five-year average price for the predicted future values of a barrel of WTI in the previous section; here we increase the price of WTI to $150 per barrel over the 2013:Q2–2014:Q4 time period. This strong jump in price represents the oil price shock. We use the same SAS code, S12.3, that was utilized in the previous example to model this scenario, with the only difference being the future values of WTI. The forecasts are presented in Table 12.4 and are very different from those reported in Table 12.3. When predicting an upward jump in oil prices, the GDP growth rates drop into negative territory in 2013:Q3 and remain negative for the forecast horizon. Moreover, the unemployment rate increases and peaks in 2014:Q4 at 9.63 percent. Industrial production and the S&P 500 index also suggest negative growth rates for 2014. We can conclude that a rise in oil prices can have negative, and significant, effects on the economy.

Figure 12.5 shows the actual and forecasted GDP growth rates in the case of an oil price shock. The forecast indicates a recession beginning in 2013.

TABLE 12.4 Forecasts Based on the Higher WTI Price Model: The Oil Price Shock Scenario

| | | | | | | | | | The Model Conditioned on the Higher (WTI) Oil Price | | | | | | | | |
Date	Annualized Real GDP	Forecasted Annualized Real GDP	CPI (YOY)	Forecasted CPI (YOY)	IP (YOY)	Forecasted IP (YOY)	SP 500 (YOY)	Forecasted SP 500 (YOY)	WTI-Pricce	Trade Weight $ (YOY)	Forecasted Trade Weight $ (YOY)	CRB Index (YOY)	Forecasted CRB (YOY)	Ten Years Treasury	Forecasted Ten Years Treasury	Unemployment Rate	Forecasted Unemployment Rate
1/1/2011	0.09	2.60	2.13	2.07	4.79	6.96	15.98	12.97	93.54	−4.21	−3.40	24.36	22.83	3.46	2.84	9.00	9.28
4/1/2011	2.47	1.60	3.35	2.72	2.86	5.39	16.22	16.46	102.23	−8.00	−5.23	24.54	23.79	3.21	3.37	9.03	8.86
7/1/2011	1.27	1.24	3.75	2.97	2.55	3.24	12.10	15.52	89.72	−6.36	−6.67	16.14	19.44	2.43	3.18	9.00	8.92
10/1/2011	4.09	0.88	3.33	2.95	3.30	1.44	1.79	6.96	94.01	0.40	−2.89	−4.99	9.69	2.05	2.30	8.67	8.93
1/1/2012	1.96	1.12	2.81	2.83	3.97	1.72	3.47	−3.69	102.88	1.13	2.30	−11.22	−4.13	2.04	1.82	8.27	8.60
4/1/2012	1.25	1.65	1.90	2.22	4.50	2.38	2.35	−1.78	93.43	5.63	3.11	−14.26	−10.30	1.83	1.83	8.17	8.18
7/1/2012	3.11	2.00	1.70	1.61	3.32	3.50	14.08	−1.60	92.18	4.93	5.34	−11.31	−11.97	1.64	1.70	8.04	8.09
10/1/2012	0.38	2.05	1.90	1.58	2.71	2.99	15.73	10.80	87.96	−0.44	3.71	−2.38	−7.63	1.71	1.60	7.83	7.96
1/1/2013	2.50	1.93	1.67	1.86	2.62	2.43	12.41	12.09	94.34	0.92	−0.25	−0.51	−0.87	1.95	1.64	7.73	7.79
4/1/2013		0.06		2.52		1.40		4.79	150.00		−0.08		2.10		1.54		7.82
7/1/2013		−0.66		2.93		0.08		−1.60	150.00		−0.81		2.53		1.27		7.98
10/1/2013		−1.25		3.07		−1.25		−6.75	150.00		−1.33		1.98		1.03		8.21
1/1/2014		−1.71		3.03		−2.50		−10.69	150.00		−1.69		1.12		0.81		8.50
4/1/2014		−2.05		2.88		−3.60		−13.46	150.00		−1.98		0.34		0.59		8.85
7/1/2014		−2.27		2.66		−4.48		−15.12	150.00		−2.25		−0.17		0.38		9.23
10/1/2014		−2.38		2.41		−5.12		−15.76	150.00		−2.52		−0.29		0.18		9.63

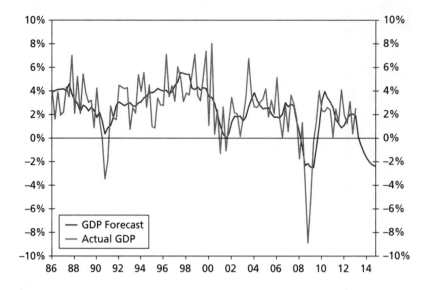

FIGURE 12.5   GDP Forecasts Conditioned on Higher WTI Prices: The Oil Price Shock Scenario

In summary, the conditional forecasting approach is very useful when analyzing different policy implications and external shocks. To show the risk to forecasts due to uncertainty, it is wise to predict different scenarios and the likely growth paths for the variables of interest. We presented only one scenario, but the basic idea to build a small-scale macro model and generate forecasts for different scenarios can be replicated for any policy change or external shock.

SUMMARY

Long-term forecasting approaches are an important element in decision making. In the case of unconditional forecasting, the BVAR approach is suggested. The BVAR approach utilizes past and current values of the dataset and generates forecasts for the target variables. In the conditional forecasting approach, a practical option is to build a small-scale macro model that can be utilized to generate forecasts for the target variables.

Both approaches are useful to public and private decision making. The benefit of unconditional forecasting is that it provides neutral forecasts and lets the data speak for itself. Conditional forecasting, in contrast, is an essential tool to analyze the impact of a policy change and/or of an external shock on the economy.

An analyst should become familiar with both approaches and utilize the SAS codes provided in the chapter for long-term forecasting.

CHAPTER **13**

The Risks of Model-Based Forecasting: Modeling, Assessing, and Remodeling

This chapter highlights risks and challenges to model-based forecasting and also provides guidelines to minimize the forecast errors stemming from those risks. The nature of forecast risks differs depending on the duration of the forecast. We divide these risks into two broad categories: (1) risks related to short-term forecasting and (2) risks related to long-term forecasting.

In short-term forecasting, the chance of a permanent shift in the behavior of a series is low, but sometimes factors, such as a hurricane or a work-related strike, can affect the outcome. Including those factors in a model is difficult due to their unexpected and temporary nature. That said, adjustments can be made to the model's forecast to reduce forecast error.

For long-run forecasting, the event's nature tends to be permanent, and the chance of significant changes, or structural breaks, is very high. For instance, trying to forecast the path of home prices during the housing boom of the late 1990s through the mid-2000s would have been very difficult. From January 1997 to December 2005, the Standard & Poor's (S&P)/Case-Shiller House Price Index (HPI) followed a strong increasing trend—a trend that many analysts speculated would continue for the foreseeable future. However, the index peaked in April 2006,

307

and a strong downward trend followed. The break in the prior trend was unexpected and therefore difficult to forecast. How could the analyst prepare for such unexpected changes in long-run data? One possible solution would be to generate scenario-based forecasts of the S&P/Case-Shiller HPI to include the possibility of a decline in prices even though prices may not have fallen in the recent past.

In this chapter, we also discuss the financial crisis of 2007 to 2009 and its effect on economic forecasts and suggest that, in some instances, even a forecaster cannot predict a financial panic. A better way to analyze likely scenarios is to closely monitor the patterns and changes of variables and to incorporate those patterns into a model's output.

In the last section of this chapter, we summarize overall thoughts about model-based forecasting and suggest three phases to model-based forecasting: (1) modeling, (2) assessing, and (3) remodeling. These three interconnected phases are essential for both short-term and long-term forecasting.

RISKS TO SHORT-TERM FORECASTING: THERE IS NO MAGIC BULLET

When devising short-term forecasting—forecasting outcomes one to two months in advance—there is little incidence of significant changes in the economic environment, and therefore little chance of a structural shift in the data. For instance, a one-month-ahead forecast of the S&P 500 index or a firm's forecast for the next quarter's earnings would not likely be subject to a significant structural change in the model. Sometimes short-term forecasting may face significant changes—for example, a natural disaster like Hurricane Katrina that shocks the data instantly. There are some occasions, however, when an analyst finds it necessary to adjust the forecast to reduce error. This may or may not include rebuilding the model. In this section, we provide suggestions as to when it is necessary to rebuild the model.

Forecasting economic and financial series is like sailing a boat. The analyst should constantly monitor the performance of the model and make adjustments to the (financial and economic) winds and currents. Many analysts, however, try to find the best forecasting model at the time and then continue to use it even if the environment has changed. Unfortunately, models often break down over time and become less accurate at predicting future movements.

Monitoring a model's performance need not be difficult. Here are some useful evaluating techniques. If the forecast misses the direction of the actual value for three consecutive months, then the analyst should revise the model.[1]

---

[1] We considered forecast error too, but it is almost impossible to get a perfect forecast every time. Therefore, we pay more attention to the directional accuracy, but if we experienced a few very large forecast errors, then we do revise the model.

Moreover, periodically the analyst can compare the model's performance to others in the field. For example, the analyst can compare the model to Bloomberg's consensus using real-time out-of-sample root mean squared error (RMSE) and directional accuracy criteria. If a model has a higher RMSE and lower directional accuracy compared to the Bloomberg consensus, then the model should be reconstructed. If a model needs to be revised, the analyst can follow the procedure described in Chapter 11.[2]

After the Great Recession of 2007 to 2009, many economic and financial data series were turned upside down, causing most forecasting models to become ineffective. We will run through an example using the Bayesian vector autoregression (BVAR) nonfarm payrolls model. Prior to the Great Recession, the analyst's model for nonfarm payrolls could have been very accurate. As markets turned and businesses shed jobs by the millions, the model broke down completely. For instance, the real-time, out-of-sample, one-month-forward RMSE of the original nonfarm payrolls model from October 2006 to February 2008 was 51,000, beating the Bloomberg consensus RMSE of 54,000. However, once the economy began to fall apart, and job growth began to contract dramatically, the analyst likely noticed his or her forecast missing the direction of growth (continuing to foresee growth in payrolls when in reality jobs were declining). At this time, if the analyst rebuilt the model, he or she would have achieved a new RMSE of 75,000 for January 2009 to August 2010. If the analyst continued to use the old model, the new RMSE would have been 110,000—significantly worse than the rebuilt model. We suggest that real-time, short-term forecasting involves three phases: (1) building new models, (2) continuously monitoring the forecasting performance of these models, and (3) constructing new models when these models break down. In an age of ever-changing economies, one model specification will not remain accurate forever. Even the best model specification will need to be revised.

One important thing to note is that the nature of the event shocking the economic data will have different influences on the accuracy of the model. Some events are temporary and affect the accuracy of the forecast for only a short duration. In this case, an analyst would not want to rebuild the models but rather create add factors.[3]

There are many real-world examples of temporary events, especially from the recent recession/recovery of 2007 to 2012. One example is Cash for Clunkers, the 2009 federal program that provided cash credit on trade-in cars

---

[2]To do so, the analyst would reselect the predictors for the model using the three-step procedure and then finalize the model based on a simulated out-of-sample RMSE.

[3]Simply, an add factor is the adjustment made to a model-based forecast. For example, if we expect a change in recent periods that we did not or could not include in the model, we may add or subtract an add factor to the forecast. For example, due to the "Cash for Clunkers" effect, we boosted our auto sales forecast to 11.6 million units from 9.9 million units (which is model based) for the July 2009. It is worth mentioning that the actual release came in as 11.3 million units.

that consumers could use to purchase a new vehicle.[4] This short-term program incentivized consumers to trade in their old vehicles, with the hope of stimulating demand for automobiles, a demand that was not likely forecasted. However, such an increase in demand might have occurred in a few years later anyway. Due to the Cash for Clunkers effect, we included add factors to the model-based forecasts for auto sales, retail sales, personal spending, and industrial production for the July–September 2009 time period.

While the Cash for Clunkers program was truly a temporary event, some economic events considered temporary tend to persist for a longer time. A good example is what is termed the Census effect. Every 10 years the U.S. Census Bureau conducts a survey of the American population. To complete the survey in a timely manner, the Census Bureau hires more than a half a million temporary workers. However, these workers are on the payroll for only a few months before they are laid off. Because this boost to hiring is expected once every 10 years, an analyst can place add factors into the model to help more accurately predict the level of nonfarm payrolls. To do this, the analyst should add additional employees to the nonfarm payroll forecast and then subtract them back out when they will likely be laid off. Since details about the workers hired and laid off by the Census Bureau are available publicly at its Web site, an analyst does not need to rebuild the non-farm payrolls forecast; rather he or she can simply add-in the expected hires.

In summary, the effective forecaster needs to constantly monitor and evaluate the accuracy of a forecast. If a model is unable to produce accurate forecasts due to a temporary event, the analyst should consider using add factors instead of rebuilding the model. Short-term forecasting is an evolving process, and due to the variable nature of economic and financial relationships, one model specification is not likely to remain accurate forever.

RISKS OF LONG-TERM FORECASTING: BLACK SWAN VERSUS A GROUP OF BLACK SWANS

When forecasting long term, the chances of significant changes in the economic environment are high. The challenge for forecasters is that the longer the forecast horizon, the degree of confidence in that forecast declines and the range of possible outcomes rises. The magnitude of the forecast error tends to increase as we lengthen the forecast horizon.

For long-term forecasting, the analyst should keep in mind that many macroeconomic variables behave differently during different phases of a business

---

[4]The Cash for Clunkers program is formally named the Car Allowance Rebate System (CARS) and was signed into law on June 24, 2009, by President Obama. The program gave cash credits of $3,500 or $4,500 to buyers who traded in used cars for ones with an improved mileage rating. For more information, visitCARS.gov.

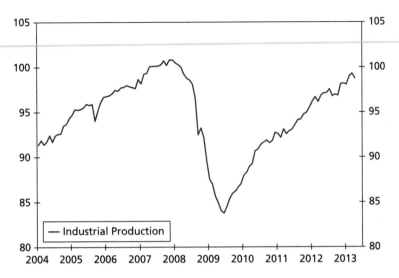

FIGURE 13.1 Industrial Production, Total Index (SIC) (Units 2007=100)
Source: Federal Reserve Board

cycle. The U.S. unemployment rate tends to rise during recessions and fall during expansions. A forecaster interested in predicting the unemployment rate for the next six to eight years should consider business cycle movements because the average business cycle duration, defined as trough to trough, since World War II, is around 70 months. Another important consideration is policy changes. The possibility of a structural change, due to internal and/or external shocks, is higher during long-term forecasting compared to short-term prediction.

For long-term forecasting, forecast errors and the potential need to rebuild the model depend on the nature of the shock (i.e., whether an economic shock creates a permanently shift in a series' trend or not). A shock can break the trend of a series. If the behavior of the series (e.g., upward or downward moving) remains the same as the pre- and post-break eras, then that break can be seen as a black swan. If, in contrast, a series depicts different behaviors for pre- and post-break periods, then the break can be labeled a group of black swans.[5] The reason to divide the break into a black swan and a group of black swans is that the forecast errors would be different for the long-term forecasting models. An analyst would treat these shocks differently during the remodeling process.

Let's first explain a black swan and then a group of black swans.

In the case of a break in the trend, or a black swan, the movements in the trend would be similar for the pre-break and post-break eras. One example is the case of the U.S. Industrial Production (IP) data in Figure 13.1. During the

---

[5]Taleb (2007) called unusual events, such as outliers, *black swans*. Here, however, we use the term to refer to a break in the long-run trend in the series. For more details, see Nassim Nicholas Taleb (2007), *The Black Swan: The Impact of the Highly Improbable* (New York: Random House).

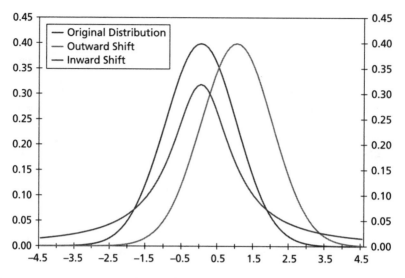

FIGURE 13.2 A Group of Black Swans: A Shift in the Distribution
Source: Authors' calculations

January 2004–December 2007 period, the IP index had an upward linear trend. After December 2007, the trend experienced a break and the IP index started falling, eventually bottoming out in June 2009. Since July 2009, the IP index has returned to its linear upward trend that was consistent with the pre-December 2007 time period. This is an example of a black swan. The economic event, in this case the Great Recession, caused a momentary change in the growth pattern of the data. Eventually, however, the data returned to its long-run growth path.

Before we discuss the consequences of a black swan to long-term forecasting, let us explain the concept of a group of black swans. If the post-break era performs differently from the pre-break regime, we call it a group of black swans—that is, a shock caused a break in the trend of a variable that did not allow the variable to recover to its previous trend after the break. Put differently, the shock created a permanent shift in the distribution of a variable. The shift can be inward, outward, and so on; see Figure 13.2.

There are two examples of a group of black swans illustrated in Figures 13.3 and 13.4 where there is a shock to the economic system that drives both series into a very different model of behavior. In the first case, the shock shifted the trend of the series (unemployment rate) upward and it stayed there (see Figure 13.3). Clearly, the unemployment rate series have two different patterns: (a) before March 2008 (break date identified as the sudden shift in the average (mean) value of the time series, here the unemployment rate), the unemployment rate follows a decreasing trend and bottoms out at February 2008 and (b) after that break date, the unemployment rate rises quickly and peaked at October 2009. From October 2009 onward, the unemployment rate stayed at an elevated level compared to the historical standard. The mean and standard

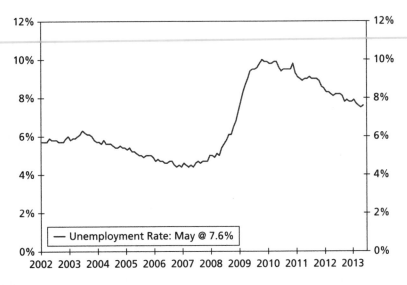

FIGURE 13.3   The Unemployment Rate
Source: U.S. Department of Labor

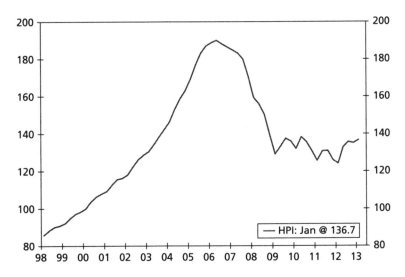

FIGURE 13.4   The S&P/Case-Shiller HPI
Source: Standard & Poor's and Case-Shiller

deviation of the pre-break date era (January 2004–February 2008) is 4.96 percent and 0.41 percent, respectively. For the March 2008–May 2013 period (after the break date), the mean is 8.40 percent and the standard deviation is 1.30 percent, both significantly higher than the values of the pre-break date era.

Figure 13.4, showing the S&P/Case-Shiller HPI, depicts the second example of a group of black swans. The index experienced an increasing trend until April 2006, which is the break date when home prices broke their upward trend and then prices started falling and the HPI bottomed out in April 2009.

After this, the HPI did not return to the pattern of the pre-break (April 2006) era and displays a completely different pattern. In addition, the mean and standard deviation for the January 2002 to April 2006 (pre-break) era are 153.1 and 24.7, respectively. The mean of the post-break era is significantly smaller than that of the pre-break era, which is 132.6 (standard deviation is 4.34). A group of black swans can change the behavior of a series completely.

What are the issues and challenges posed by a single black swan and a group of black swans? In the case of a black swan, since a variable follows a consistent pattern with the pre-break era, the model used prior to the break date may still produce reliable forecasts. The reason is that a shock may break the trend, but the movements (upward or downward) would remain the same once a series bottoms out (or peaks). For instance, the IP peaked in December 2007 and then started falling before bottoming out in June 2009. After June 2009, the IP followed an upward trend consistent with the pre-December 2007 trend. Therefore, a model built for the pre-December 2007 era may be still appropriate to utilize, all else being equal. The issue, however, would be to know when a series is bottoming out. This implies that the forecaster must observe the target variable (IP index) and its potential predictors to judge the changes in the series.

The case of a group of black swans is more challenging because we do not know what pattern the series will follow in the post-break era. In the two examples provided in the previous section (unemployment rate and house prices), the post-break eras followed a different pattern from the pre-break periods. Therefore, the chances of uncertainty are much higher with a group of black swans than with a black swan. Another difference is that a forecaster is better off building a new model because the original model was built around relationships between variables that have likely broken down in the new economic environment. A new model, based on new relationships and new environments, will be needed.

For long-term forecasting, we suggest generating different scenarios instead of one forecast because the chances of a shock are higher. If the shock is a black swan, the old model may be utilized for forecasting. If the shock is a group of black swans, a new model must be built for future forecasting.

MODEL-BASED FORECASTING AND THE GREAT RECESSION/FINANCIAL CRISIS: WORST-CASE SCENARIO VERSUS PANIC

The Great Recession and financial crisis posed a great challenge to short-term and long-term model-based forecasting. Many economic and financial series experienced a structural break and became very volatile. The financial crisis raised many questions about the credibility of model-based forecasting.

We believe for three primary reasons that model-based forecasting remains a reliable tool in the decision-making process. First, model-based forecasting is an evolving and flexible process that allows for current-period information and future expectations to be incorporated in the model.

Second, in scenario-based forecasting, a forecaster generates different forecasts, including the worst-case scenario, to prepare for different future scenarios. However, there is always an even worse case within a worst-case scenario, more appropriately called a panic. There is a threshold between a worst-case scenario and a panic. Once the threshold is crossed, the worst-case scenario converts to a panic. Unfortunately, the threshold that converts a worst-case scenario into a panic is unknown. But analysts and decision makers can feel when a worst-case becomes a panic. Several panics occurred during the financial crisis. One was the failure of Lehman Brothers, which filed for bankruptcy on September 15, 2008, igniting the global financial meltdown. Lehman's bankruptcy triggered a series of global events that included bank failures across the world. Lehman's collapse turned the worst-case scenario into a panic. Typically, financial institutions have reserves to deal with uncertain situations (worst-case scenarios); when people lose confidence in these institutions, it is hard for those banks to survive as a run on them ensues. This is a panic. In the case of a panic, financial institutions are unable to do anything except for file for bankruptcy. Therefore, in our view, the panic during the financial crisis was a major cause of the failure of forecasts.

Unfortunately, in the case of a panic, a forecaster is unable to do much in terms of predictions. But there is much to be learned after a panic.

Finally, economies tend to reach a new equilibrium where new economic relationships tend to be established. Only rarely do economic systems become explosive and collapse leading to a complete break in economic organizations— Weimar Germany being a notable example. Since a new set of economic relationships tend to be established, the employment of model-based-forecasting becomes effective once more.

SUMMARY

Model-based forecasting, whether short term or long term, consists of three phases: modeling, assessing, and remodeling. It is critical that the forecaster continuously monitors and analyzes the performance of the model and, if inaccuracy persists, rebuilds it.

In certain cases, more common in short-term forecasting, due to temporary events, a forecaster would need to incorporate add factors into the model to reduce forecast error. In some cases, remodeling will not be necessary. In long-term forecasting, we suggest producing multiple scenario-based forecasts instead of a single forecast. In addition, the nature of a break (think black swan or a group of black swans) determines whether the forecaster will need to construct a new model.

CHAPTER **14**

Putting the Analysis to Work in the Twenty-First-Century Economy

During the current business recovery, the economic performance of the United States has been very different from what many analysts had expected. Decision makers in both private and public sectors faced a set of mixed economic and financial indicators that offered a confused picture of the state of the economic recovery, the pace of that recovery, and the character of the structural challenges facing the economy.

At the start of America's journey to recovery, three major trends characterized the confusion. First, gross domestic product (GDP) growth had been unusually low and uneven relative to economic recoveries since World War II. During the recovery, the economy accelerated after an initial stimulus from the Federal Reserve (the Fed) and the federal government but then lost momentum as the stimulus generated no follow-on acceleration in growth. Decision makers had the difficult challenge of identifying what was the true trend in the economy and what was the cycle around that trend. Had trend economic growth fundamentally downshifted in the United States?

Second, job growth had become the number one political issue for both parties. But job growth appeared soft and out of line with GDP growth as the business cycle progressed. Further, weak job growth intimated a sharp structural break in both private and public sector decision makers' preconceived understanding of the relationship between employment and population growth, where employment levels rose alongside population growth. Had there been a structural break between employment and population growth and/or between employment and output growth? Why have exceptionally low mortgage interest rates not spurred a pickup in housing, as in prior recoveries? Had this relationship experienced a structural break as well?

Third, corporate profits, business equipment spending, and industrial production improved in this cycle in a way reminiscent of prior recoveries despite the overall perception that the economic recovery had been subpar. How can we identify economic series that appear to behave in typical cyclical fashion compared to those that do not?

In this final chapter, we look at the benchmark economic series that frame good decision making: output, employment, profits, interest rates, and the dollar exchange rate.

To address these issues effectively, let's recall our work returns to an earlier tradition of applied research. In contrast, our approach in this text differs from the theoretical econometrics text, which is almost all technique with little to no real-world application, or an economics text with primarily economic theory approach with no applied techniques and only hypotheses about economic behavior in the real world.

Due to the Great Recession (2007–2009) and the accompanying financial crisis, the need for effective economic analysis, especially the identification of time series and then accurate forecasting of economic and financial variables, has significantly increased. Our approach provides a comprehensive yet practical process to quantify and accurately forecast key economic and financial variables.

Different economic and financial variables—economic growth, final sales, employment, inflation, interest rates, corporate profits, financial ratios, and the exchange value of the dollar—exhibit differential behavior over the business cycle and over time.

A strategic vision with a context for where the economy is headed is thus needed. This vision requires the effective application of time series techniques to address both private and public sector decisions. Economic analysis is an essential element in effective due diligence, and our focus emphasizes the five key economic fundamentals: growth, inflation, interest rates, profits, and the dollar.

BENCHMARKING ECONOMIC GROWTH

Throughout this chapter, we discuss the various elements of bias in decision making. With respect to projecting the growth of the economy, the presence of an anchoring bias must be recognized. This bias makes its appearance as an analyst anchors expectations of the future based on an anticipation that it will look a lot like the past. Expressed differently, does the path of the mean of a series revert back to a past value after a shock?[1]

Our view is that the U.S. economy's growth from the 1950s through the mid-1970s reflected a closed economy with a store of savings from the World War II era and a history of low inflation and interest rates. However, the context of the economy differs markedly today. Since the mid-1970s, the global price of energy has risen dramatically. Changes in Canadian and Japanese trade policy have introduced competition into many sectors. This global competition aspect has been magnified with the North American Free Trade Agreement, and the rise of China as a major economic power and its entrance into the World Trade Organization has also increased competition. The evolution of the economy represents a constant challenge to the temptation to anchor analysis to the past. Here we begin a test for mean reversion in the post-inflation era beginning in 1982.

Benchmarks: Economic Growth and the Labor Market

To provide better guidance for decision makers, we focus on two broad areas of the U.S. economy: economic growth (output) and the labor market. The Great Recession produced the largest losses in terms of output (as measured by GDP) and jobs (nonfarm payrolls) in the post–World War II era. After experiencing such deep and severe losses, can the economy ever get back to the "normal" level? Will we see mean reversion? To answer these questions, we test the behavior of U.S. GDP and industrial production to proxy output in the economy and two indicators of the labor market: the unemployment rate and nonfarm payrolls.

Testing, Not Assuming, Economic Values for Good Decision Making

Fortunately for decision makers, econometric techniques can frame the behavior of strategic variables that define our economic baseline for strategy. Here we wish to determine whether a series is mean reverting. In Chapter 4 we introduced the concept of unit root testing and our preferred test, the augmented Dickey-Fuller (ADF) test, as the process to quantify whether a series is mean reverting. Recall that the null hypothesis of the ADF test is that the underlying series is not mean reverting (nonstationary) and the alternative hypothesis is that the data series is mean reverting (stationary). If a series is nonstationary,

---

[1] See John E. Silvia (2011), *Dynamic Economic Decision Making* (Hoboken, NJ: John Wiley & Sons). The anchoring bias is covered, for example, on pp. 71–73. The book also covers other decision-making biases, such as the confirmation bias and the recency bias.

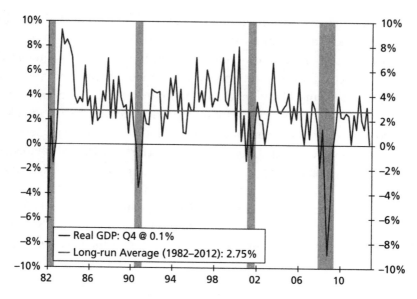

FIGURE 14.1 Real GDP Growth: Compound Annual Growth Rate
Source: U.S. Department of Commerce and authors' calculations

then the behavior or change from one period to another is random and the future values are unpredictable.

The goal of a forecaster is to predict the movement of data over time. To evaluate the movement of a time series, a decision maker can employ ordinary least squares (OLS) regression analysis, which will provide the estimated mean value of the time series. However, since stationarity of the data, or constant variance, is a critical assumption of OLS regression, we utilize the ADF unit root test to evaluate whether we can take the mean as given or if the results are spurious. If the ADF test proves the data to be nonstationary, then we have violated an underlying assumption of OLS regression analysis and cannot draw any conclusions from the results. However, if the ADF test proves the data to be stationary, the next step is to define the stationary behavior of the data. Three possibilities exist regarding stationary behavior. A data series can be: zero mean, which identifies the mean of the data series as zero; single mean, which defines the data series as having a constant mean that is not zero; and trend growth, meaning that the data series does not have a constant mean over the time period but follows a consistent time trend with finite error terms. Examining the time series in chart form is often very helpful in determining the form of stationarity of that data series.

Our Benchmark for Real GDP Growth: 2.75 Percent

Over the sample period, Q1-1982 to Q4-2012, the average annualized growth rate of real GDP in the United States was 2.75 percent, as illustrated in Figure 14.1

TABLE 14.1 GDP ADF Results Exhibit Stationarity

Type	Tau Statistic	Pr < Tau
Zero Mean	−2.3375	0.02*
Single Mean	−4.3891	0.00*
Trend	−5.3303	0.00*

Estimated Mean Value		
Estimated Mean	2.75*	
t-value	10.98	

*Significant at 5 percent level
Source: U.S. Department of Commerce and authors' calculations

and confirmed with the OLS analysis in Table 14.1. Is this a reasonable benchmark to guide our expectations? The results in Table 14.1 show no evidence of a shift or long-term deviation from the long-run average rate of GDP growth. Therefore, the GDP data series appears stationary and exhibits mean reversion back to its 2.75 percent value.

In the ADF unit root test illustrated in the top portion of Table 14.1, we can reject the null hypothesis of mean diversion or nonstationary growth of GDP at the 5 percent significance level.[2] While the table demonstrates the possibility of zero mean, single mean, and trend growth, we identify the series as single mean using the value of the mean from the OLS analysis. The OLS analysis finds that a mean of 2.75 percent is significant, and the chart also confirms our suspicions of a mean-reverting data series around 2.75 percent.

We can thus conclude that GDP growth is mean reverting. For decision makers, the benchmark for strategic thinking is that growth will more likely be 2.75 percent over time; therefore, divergent views from this growth rate are less than an even bet. This is especially true for outlooks beyond the next two years that really reflect the longer-term trend of growth. In this case, the trend is more likely to fall around 2.75 percent rather than values such as 4 percent plus or a drop to zero growth. Finally, the evidence, so far, does not imply a fundamental downshift in economic growth in recent years, even though the average growth rate has been below 2.75 percent for several years. There is just not enough evidence to advocate a fundamental, statistically significant, shift in the growth rate of GDP.

---

[2] Recall that the value of Pr < Tau of the ADF test identifies whether we accept or fail to accept the null hypothesis of nonstationarity. In this report we apply the 5 percent significance level; therefore, any probability value less than 0.05 identifies a significant relationship, implying that the series is stationary. Therefore, we can progress with the OLS regression model.

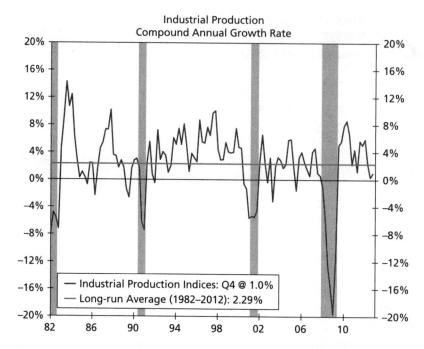

FIGURE 14.2   Industrial Production: Compound Annual Growth Rate
Source: Federal Reserve Board and authors' calculations

INDUSTRIAL PRODUCTION: ANOTHER CASE OF STATIONARY BEHAVIOR

In a similar way, the OLS regression analysis estimates an average quarterly annualized growth rate of 2.29 percent for industrial production over the sample period. The unit root test demonstrates that industrial production data is stationary; therefore, we can validate the long-run average growth of industrial production to remain around 2.29 percent. As can be seen in Figure 14.2, industrial production growth demonstrates a cyclical pattern—falling during recession and bouncing back during the early phases of recovery as we reviewed in Chapter 1. However, these anticipated deviations from the long-run mean are temporary in nature. Therefore, a decision maker can anticipate industrial production growth around its long-term trend despite its cyclical pattern. Table 14.2 illustrates the results of our test for stationarity, which indicates that the industrial production growth series is stationary over time despite the constant ups and downs over various business cycles.

Decisions based on any movement away from the mean of stationary series are subject to a confirmation bias—the tendency of an observer to view new information in a way that confirms the observer's prior beliefs. Earlier in this economic recovery, we witnessed three examples of the confirmation bias in action. First, as illustrated in Figure 14.3, real GDP rose sharply with the initial

TABLE 14.2   ADF Results Indicate Stationarity for Industrial Production(2)

Type	Tau Statistic	Pr < Tau
Zero Mean	−4.3778	0.00*
Single Mean	−5.4489	0.00*
Trend	−5.7754	0.00*

OLS Estimated Mean Value		
Estimated Mean	2.29*	
t-value	4.91	

Source: Federal Reserve Board and authors' calculations
*Significant at 5 percent level

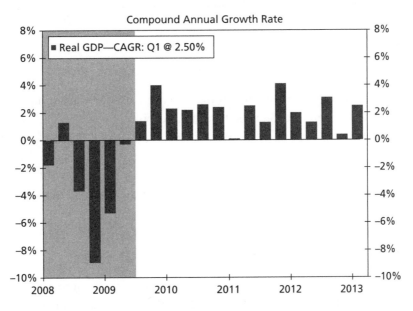

FIGURE 14.3   Real GDP: Compound Annual Growth Rate
Source: U.S. Department of Commerce

fiscal stimulus program in 2009. However, this pace of growth was not sustained as growth quickly moderated to a 2 percent pace, where it has remained throughout this economic expansion.

In a similar way, existing homes sales jumped in 2009 in response to the enactment of the first-time home buyer credit.[3] As evidenced in the Figure 14.4, the jump in sales was quickly eroded and did not sustain a recovery in existing

---

[3]The First-time Homebuyer Tax Credit was enacted, along with the fiscal stimulus program, in 2009.

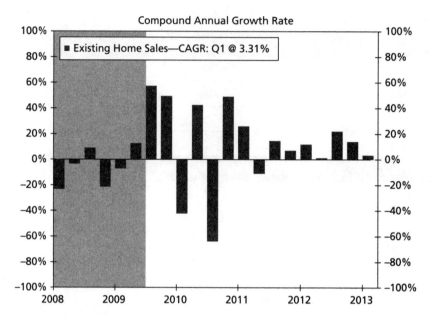

FIGURE 14.4 Existing Home Sales
Source: U.S. Department of Commerce

home sales. The Cash for Clunkers program gave rise to a sharp jump in light vehicle sales but then was followed by a sharp drop-off and very little sustained improvement in sales the next two years (see Figure 14.5).[4] The confirmation bias comes into play when the early successes of these or any change in trends are extrapolated by proponents into permanent changes in the pace of economic activity. In economics, the general principle demonstrated here is that temporary programs do not alter long-run behavior of households or businesses.

EMPLOYMENT: JOBS IN THE TWENTY-FIRST CENTURY

Growth in employment stands as a primary input for any accurate estimate of the state of the American consumer. Retail and auto sales for the private sector, sales tax revenues/auto registrations for state and local government, and federal payroll and income taxes are three estimates that start with job gains. Meanwhile, policy goals for the Federal Reserve, the president, and Congress are defined by their ability to reach certain levels of unemployment and monthly job gains. Finally, the impact of many policy actions, such as regulations, minimum wage changes, and eligibility for certain programs such as disability payments, are benchmarked by their impact on the job market.

---

[4]The Car Allowance Rebate System (CARS), commonly referred to as Cash for Clunkers, was a new federal program that gives buyers up to $4,500 toward a new, more environmentally friendly vehicle when they trade in their old gas-guzzling cars or trucks. This program began July 2009.

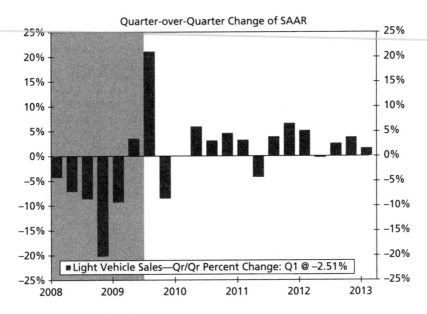

FIGURE 14.5 Light Vehicle Sales
Source: U.S. Department of Commerce

For policy makers in the current recovery, the behavior of the unemployment rate has become the standard to judge the effectiveness of economic policy. We begin here.

Unemployment Rate Measured by U-3: A Surprising Result of Stationarity

The unemployment rate, measured by the U-3 definition that is commonly reported in the media and serves as a benchmark for stress testing advocated by the Federal Reserve, displays stationarity (see Figure 14.6).[5] These results may be surprising to some commentators and decision makers, especially given the persistently high, and seemingly outsized, unemployment rates since the latest recession. The results in Table 14.3 indicate that the official unemployment rate is mean reverting around a long-term average rate of 6.37 percent. The long-run average is surprisingly close to the Federal Reserve's guidepost of 6.5 percent for raising the federal funds rate.

Unfortunately, an unemployment rate of 6.375 is higher than what is perceived as full employment by those with an anchoring bias looking at the past. Yet our statistical evidence indicates that the unemployment series does not

---

[5]The U-3 measurement of the unemployment rate counts the total number of unemployed persons as a percentage of the civilian labor force. This is the official unemployment rate that is most frequently cited in the media and is most familiar to the public and many decision makers.

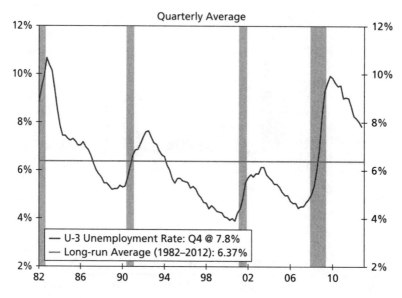

FIGURE 14.6 Unemployment Rate: U-3
Source: U.S. Department of Labor and authors' calculations

TABLE 14.3 Stationarity For the U-3 Measure of Unemployment: The ADF Results

Type	Tau Statistic	Pr < Tau
Zero Mean	−1.4847	0.13*
Single Mean	−3.8003	0.00*
Trend	−3.6525	0.03*

OLS Estimated Mean Value		
Estimated Mean	6.37*	
t-value	41.67	

Source: U.S. Department of Labor and authors' calculations
*Significant at 5 percent level

exhibit any drift in the values over time since 1982 and implies that percep-tions that the long-term level of unemployment has shifted upward since the Great Recession are misplaced. So far no statistical evidence exists of a funda-mental shift in this series in the post-recession period.

Employment Growth: Surprisingly Stationary Despite Impressions

In addition, we find that the growth in payrolls (see Figure 14.7) is surprisingly sta-tionary. Public impressions today fall prey to the recency bias that assumes that the

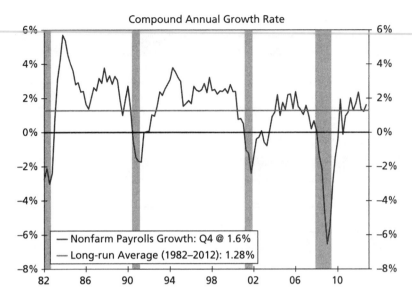

FIGURE 14.7 Nonfarm Payrolls
Source: U.S. Department of Labor, and authors' calculations

most recent experience is a signal of the future that is distinct from the past.[6] Yet the evidence shows that the annualized quarterly growth rate of nonfarm employment is actually a stationary series that is mean reverting. The average growth rate is estimated at 1.28 percent over the Q1-1982 to Q4-2012 period. In Q4-2012, payrolls were growing at a 1.64 annualized rate, above the long-term trend.

In Table 14.4, we show the statistical test results indicating stationarity of the growth in payroll employment over the sample period. This would appear surprising to those analysts who focus on the variation over the cycle. Here, however, we are more interested in the trend over time and that trend growth rate appears to be stationary over the sample period.

Patterns of employment open up the door to biases in decision making that may lead us astray. In Figure 14.8, the monthly gains in nonfarm employment are illustrated for the current recovery. While our earlier statistical analysis would indicate stationarity in the growth of employment, some took the spike in employment by hiring Census workers in 2010 as a signal of a robust job market. Why? Unfortunately, the job gains coincided with some analysts' projections that the fiscal stimulus would lead to a rapid gain in economic growth in 2010. For decision makers, this is an excellent example of the confirmation bias—the interpretation of data/observations as a confirmation of an anticipated outcome. Some analysts anticipated job gains, they saw some job gains, and therefore they judged the economy to be taking on the path of rapid

---

[6] See Silvia (2011), pp. 208–210.

TABLE 14.4 Employment Growth as a Stationary Series: The ADF Results

Type	Tau Statistic	Pr < Tau
Zero Mean	−3.1225	0.00*
Single Mean	−4.2621	0.00*
Trend	−5.2546	0.00*

OLS Estimated Mean Value		
Estimated Mean	1.28*	
t-value	6.98	

Source: U.S. Department of Labor, and authors' calculations
*Significant at 5 percent level

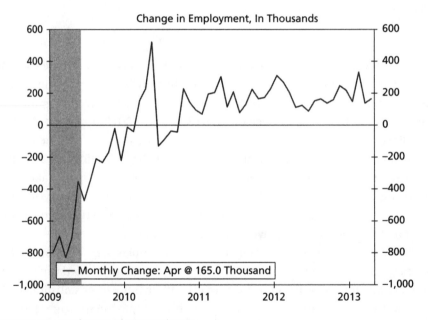

FIGURE 14.8 Nonfarm Employment Change
Source: U.S. Department of Labor

growth. Yet the pattern of employment after the spring of 2010 did not show any evidence of this prediction.

The change in character of the U.S. labor market is also evident by the rise in the proportion of the labor force that is composed of part-time workers and the rise in underemployment where many workers are in jobs below their level of education and skills. Further evidence of the structural change in the labor market is revealed in the following discussion on the Beveridge curve.

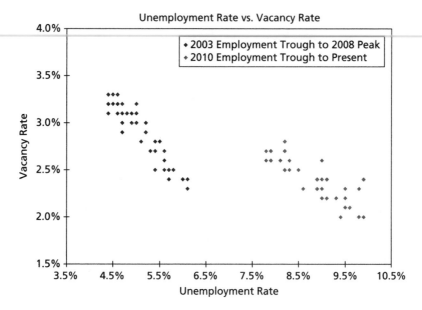

FIGURE 14.9 Beveridge Curve in Employment Recoveries
Source: U.S. Department of Labor

The Beveridge Curve: Yet to Shift Inward

While some analysts have argued that the structural shift in labor markets, as evidenced by the Beveridge curve, is a temporary cyclical phenomenon, after four years of economic expansion, this shift seems like a more fundamental change.[7] Even as the headline U-3 unemployment rate has improved in the typical, albeit slow, cyclical fashion, other labor market indicators suggest that today's labor market environment has changed. Job vacancies have become more plentiful as the economy has recovered. However, as shown in Figure 14.9, the unemployment rate remains high relative to the rate of job openings in previous cycles and intimates more frictions in matching the unemployed with available jobs.

It has been argued that the outward swing in the Beveridge curve is typical during the early stages of a labor market recovery. While some skills mismatch is normal as the economy undergoes significant periods of restructuring following a recession, more than four years into the recovery, the Beveridge curve remains above its path during the last economic expansion. The Great Recession a challenge to structural frictions beyond the typical pattern. The share of unemployed workers out of a job for more than 27 weeks remains historically high. The longer these workers are out of a job, the higher the risk

---

[7]The Beveridge curve illustrates the relationship between unemployment (measured by the U-3 unemployment rate, plotted on the *x*-axis) and job availability (measured by the vacancy rate, plotted on the y-axis). The curve is downward sloping as unemployment rises and job vacancies fall in times of weak economic growth.

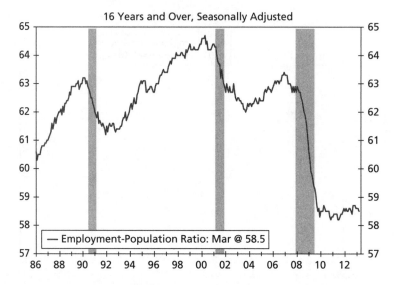

FIGURE 14.10 Employment–Population Ratio
Source: U.S. Department of Labor

that the slow cyclical recovery results in a longer-lasting structural mismatch as these workers' skills become increasingly out of date.

Structural Change in the U.S. Labor Market: Two Illustrations

Two indications of structural change in the labor market not captured by apparent stationarity of the U-3 unemployment rate are the sharp downdraft in the employment–population ratio (see Figure 14.10) and the decline in the labor force participation rate (see Figure 14.11).

According to the employment-population ratio, there are far fewer workers as a share of the working-age population than in the past. This creates two problems. First, to achieve any given pace of economic output, productivity must improve significantly for the fewer current workers. Second, when inverted, this employment-population ratio hints that a far smaller share of the population is supporting the rest of the population through government spending, especially entitlement programs, than in the past.

Structural change in the labor market not captured by the U-3 unemployment measure is also indicated by the drop in labor force participation (see Figure 14.11). In recent years, a decline in labor force participation for both male and female workers reinforces the view that the future pace of GDP growth may downshift from current perceptions. This downshift in future economic growth represents a challenge to decision makers. Many analysts will ignore the changes in the labor market and its implications. Anchored in the past, they have a biased, out-date-view of the labor market, which leads to an overestimate of potential future economic growth as well as the potential of that growth to solve the structural unemployment problems of today.

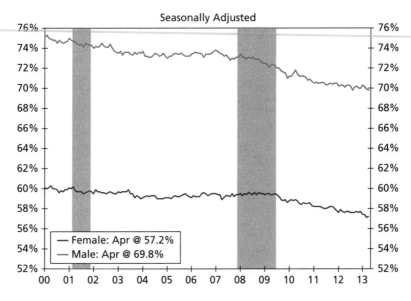

FIGURE 14.11 Labor Force Participation Rate
Source: U.S. Department of Labor

Decision makers are also subject to the availability bias in their view of the labor market by judging the state of the economy on the most visible, available statistic—the U-3 unemployment rate. They fail to recognize the problems of underemployment, as represented by the U-6 statistics (which are less visible to many observers but also more accurate representations of the true nature of the economy). These problems include the increasing substitution of part-time for full-time employment and the mobility problems of many workers due to depressed home prices or skills mismatch.

INFLATION

Inflation measures are a major input to the cost-of-living adjustments to programs such as Social Security and in the setting of wage and benefits compensation baselines in the private sector. Inflation assumptions also impact estimates of valuation for financial assets. For example, despite current commentary that inflation is low, inflation still is in excess of returns to savers in money market funds and short-maturity U.S. Treasury bills and notes. It thus influences the investment behavior of investors and the flow of funds in the U.S. economy.

In the past, the pattern of inflation has influenced decision makers, especially investors, and has given rise to the recency bias that we need to recognize, given that inflation cycles evolve over time and that a focus on the recent behavior of inflation leaves us open to missing the next move of inflation in the future. For example, in the early 1980s, inflation expectations were based on the high inflation rates of the 1970s not changes in monetary policy under Fed

FIGURE 14.12 TIPS Inflation Compensation
Source: Federal Reserve Board and University of Michigan

chairman Paul Volcker and the conservative philosophy of President Ronald
Reagan and his drive to cut taxes. Without this perspective, decision makers
could not recognize that the future pattern of inflation would be very different
and lower going forward. Those influenced by the recency bias bases future
expectations on the most recent past information without allowing for changes
in the economy.

Inflation and Inflation Expectations

Investors should examine the argument that inflation expectations are well
anchored more closely. We believe that investors should follow the observation
of David Romer: Monetary policy has an inherent inflationary bias.[8]

One measure of inflation expectations is the five-year implied inflation
expectations from the Treasury Inflation-Protected Securities (TIPS) yield,
illustrated in Figure 14.12. This figure indicates that, since 2010, there has been
a steady but very modest rise in inflation expectations. As implied earlier, inflation expectations are rising but not at the pace that would likely prompt any
change in monetary policy soon. Whether these patterns indicate that inflation
expectations are well anchored is another issue. More important for decision
makers, the recent pattern of rising inflation expectations, although modest,
intimates that nominal yields may not cover the actual inflation experience
over time, a fact that must be brought into the investment calculus.

---

[8]David Romer 2012,. *Advanced Macroeconomics* (New York: McGraw-Hill Irwin), Chapter 10, p. 496.

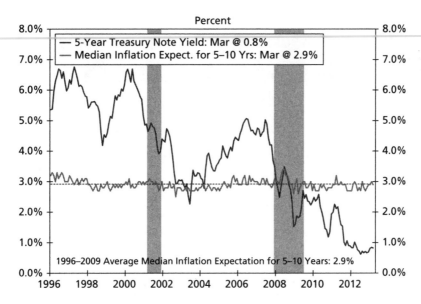

FIGURE 14.13 Inflation and the Real Yield
Source: Federal Reserve Board and University of Michigan

In Figure 14.13, inflation expectations, as measured from a University of Michigan survey, appear well anchored—unfortunately *too* well anchored. The series appears to stay remarkably close to 3 percent inflation, leaving little reason for policy tightening or easing over the past 16 years. Certainly there is no case for Fed actions to fight deflation fears in 2002 to 2004 or in 2007 to 2008. Yet the Fed took aggressive action through expanding its balance sheet. If this series is perhaps a benchmark for inflation expectations, then it should work on both the upside and the downside. Analysts who are complacent today may face a rude shock when inflation makes an unscripted return.

One cautionary note for decision makers: The perceived volatility in inflation is actually higher when the average inflation rate is lower, which sets up a position that the risk of inflation volatility is actually greater. This result will surprise many analysts. As shown in Table 14.5, the stability ratio actually has been higher in recent business cycles. Counterintuitive but true nonetheless.

Inflation: A (Small) Bias to the Upside

Current modest inflation, as measured by the consumer price index and illustrated in Figure 14.14, provides time for credit markets to continue to improve and also allows the Fed to continue current policy. A few market signals hint that inflation pressures are rising, although they are still not at a pace that would prompt the Federal Open Market Committee which sets monetary policy at the Federal Reserve System to alter its current policy.

TABLE 14.5 Business Cycles and Consumer Inflation

Business Cycles*	CPI (Year-over-Year)		
	Mean	S.D.	Stability Ratio
1982:Nov–1991:Mar	3.91	1.15	29.34
1991:Mar–2001:Nov	2.77	0.70	25.17
2001:Nov–2009:Jun	2.59	1.35	52.26
2009:Jun–2013:Apr†	1.87	1.36	72.99
1982:Nov–2013:Apr	2.93	1.27	43.20

S.D. = Standard deviation
*Trough to trough
†Not a complete business cycle
Source: U.S. Department of Labor and authors' calculations

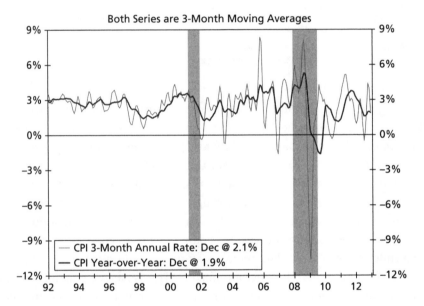

FIGURE 14.14 U.S. Consumer Price Index
Source: U.S. Department of Labor

Ten-year inflation expectations, Figure 14.15, have trended upward since 2010 and currently have returned to the levels that existed prior to the recession of 2007 to 2009. Similar to the five-year measure of inflation expectations, the current level of inflation expectations is not high enough to move the Federal Open Market Committee to alter its current policy.

Finally, gold prices have risen steadily since the recovery began in 2009, yet have leveled off in 2012 (see Figure 14.16). Gold prices, like many other prices, respond to several factors beyond overall inflation expectations. But many analysts utilize gold prices as an inflation proxy, and the message from gold prices now is that inflation n expectations do not appear to be accelerating. Moreover,

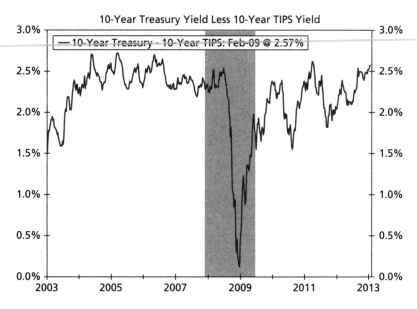

FIGURE 14.15 10-Year Implied Inflation Expectations
Source: Federal Reserve Board

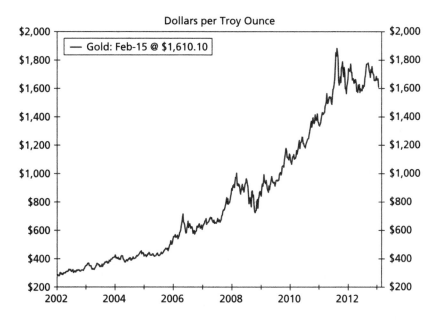

FIGURE 14.16 Gold Price
Source: Bloomberg LP

gold is a globally traded commodity and is not well correlated to the pace of domestic inflation in the United States, as illustrated in Figure 14.17.

Finally, Figure 14.18 demonstrates the rapid decline in velocity, or the turnover of money in the economy, as measured by the ratio of nominal GDP

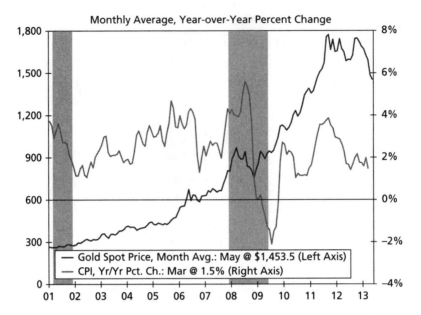

FIGURE 14.17 Gold Spot Price and Price Inflation
Source: Bloomberg LP and U.S. Department of Labor

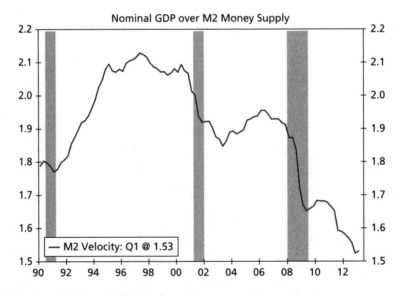

FIGURE 14.18 M2 Money Supply Velocity
Source: Federal Reserve Board and U.S. Department of Commerce

to the M2 measure of the money supply where M2 includes checking, savings and money market funds for example. This decline in velocity illustrates the break down in the link between money and inflation. While this relationship appeared very strong even over short periods in the 1960s and 1970s, it began to crumble in the 1980s. This fact again shows that some analysts continue to succumb to their anchoring bias and base their projections of inflation on their experience from decades ago. The global economy has evolved in such a way that the U.S. currency is employed globally, reducing the domestic link of money to inflation. Analysts would be better served if they developed a model for inflation going forward, a rational expectations approach, that reflects the changing character of the application of money in the global economy and the myriad of influences on inflation in the short and long run.[9]

INTEREST RATES

Interest rates and changes in those rates, both anticipated and unanticipated, are two of the driving forces of economic activity. Our focus on the role of interest rates as the price of credit reflects the realization that interest rates are a major factor influencing the pace of home purchases and refinances. During the last decade, fluctuations in the level of interest rates were a major force supporting both the boom and the bust in housing. For the business sector, interest rates represent one cost of credit or capital and a hurdle that an investment must overcome if that investment is to be pursued.

For investors, interest rates indicate the rate of return on savings accounts, money market accounts, and fixed income investments such as public and private bonds. For state and local governments, interest rates are the cost of borrowing, which is often benchmarked off the yield on Treasury interest rates. We turn to those rates shortly.

Interest rate expectations are subject to a set of biases for decision makers that can be, and have been, very expensive in terms of economic performance. During the 1970s, inflation rapidly outpaced interest rates, and real interest rates were negative. At the time, analysts rationalized this deviance (the normalization of deviance) in traditional behavior (nominal interest rates typically exceed inflation) to their own cost as rapid inflation and interest rate increases later in the decade led to large capital losses for investors. Early in the 1980s, many analysts complained that the level of interest rates was too low and that interest rates, along with inflation, would rise quickly as the economy picked up steam and the Fed loosened up on the money supply. This return to the past represented the anchoring bias.

Today, with inflation again outpacing the level of short-term interest rates, decision makers are again faced with the challenge that the current environment is not sustainable over time. In addition, the pace of home price increases is once again exceeding mortgage rates, which is reminiscent of the period from 2004 to 2007. Is another housing bubble looming? These issues require

---

[9]For more on adaptive and rational expectations, see N. Gregory Mankiw (2010), *Macroeconomics* 7th ed. (New York: Worth), pp. 390–398.

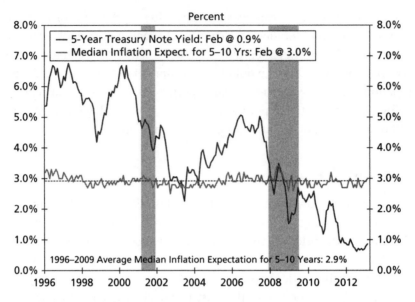

FIGURE 14.19 Inflation and the Real Yield
Source: Federal Reserve Board and University of Michigan

an assessment of the balance between real and nominal interest rates to which we now turn.

Inflation and Real Yields: A Signal of Financial Imbalances

From our viewpoint, one sign of financial imbalances in the economy is the extent to which inflation expectations are not reflected in current five-year Treasury yields (see Figure 14.19). In the early years of an economic recovery, Treasury yields often decline in line with easing monetary policy, as evidenced in 2002 to 2004. However, the current period indicates that yields are far below inflation expectations and have been there for some time. This shows that the extent of Fed buying of Treasury debt, along with purchases of U.S. Treasury debt by the Japanese and Chinese central banks, has distorted pricing in the Treasury market.

IMBALANCES BETWEEN BOND YIELDS AND EQUITY EARNINGS

Another signal of the unusual circumstances in today's capital markets is the inversion in the ratio between Baa corporate bond yields and Standard & Poor's (S&P) earnings, as illustrated in Figure 14.20. Bond yields appear low relative to equity earnings, even though general equities have historically yielded more (1990–2007) and are considered riskier investments.

Credit default swap (CDS) premiums provide the analyst a measure of the risk assessment in the marketplace for any financial instrument. A CDS is a financial agreement that the seller of the CDS will compensate the buyer in the

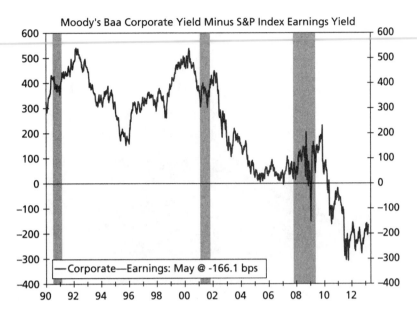

FIGURE 14.20 Baa Corporate Yield over S&P Index Earnings
Source: Moody's Analytics, S&P

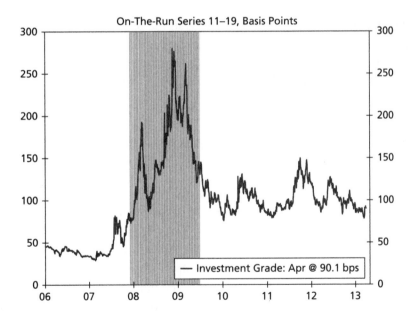

FIGURE 14.21 Investment-Grade CDS Index
Source: Mark-It Partners and Bloomberg LP

event of a loan default or other credit event (e.g., a downgrade). The buyer of the CDS makes a series of payments (the CDS "fee" or "spread") to the seller and, in exchange, receives a payoff if the loan defaults.

In Figure 14.21, these premiums spiked during the recession period to reflect the rapid rise in the risk that an issuer of investment grade bonds might default or

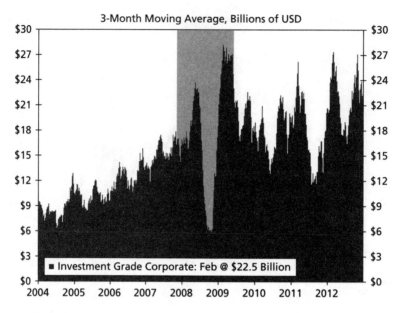

FIGURE 14.22 Investment-Grade Corporate Issuance
Source: IFR Markets

would be downgraded. In addition, spreads in the post-recession period remain wider relative to the spreads prior to the latest recession. This suggests that market participants have adjusted their risk assessments to be a bit more risk averse than before the recession and reflects an adjustment in risk perceptions that would nullify the anchoring bias that might have led to a return to prior narrow spreads.

Healthy Bond Issuance Consistent with Functioning Credit Market Expansion

Bond issuance in 2012 was a strong signal that credit markets were again functioning normally. As illustrated in Figure 14.22, investment-grade bond issuance has been at a consistent and solid pace for several years now. In addition, high yield issuance (see Figure 14.23) has accelerated in recent years as the recovery/expansion matures. These developments support our view that credit markets are functioning normally as far as the corporate bond market is concerned.

Unfortunately, there are now new worries for bondholders.[10] Low interest rates and more optimistic views of the economy, compounded by an accommodating bond market as illustrated by the strength of issuance, has given some investors the opportunity to pursue leveraged buy-outs. These buy-outs, financed by debt issuance, could possibly lead to downgrades of corporate debt

---

[10]Patrick McGee and Matt Wirz (2013), "New Worry for Bondholders: LBOs," *Wall Street Journal,* February 3.

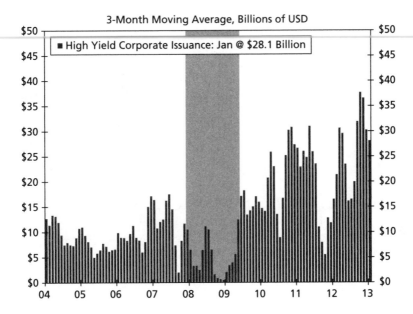

FIGURE 14.23 High-Yield Corporate Issuance
Source: IFR Markets

and investor losses. At present, the risk of leveraging activity has increased. Decision makers need to consider whether the current low-interest-rate policy has stayed too long and thereby is encouraging a more aggressive risk-taking appetite than perhaps the Fed anticipated.[11]

Finally, current Aaa and Baa corporate bond spreads (see Figure 14.24) have traveled in a range slightly higher than during the boom period of 2005–2006, indicating that a risk premium in the market today provides a better risk/return balance than during the boom period. It is reassuring that the market is pricing risk in a better way than it did in the past decade.

Two-Year Treasury Yield: Benchmark for the Short End of Yield Curve

Over the sample period, Q1-1982 to Q4-2012, the two-year Treasury yield, expressed commonly in level form, was nonstationary. That is, the two-year Treasury yield actually declined over the sample period, as illustrated in Figure 14.25 and this decline was statistically significant. The two-year Treasury yield,

---

[11] For more on the possible current risks in the financial markets, see Jeremy Stein (2013), "Overheating in the Credit Markets: Origins, Measurement and Policy Responses," Research Symposium, sponsored by the Federal Reserve Bank of St. Louis, St. Louis, Missouri, February 7; and John E. Silvia (2013), "Brave New World or Just Revisiting Desolation Row," January 22, available upon request.

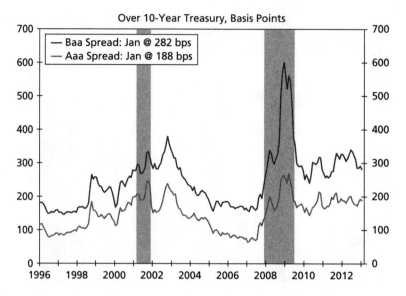

FIGURE 14.24 Aaa and Baa Corporate Bond Spreads
Source: IHS Global Insight

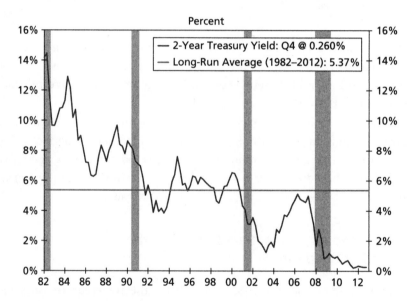

FIGURE 14.25 2-Year Treasury Yield
Source: Federal Reserve Board and authors' calculations

reflects the expected path of interest rates over the next eight quarters since, for example, an investor could buy a one-year Treasury bill and then reinvest those proceeds with the result that her return on that strategy would equal the return on the two-year note today. This two-year yield then indicates the expected path of interest rates and that is critical for decision makers to judge their expected financing costs over this two-year period.

TABLE 14.6 Evidence of Nonstationarity of the Two-Year Yield: ADF Results

Type	Tau Statistic	Pr < Tau
Zero Mean	−1.5369	0.12
Single Mean	−1.1645	0.69
Trend	−3.31	0.07

	Estimated Mean Value	
Estimated Mean	5.37*	
t-value	18.47	

Source: Federal Reserve Board and authors' calculations
*Significant at 5 percent level

In the augmented Dickey-Fuller unit root tests illustrated in Table 14.6, the probability of a unit root at a 5 percent level of significance implies that we cannot reject the null hypothesis of the nonstationary character of the level value of the two-year Treasury yield that appears in so many economic surveys. Therefore, the two-year Treasury rate is not mean reverting and, as can be seen in Figure 14.25, has followed a downward time trend. Formal trend testing reveals that the two-year Treasury yield has a linear, downward trend over our sample time period.

For decision makers, the benchmark for strategic thinking for the two-year Treasury yield is that it is not mean reverting. Therefore, a thoughtful economic estimate would have to alter the two-year yield level in some way to generate a stationary series.

Adjusting the Two-Year Treasury Yield to Achieve Stationarity

Once we have identified that a series, the two-year Treasury yield in our case, is nonstationary at level form, then we need to determine the type/source of nonstationarity. Recall that that there are two major types of nonstationary behavior: difference stationary (DS) and trend stationary (TS). It is important to identify the character of a time series as either DS or TS because both sources of nonstationarity have different implications for the future path of the variable. If a series follows the DS pattern, then the effect of any shock will be permanent. To convert the series into a stationary process, an analyst would have to generate the first difference of the series. A common source of nonstationarity is TS behavior, which implies that the series has a deterministic trend (upward or downward) over time. To convert a TS series into a stationary form,

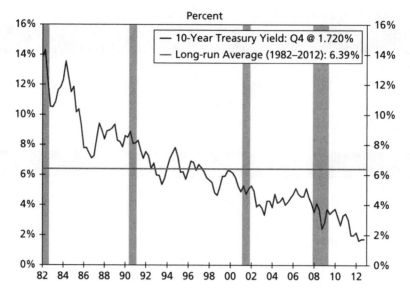

FIGURE 14.26   10-Year Treasury Yield
Source: Federal Reserve Board and authors' calculations

we have to de-trend the series, meaning regress the variable of interest on a time dummy variable.[12]

The two-year Treasury series appears to exhibit TS behavior, implying that it does not have a constant mean; the mean changes over time and a benchmark average rate for the two-year Treasury yield should not be applied to future forecasts. We propose that the two-year Treasury yield contains a TS behavior for two reasons: (1) The graph of the series (see Figure 14.25) shows a clear deterministic downward trend; and (2) we employed regression analysis to determine the type of trend (i.e., to determine whether the trend is linear [constant growth rate over time], nonlinear [nonconstant growth rate], or log-linear [the log of the series has a constant growth rate]). The regression results indicate that the two-year Treasury yield contains a linear downward time trend.

10-Year Treasury Yields: Not Mean Reverting

In a similar way, when expressed in level form, the 10-year Treasury yield (see Figure 14.26) is a nonstationary series with trend behavior. As illustrated in Table 14.7, the probability calculation, Pr < Tau, is significantly greater than the 5 percent significance level for both the zero mean and the single mean, such

---

[12]For a detailed discussion about the nonstationary concept, see G. S. Maddala and In-Moo Kim (1998), *Unit Roots, Cointegration, and Structural Change* (Cambridge, U.K.: Cambridge University Press).

TABLE 14.7 Ten-Year Treasury: The ADF Results

Type	Tau Statistic	Pr < Tau
Zero Mean	−1.7336	0.08
Single Mean	−1.1398	0.7
Trend	−3.7946	0.02*

OLS Estimated Mean Value		
Estimated Mean	6.39*	
t-value	25.4	

Source: Federal Reserve Board and authors' calculations
*Significant at 5 percent level

that we cannot reject the hypothesis of a unit root or nonstationary behavior of the 10-year Treasury yield. But the Pr < Tau is less than 0.05 in the case of "trend," indicating the 10-year Treasury rate contains TS behavior.

Once again, we can achieve stationarity for the 10-year Treasury yield series by de-trending the series. Regression results imply that a nonlinear (U-shaped) trend better fits the series. That is, a de-trended 10-year Treasury rate is mean reverting and thereby can be utilized in the econometric analysis and forecasting.

A NOTE OF CAUTION ON PATTERNS OF INTEREST RATES

While the pattern for interest rates on 2- and 10-year Treasury securities has been a gradual decline since 1982, there is also a question of the longer-term cycles in interest rates in history. For example, interest rates rose steadily from 1900 to 1920 and again from 1946 to 1981. In contrast, rates fell steadily between 1920 and 1946 and, of course, in the recent period. As a result, analysts must put any trend in rates in the context of the longer-term movements in the economy, inflation, and the overall credit markets.

In his seminal paper on business cycle modeling, Nobel Prize–winning economist Robert E. Lucas reinforced this message by finding that the welfare gain from stabilization policy is small.[13] While the benefits from stabilization may be greater than what Lucas cites (see Clark, Laxton, and Rose, 1996), there does not appear to be a clear case for a stabilization policy that seeks growth above a trend pace of 2.75 percent and also does not account for the

---

[13] Robert E. Lucas (1987), *Models of Business Cycles* (Oxford, U.K.: Basil Blackwell).

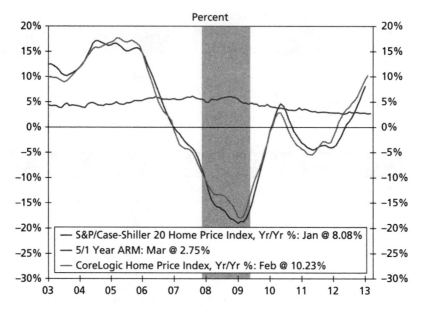

FIGURE 14.27 Home Price Growth versus Mortgage Rates
Source: Standard & Poor's, Bloomberg LP, and CoreLogic

distortions created in the credit markets at the same time when those stabilization efforts are undertaken.[14]

For investors and decision makers, we would advocate a high degree of skepticism regarding the claim that there is no evidence that U.S. central bank purchases have impaired the functioning of financial markets (and the real economy as well). In fact, we see distortions developing in the housing market today similar to those that gave rise to the housing boom of 2004 to 2007. As evidenced in Figure 14.27, the current pace of home price inflation exceeds the going rate on home mortgages—as was the case during the period from 2004 to 2006. In effect, home price inflation is increasing faster than the rise in the burden of home finance, which is exactly the problem that gave rise to prior housing excesses. It is possible, therefore, that housing decisions are in fact being distorted.

Decision makers need to give greater thought to tempering purchases of mortgage-backed securities as the level of housing starts are not part of the Fed's mandate. The housing market reflects the experience of two-decision making biases that analysts must recognize:

1. The traditional model of monetary policy easing led to lower interest rates, and a housing rebound did not occur with anything like the response many analysts expected. Instead, the responsiveness of housing was very weak, reflecting the anchoring bias of analysts who rely

---

[14]Peter Clark, Douglas Laxton, and David Rose (1996), "Asymmetry in the U.S. Output-Inflation Nexus," *IMF Staff Papers* 43(March): 216–251.

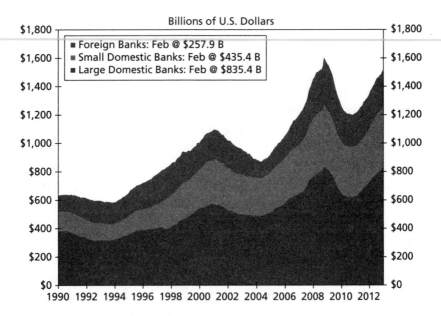

FIGURE 14.28 Commercial and Industrial Loans by Bank Type
Source: Federal Reserve Board

on models based on past behavior rather than recognizing changes in the economy during the recent 2009–2012 period and therefore reflecting the context of the economy (lower consumer confidence) and credit markets (restrictions on bank capital and new bank lending regulations) around any easing policy at that time.

2. The home price decline created a sunk cost bias among homeowners to sell their home at a loss.

Both biases reflect thinking that was not in vogue prior to the recession, and therefore are warnings to analysts to recognize the constant evolution of the economy over time.

Whereas the role of a central bank is to provide liquidity when needed, and we have ample liquidity in markets today, specifically targeting housing and how Fed supplied credit market liquidity is employed will create pricing distortions for investors and decision makers alike.

BUSINESS CREDIT: PATTERNS REMINISCENT OF CYCLICAL RECOVERY

Finally, the gains in commercial and industrial loans for all three categories of banks (see Figure 14.28) indicate that credit is being made available. For some analysts, this fact reduces the case that further aggressive policy easing is needed. Here, in contrast to housing, business lending appears to be taking on the pattern of a cyclical recovery and does not provide evidence of a structural break in credit availability.

PROFITS

Profits are rewards for economic success and incentives for innovation and change in the business sector. Profits also provide the source of capital for investments that will increase productivity and the standard of living for any society over time. However, profits are very cyclical. Interpreting short-term trends in profits can lead to extrapolations of recent profit gains that would be inconsistent with the cyclical character of profit growth. For example, above-average profit growth in the early phase of the economic recovery tends to encourage analysts to extrapolate into the future. This is the familiar pattern of the bias of the normalization of deviance, where deviations from trend, on both the upside and the downside, are treated as new trends. In a bull market for equities, prices and earnings can only go up. In a recession, prices and profits will never recover. Such are the sentiments of fear and greed in the market. As the next analysis illustrates, the share of GDP that goes to profits is very cyclical but also is mean reverting.

Corporate Profits: Surprising Stability

Although current corporate profits are at a record share of GDP (see Figure 14.29), econometric testing indicates that this situation may be only temporary

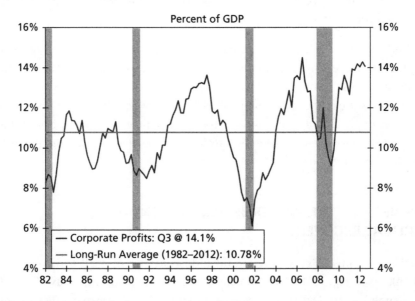

FIGURE 14.29 Corporate Profits
Source: U.S. Department of Commerce and authors' calculations

and may more accurately be a statement of where the business cycle is than of any long-term trend. The corporate profit share of GDP is a stationary series and is mean reverting. The calculation of Pr < Tau in Table 14.8 shows that we can reject the null hypothesis. We estimate that corporate profits, on average, are 10.78 percent of GDP, and deviations from that mean are only temporary in nature.

Some commentators have noted that corporate profits have recorded an outsized performance compared to the past. The analysis here indicates that profits growth has indeed been stronger than the long-run average. However, the current cycle has not yet been completed, and profits growth tends to moderate farther into the business cycle. As illustrated in Table 14.9, corporate profits growth in the 2001 to 2009 cycle averaged 6.40 percent, which was below the average of 7.95 percent in the 1948 to 2012 period. Moreover, the volatility of these profits, as measured by the stability ratio, is above that of the long-run average. The fastest pace of growth for profits appeared in the 1975 to 1980 period of high inflation, while the most volatile period appeared to be the 1954 to 1958 period.

FINANCIAL MARKET VOLATILITY: ASSESSING RISK

For financial markets, risk is often measured by volatility. Tables 14.10 and 14.11 show calculations for volatility in the S&P 500 index and 10-year Treasury yield, two financial benchmarks. For the S&P 500, we find that the previously completed business cycle of 2001 to 2009 had been the worst period for average S&P performance since the early 1970s, when rising oil prices, rapid inflation, and high interest rates plagued the economy. The volatility of the 2001 to 2009 period was also quite high. The 1970 to 1975 period, however, remains

TABLE 14.8 Stationarity for Corporate Profits: ADF Results

Type	Tau Statistic	Pr < Tau
Zero Mean	0.1631	0.73
Single Mean	−2.97	0.04*
Trend	−3.1846	0.09

OLS Estimated Mean Value		
Estimated Mean	10.78*	
t-value	63.14	

Source: U.S. Department of Commerce and authors' calculations
*Significant at 5 percent level

TABLE 14.9   Corporate Profits (Year over Year) S.D.

Business Cycles*	Mean	S.D	Stability Ratio
1949:Q4–1954:Q2	5.60	19.78	353.25
1954:Q2–1958:Q2	4.32	17.51	405.85
1958:Q2–1961:Q1	6.26	20.29	324.13
1961:Q1–1970:Q4	5.00	10.08	201.40
1970:Q4–1975:Q1	8.15	24.61	302.06
1975:Q1–1980:Q3	11.58	16.39	141.51
1980:Q3–1991:Q1	7.91	13.60	171.87
1991:Q1–2001:Q4	5.83	8.13	139.49
2001:Q4–2009:Q2	6.40	14.71	229.87
2009:Q2–2012:Q4†	16.40	15.76	96.11
1948:Q1–2012:Q4	7.95	14.13	177.80

Source: U.S. Department of Commerce and authors' calculations
S.D. = Standard deviation
*Trough to trough
†Not a complete business cycle

TABLE 14.10   S&P 500 (Year over Year)

Business Cycles*	Mean	S.D	Stability Ratio
1949:Oct–1954:May	12.13	9.83	81.01
1954:May–1958:Apr	16.26	18.30	112.53
1958:Apr–1961:Feb	10.30	15.38	149.31
1961:Feb–1970:Nov	4.95	13.15	265.43
1970:Nov–1975:Mar	−0.02	17.68	−116,177.63
1975:Mar–1980:Jul	6.66	11.41	171.38
1980:Jul–1991:Mar	12.45	16.26	130.60
1991:Mar–2001:Nov	13.55	14.12	104.22
2001:Nov–2009:Jun	−1.32	18.51	−1,398.82
2009:Jun–2012:Dec†	11.13	15.76	141.62
1948:Jan–2012:Dec	8.43	15.93	189.07

Source: Standard & Poor's, and authors' calculations
S.D. = Standard deviation
*Trough to trough
†Not a complete business cycle

TABLE 14.11 10-Year Treasury

Business Cycles*	Mean	S.D	Stability Ratio
1954:May–1958:Apr	3.06	0.47	15.20
1958:Apr–1961:Feb	3.99	0.48	12.03
1961:Feb–1970:Nov	4.99	1.18	23.71
1970:Nov–1975:Mar	6.74	0.64	9.54
1975:Mar–1980:Jul	8.51	1.24	14.53
1980:Jul–1991:Mar	10.32	2.23	21.60
1991:Mar–2001:Nov	6.27	0.89	14.26
2001:Nov–2009:Jun	4.25	0.59	13.84
2009:Jun–2012:Dec†	2.75	0.77	28.14
1948:Jan–2012:Dec	6.17	2.75	44.65

Source: Federal Reserve Board, and authors' calculations
S.D. = Standard deviation
*Trough to trough
†Not a complete business cycle

the most volatile period for the S&P 500 index. Both periods were character-ized by disappointing performance relative to the average gain of 8.4 percent over the 1948 to 2012 period as well as weak equity market performance and a difficult period for household wealth and confidence.

DOLLAR

International economic and financial linkages between the U.S. economy and the global economies take place through the exchange value of the dollar. Relative dollar valuations against other currencies provide the benchmark for trade/price competitiveness judgments and influence the flow of credit and trade. Changes in the value of the dollar are reflected in the prices of imports and exports and they impact the value of trade flows and GDP of the United States as well as other countries.

Effective economic policy is generally associated with a stable exchange rate, which allows for better long-run planning by both private and public sec-tors. A weaker dollar, in contrast, is associated with higher import prices and an upward bias to inflation over time. For both importers of goods and investors, a weaker dollar/higher inflation combination would generally not be consistent with an improving economy. This pattern was apparent in the late 1970s in the United States. In contrast, a stronger dollar is associated with lower import prices, overall inflation and generally a stronger economy as we have seen in the U.S. in the early 1980s.

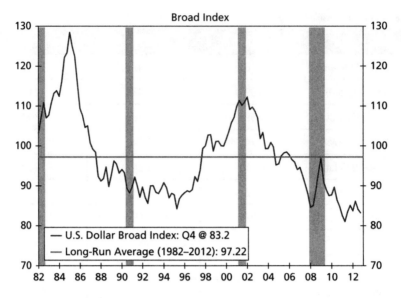

FIGURE 14.30 U.S. Dollar Index
Source: Federal Reserve Board and authors' calculations

Dollar Exchange Rate: A Strong Dollar Is Not the Real Story

Another interesting development is that the trade-weighted dollar index (see Figure 14.30) shows evidence of nonstationary behavior. As shown in Table 14.12, the Pr < Tau provides proof that we cannot reject the null hypothesis and that the series is not mean reverting.

The regression analysis indicates a log-linear time trend for the dollar index. That is, the log-form of the trade-weighted dollar has a linear trend over time. We can produce a stationary series by de-trending the dollar index. That de-trended series should be employed in further analysis owing to it is a mean-reverting series. Also, notice that the trend estimate is −5.65, which intimates that the dollar index is trending downward over time. The value of the dollar is not stable, but is declining over time.

This pattern implies that the dollar has drifted downward since 1982 and may reflect the rise of many economically competitive nations such that the premium to be paid for security in the dollar is less today than in the past. Returning the dollar to prior values would reflect an anchoring bias and, in reality, would not likely succeed given the diversification of goods and financial flows today.

Volatility in the Dollar over Time

Another useful benchmark to evaluate any economic series over time, is the examination of the stability ratio of the dollar, as illustrated in Table 14.13.

TABLE 14.12 Nonstationary Behavior of the Dollar: ADF Results

Type	Tau Statistic	Pr < Tau
Zero Mean	−0.7877	0.37
Single Mean	−1.7591	0.4
Trend	−2.0477	0.57

OLS Estimated Mean Value		
Estimated Mean	97.22*	
t-value	104.65	

Source: Federal Reserve Board and authors' calculations
*Significant at 5 percent level

TABLE 14.13 Business Cycles and the U.S. Dollar

Business Cycles*	Dollar (Level)		
	Mean	S.D.	Stability Ratio
1982:Nov–1991:Mar	102.63	11.84	11.54
1991:Mar–2001:Nov	94.50	7.98	8.44
2001:Nov–2009:Jun	98.04	7.32	7.47
2009:Jun–2013:Apr†	85.28	2.68	3.14
1982:Nov–2013:Apr	96.78	10.32	10.66

Source: Authors' calculations
S.D. = Standard deviation
*Trough to trough
†Not a complete business cycle

Note that the average value of the dollar has declined since the 1980s, as has the volatility of the dollar as measured by the stability ratio. By employing the stability ratio in our analysis, we can provide a context to decision makers so that they can better judge the riskiness of any key economic series important in making investment decisions.

ECONOMIC POLICY: IMPACT OF FISCAL POLICY AND THE EVOLUTION OF THE U.S. ECONOMY

Looking forward, analysts will be challenged in their application of both economics and time series techniques when tracking and predicting the impact of significant changes in recent monetary and fiscal policy. They will need to recognize the magnitude and the unusual nature of our monetary and fiscal policy. Moreover, due to the overconfidence bias, forecasts of policy effectiveness for both fiscal and monetary policy have been too optimistic relative to actual outcomes. As mentioned, forecasts of the effectiveness of the 2009 fiscal stimulus and the first-time homebuyers' credit did not deliver.

Will our economic/statistical model of the impact of entitlement spending and debt-to-GDP ratios on the economy be wrong in a similar way? If our estimate of 2.75 percent trend growth is really the path of the future, will the clash of fiscal spending promises and continued monetary ease prove inconsistent with low inflation and interest rates? In addition, what happens if the long-term cycles of interest rates tend to move upward, as interest rates did in fact rise at the beginning of the post–World War II period, and as a result large fiscal deficits will be continuingly financed at higher nominal interest rates? Will there be a temptation to resort to inflation-financed federal deficits in the future? Should we also expect higher future taxes to pay for government spending? While we may be uncertain on how the economy will evolve, we know that something will change in the patterns of growth, inflation, interest rates, and the dollar we have evaluated so far. We cannot evaluate the patterns here, but let us take a look at the context of fiscal issues at least to provide a research agenda for the future.

Large and Persistent Deficits: A Brave New World of Fiscal Policy

As apparent in Figure 14.31, there has been a clear shift in the position of fiscal policy today compared to prior years and prior economic recoveries. Yet conventional measures of the fiscal deficit have misrepresented the true federal budget situation for more than 40 years. The unfunded liabilities of the entitlement programs reflect a commitment to spend in the future without any set-aside out of current revenues (see Figure 14.32).

As a result, the current federal budget appears to be much closer to balance since the unfunded liabilities are not accounted for in today's budget calculations. By not accounting for these liabilities, the public budget calculations for the past 40 years seriously overstated the positive position of federal, state, and local budgets within the U.S. economy. Only in recent years have taxpayers learned the true state of fiscal deficits as the retirement and healthcare bills begin to accumulate. As illustrated in Figure 14.33, estimates by the Congressional Budget Office indicate that the burden of these unfunded liabilities will alter fiscal policy expectations.[15] These bills represent the risk of higher taxes, reduced

---

[15] Congressional Budget Office, (2013). The Budget and Economic Outlook: Fiscal Years 2013 to 2023. Government Printing Office, Washington, D.C.

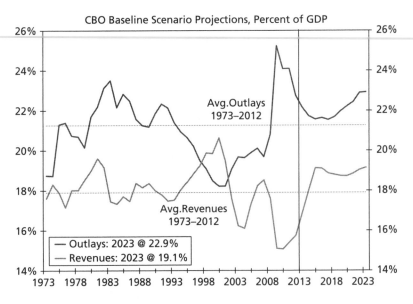

FIGURE 14.31 U.S. Budget Gap
Source: Congressional Budget Office

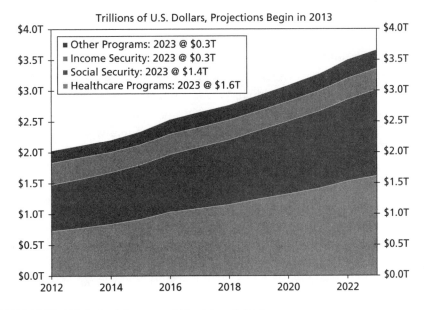

FIGURE 14.32 U.S. Federal Government Mandatory Outlays
Source: Congressional Budget Office

after-tax incomes, and the potential for a lower standard of living for taxpayers than they had anticipated. The federal government might have to resort to central bank financing of the deficit to pay its bills. This would increase the risk of higher inflation, higher interest rates, and lower real growth and job gains in the future. This fiscal policy framework certainly alters the decision-making

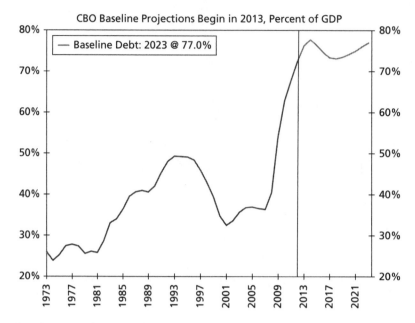

FIGURE 14.33   U.S. Debt Held by the Public
Source: Congressional Budget Office

calculus for investors, savers, and business decision makers as they evaluate the path of growth, inflation, and interest rates going forward. Moreover, the time horizon for federal tax and spending policy has shortened dramatically in recent years with increased partisanship in Washington. As a final note, the pattern of mandatory outlays was tested for mean reversion, and the results exhibit a nonstationary pattern over, indicating no mean reversion in any sense.

Budget Limits with 2.75 Percent Trend Economic Growth

Unfunded liabilities at any level of government will, in some combination, increase future taxes, lower direct government spending, and require greater debt financing, all problems evident during the past four years as government budgets have become tight in light of slower economic and revenue growth. At the federal level, the genesis of these problems began with Social Security, Medicare, Medicaid, and a number of stimulus programs under both Democratic and Republican administrations, underscoring their bipartisan nature. The longer-term fiscal outlook places the economy in a territory outside past experience, as the U.S. debt held by the public rises far above previous experience (see Figure 14.33).

In the short run, hard choices have been avoided by employing off-budget spending, emergency spending programs, mandates imposed on the private sector, and unrealistic budget and economic forecasts (the rosy scenario) that cover up the real nature of the fiscal problems. But not tackling these problems has had an economic impact on the real economy. The lack of the relationship

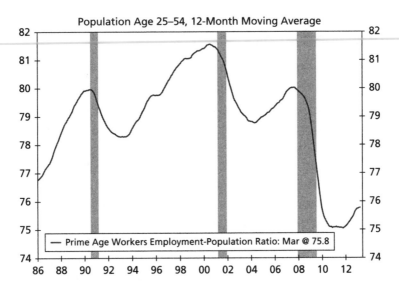

FIGURE 14.34 Prime Employment–Population Ratio
Source: U.S. Department of Labor

between the reported fiscal deficit and the true budget imbalance has not addressed as well as the real choices needed to sustain a steady, or at least predictable, fiscal policy over time.

Auerbach, Gale, Orszag, and Potter build a case that current fiscal policies are far from addressing the federal government's real budget constraint.[16] The demographic pressure on entitlement programs indicates that the ratio of working-age adults relative to those over 65 will decline in the decades ahead. In fact, the sharp drop in the employment-to-population ratio in recent years (see Figure 14.34) already signals a fiscal problem as fewer workers begin to support a larger entitlement-benefiting cohort. In addition, medical care technology continues to put upward pressure on medical spending, while current life expectancies exceed the expectations that existed when most of these entitlement programs were established. These forces are large and persistent. A widening gap between spending and revenues in the future will exist. In turn, investors and business decision makers will have to reevaluate their expectations regarding growth, inflation, and interest rates in such an environment where the federal budget will be unlikely to be balanced over the economic cycle and sudden changes in tax and spending policy could appear. Many policy adjustments will be needed, and they will influence the path of expected real after-tax incomes and profits. These policy options include some combination of tax increases, spending cuts, or higher inflation to reduce the real value of the federal debt.

---

[16]A. J. Auerbach, W. G. Gale, P. R. Orszag, and S. R. Potter (2003), "Budget Blues: The Fiscal Options for Reform," in H. Aaron, J. Lindsay, and P. Nivola, eds., *Agenda for the Nation*, pp. 109–143 (Washington, DC: Brookings Institution).

THE LONG-TERM DEFICIT BIAS AND ITS ECONOMIC IMPLICATIONS

The theme of a deficit bias in fiscal policy is evident in the sovereign debt issues in Europe and the United States. For years, many decision makers have argued for a balanced budget, but disagreements between the political parties have made such a goal seemingly impossible. There is little evidence that policy follows a cyclical pattern trending toward balance.

How does this deficit bias come about? James Buchanan and Richard Wagner argue that the benefits of high purchases and low taxes are direct and evident, while the costs lower future purchases. Higher future taxes are indirect and less obvious. If voters do not recognize the extent of the costs or assume they will not pay these costs, then there is a tendency toward excessive deficits.[17] This bias becomes even more accentuated when some voters perceive that they will not bear the tax burden of current and future spending.

The euro crisis reflects the fundamental disconnect with patterns of current fiscal policy spending that could not be sustained over time, giving an ever-rising ratio of debt to GDP. The shock of the 2007 to 2009 recession made the debt-to-GDP imbalance an immediate crisis. Belated attempts to deal with the crisis resulted in sharp contractions in fiscal policy, a large decline in aggregate demand, major repercussions for capital and foreign exchange markets, and the potential for government default.

The euro experience follows a long history of financial crises that illustrate transitions from an unsustainable fiscal deficit position are rarely smooth, especially when the markets recognize that such a debt position is unsustainable. For example, we have witnessed a default in the case of Greece in recent years, or periods of sharply lower real exchange rates, increased inflation, and recessions, such as the case in Mexico. These crises disrupt capital markets, lower real investment, and reduce real economic growth.

Interest Rates Trend Reversal: Test to Come Ahead

For the United States, one path to a fiscal crisis is to not recognize that the trend growth for the country is closer to 2.75 percent in the near term than to the 4 percent that some forecasters estimate for the next two years or to sustain the belief that long-run trend growth is more like 3 to 3.5 percent (see Figure 14.35). Unfortunately, we are already seeing this disconnect in regard to pension and healthcare benefits promised over the past 40 years by federal, state, and local governments. These promises were made with expectations of growth

---

[17]J. M. Buchanan and R. E. Wagner (1977), *Democracy in Deficit: The Political Legacy of Lord Keynes* (New York: Academic Press).

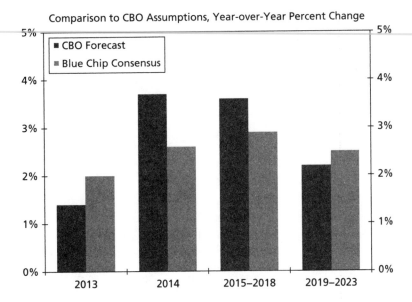

FIGURE 14.35 Real GDP Growth Estimates
Source: Blue Chip and Congressional Budget Office

stronger than we are currently experiencing and stronger than we anticipate going forward. Simply stated, based on current projections of economic and job growth, there is not likely to be enough tax revenue to pay the entitlement bills. When private and public investors recognize this weaker trend growth, they will begin to migrate away from U.S. Treasuries at current interest rates and the current exchange rate.

This process may already be starting. The Bank of Japan has decided to follow Prime Minister Abe's program to ease monetary policy and promote an increase in inflation. In this case, the implication is that the yen would depreciate against the dollar. Yet a policy of monetary ease would also indicate a decreased interest by the Bank of Japan to buy Treasury debt. With Japan as one of three dominant buyers of Treasury debt (along with China and the Fed), Japan's decision would put some upward pressure on U.S. interest rates even while the size of Treasury debt issuance remains large. As in many markets, when traders and investors in China and the Cayman Islands sense that the direction of the bond market has changed, market rates will likely rise much faster than generally has been incorporated in current forecasts.

Credit Imbalance: The U.S. Treasury Market

Persistent, large future federal deficits, as illustrated in Figure 14.36, create significant uncertainties in financial markets. Will continued large federal deficits find sufficient demand at current interest rates, dollar exchange rates, and

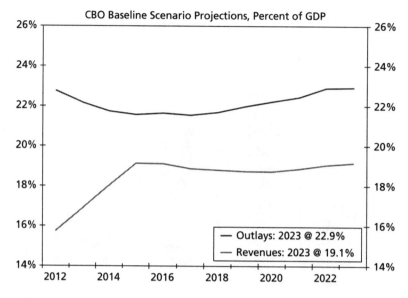

FIGURE 14.36 U.S. Budget Gap
Source: Congressional Budget Office and U.S. Department of the Treasury

levels of inflation? How much will large federal financing squeeze out private sector investment? Something has to give, especially given the dominant role played by central bank Treasury-buying policies in Japan, China, and, ultimately, by Federal Reserve in the United States. Since these institutions are not motivated by profits but rather by concerns about exchange rate stability and/ or unemployment, policy can change the demand for U.S. Treasury debt at a moment's notice, and for non–market-related factors.

On the supply side of the Treasury debt market, consider that the model for fiscal policy today is for permanent deficits that must be financed. It is likely that household and business behavior would be different from under the traditional model. Since this model is different from what is commonly assumed, this behavior will likely evolve into another kind of economic outcome than what some have projected.

First, the economic impact of fiscal deficits that are perceived to be permanent and unsustainable will be different from the impact of deficits that are temporary and self-correcting. Permanent deficits must be financed by taxes/debt finance and possibly rising inflation over time. In addition, when deficits are perceived to be unsustainable, the risk is that future taxes will rise, debt finance will grow, and inflation has a strong upside bias. Higher future taxes cause greater caution among taxpayers who anticipate that higher future taxes will reduce their after-tax disposable income. Greater future debt finance increases the probability of higher taxes and/or higher inflation. Finally, permanent, unsustainable future deficits prevent the use of traditional fiscal policy models based on the customary assumption of temporary and self-correcting deficits. The framework of fiscal policy has changed, and the anchoring bias of basing current economic estimates on outdated models is very obvious today.

Second, current deficits finance current consumption. This also is a significant change from the past, when deficit finance focused on public infrastructure, such as highways. Those past deficits added to the nation's physical capital and to the potential improvement in long-run growth of the economy. Financing current consumption through transfer payments such as Social Security and Medicare supports current consumption, of course, but detract from the capital needed for long-run growth. These unfunded liabilities—entitlements—allowed the U.S. economy to exhibit above-average consumption in recent years, which was above the pace of consumption consistent with income gains. Those deficits allowed the U.S. economy to appear to be doing better than it really was. The U.S. economy is living on borrowed time and reducing the wealth of future generations either through higher future taxes or inflation to pay the debt.

Finally, time shifting in taxation and deficit finance provides a bias for more spending today. Current fiscal policy—government-financed consumption—favors today's voters at the cost of the young and future generations who are not yet voters. This helps explain the unfunded liabilities of entitlements at the federal, state, and local levels. These liabilities reinforce the risk to current workers, who are not entitlement recipients, of higher taxes/debt finance/ higher inflation over time while limiting their spending today when deficits are perceived to be permanent and unsustainable. When faced with the choice of "pay me now" or "have someone else pay later," current entitlement recipients and policy makers shift the burden to future taxpayers (nonvoters).

The altered model of fiscal policy, permanent large deficits as illustrated above in Figure 14.36, helps to show why current spending did not generate the economic growth or jobs that were promised. The lack of stimulus follow-through on the demand side also helps to show why interest rates have not risen as some anticipated, although the impact of the supply of credit from China and Japan as foreign buyers of U.S. Treasuries (Figure 14.37), and the Federal Reserve as well helps explain the continued low interest rates. Some analysts have argued that the failure to see higher interest rates indicates that deficit financing did not have a negative impact and therefore that federal, state, and local governments can spend even more money. However, that argument only takes a pure demand-side view of the credit market. It overlooks the impact of the supply of credit from China and other nations, the depressing effect on current consumption and higher saving, and/or the deleveraging of current taxpayers who are discounting the impact of higher future taxes on their disposable incomes. Deficits without tears?

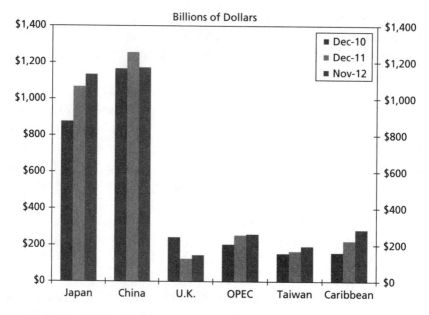

FIGURE 14.37 Top Holders of U.S. Treasuries
Source: Congressional Budget Office and U.S. Department of the Treasury

Fiscal deficits have delivered a stretch of subpar economic growth of 2 percent over the past three years as well as two years of job growth of 180,000 per month on average for each year, a disappointing number. The price of temporary programs, policy uncertainty, and model uncertainty has been subpar economic growth. Moreover, federal debts are paid in a fiat currency, the dollar, the supply of which the Fed has increased dramatically over the past five years. This increases the risk of higher inflation sometime in the future.

SUMMARY

The relationship between economic and financial variables evolves over time. In addition, the behavior of individual data series also changes with the passage of time. There is a tendency either to believe in the past findings (e.g., that GDP growth rate and unemployment rate, Okun's law, has a statistically significant relationship) or to make an assumption about the behavior of an individual variable (e.g., inflation rate is mean reversion) in decision making. Our approach is to test/quantify statistical relationships between variables of interest using econometric techniques and the most recent dataset instead of making assumptions of about the relationships.

Statistical software enables analysts to use major econometric techniques to characterize a variable and/or to quantify a statistical relationship between variables of interest. Without learning the tedious math, analysts can employ these statistical tools to perform the required tests.

Users must be aware, however, that statistical software produces results without considering the type of input dataset. It is an analyst's job to make sure the input dataset fulfills economic/financial theory and matches the statistical properties of the underlying tests.

The challenges for analysts going forward require that we anticipate change in our economic and financial benchmarks and model those changes. We await the results.

Useful References for SAS Users

The best resource for interested SAS users is SAS's Web site (www.sas .com). The Web site offers manuals about several SAS products including SAS/ETS 9.3 (the latest version of the ETS at the time of this writing) and is available free of cost. The ETS manual provides detailed discussion about all the procedures (related to the ETS) including PROC ARIMA, PROC AUTOREG, PROC MODEL, and others. Furthermore, it shows useful SAS codes and examples of SAS output. In our view, the SAS Web site is the single best source for all level of SAS users, from beginner to advanced.

For the beginner, *The Little SAS Book: A Primer*, 5th ed., by Lora Delwiche and Susan Slaughter (Cary, NC: SAS Institute, 2012), is one of the most useful books for SAS users. It offers a detailed discussion about the DATA and the PROC steps, provides very useful tips for SAS users, and is user friendly.

Applied Statistics and the SAS Programming Language, 5th ed., by Ron P. Cody (Upper Saddle River, NJ: Pearson, 2005), is a good reference book for experienced SAS users and a good source for the PROC steps.

Statistical Programming with SAS/IML Software by Rick Wicklin (Cary, NC: SAS Institute, 2010) is a book for very advanced SAS users interested in writing their own programs, as SAS/IML is a programming language tool.

About the Authors

JOHN E. SILVIA

John Silvia is a managing director and the chief economist for Wells Fargo. Prior to his current position, John worked on Capitol Hill as senior economist for the U.S. Senate Joint Economic Committee and as chief economist for the U.S. Senate Banking, Housing and Urban Affairs Committee. Before that, he was chief economist of Kemper Funds and managing director of Scudder Kemper Investments, Inc. John was formerly a director of NABE and was former president of the Charlotte Economics Club. He has also served on economic advisory committees to the Federal Reserve Bank of Cleveland, the Federal Reserve Bank of Chicago, and the Public Securities Association.

John was awarded a NABE Fellow Certificate of Recognition in 2011 for outstanding contributions to the Business Economics Profession and Leadership Among Business Economists to the Nation. For the second time in three years, he was awarded the best overall forecast by the Federal Reserve Bank of Chicago as well as the best unemployment rate forecast for 2011. John has been awarded the Adolph Abramson award for the best article in economics published in *Business Economics* for a given year. John holds B.A. and Ph.D. degrees in economics from Northeastern University in Boston and has a master's degree in economics from Brown University. John's book *Dynamic Economic Decision Making* was published by John Wiley & Sons in August 2011.

AZHAR IQBAL

Azhar Iqbal is an econometrician at Wells Fargo and is responsible for providing quantitative analysis to the Economics group, including modeling and forecasting of macro and financial variables. He also teaches advanced business and economic forecasting to graduate students at the University of North Carolina, Charlotte. He was previously an economist and course instructor at the Applied Economics Research Center at the University of Karachi in Pakistan, teaching econometrics, microeconomics, and urban economics. He has also worked as an economist at the United Nations, at the Arif-Habib Investment Bank, and for projects funded by the government of Pakistan.

Azhar received his bachelor's degree in economics from the University of Punjab and has three master's degrees. He earned his master's degree in economic forecasting from the University at Albany, State University of New York, where he also earned a Certificate of Graduate Study in economic forecasting. He also has master's degrees in applied science and applied economics from the University of Karachi, and in econometrics and mathematics from the University of the Punjab in Lahore, Pakistan.

His interests focus on forecasting, time series, panel data, and macroeconomics. Azhar has presented research papers at the American Economic Association, Econometric Society meetings, the Panel Data Conference, and other international conferences. He has published several papers in the *Canadian Journal of Economics*, *Global Economy Journal*, *Business Economics*, and other refereed articles listed in the *Journal of Economic Literature*.

KAYLYN SWANKOSKI

Kaylyn Swankoski is currently pursuing a graduate degree in economics at Duke University. Previously she worked as an economic analyst at Wells Fargo Securities. She received her B.A. in economics from Elon University in North Carolina.

SARAH WATT

Sarah Watt is an economist with Wells Fargo Securities. She received her B.A. in economics and political economy from Tulane University and her MSc from the London School of Economics. Sarah is a member of the National Association of Business Economics and the Charlotte Economics Club.

SAM BULLARD

Sam Bullard is a managing director and senior economist at Wells Fargo Securities, providing analysis on the macro U.S. economy, major foreign economies, and the financial markets. Sam has a BBA in finance from the University of Georgia (1994) and an MBA from Wake Forest University (2006). His work has been published in *Business Economics*, and his comments on the economy regularly appear in *The Wall Street Journal*, *Financial Times*, *USA Today*, Associated Press, and Reuters. Sam is a member of the National Association of Business Economics and the Charlotte Economics Club.

Index